A Workout in Computational Finance

For other titles in the Wiley Finance series
please see www.wiley.com/go/finance

A Workout in Computational Finance

Michael Aichinger
Andreas Binder

WILEY

This edition first published 2013
© 2013 Michael Aichinger and Andreas Binder.

Registered office
John Wiley & Sons Ltd, The Atrium, Southern Gate, Chichester, West Sussex, PO19 8SQ, United Kingdom

For details of our global editorial offices, for customer services and for information about how to apply for permission to reuse the copyright material in this book please see our website at www.wiley.com.

Wiley publishes in a variety of print and electronic formats and by print-on-demand. Some material included with standard print versions of this book may not be included in e-books or in print-on-demand. If this book refers to media such as a CD or DVD that is not included in the version you purchased, you may download this material at http://booksupport.wiley.com. For more information about Wiley products, visit www.wiley.com.

Designations used by companies to distinguish their products are often claimed as trademarks. All brand names and product names used in this book are trade names, service marks, trademarks or registered trademarks of their respective owners. The publisher is not associated with any product or vendor mentioned in this book.

Limit of Liability/Disclaimer of Warranty: While the publisher and author have used their best efforts in preparing this book, they make no representations or warranties with the respect to the accuracy or completeness of the contents of this book and specifically disclaim any implied warranties of merchantability or fitness for a particular purpose. It is sold on the understanding that the publisher is not engaged in rendering professional services and neither the publisher nor the author shall be liable for damages arising herefrom. If professional advice or other expert assistance is required, the services of a competent professional should be sought.

Library of Congress Cataloging-in-Publication Data

Aichinger, Michael, 1979–
   A workout in computational finance / Michael Aichinger and Andreas Binder.
      pages cm
   Includes bibliographical references and index.
   ISBN 978-1-119-97191-7 (cloth)
   1. Finance—Mathematical models.   I. Binder, Andreas, 1964–   II. Title.
   HG106.A387 2013
   332.01'51—dc23

                                                          2013017386

A catalogue record for this book is available from the British Library.

ISBN 978-1-119-97191-7 (hardback) ISBN 978-1-119-97348-5 (ebk)
ISBN 978-1-119-97349-2 (ebk)   ISBN 978-1-119-97350-8 (ebk)

Cover image: Shutterstock.com

Set in 10/12pt Times by Aptara, Inc., New Delhi, India
Printed in Great Britain by CPI Group (UK) Ltd, Croydon, CR0 4YY

To Elke, Michael, Lisa and Florian

To Julian

Contents

Acknowledgements

The authors would not have been able to write this book without the support of their colleagues: Johannes Fürst and Christian Kletzmayr provided a lot of detailed calculations. Sascha Kratky has been an invaluable help for technical support. Andreas Obereder tried (but did not always succeed) to organize tight deadlines. Michael Schwaiger, as the UnRisk product manager, was a great help in providing software parts. Stefan Janecek is the one who improved the English language of the first version.

AB wants to thank Heinz W. Engl for being his academic teacher and mentor for the last 30 years.

MA wants to thank Herbert Exner for many fruitful discussions that led to valuable insight.

MA and AB are grateful to Wiley for their understanding when deadlines did not hold.

About the Authors

Michael Aichinger

Michael Aichinger, FRM, obtained his Ph.D. in Theoretical Physics from the Johannes Kepler Universität Linz with a thesis on numerical methods in density functional theory and their application to 2D finite electron systems. A mobility grant led him to the Texas A&M University (2003) and to the Helsinki University of Technology (2004). In 2007, Michael Aichinger joined the Industrial Mathematics Competence Center, where he has been working as a senior researcher and consultant in the field of quantitative finance for the last five years. He also works for the Austrian Academy of Sciences at the Radon Institute for Computational and Applied Mathematics, where he is involved in several industrial mathematics and computational physics projects.

Andreas Binder

Andreas Binder obtained his Ph.D. in Industrial Mathematics from the Johannes Kepler Universität Linz with a thesis on continuous casting of steel. A research grant led him to the Oxford Centre for Industrial and Applied Mathematics, UK, in 1991. After returning to Linz, he became assistant professor at the Industrial Mathematics Institute. In 1996, he left university and became managing director of MathConsult GmbH. Andreas Binder has authored two introductory books on mathematical finance and 25 journal articles in the fields of industrial mathematics and of mathematical finance.

1

Introduction and Reading Guide

PROLOGUE

We wrote this book with the aim of giving practitioners in computational finance a sound overview of relevant numerical methods. Some of the methods presented in this book are widely used today, while others should, in our opinion, gain more importance in the future. By, "computational finance" we loosely refer to all tasks related to the valuation of financial instruments, risk analysis and some aspects of risk management. Together with our colleagues at MathConsult GmbH, we have been working on a wide range of computational finance projects since 1997. During that time, we have observed that the numerical quality of software used in financial institutions widely varies.

Particular attention is thus given to working out the strengths and weaknesses of the different methods, and to reveal possible traps in their application. We have used real-world examples of valuation, risk analysis and calibration of specific financial instruments and models to introduce each method. A strong emphasis is laid on stable and robust schemes for the numerical treatment.

We have named the book "A Workout in Computational Finance" because due to our experience in training finance professionals, it is our strong belief that computational methods are best studied in a practical, hands-on approach, requiring the student to write at least part of the program code herself. To facilitate this style of learning, the book comes with accompanying software distilled from the UnRisk software package.[1]

The reader is assumed to have a basic knowledge of mathematical finance and financial derivatives, and a strong interest in quantitative methods. The typical reader of the book is a "junior quant" at a financial institution who wants to gain deeper insight into numerical methods, or, if she has a background in economy, wants to take first steps towards a more quantitative approach. Alternatively, university students at the graduate level may find the topics in this book useful when deciding on a possible future career in finance.

WHAT YOU CAN EXPECT FROM THE DIFFERENT CHAPTERS

In the following, we give a short overview of the contents of the different chapters. Together with the reading guide this should allow the reader to select her topics of interest.

Chapter 2: Binomial Trees

Binomial trees a conceptionally elegant method for valuating derivatives: They are explicit (i.e., no system of equations needs to be solved), and they intrinsically include no-arbitrage

---

[1] The UnRisk ENGINE and the UnRisk FACTORY are software packages for valuation and risk management of financial instruments and portfolios thereof. UnRisk has been developed by MathConsult since 1999 and now contains more than 1 million lines of multi language code. UnRisk is a registered trademark of MathConsult. Details: www.unrisk.com

conditions. From a numerical point of view, their lack of adaptivity as well as stability problems limit their range of applicability.

Chapter 3: Finite Differences and the Black-Scholes PDE

In this chapter the derivation of the Black-Scholes partial differential equation is explained in detail. The differential operators are discretized using finite difference formulae, and various methods for the time discretization are introduced. Stability issues resulting from the chosen spatial and time discretizations are discussed. The application of the finite difference method to the prototype model of the heat equation concludes the chapter.

Chapter 4: Mean Reversion and Trinomial Trees

When models exhibit mean reverting behavior, such as the Vasicek model for interest rates, binomial trees do not recombine anymore. Trinomial trees have been introduced to cure this problem. To retain their stability, up- and down-branching is used, cutting off the calculation domain and therefore implicitly changing the boundary conditions.

Chapter 5: Upwinding Techniques

Particular finite difference formulae need to be applied to cure the instabilities occurring if partial differential equations arising from mean reverting models are discretized. These formulae are derived in Chapter 5 and their ability to cope with the instabilities is examined. The chapter concludes with a detailed example of the application of upwinding techniques to a putable fixed rate bond under a one factor short rate model.

Chapter 6: Boundary, Terminal and Interface Conditions

To valuate a specific financial instrument, its term sheet must be translated into boundary-, terminal- and possibly also interface conditions (for coupons or callabilities) for the differential equation to be solved. These conditions are formulated for a range of instruments. It turns out that for heavily path-dependent instruments, Monte Carlo techniques may be the more appropriate choice. For the case of mean reverting interest rate models, the influence of artificial boundary conditions is studied.

Chapter 7: Finite Element Methods

The basic concepts of the finite element method are described, and for a number of different elements, the element matrices are derived. Particular emphasis is laid on the assembling process of the global matrices and the incorporation of boundary conditions. Similarly to the finite difference technique, stabilization terms need to be added if the finite element method is applied to convection-diffusion-reaction problems. An example comparing the numerical results obtained with the finite element method to results obtained with tree techniques concludes the chapter.

Chapter 8: Solving Systems of Linear Equations

In Chapters 3, 5, 7 and 13 different discretization techniques for partial (integro) differential equations are discussed, all of them leading to systems of linear equations. This chapter provides an overview of different techniques to solve them. Dependent on the type of problem and the problem size, direct methods or iterative solvers methods may be preferable. A number of basic algorithms for both types of methods are discussed and explained based on small examples.

Chapter 9: Monte Carlo Simulation

The principles of Monte Carlo integration techniques and their application for the pricing of derivatives are explained. Furthermore, different discretization techniques for the stochastic differential equations used to model the propagation of the underlying risk factors are discussed. The Libor market model is examined as an example of a high-dimensional model where Monte Carlo methods are typically applied to valuate derivatives. The final part of the chapter emphasizes random number generation, which is one of the major building blocks of every Monte Carlo-based pricing routine.

Chapter 10: Advanced Monte Carlo Techniques

Different techniques exist to reduce the variance of Monte Carlo estimators. Some of the more general algorithms are explained based on examples such as the pricing of exotic options. In contrast to the Monte Carlo method, Quasi Monte Carlo methods do not use sequences of pseudo-random numbers, but use sequences of low-discrepancy numbers instead. The most important sequences are introduced and applied to the pricing of a structured interest rate product under the Libor market model. As a technique to speed up Monte Carlo as well as Quasi Monte Carlo simulations the Brownian bridge method is outlined.

Chapter 11: Least Squares Monte Carlo

A well-known problem when using Monte Carlo methods for pricing is the inclusion of American or Bermudan call- or putability. We present a detailed outline of a Least Squares Monte Carlo algorithm in this chapter and apply this algorithm to a number of structured interest and foreign exchange rate instruments.

Chapter 12: Characteristic Function Methods for Option Pricing

For many distributions the density functions are not known or are not analytically tractable, but their corresponding Fourier transforms, the characteristic functions, are. This circumstance provides the basis for the methods presented in two fast and reliable methods for the valuation of European vanilla options based on the Fast Fourier Transformation and cosine series expansion are discussed. An overview of equity models beyond Black-Scholes is given in this chapter, as the calibration of these models is one of the major areas where the characteristic function methods can be applied.

Chapter 13: Numerical Methods for the Solution of PIDEs

The extension of the methods discussed in Chapters 3, 5 and 7 to cope with partial integro differential equations is discussed in this chapter.

Chapter 14: Copulas and the Pitfalls of Correlation

In the first two parts of this chapter, a number of common measures for dependence and basic concepts of copulas are presented. Subsequently, the most important copulas applied in finance are discussed and some estimation and sampling methods for them are outlined. An example showing the impact of different copula functions on the probability of default closes the chapter.

Chapter 15: Parameter Calibration and Inverse Problems

Market data are changing more or less continuously. To reflect this fact in the valuation of financial instruments, the parameters of the mathematical models describing the movement of underlyings have to be (re)calibrated on a regular basis. This is a classical inverse problem, and therefore instabilities are to be expected. Several examples for equity and for interest rate models are discussed in detail.

Chapter 16: Optimization Techniques

To solve the calibration problems outlined in Chapter 15, optimization techniques need to be applied. We differentiate gradient-based and heuristically motivated methods, discuss algorithms for both types and show that hybrids of the two worlds can successfully be applied to estimate parameters, using the calibration of a Heston model as an example. For constrained optimization problems we introduce the interior point method and show the capability of this method in the field of portfolio optimization.

Chapter 17: Risk Management

Many of the methods discussed up to this point in the book can be used to value single instruments or portfolios. Frequently, such algorithms are used as building blocks in a risk management system where these valuations must be performed over thousands of different scenarios. In this chapter we will discuss the different possibilities to generate such scenarios and how to assess the risk measures from the simulation results. A short outline of extreme value theory and its application to the calculation of Value at Risk and Expected Shortfall concludes the chapter.

Chapter 18: Quantitative Finance on Parallel Architectures

In many fields of quantitative finance it is necessary to perform thousands or even millions of valuations of often highly structured instruments. Parallel computation techniques are used to significantly speed up these valuations. Multicore CPUs and recent GPUs, have fueled this trend by providing affordable and readily available parallel hardware. Based on examples we examine how different parallelization techniques can successfully be applied.

Chapter 19: Building Large Software Systems for the Financial Industry

This is a short chapter on the authors' experiences in building a large software system for risk management of financial instruments.

ACCOMPANYING SOFTWARE

The buyer of the book is entitled to download the accompanying software from www.unrisk.com/Workout after registration. A tutorial on how to use the software together with the book is available on the webpage.

READING GUIDE

The diagram below shows the interrelations between different chapters and the suggested order of reading. Vertical arrows indicate suggested order of reading within a group of associated chapters, all other arrows indicate relations between different groups. For example, the Chapters on P(I)DE methods should be read in the order 3, 5–7, 13, and Chapter 8 (Solving Systems of Linear Equations) depends on material covered the P(I)DE chapters.

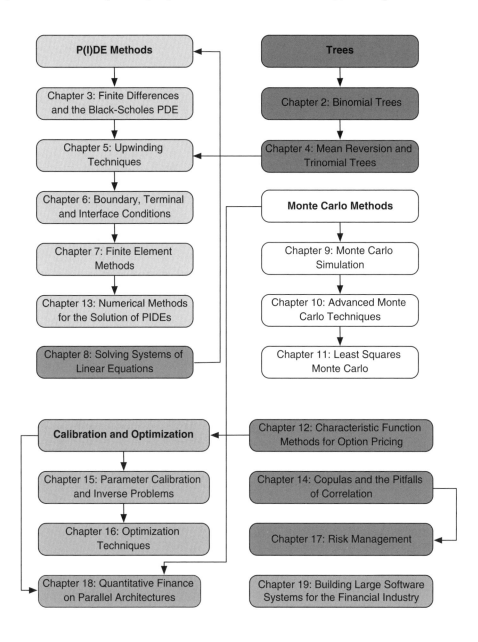

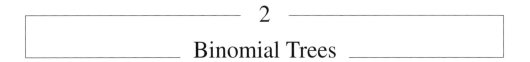

2

Binomial Trees

Binomial trees are widely used in option pricing, but are, as will be discussed later, not our preferred method.[1] In this chapter, we will present the basic binomial tree algorithm and some of its refinements. As we want to apply binomial trees to the valuation of options, we will discuss options beforehand.

2.1 EQUITIES AND BASIC OPTIONS

An equity (stock, share) is a specified portion of ownership of a company, giving the holder of the share several rights, e.g., to participate in the annual general meeting and in the elections there and to obtain a dividend as a part of the profit of the company. Throughout this book, we assume that the stock is exchange-traded, so that the actual trading price of the share can be obtained (maybe with some time delay) by consulting the exchange's homepage or a Reuters or Bloomberg screen. With the exception of an initial public offering or an increase in capital, a change in the share price does not change the firm's capital or liquidity, but is – at least in an ideal world – the investors' consensus on the value of the share. If the universe of investors thinks that the iPhone will be a cash cow, then the stock price of Apple will increase.

As experience during the last years showed, equity prices cannot only rise, but also can drop significantly. In order to limit the impact of downward moves of an investment at a certain point in time, a European call option may be an appropriate instrument:

European call and put options: A European call option on an underlying S gives the holder of the option the right, but not the obligation, to buy one share of the equity S at a future time T the expiry time, for a fixed price K, the strike price.

A European put option on the underlying S gives the holder of the option the right, but not the obligation, to sell one share of the equity S at a future time T the expiry time, for a fixed price K, the strike price.

Thus, at expiry, the payoffs of European options are as shown in Figure 2.1.

While European options may only be exercised at the date of expiry, American options may be exercised at any time during their lifetimes; Bermudan options may be exercised only at certain but known dates. Bermudan style exercise is quite popular in the fixed income world, where bonds are sometimes equipped with an early redemption right for the issuer. This early redemption typically takes place on coupon days.

Call and put options on liquid underlyings are actively traded for different strike prices and for different expiries. Of course, a (call or put) option always has a non-negative value. Holding, e.g., a call option provides an insurance against movements of the underlying below the strike price. The value of the option can therefore be interpreted as the premium to be paid for this insurance. Calculating fair values of a wide variety of options and other derivative or structured

---

[1] If you google for the combination of "binomial tree" and "option pricing", you obtain 34 200 results (date of search: November 24, 2010).

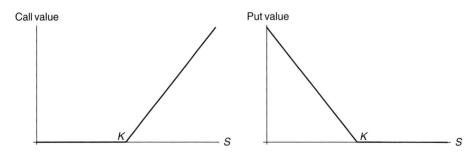

Figure 2.1 Payoff of a call and of a put option at expiry as functions of the equity price S. Both options have a strike price K.

instruments, analyzing their values under different scenarios and ultimately managing their risks is one of the main purposes of computational finance as the authors understand it.

2.2 THE ONE PERIOD MODEL

Consider (at time 0) an option written on an equity that can, at the expiry T, assume only two possible states s_1 and s_2 and assume that the random variable S_T has the distribution

$$S_T = \begin{cases} s_1 & \text{with probability } p, \\ s_2 & \text{with probability } 1 - p. \end{cases} \tag{2.1}$$

The payoff of the option should then, depending on the price of the underlying, have the value $V_T(s_1) = v_1$ and $V_T(s_2) = v_2$. Is it possible to construct a portfolio P consisting of cash (which is assumed to pay interest at a continuous rate[2] r) and shares of the equity in such a way that the portfolio replicates the option value independent of the outcome of the random process for the equity?

At time 0, let our portfolio consist of a_1 units of cash and of a_2 shares. Its value P_0 at time 0 is then

$$P_0 = a_1 + a_2 s_0. \tag{2.2}$$

At time T the cash amount has increased to $a_1 e^{rT}$ whereas the equity portion's value has changed to $a_2 s_1$ or $a_2 s_2$, respectively. If the portfolio is to replicate the option value, the unknowns a_1, a_2 must satisfy

$$v_1 = a_1 e^{rT} + a_2\, s_1,$$
$$v_2 = a_1 e^{rT} + a_2\, s_2,$$

with the solutions

$$a_2 = \frac{v_1 - v_2}{s_1 - s_2},$$

$$a_1 = e^{-rT} \left(v_1 - \frac{(v_1 - v_2)s_1}{s_1 - s_2} \right).$$

---

[2] See section 4.1.1 for compounding.

Hence, if we choose the weights a_1 and a_2 accordingly, P replicates the option and therefore the option value equals the portfolio value also at time 0. Hence, we obtain

$$v_0 = P_0 = s_0 \left(\frac{v_1 - v_2}{s_1 - s_2} \right) + e^{-rT} \left(v_1 - \frac{(v_1 - v_2)s_1}{s_1 - s_2} \right). \tag{2.3}$$

Note that the formula for the option value does not depend on the probability p of the outcomes s_1, s_2! We would have obtained the same result by discounting the expected outcome (at time T) with the expectation value taken under a probability q for s_1 and $1 - q$ for s_2 with

$$q = \frac{S_0 e^{rT} - s_2}{s_1 - s_2}. \tag{2.4}$$

The measure implied from this change of probability is called the risk neutral measure of the binomial model, whereas the physical measure is the one with the probability p. For a more detailed discussion concerning the measure theoretic foundation of risk neutral valuation, see, e.g., Delbaen and Schachermayer (2006). In the risk neutral measure, the expected value of the share price grows with the risk free rate r independent of the physical growth rate implied by s_1 and s_2 and their physical probabilities. In order to obtain a probability q in the interval $(0, 1)$, it is required that the risk-free forward value $S_0 e^{rT}$ lies between s_1 and s_2. If $S_0 e^{rT}$ was outside this interval, arbitrage (a guaranteed profit at a higher rate than the risk-free rate) would be possible.

2.3   THE MULTIPERIOD BINOMIAL MODEL

The assumption of only two possible states for the price of the equity at the expiry of the option is not a very realistic one. However at least in theory, it might be a reasonable assumption if the time interval under consideration is sufficiently small. Therefore, we recursively build an N-level tree as indicated in the following figure. Note that the random variables which choose the up or the down branch are assumed to be identical for all time steps. This is an essential assumption for the convergence analysis utilizing the central limit theorem.

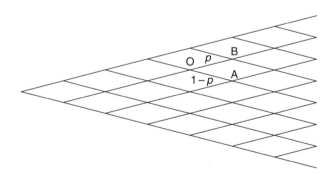

Following this construction, each node O has two successor nodes A and B in this multi-period binomial tree. The distribution (in the physical measure) of reaching A or B from O is assumed to be

$$S_{nT/N} = \begin{cases} (1 + b(N))S_{(n-1)T/N} \text{ with probability } p \text{ (Point B)} \\ (1 + a(N))S_{(n-1)T/N} \text{ with probability } 1 - p \text{ (Point A)} \end{cases} \tag{2.5}$$

with the up and down factors $(1 + b(N))$ and $(1 + a(N))$, respectively, where N is the number of time levels used.

In order to obtain a recombining tree in the figure, we implicitly assumed that the up and down factors are constant during the lifetime of the option. Otherwise, a bushy tree with up to 2^N branches would be the result. If the option value at A and B is known one can calculate the fair value of the option at node O by a one-period binomial as shown in the previous section. The corresponding risk neutral probability is

$$q = \frac{e^{rT/N} - 1 - a(N)}{b(N) - a(N)}. \tag{2.6}$$

As the option value is known for all nodes at expiry (the payoff function of the option), we can recursively calculate the values at all nodes.

As an example after some manipulation (and after taking into account the independence of branching also in the risk-free measure), we obtain for the fair value of a European call option (with strike price K and an initial stock price of S_0)

$$V_0(N) = \underbrace{e^{-rT}}_{(DF)} \underbrace{\sum_{n=0}^{N} \binom{N}{n} q^n (1-q)^{N-n}}_{(PD)} \underbrace{\left((1 + b(N))^n (1 + a(N))^{N-n} S_0 - K \right)^+}_{(PO)}, \tag{2.7}$$

with the interpretations (DF) discount factor, (PD) probability density of the binomial distribution in the risk-free measure and (PO) payoff of the contingent claim, here the call option. For a real-valued argument h, we used the notation

$$(h)^+ := \max(h, 0). \tag{2.8}$$

Until now, we have not specified the dependence of $a(.)$ and $b(.)$ on the number of time levels N. Obviously, if the tree should not explode for $N \to \infty$, $a(N)$ and $b(N)$ must be chosen (and tend to zero) appropriately. This leads us to the Black-Scholes model.

2.4 BLACK-SCHOLES AND TREES

In the Black-Scholes model, the time-dependent evolution of the price of an equity S starting in S_0 at time 0 is modeled by

$$dS_t = \mu S dt + \sigma S dW, \tag{2.9}$$

with S_t being the stock price at time t, dS its incremental change in the infinitesimal time interval $(t, t + dt)$, σ the annualized *volatility*, and dW the increment of a standard Wiener process. The parameter μ is the expected growth rate in the physical measure.

The equation for valuating an option on an underlying equity following (2.9) will be derived in Chapter 3. There, the risk neutral measure induced by the replicating portfolios will replace μ by the risk-free interest rate r.

It can be shown that the random variable S_T/S_0 is (in the physical measure) normally distributed with mean $(\mu - \sigma^2/2)T$ and variance $\sigma^2 T$. In the risk neutral measure, μ must be replaced by r.

If the N-level binomial tree with time step $\Delta T = (T/N)$ is to be a numerical approximation for the Black-Scholes model, the parameters $a(N)$ and $b(N)$ must be chosen in such a way that the corresponding distribution in the binomial model approaches the log-normal distribution of the Black-Scholes model in the risk neutral measure for $N \to \infty$ (to be more specific: convergence in distribution will be obtained).

There are (infinitely) many ways to choose the up/down parameters $a(.)$ and $b(.)$. Following Korn and Müller (2010), the way to choose a, b and the physical probability p is such that mean and variance of the Black-Scholes return in the risk-free measure are matched. Note that, for the valuation process in the binomial tree, the physical probability p disappears, therefore this mingling of physical and risk-free measures is justified. Prominent examples of tree parameters are:

Cox-Ross-Rubinstein

$$(1 + b) = e^{\sigma\sqrt{\Delta T}} \quad (1 + a) = e^{-\sigma\sqrt{\Delta T}} \tag{2.10}$$

Forward Tree

$$(1 + b) = e^{r\Delta T + \sigma\sqrt{\Delta T}} \quad (1 + a) = e^{r\Delta T - \sigma\sqrt{\Delta T}} \tag{2.11}$$

Note that in the literature our "Forward Tree" is sometimes named Cox-Ross-Rubinstein.

Rendleman-Bartter

$$(1 + b) = e^{(r-\sigma^2/2)\Delta T + \sigma\sqrt{\Delta T}} \quad (1 + a) = e^{(r-\sigma^2/2)\Delta T - \sigma\sqrt{\Delta T}} \tag{2.12}$$

Depending on the preferred choice of the tree, there may be upper bounds for ΔT in order to guarantee the no-arbitrage condition $q \in (0, 1)$ for q as in (2.6). For the forward tree, this is always fulfilled. The Cox-Ross-Rubinstein tree must restrict Δt for r large and σ small, the Rendleman-Bartter tree for large σ. Working out the conditions on ΔT in detail is an easy exercise and left to the reader.

The convergence in distribution of the discrete N-level trees towards the Black-Scholes model can be shown for all the trees mentioned above. The central limit theorem is the key tool for proving convergence (Kallenberg, 2006). It can be shown that with $N \to \infty$, the tree value $V_0(N)$ as in (2.7) converges to

$$V_0 = \underbrace{e^{-rT}}_{(DF)} \int_0^\infty \underbrace{\frac{1}{\sigma S \sqrt{2\pi T}} e^{-\alpha^2/2}}_{(PD)} \underbrace{\left(S - K\right)^+}_{(PO)} dS, \tag{2.13}$$

with $\alpha = \frac{1}{\sigma\sqrt{T}}(\log(S/S_0) + (r - \sigma^2/2)T)$.

2.5 STRENGTHS AND WEAKNESSES OF BINOMIAL TREES

2.5.1 Ease of Implementation

The following piece of code is an example of a forward tree realized in Mathematica. By changing the settings for the up and the down parameters, one can easily obtain a Cox-Ross-Rubinstein or a Rendleman-Bartter tree.

```
BinomialEuropeanCall2[S_, K_, r_, sigma_, T_, n_] :=
  Module[{dt, forward, up, down, P, Q, Probup, Probdown, BinomTree,
  value, level},
  dt = T/n; forward = Exp[r*dt];
  up = Exp[sigma*Sqrt[dt]]*forward;
  down = Exp[-sigma*Sqrt[dt]]*forward;
  Probup = (forward - down)/(up - down);
  Probdown = 1 - Probup;
  P = Probup*Exp[-r*dt];(* Discounting per timestep *)
  Q = Probdown*Exp[-r*dt];(* Discounting per timestep *)
  BinomTree =
   Table[Max[S*down^node*up^(n - node) - K, 0], node, 0, n];
   (* Terminal condition of a call option *)
     Do[BinomTree = Table[
       {P, Q}.{BinomTree[[node]], BinomTree[[node + 1]]},
       {node, 1,level]},
       (* In the case of an American option, compare here against
       the exercise value: BinomTree= Max[BinomTree, exercise value]
       or add knock-out conditions of barrier options here *)
     {level, n, 1, -1}];
  value = BinomTree[[1]];
  Clear[BinomTree];
  value]
```

The main advantage of the binomial tree method is its ease of implementation, also for options which may be exercised early like American or Bermudan ones. It is an explicit method so that no systems of equations have to be solved (see also Chapter 3 for a comparison of explicit/implicit methods in the finite difference framework).

2.5.2 Oscillations

How fast do binomial trees converge? Figure 2.2 shows the binomial tree values of a European call option (strike price 100, expiry 1 year, current equity price 100, interest rate 0.03, volatility 0.35) for the different binomial trees described in the previous section. Valuation has been performed for $N = 2$ to 100.

We notice the oscillating behavior (between "even values" and "odd values") for all tree implementations; the amplitude of the oscillations is typically larger for the Cox-Ross-Rubinstein tree than for the Forward and Rendleman-Bartter trees. To obtain a guaranteed relative accuracy of 0.05 % for this specific example (in the sense the result stays below this error level for all larger numbers of time levels), N must be greater than 437 (Cox-Ross-Rubinstein), 277 (Forward tree), 255 (Rendleman-Bartter), resulting in trees with at least 30 000 nodes.

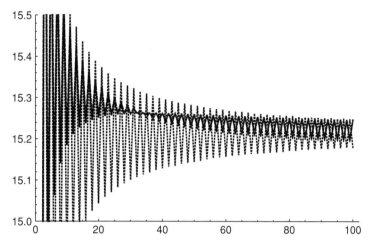

Figure 2.2 Binomial tree value as a function of the number of time steps. Dotted: Cox-Ross-Rubinstein, Dashed: Forward Tree, Solid: Rendleman-Bartter. $S = 100$, $K = 100$, $T = 1$, $r = 0.03$, $\sigma = 0.35$. The analytical Black-Scholes value is 15.2142.

The main reason for the oscillations is the non-smooth payoff of the call option (whose first derivative jumps at the strike price). Presmoothing the end condition by applying, e.g., the analytical Black-Scholes formula close to the expiry date might help. We do not carry out this procedure here, because it is feasible only when an analytical formula is available at least in the vicinity of discontinuities.

We have seen in the previous section that Cox-Ross-Rubinstein and Rendleman-Bartter trees may violate the no-arbitrage condition for large time steps and for certain parameter settings. We give two examples in Figures 2.3 and 2.4.

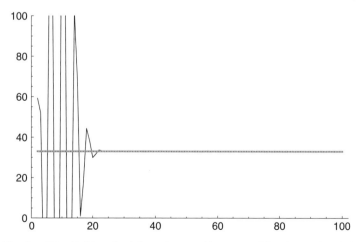

Figure 2.3 The Cox-Ross-Rubinstein violates the no-arbitrage condition for small volatilities and large time steps. Here $S = 100$, $K = 100$, $T = 8$, $r = 0.05$, $\sigma = 0.02$. Even (wrong) negative option values could result. The forward and Rendleman-Bartter trees converge fast in this case.

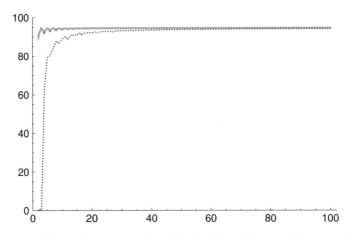

Figure 2.4 The Rendleman-Bartter tree (dotted line) violates the no-arbitrage condition for large volatilities and large time steps. Here $S = 100$, $K = 100$, $T = 8$, $r = 0.05$, $\sigma = 1.3$. Forward tree and Cox-Ross-Rubinstein exhibit oscillations, as expected.

2.5.3   Non-recombining Trees

As long as one deals with options on underlyings which either do not pay dividends (such as foreign currencies) or pay dividends proportional to the price of the equity, recombining trees can be constructed. However, if the dividend is a fixed amount of cash, then, in general, trees do not recombine anymore but become bushy as shown in Figure 2.5.

Other sources for non-recombining trees are up/down factors that are not constant on the tree. As these factors are matched to market data for interest rates and volatilities, this occurs quite frequently.

2.5.4   Exotic Options and Trees

Obviously, when there is an analytic solution available (as is the case for vanilla options in the Black-Scholes model), it does not make too much sense to calculate their value by using binomial trees or any other numerical procedure. Numerical methods only begin to play a role

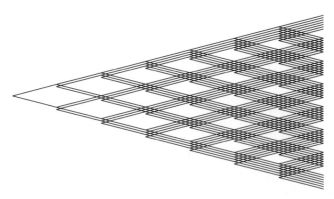

Figure 2.5   Bushy trees arising from discrete dividends.

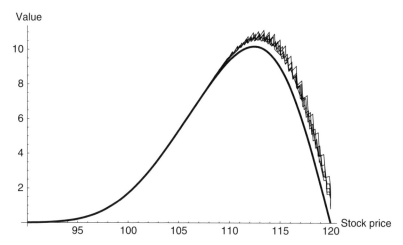

Figure 2.6 Up-and-out call option with barrier $B = 120$ (continuously observed), strike $K = 100$, 7 days to expiry, $r = 0.05$, $\sigma = 0.30$. The plot shows the value as a function of the current stock price. Thick black line: analytical value. Thin black curves: Forward trees with $N = 80, 110, 140, 170, 200$. Note the zigzagging.

when there is no analytic solution for the considered instrument (e.g., for American put options or more exotic instruments), or when the mathematical model describing the underlying is not suitable for an analytic solution.

In the next example (Figure 2.6) we study an up-and-out call option. This is a call option with the additional feature that as soon as the underlying goes above a prescribed barrier, the option becomes worthless for the holder. Such knockout options are, depending on the barrier level, significantly cheaper than plain vanilla options. For constant parameters r, σ and a constant barrier B, there is an analytic solution available (see, e.g., Wilmott (1998)). This is not the case anymore as soon as r, σ or B are time-dependent.

2.5.5 Greeks and Binomial Trees

Numerical methods in computational finance are not only used for the valuation of derivative or structured instruments, but also for determining the Greeks (see Chapter 3) for hedging purposes. We try to calculate the first derivative *Delta* of the option value with repect to the underlying S by numerical differentiation. Here we use a central difference quotient

$$\text{Delta} = \frac{V(S + \Delta S, t) - V(S - \Delta S, t)}{2\Delta S}. \tag{2.14}$$

The Delta results for a barrier option obtained by the forward tree are reported in Figure 2.7.

2.5.6 Grid Adaptivity and Trees

In order to obtain a recombining tree, all branches of the tree must look the same. This means that in order to have small time steps or a fine discretization of the underlying in one region, one needs to use a fine grid everywhere unless sophisticated extensions are made to the tree.

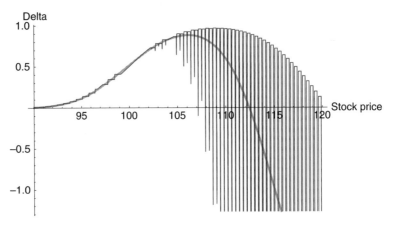

Figure 2.7 Up-and-out call option with barrier $B = 120$ (continuously observed), strike $K = 100$, 7 days to expiry, $r = 0.05$, $\sigma = 0.30$. The plot shows the delta value as a function of the current stock price. Curve: analytical value. Thin line: Numerical differentiation with $\Delta S = 0.01$ applied to a forward tree with $N = 140$. Note that the calculated binomial delta is not only inaccurate but frequently has even the wrong sign. Instead of reducing the risk by delta hedging, it is increased.

We will see in several chapters of this book how easily grid-adaptivity can be achieved with other numerical methods, e.g., finite elements.

2.6 CONCLUSION

Binomial trees can be implemented intuitively and easily. As it turned out on the previous pages, binomial trees work fine for simple models, simple derivative constructs and if computing time does not play a major role. For more complex instruments, the valuation may become inaccurate. This is even more the case for calculating Greeks by utilizing binomial trees.

3

Finite Differences and the
Black-Scholes PDE

In the preceding chapter, we have outlined how to calculate an explicit solution for the price of a European call/put option as the limit of the binomial tree setup. A different method to obtain the same solution is the transformation of the Black-Scholes stochastic differential equation (SDE) into the corresponding partial differential equation (PDE) (Wilmott, 1998).

3.1 A CONTINUOUS TIME MODEL FOR EQUITY PRICES

In this section we summarize mathematical foundations required for the derivation of the Black-Scholes PDE (Hull, 2002). Readers familiar with stochastic differential equations, Wiener processes and the Itô calculus can skip this section.

Returns

Let S_n be the price of an asset at the end of trading day n. Then, we can calculate the log-return,[1]

$$\log\left(\frac{S_n}{S_{n-1}}\right). \tag{3.1}$$

The log-return over a time period of k days is simply calculated by the sum over the respective daily log-returns,

$$\log\left(\frac{S_k}{S_0}\right) = \log\left(\frac{S_1}{S_0}\right) + \cdots + \log\left(\frac{S_k}{S_{k-1}}\right). \tag{3.2}$$

Assuming that log-returns of disjunct time intervals of equal length are independent and identically distributed, the central limit theorem states that the log-returns (3.2) are approximately normally distributed.[2]

Brownian Motion

The geometric Brownian motion (Shreve, 2008) is a process that is continuous in time and produces normally distributed log-returns at each point in time. A formal definition of the (arithmetic) Brownian motion reads:

---

[1] The relative daily return for such an asset would be $S_n/S_{n-1} - 1$. Comparing the relative daily return with the log-return shows that they are very similar (Taylor expansion).

[2] In the sense that the log-return can be seen as a sum over finitely many small independently and identically distributed random variables with finite variance.

A Brownian motion (or Wiener process) is a stochastic process $(W_t : t \in \mathbb{R})$ with the following properties:

(i) $W_0 = 0$ with probability 1 and W_t is a continuous function in t,
(ii) For each $t \geq 0$ and $h > 0$ the increment $W_{t+h} - W_t$ is normally distributed with mean 0 and variance h,

$$W_{t+h} - W_t \sim N(0, h).$$

(iii) For each n and for arbitrarily chosen points in time $t_0 < t_1 < \ldots t_{n-1} < t_n$, the increments $W_{t_j} - W_{t_{j-1}}$ $(j = 1, \ldots, n)$ are independent.

It can be shown from these properties that for each t, W_t itself is normally distributed with mean 0 and variance t. Furthermore, the increments of W_t are stationary, i.e., the distribution of the increment ΔW_t is independent of t,

$$\Delta W_t := W_{t+\Delta t} - W_t \sim \epsilon \sqrt{\Delta t}, \tag{3.3}$$

where ϵ is a normally distributed random variable with $\mu = 0$ and $\sigma = 1$. Taking the limit $\lim_{\Delta t \to 0} : \Delta W_t \to dW_t$ is formally equivalent to

$$dW_t \sim \epsilon \sqrt{dt}. \tag{3.4}$$

With the definitions and properties of dW_t at hand, we can now define the stochastic integral (Protter, 2004) for suitable functions f,

$$\int_0^T f(t)\, dW_t := \lim_{n \to \infty} \sum_{j=1}^n f(t_{j-1})\left(W_{t_j} - W_{t_{j-1}}\right), \tag{3.5}$$

where $t_j = \frac{jT}{n}$. At this point our argumentation is mainly a heuristic one, nonetheless we want to discuss some of the properties of the stochastic integral defined in (3.5):

- In contrast to the Riemann integral, the function must always be evaluated at the left interval boundary.
- If $f = 1 : \int_0^T dW_t = W_T$.
- Using the moments of the normal distribution, it can be easily shown that

$$\lim_{n \to \infty} \mathbb{E}\left[\left(\sum_{j=1}^n (W_{t_j} - W_{t_{j-1}})^2 - T\right)^2\right] = 0. \tag{3.6}$$

Again assuming $f = 1$, we heuristically obtain

$$\int_0^T (dW_t)^2 = T \tag{3.7}$$

or

$$(dW_t)^2 = dt. \tag{3.8}$$

SDE with Brownian Dynamics

Starting with the infinitesimal increment dW_t, we can define a whole class of stochastic processes with Brownian dynamics,

$$dX_t = \mu(X_t, t)\,dt + \sigma(X_t, t)\,dW_t, \tag{3.9}$$

where $\mu(x, t) : \mathbb{R} \times \mathbb{R}^+ \to \mathbb{R}$ and $\sigma(x, t) : \mathbb{R} \times \mathbb{R}^+ \to \mathbb{R}$ are deterministic functions. Equations of this type are also known as Itô processes. The notation above is equivalent to

$$\int_0^t dX_s = \int_0^t \mu(X_s, s)\,ds + \int_0^t \sigma(X_s, s)\,dW_s. \tag{3.10}$$

In the following, we will frequently use continuously differentiable functions $f(X_t, t)$, where X_t is a process following (3.9). Itô's lemma (Protter, 2004) states that for such functions, the following relation holds with probability 1:

$$df(X_t, t) = \left(\frac{\partial f}{\partial X_t} \mu(X_t, t) + \frac{\partial f}{\partial t} + \frac{1}{2} \frac{\partial^2 f}{\partial X_t^2} \sigma^2(X_t, t) \right) dt + \frac{\partial f}{\partial X_t} \sigma(X_t, t)\,dW_t. \tag{3.11}$$

3.2 BLACK-SCHOLES MODEL: FROM THE SDE TO THE PDE

The Black-Scholes SDE

The simplest model for stock price movements still in use today is the Geometric Brownian motion,[3]

$$dS_t = S_t(\mu\,dt + \sigma\,dW_t) \quad (\mu, \sigma \quad \text{const.}). \tag{3.12}$$

We denote μ as the expected return rate (drift) and σ as the volatility. The process described above is a special case of the Itô process (3.10) with $\mu(S_t, t) = S_t\mu$ and $\sigma(S_t, t) = S_t\sigma$. The model is named after Fischer Black and Myron Scholes due to their seminal work in deriving analytical formulae for option prices using stochastic methods.[4]

We would now like to briefly point out a number of important properties of the Black-Scholes SDE:

- Applying Itô's Lemma with $f(S_t, t) = \log S_t$, we obtain

$$d(\log S_t) = \left(\mu - \frac{\sigma^2}{2} \right) dt + \sigma\,dW_t.$$

- With $W_0 = 0$ and for each $T \geq 0$:

$$\log S_t - \log S_0 = \left(\mu - \frac{\sigma^2}{2} \right) T + \sigma(W_T - W_0) = \left(\mu - \frac{\sigma^2}{2} \right) T + \sigma W_T.$$

---

[3] Historically Louis Bachelier was the first to use the arithmetic Brownian motion to model asset prices on stock exchanges in 1900 with the disadvantage of the possibility of negative stock prices. Paul A. Samuelson modified the model using the geometric Brownian motion for the dynamics of the stock price. Recently, due to extremely low interest rates in some economies, the Bachelier model gained new popularity as an alternative to Black76.

[4] Robert Merton has also made contributions to the work but published a separate article. For their work, Merton and Scholes got the Nobel Prize in 1997 (Black had died in 1995).

- From the normal distribution of W_t, it follows that

$$\log S_t \sim N\left(\log S_0 + \left(\mu - \frac{\sigma^2}{2}\right)T, \sigma^2 T\right).$$

- In the model of the geometric Brownian motion, the stock price at each point in time T is log-normally distributed with mean

$$\mathbb{E}(S_T) = S_0 e^{\mu T}$$

and variance

$$\mathrm{Var}(S_T) = S_0^2 e^{2\mu T}\left(e^{\sigma^2 T} - 1\right).$$

- We can get a clear interpretation of the parameters μ and σ (as parameters of the corresponding normal distribution) by discretizing the SDE,

$$\frac{\Delta S_t}{S_t} = \mu \Delta t + \sigma \epsilon \sqrt{\Delta t} \sim N(\mu \Delta t, \sigma^2 \Delta t),$$

where $\Delta S_t = S_{t+\Delta t} - S_t$ is the change of the stock price S in a reasonably small time interval ΔT and $\epsilon \sim N(0, 1)$.

The Black-Scholes PDE

Let $C(S, T)$ be the price of a European call at its expiry date (terminal condition), on an underlying with price process $S = S_t$ following a geometric Brownian motion (3.12). Furthermore assume π_t to be the value of a portfolio at time t consisting of such a call and a number Δ of short positions in the underlying,

$$\pi_t = C(S, t) - \Delta \cdot S. \tag{3.13}$$

The purpose of the short positions is to hedge[5] the variability of the call. In a time interval of length dt the value of the portfolio will change as

$$d\pi_t = dC - \Delta \cdot dS. \tag{3.14}$$

From Itô's lemma we obtain

$$dC = \left(\frac{\partial C}{\partial S}\mu S + \frac{\partial C}{\partial t} + \frac{1}{2}\frac{\partial^2 C}{\partial S^2}\sigma^2 S^2\right)dt + \frac{\partial C}{\partial S}\sigma S\, dW_t, \tag{3.15}$$

and thus we get for the value of the portfolio

$$d\pi_t = \left(\frac{\partial C}{\partial t} + \frac{1}{2}\frac{\partial^2 C}{\partial S^2}\sigma^2 S^2\right)dt + \left(\frac{\partial C}{\partial S} - \Delta\right)dS. \tag{3.16}$$

It is straightforward to see that we can eliminate the stochastic component (represented by dS) in the above equation if we hold a number of

$$\Delta = \frac{\partial C}{\partial S} \tag{3.17}$$

---

[5] Making immune to the risk of adverse price movements. Normally a hedge is established by taking an offsetting position in a related security.

short positions in the underlying at time t. Since the resulting portfolio is then risk-free (i.e., does not have a stochastic component), and keeping in mind that we assume σ is a known quantity,

$$d\pi_t = r\pi_t \, dt \tag{3.18}$$

must hold due to the no-arbitrage condition[6] – otherwise a risk-less profit would be possible! These arguments lead to the Black-Scholes PDE,

$$\frac{\partial C}{\partial t} + \frac{\sigma^2 S^2}{2} \frac{\partial^2 C}{\partial S^2} + rS \frac{\partial C}{\partial S} - rC = 0, \tag{3.19}$$

a linear parabolic partial differential equation. Again, constructing the risk free portfolio π led us to the risk-free measure implied by the risk-free rate. Therefore, the physical growth rate μ does not occur in the Black-Scholes PDE anymore, and the stochastic behavior is reflected by the remaining parameter σ alone. The determination of σ is a central task in quantitative finance. It can be performed either by historical estimates or by parameter identification (see Chapter 15) from the market prices of options. Note that the specific structure of the payoff did not enter the derivation of the Black-Scholes equation – the equation holds for all European derivatives in the Black-Scholes model. To calculate the price of a specific instrument, the terminal payoff at time T is needed,[7] and is propagated backwards in time. Furthermore, due to the no-arbitrage condition, the boundary conditions

$$C(0, t) = 0, \qquad \lim_{S \to \infty} \frac{\partial C(S, t)}{\partial S} = 1 \tag{3.20}$$

must be fulfilled for all $t \in [0, T]$.

The Greeks

In the derivation of the Black-Scholes equation we have used

$$\Delta = \frac{\partial C(S_t, t)}{\partial S_t} \tag{3.21}$$

to hedge away all risky quantities. If we choose Δ in this specific way, we hold a *delta neutral position*. The value of Δ, however, depends on time t, and the portfolio thus needs to be rebalanced continuously.

In practice it is only possible to re-hedge at discrete points in time which leads to a hedge error.[8] By definition, Δ is a sensitivity measure for the derivative price with respect to the underlying asset S_t.

Another important Greek is

$$\Gamma := \frac{\partial^2 C}{\partial S_t^2}, \tag{3.22}$$

---

[6] This argumentation is the continuous version of the arguments used for the weights in the binomial tree (2.3).

[7] For example $C(S, T) = \max(S - K, 0)$ for a European call option.

[8] In the real world, transaction costs have to be paid for each deal, making a continuous rebalancing prohibitively costly. Transaction costs have not been taken into account in the derivation of the Black-Scholes PDE. More sophisticated models incorporate transaction costs (Kabanov and Safarian, 2010) and the resulting prices are adjusted.

which measures the sensitivity of Δ with respect to S_t. The sensitivity of the derivative's price with respect to time is denoted by Θ,

$$\Theta := \frac{\partial C}{\partial t}. \tag{3.23}$$

The sensitivity with respect to the volatility is measured by

$$\text{Vega} := \frac{\partial C}{\partial \sigma}, \tag{3.24}$$

and the sensitivity with respect to the interest rate is denoted by

$$\rho := \frac{\partial C}{\partial r}. \tag{3.25}$$

Continuous Dividends

Under the assumption that dividends are paid in the form of a continuous yield (Hull, 2002) at a constant level, the price of the underlying asset decreases in each time interval dt by an amount

$$\delta S \, dt \quad \text{with} \quad \delta \geq 0. \tag{3.26}$$

The corresponding Black-Scholes equation for a contingent claim V then reads

$$\frac{\partial V}{\partial t} + \underbrace{\frac{\sigma^2 S^2}{2} \frac{\partial^2 V}{\partial S^2}}_{\text{Diffusion}} + \underbrace{rS \frac{\partial V}{\partial S}}_{\text{Convection}} \underbrace{- (r - \delta)V}_{\text{Reaction}} = 0. \tag{3.27}$$

Discrete dividends lead to an interface condition on the date the dividend is paid and will be discussed in more detail in Chapter 6.

Solution of the Black-Scholes PDE

Numerical problems arise from subdomains where convection dominates if the Black-Scholes equation is implemented in the form (3.27), see also Chapter 5. Here, we avoid this problem by a transformation that simplifies the numerical treatment if r, δ and σ are constant. We use the substitutions

$$S = Ke^x, \qquad t = T - \frac{2\tau}{\sigma^2}, \qquad q = \frac{2r}{\sigma^2}, \qquad q_\delta = \frac{2(r - \delta)}{\sigma^2}, \tag{3.28}$$

and define the value of the contingent claim V at time t as

$$V(S, t) = V\left(Ke^x, T - \frac{2\tau}{\sigma^2}\right) = v(x, \tau). \tag{3.29}$$

With the definition

$$v(x, \tau) = K \exp\left\{-\frac{1}{2}(q_\delta - 1)x - \left(\frac{1}{4}(q_\delta - 1)^2\right) + q\tau\right\} u(x, \tau), \tag{3.30}$$

the Black-Scholes equation (3.27) is transformed into a simple heat equation,

$$\frac{\partial u}{\partial \tau} = \frac{\partial^2 u}{\partial x^2}. \tag{3.31}$$

In addition, the terminal and boundary conditions of the Black-Scholes PDE have to be transformed into the new coordinate system, resulting in initial and boundary conditions for Eq. (3.31). The original maturity $t = T$ is now at $\tau = 0$. Since $t = 0$ is transformed to $\tau = \frac{1}{2}\sigma^2 T$, we can argue that τ represents the remaining life-time of the option up to a scaling factor $\frac{1}{2}\sigma^2$. The domain changes from

$$S > 0, \quad 0 \le t \le T \tag{3.32}$$

to

$$-\infty < x < \infty, \quad 0 \le \tau \le \frac{1}{2}\sigma^2 T. \tag{3.33}$$

After the solution $u(x, \tau)$ of (3.31) has been obtained, it can be transformed back using the transformation equations defined in (3.28)–(3.30). To show how the terminal condition changes, we will again use the European call ($V(S, T) = C(S, T)$) as an example,

$$C(S, T) = \max(S - K, 0) = K \max(e^x - 1, 0) = K \exp\left\{-\frac{x}{2}(q_\delta - 1)\right\} u(x, 0). \tag{3.34}$$

Therefore,

$$u(x, 0) = \exp\left\{\frac{x}{2}(q_\delta - 1)\right\} \max(e^x - 1, 0) = \tag{3.35}$$

$$= \begin{cases} \exp\left\{\frac{x}{2}(q_\delta - 1)\right\}(e^x - 1) & \text{for} \quad x > 0 \\ 0 & \text{for} \quad x \le 0 \end{cases}. \tag{3.36}$$

The original terminal condition has been transformed into an initial condition, which can be written as a max condition for the European call,

$$u(x, 0) = \max\left(\exp\left\{\frac{x}{2}(q_\delta + 1)\right\} - \exp\left\{\frac{x}{2}(q_\delta - 1)\right\}, 0\right), \tag{3.37}$$

by using the identity

$$\exp\left\{\frac{x}{2}(q_\delta - 1)\right\}(e^x - 1) = \exp\left\{\frac{x}{2}(q_\delta + 1)\right\} - \exp\left\{\frac{x}{2}(q_\delta - 1)\right\}. \tag{3.38}$$

It still remains to determine boundary conditions for $x \to -\infty$ and $x \to \infty$ to complete the boundary value problem. We will address this issue later in this chapter.

3.3 FINITE DIFFERENCES

Finite differences are an important method in numerical analysis, especially in the field of the numerical solution of differential equations (Quarteroni, Sacco and Saleri, 2002). We start by defining a grid in d spatial dimensions as a discretization of the computational domain,

$$[a_k, b_k]^d \times [0, t_{\max}] = [a_1, b_1] \times \cdots \times [a_d, b_d] \times [0, t_{\max}] = \left(\prod_{k=1}^{d} [a_k, b_k]\right) \times [0, t_{\max}], \tag{3.39}$$

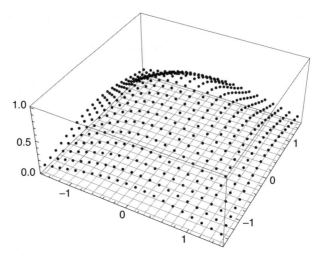

Figure 3.1   Representation of a function $f(x, t)$ on a discrete, equidistant grid.

and use $N_k + 1$ points for the spatial discretization, and $M + 1$ points for the time discretization.

The corresponding indices are $i_k \in \{0, \dots N_k\}$ on the spatial grid in the k-th dimension and $j \in \{0, \dots M\}$ on the time grid,[9] resulting in the discrete grid

$$\left\{(x_{1\,i_1}, \dots, x_{d\,i_d}, t_j) : \forall i_k \in \{0, \dots N_k\}, j \in \{0, \dots M\}\right\}. \tag{3.40}$$

Here, we will focus on equidistantly spaced grids; when adaptivity is required, the finite element method described in Chapter 7 is preferred. On such a grid, the space grid points $x_{k\,i_k}$ are calculated using the space step size h_k,

$$x_{k\,i_k} = a_k + i_k h_k, \quad h_k = \frac{b_k - a_k}{N_k}, \tag{3.41}$$

and the time grid points are calculated using the time step size Δt,

$$t_j = j\Delta t, \quad \Delta t = \frac{t_{max}}{M}. \tag{3.42}$$

A function $f(x_1, \dots, x_d, t)$ can be represented by its values on the grid using $(M + 1)\Pi_{k=1}^d (N_k + 1)$ points,

$$f(x_1, \dots, x_d, t) \rightarrow \left\{f^j_{i_1 \dots i_d} = f\left(x_{1\,i_1}, \dots, x_{d\,i_d}, t_j\right)\right\}. \tag{3.43}$$

A function can be visualized on such a grid as shown in Figure 3.1. If the form of the function f is unknown, its derivatives need to be approximated numerically. One way to construct such finite difference formulae for the first and higher derivatives for different orders of accuracy is based on Taylor series expansions. For clarity of presentation, we restrict ourselves to one dimension and omit the time index. Later in this chapter we will come back to the more general

---

[9] The number of intervals is therefore N_k in each spatial and M in the time dimension.

case. Consider the expansion of the functions $f(x + h)$ and $f(x - h)$,

$$f(x + h) = f(x) + \frac{h}{1!} f'(x) + \frac{h^2}{2!} f''(x) + \frac{h^3}{3!} f'''(x) + \cdots \qquad (3.44)$$

$$f(x - h) = f(x) - \frac{h}{1!} f'(x) + \frac{h^2}{2!} f''(x) - \frac{h^3}{3!} f'''(x) + \cdots \qquad (3.45)$$

Rearranging the terms in (3.44),

$$f'(x) = \frac{f(x + h) - f(x)}{h} + \underbrace{\left(-\frac{h}{2!} f''(x) - \frac{h^2}{3!} f'''(x) - \cdots \right)}_{O(h)}, \qquad (3.46)$$

yields the so called *forward difference quotient*, which is a first-order approximation of the first derivative,[10]

$$f'(x) \approx \frac{f(x + h) - f(x)}{h} + O(h). \qquad (3.47)$$

Performing the same steps with (3.45), we obtain the *backward difference quotient*,

$$f'(x) \approx \frac{f(x) - f(x - h)}{h} + O(h), \qquad (3.48)$$

another first-order approximation of the first derivative. Using the index notation introduced for the discrete representatation of a function on the grid, Equation (3.43), the forward and backward difference quotients at position x_i can be written in more compact notation,

$$f'_i = \frac{f_{i+1} - f_i}{h} \quad \text{and} \quad f'_i = \frac{f_i - f_{i-1}}{h}. \qquad (3.49)$$

To obtain a higher order formula for the first derivative, we subtract (3.45) from (3.44),

$$f(x + h) - f(x - h) = 2hf'(x) + 2\frac{h^3}{3!} f'''(x) + \cdots . \qquad (3.50)$$

Rearranging this equation yields a second-order formula for the first derivative, the *central difference quotient*,

$$f'(x) = \frac{f(x + h) - f(x - h)}{2h} + O(h^2). \qquad (3.51)$$

Again, in index notation $f'(x_i)$ can be written as

$$f'_i = \frac{f_{i+1} - f_{i-1}}{2h}. \qquad (3.52)$$

To obtain an approximation for the second-order derivative we add (3.45) to (3.44) and obtain

$$f(x + h) + f(x - h) = 2f(x) + 2\frac{h^2}{2!} f''(x) + 2\frac{h^4}{4!} f^{(iv)}(x) + \cdots . \qquad (3.53)$$

---

[10] $O(h)$ describes the order of the error induced by the used finite difference formula. For more details see Stoer and Bulirsch (2002).

Solving for $f''(x)$ yields

$$f''(x) = \frac{f(x+h) - 2f(x) + f(x-h)}{h^2} + O(h^2), \tag{3.54}$$

which in index notation reads

$$f_i'' = \frac{f_{i+1} - 2f_i + f_{i-1}}{h^2}. \tag{3.55}$$

If we want to derive higher derivatives or higher order formulae for the first as well as for higher derivatives, we need to derive Taylor expansions for $f(x + ih)$ with $i \in \{2, 3, \dots\}$ and calculate linear combinations. An alternative way to derive finite difference formulae using Lagrange interpolation will be presented in the hands-on exercises accompanying this chapter.

The generalization of the finite difference formulation to d dimensions is straightforward. The central difference quotient for the first derivative can be formed analogously to the one-dimensional case by keeping all dimensions but the one in which the derivative should be calculated for fixed, yielding

$$\frac{\partial f(x_1, x_2, \dots, x_d)}{\partial x_j} \approx \frac{f(x_1, x_2, \dots, x_j + h_j, \dots, x_d) - f(x_1, x_2, \dots, x_j - h_j, \dots, x_d)}{2h_i} \tag{3.56}$$

In index notation, this formula reads

$$\frac{\partial f_{i_1 i_2 \dots i_d}}{\partial x_j} \approx \frac{f_{i_1 i_2 \dots i_j+1 \dots i_d} - f_{i_1 i_2 \dots i_j-1 \dots i_d}}{2h_j}. \tag{3.57}$$

Second derivative formulae for the higher-dimensional case are simply obtained by summing up the one-dimensional formulae keeping the other coordinates fixed.

$$\Delta f(x_1, x_2, \dots, x_d) =$$

$$\frac{f(x_1 + h_1, x_2 \dots, x_d) - 2f(x_1, x_2, \dots, x_d) + f(x_1 - h_1, x_2, \dots, x_d)}{h_1^2} +$$

$$\frac{f(x_1, x_2 + h_2 \dots, x_d) - 2f(x_1, x_2, \dots, x_d) + f(x_1, x_2 - h_2, \dots, x_d)}{h_2^2} + \dots +$$

$$\frac{f(x_1, x_2, \dots, x_d + h_d) - 2f(x_1, x_2, \dots, x_d) + f(x_1, x_2, \dots, x_d - h_d)}{h_d^2} \tag{3.58}$$

$$\Delta f_{i_1 i_2 \dots i_d} =$$

$$\frac{f_{i_1+1 i_2 \dots i_d} - 2f_{i_1 i_2 \dots i_d} + f_{i_1-1 i_2 \dots i_d}}{h_1^2} +$$

$$\frac{f_{i_1, i_2+1 \dots i_d} - 2f_{i_1, i_2 \dots i_d} + f_{i_1 i_2-1 \dots i_d}}{h_2^2} + \dots +$$

$$\frac{f_{i_1 i_2 \dots i_d+1} - 2f_{i_1 i_2 \dots i_d} + f_{i_1 i_2 \dots i_d-1}}{h_d^2} \tag{3.59}$$

Suppose we have a two-dimensional grid in two spatial dimensions x_1 and x_2 with equidistant grid spacing. Then, the discrete representation of the Laplace operator is the five-point stencil

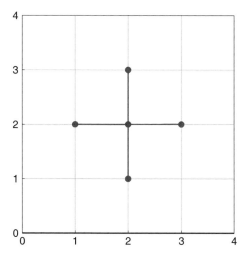

Figure 3.2   Five point stencil of a point in the grid is made up of the point itself together with its four neighboring points. It represents a discrete $\mathcal{O}(h^2)$ approximation of the Laplace operator Δ.

shown in Figure 3.2. The action of a finite difference operator on a function defined on the grid can be easily calculated using the matrix representation of the operator. Depending on the order used, the discretization of the differential operators leads to band matrices (Stoer and Bulirsch, 2002). The discrete approximation of the Laplace operator in one dimension can be represented by a simple tridiagonal matrix,

$$
\mathbf{A} = \begin{pmatrix}
-2 & 1 & 0 & \cdots & 0 \\
1 & -2 & 1 & \ddots & \vdots \\
0 & 1 & \ddots & \ddots & 0 \\
\vdots & \ddots & \ddots & \ddots & 1 \\
0 & \cdots & 0 & 1 & -2
\end{pmatrix}. \tag{3.60}
$$

Due to the sparsity of these matrices, see for instance Figure 3.3, multiplications between them can be performed efficiently, as only the non-zero components have to be taken into account.

3.4   TIME DISCRETIZATION

Formulae for time derivatives can be derived in the same way as those for spatial derivatives earlier in this chapter. Again, we partition the region of interest $[0, T]$ into a discrete set of points in time,

$$
0 = t_0 < t_1 < t_2 < \ldots < t_{n-2} < t_{n-1} < t_n = T. \tag{3.61}
$$

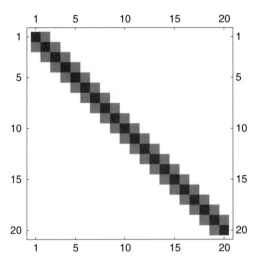

Figure 3.3   Density of entries for the discrete approximation of the Laplace operator in one dimension. The sparsity is obvious.

Consider a time-dependent partial differential equation for a scalar quantity f,

$$\frac{\partial f}{\partial t} = b - Lf, \tag{3.62}$$

where L is a linear differential operator containing all spatial derivatives,[11] and b is a function of (x, t). We can again write the time variation of the quantity f in the discrete time interval of length Δt between t and $t + \Delta t$ using a Taylor expansion,

$$f(t + \Delta t) = f(t) + \Delta t \frac{\partial f}{\partial t} + \frac{\Delta t^2}{2} \frac{\partial^2 f}{\partial t^2} + \cdots . \tag{3.63}$$

Neglecting terms of order higher than one, we can approximate the time derivative with a term accurate up to first order

$$\frac{\partial f(t)}{\partial t} \approx \frac{f(t + \Delta t) - f(t)}{\Delta t} + O(\Delta t). \tag{3.64}$$

Evaluating the right hand side of (3.62) at time t we obtain

$$\frac{f(t + \Delta t) - f(t)}{\Delta t} = b(t) - L(t)f(t), \tag{3.65}$$

and, in turn, the explicit time-stepping scheme

$$f(t + \Delta t) = f(t) + \Delta t(b(t) - L(t)f(t)). \tag{3.66}$$

---

[11] Here L is only used in a formal way to shorten the notation. $L(\cdot)f(\cdot)$ denotes the action of the linear operator $L(\cdot)$ on a function $f(\cdot)$.

Table 3.1   Different time-stepping schemes.

Θ	Name of the Scheme	Description
0	Forward difference method	Fully explicit scheme
1	Backward difference method	Fully implicit scheme
0.5	Crank-Nicolson method	Semi-implicit scheme

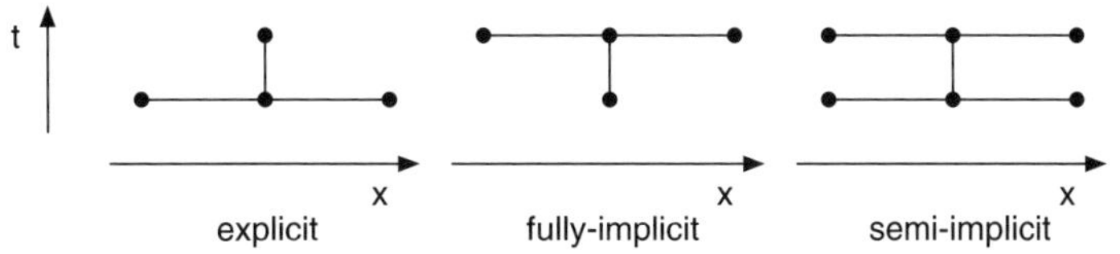

Figure 3.4   Characteristic patterns for the explicit, implicit and semi-implicit time-stepping schemes in the space-time domain.

For this explicit scheme it is not necessary to solve a system of linear equations. For the fully implicit scheme, on the other hand the basic equation is

$$\frac{f(t + \Delta t) - f(t)}{\Delta t} = b(t + \Delta t) - L(t + \Delta t)f(t + \Delta t), \qquad (3.67)$$

and the propagation equation requires the solution of a system of linear equations

$$(1 + \Delta t L(t + \Delta t)) f(t + \Delta t) = f(t) + \Delta t b(t + \Delta t). \qquad (3.68)$$

Both of the above methods are of order Δt.

By introducing a new parameter Θ such that

$$\frac{f(t + \Delta t) - f(t)}{\Delta t} = (1 - \Theta)(b(t) - L(t)f(t)) + \Theta(b(t + \Delta t) - L(t + \Delta t)f(t + \Delta t)), \quad (3.69)$$

we can construct different transient schemes (Quarteroni, Sacco and Saleri, 2002) for different values of Θ, see Table 3.1. The different time-stepping schemes have characteristic patterns in the space (x) and time (t) domain as shown in Figure 3.4. Setting $\Theta = 1/2$, we obtain a semi-implicit scheme of order $(\Delta t)^2$, the so-called Crank-Nicolson method,

$$\left(1 + \frac{1}{2}\Delta t L(t + \Delta t)\right) f(t + \Delta t) = \left(1 - \frac{1}{2}\Delta t L(t)\right) f(t) + \frac{1}{2}\Delta t (b(t + \Delta t) + b(t)). \qquad (3.70)$$

If either L or b depend on the unknown quantity f, Equation (3.62) becomes nonlinear. In order to avoid having to solve a nonlinear system of equations in each time step when applying one of the implicit time-stepping methods, one can, for instance, linearize the system. This can be done, among others, by applying the predictor-corrector[12] or the Runge-Kutta[13] methods to the problem. In financial engineering, nonlinearities occur when generalized Black-Scholes equations are used for nonlinear volatility or problems with transactions costs (Kabanov and Safarian, 2010).

---

[12] A predictor-corrector method is an algorithm that proceeds in two steps: the prediction step calculates a rough approximation of the desired quantity, the corrector step refines the initial approximation.

[13] Runge-Kutta methods are a family of methods for the approximation of the solution of ordinary differential equations.

3.5 STABILITY CONSIDERATIONS

An exact analysis of the stability of different time-stepping schemes is beyond the scope of this book, but can be found in many textbooks on numerical analysis (Quarteroni, Sacco and Saleri, 2002). Here, we only summarize the most important issues. The explicit time-stepping method for solving (3.31) is stable only if

$$0 < \Delta t \leq \frac{h^2}{2}. \tag{3.71}$$

We give a derivation of this stability condition in the appendix of this chapter. Due to (3.71), the parameters h and Δt (and in turn the number of points in the combined space-time grid) cannot be chosen independently. In many practical applications this leads to infeasibly small time steps. The tree methods presented in Chapter 2 are explicit methods where (3.71) is implicitly fulfilled by the choice of the tree parameters (2.10), (2.11) or (2.12). The fully implicit time-stepping scheme is unconditionally stable, i.e., stable for all $\Delta t > 0$. Both the explicit and the implicit method are of order $O(\Delta t)$. It seems advantageous to use an unconditionally stable scheme of a higher order. Fortunately, the Crank-Nicolson method fulfills both criteria – the scheme is stable for all $\Delta t > 0$ and is of order $O(\Delta t^2)$. The Crank-Nicolson scheme is widely used for this reason, although it can cause spurious oscillations, in particular near the strike price and near barriers. Duffy has suggested using an extrapolated fully implicit scheme to obtain second order accuracy and at the same time avoid such oscillations (Duffy, 2006). In addition to the methods discussed so far, advanced time discretization schemes have been developed and are used in different fields of applied mathematics and computational physics (Landau, Paez and Bordeianu, 2011).

Boundary Conditions

In physics and engineering, initial and boundary conditions are usually dicated by the physical setup.[14] When pricing financial derivatives, on the other hand, it is not possible to determine the product value or its derivatives at the boundaries of the computational domain, except for very simple instruments. We will discuss several methods to circumvent this problem and different forms of boundary conditions in Chapter 6.

3.6 FINITE DIFFERENCES AND THE HEAT EQUATION

In this section, we apply the finite difference method to the transformed Black-Scholes equation (3.31). If $x \in \mathbb{R}$, one must choose a bounded computational domain $[a, b]$ and impose artificial boundary conditions at $x = a$ and $x = b$ for all t. Different types of boundary conditions can be used:[15]

• Dirichlet boundary conditions:

$$u(a, t) = g_a(t) \quad \text{and} \quad u(b, t) = g_b(t) \tag{3.72}$$

---

[14] For example when solving a heat equation problem, one normally has an initial temperature (initial condition) and conditions on the spatial boundaries. These conditions can either be fixed values for the temperature on some parts of the boundary or some information about the heat flux induced either by convection or radiation.

[15] More boundary conditions than Dirichlet or Neumann can be applied to the equation. For a detailed discussion of this topic we refer to Chapter 6.

- Neumann boundary conditions:

$$\frac{\partial u(a,t)}{\partial x} = g_a(t) \quad \text{and} \quad \frac{\partial u(b,t)}{\partial x} = g_b(t) \tag{3.73}$$

The derivatives occuring in the boundary conditions can be approximated using the one-sided finite differences (3.49), yielding

$$\frac{u_1^j - u_0^j}{h} = g_a(t_j), \qquad \frac{u_N^j - u_{N-1}^j}{h} = g_b(t_j) \quad \text{for } j = 0, \dots, M. \tag{3.74}$$

Subscript indices are used for the spatial domain and superscript indices are used for the time domain. Using the finite difference formulae derived previously, one can replace the PDE (3.31) by a set of algebraic equations. In the following, we describe the workflows necessary for applying the different time-stepping schemes:

- **Explicit (Euler) finite difference scheme**

$$\frac{u_i^{j+1} - u_i^j}{\Delta t} - \frac{u_{i+1}^j - 2u_i^j + u_{i-1}^j}{h^2} = 0 \tag{3.75}$$

for $j = 0, \dots, M-1$ and $i = 1, \dots, N-1$ (see Figure 3.5).

Workflow for the explicit time-stepping scheme
1. Initialization

$$u_i^0 = u(x_i, 0) \qquad i = 0, \dots, N \tag{3.76}$$

2. For $j = 0, \dots, M-1$:

$$u_i^{j+1} = \frac{\Delta t}{h^2} u_{i+1}^j + \left(1 - 2\frac{\Delta t}{h^2}\right) u_i^j + \frac{\Delta t}{h^2} u_{i-1}^j \quad i = 1, \dots, N-1 \tag{3.77}$$

If Dirichlet boundary conditions are used:

$$u_0^{j+1} = g_a(t_{j+1}) \qquad u_N^{j+1} = g_b(t_{j+1}) \tag{3.78}$$

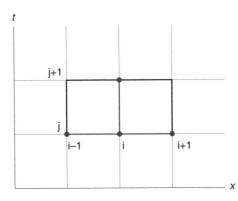

Figure 3.5 Discretization points in space and time used to propagate point i from time t_j to t_{j+1} using an explicit time discretization.

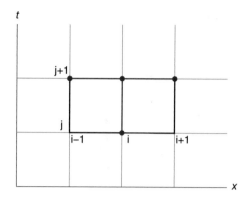

Figure 3.6 Discretization points in space and time used to propagate point x_i from time t_j to t_{j+1} using an implicit time discretization.

If Neumann boundary conditions are used:

$$u_0^j = u_1^j - hg_a(t_j) \qquad u_N^j = u_{N-1}^j + hg_b(t_j) \tag{3.79}$$

- **Implicit finite difference scheme**

$$\frac{u_i^{j+1} - u_i^j}{\Delta t} - \frac{u_{i+1}^{j+1} - 2u_i^{j+1} + u_{i-1}^{j+1}}{h^2} = 0 \tag{3.80}$$

for $j = 0, \ldots, M - 1$ and $i = 1, \ldots, N - 1$ (see Figure 3.6).

Workflow for the implicit time-stepping scheme
1. Initialization

$$u_i^0 = u(x_i, 0) \qquad i = 0, \ldots, N \tag{3.81}$$

2. For $j = 0, \ldots, M - 1$:
   Solve:

$$-\frac{\Delta t}{h^2} u_{i+1}^{j+1} + \left(1 + 2\frac{\Delta t}{h^2}\right) u_i^{j+1} - \frac{\Delta t}{h^2} u_{i-1}^{j+1} = u_i^j \quad i = 1, \ldots, N - 1 \tag{3.82}$$

If Dirichlet boundary conditions are used:

$$u_0^{j+1} = g_a(t_{j+1}) \qquad u_N^{j+1} = g_b(t_{j+1}) \tag{3.83}$$

For the treatment of Neumann boundary conditions, see the general Θ-scheme below.

- **Θ-finite difference scheme**
  With the parameter $\Theta \in [0, 1]$, the resulting scheme is a combination of explicit and implicit schemes (see Figure 3.7).

$$\frac{u_i^{j+1} - u_i^j}{\Delta t} - \left[(1 - \Theta)\frac{u_{i+1}^j - 2u_i^j + u_{i-1}^j}{h^2} + \Theta\frac{u_{i+1}^{j+1} - 2u_i^{j+1} + u_{i-1}^{j+1}}{h^2}\right] = 0. \tag{3.84}$$

To analyze this equation we introduce a matrix notation:
  With the column vector **u**,

$$\mathbf{u}^j = (u_0^j, u_1^j, \ldots, u_{N-1}^j, u_N^j)^T, \tag{3.85}$$

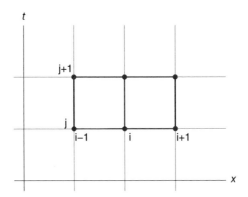

Figure 3.7   Discretization points in space and time used to propagate point i from time t_j to t_{j+1} using a Crank-Nicolson ($\Theta = 1/2$) time discretization.

an $N + 1 \times N + 1$ identitiy matrix $\mathbf{I}$, and the tridiagonal matrix $\mathbf{A}$ from equation (3.60), we can write the finite difference Θ-scheme in matrix form

$$\underbrace{\left(\mathbf{I} + \Theta \frac{\Delta t}{h^2} \mathbf{A}\right)}_{\mathbf{B}} \mathbf{u}^{j+1} = \underbrace{\left(\mathbf{I} - (1 - \Theta) \frac{\Delta t}{h^2} \mathbf{A}\right)}_{\mathbf{C}} \mathbf{u}^j, \tag{3.86}$$

or, shorter, as

$$\mathbf{B}\mathbf{u}^{j+1} = \mathbf{C}\mathbf{u}^j. \tag{3.87}$$

Homogeneous Dirichlet boundary conditions ($u_0^j = 0$ and $u_N^j = 0$) can be incorporated by updating the first and the last row vectors $\mathbf{b}_0$, $\mathbf{c}_0$, $\mathbf{b}_N$ and $\mathbf{c}_N$ of the matrices $\mathbf{B}$ and $\mathbf{C}$ according to

$$\mathbf{b}_0 = \mathbf{c}_0 = (1, 0, \dots, 0) \quad \mathbf{b}_N = \mathbf{c}_N = (0, \dots, 0, 1). \tag{3.88}$$

Workflow for the Θ time-stepping scheme
1. Initialization,

$$\mathbf{u}^0 = (u_0^0, u_1^0, \dots, u_{N-1}^0, u_N^0)^T, \tag{3.89}$$

where u_0^0 and u_N^0 depend on the boundary conditions.
2. For $j = 0, \dots, M - 1$:

$$\mathbf{u}^{j+1} = \mathbf{B}^{-1}\mathbf{C}\mathbf{u}^j, \tag{3.90}$$

where the multiplication with the inverse of $\mathbf{B}$ amounts to solving a linear system.

Θ-scheme for inhomogeneous Dirichlet boundary conditions:
For inhomogeneous Dirichlet conditions (3.72), we define

$$\mathbf{u}^j = (\Theta g_a^{j+1} + (1 - \Theta)g_a^j, u_1^j, \dots, u_{N-1}^j, \Theta g_b^{j+1} + (1 - \Theta)g_b^j)^T. \tag{3.91}$$

Θ-scheme for Neumann boundary conditions:
Assuming Neumann conditions (3.73), we define

$$\mathbf{u}^j = (\Theta h g_a^{j+1} + (1 - \Theta)h g_a^j, u_1^j, \dots, u_{N-1}^j, \Theta h g_b^{j+1} + (1 - \Theta)h g_b^j)^T, \tag{3.92}$$

and update the first and the last row vectors $\mathbf{b}_0$, $\mathbf{c}_0$, $\mathbf{b}_N$ and $\mathbf{c}_N$ of the matrices $\mathbf{B}$ and $\mathbf{C}$ according to

$$\mathbf{b}_0 = \mathbf{c}_0 = (-1, 1, 0, \dots, 0) \quad \mathbf{b}_N = \mathbf{c}_N = (0, \dots, 0, 1, -1). \tag{3.93}$$

3.6.1 Numerical Results

To compare the different time-stepping schemes, we have solved the heat equation (3.31) on the computational domain (space $\times$ time)

$$[-1; 1] \times [0, 0.2].$$

Throughout the following sections, we have chosen $N = 200$, resulting in $h = 0.01$. The initial condition has been chosen as

$$u(x, 0) = \exp\left\{ -\left(\frac{x}{0.1}\right)^2 \right\},$$

and the Dirichlet boundary conditions are

$$u(-1, t) = 0 \quad \text{and} \quad u(1, t) = 0.$$

Implicit Time Stepping

As pointed out before, the implicit time-stepping scheme is unconditionally stable. Figure 3.8 shows the evolution of $u(x, t)$ in time starting with the initial function $u(x, 0)$ for $\Delta t = 0.01$ and $n_t = 20$.

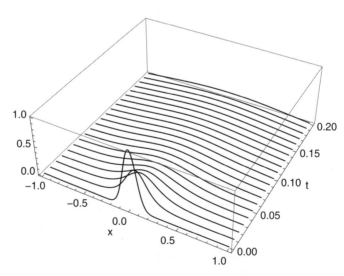

Figure 3.8   The figure shows the evolution of $u(x, t)$ in time between $t = 0$ and $t = 0.2$ using an implicit, and therefore unconditionally stable, time-stepping scheme.

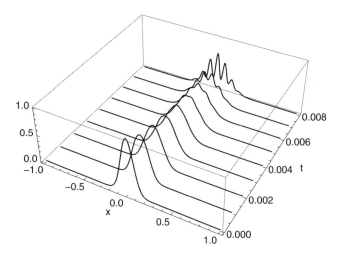

Figure 3.9 The figure shows the evolution of $u(x, t)$ in time between $t = 0$ and $t = 0.008$ using an explicit time-stepping scheme that violates (3.71). Within a few iterations oscillations occur.

Explicit Time Stepping

The explicit time-stepping scheme is only stable if condition (3.71) is satisfied. Violating the stability condition by choosing $\Delta t = 0.001$ leads to the onset of oscillations within a few time steps as can be seen in Figure 3.9. Figure 3.10 shows a detailed plot of the oscillations at $t = 0.008$.

Crank-Nicolson Time Stepping

Although unconditionally stable (Thomas, 1995), the Crank-Nicolson scheme can produce oscillations in the approximated solutions, depending on Δt. These oscillations are damped

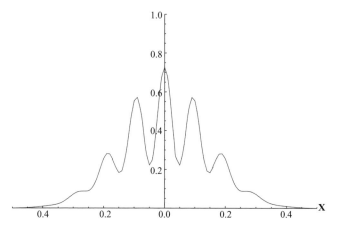

Figure 3.10 The figure shows $u(x, 0.008)$. The oscillations/instabilities induced by using an explicit time-stepping scheme violating (3.71) are obvious.

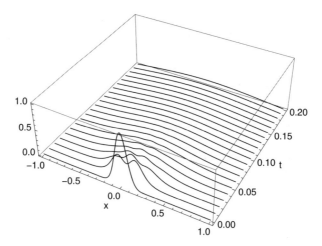

Figure 3.11 The figure shows the evolution of $u(x, t)$ in time between $t = 0$ and $t = 0.2$ using the Crank-Nicolson time-stepping scheme with $\Delta t = 0.01$. The oscillations are damped out during the time propagation.

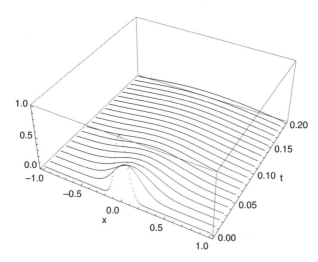

Figure 3.12 The figure shows the evolution of $u(x, t)$ in time between $t = 0$ and $t = 0.2$ using the Crank-Nicolson time-stepping scheme with $\Delta t = 0.001$. The oscillating noise is significantly reduced.

during the evolution in time. Figures 3.11 and 3.12 compare the solution of the heat equation (3.31) using the Crank-Nicolson time-stepping scheme for $\Delta t = 0.01$ and $\Delta t = 0.001$. Reducing Δt significantly reduces the oscillating noise.

3.7 APPENDIX: ERROR ANALYSIS

To demonstrate the convergence of the above schemes, we will explore its consistency and stability. The consistency error q_i^j measures the quality of the approximation of the equation. A scheme is called consistent if its consistency error goes to zero as $h \to 0$, $\Delta t \to 0$. Estimating the consistency error for the heat equation in terms of the mesh width h and the time step size Δt yields[16]

$$|q_i^j| \leq C(h^2 + \Delta t) \quad 0 \leq \Theta \leq 1 \tag{3.94}$$

and

$$|q_i^j| \leq C(h^2 + \Delta t^2) \quad \Theta = \frac{1}{2}, \tag{3.95}$$

where C depends on the exact solution $\tilde{u}(x,t)$. Note that these inequalities only hold for sufficiently smooth exact solutions $\tilde{u}(x,t)$.

For the stability analysis, we define the discretization error vector $\mathbf{e}^j$ at time t_j,

$$e_i^j = \tilde{u}(x_i, t_j) - u_i^j. \tag{3.96}$$

The error vectors satisfy

$$\frac{1}{\Delta t} \mathbf{B} \mathbf{e}^{j+1} - \frac{1}{\Delta t} \mathbf{C} \mathbf{e}^j = \mathbf{q}^j, \tag{3.97}$$

or, in explicit form,

$$\mathbf{e}^{j+1} = \mathbf{A}_\Theta \mathbf{e}^j + \Delta t \mathbf{B}^{-1} \mathbf{q}^j, \tag{3.98}$$

where $\mathbf{A}_\Theta = \mathbf{B}^{-1}\mathbf{C}$ is called the amplification matrix. We recall the definitions of $|| : ||_2$ for a vector

$$||\mathbf{v}||_2 := \sqrt{v_1^2 + \cdots + v_N^2}, \tag{3.99}$$

and a matrix

$$||\mathbf{M}||_2 := \sup_{\mathbf{v} \neq 0} \frac{||\mathbf{M}\mathbf{v}||_2}{||\mathbf{v}||_2}. \tag{3.100}$$

It is well known that a finite difference scheme converges as $M \to \infty$ and $N \to \infty$ if

$$||\mathbf{A}_\Theta||_2 \leq 1 \tag{3.101}$$

holds. In the case of a symmetric matrix, $|| : ||$ can be calculated using

$$||\mathbf{M}||_2 = \max_{1 \leq l \leq N} |\lambda_l|, \tag{3.102}$$

where λ_l with $1 \leq l \leq N$ are the eigenvalues of matrix $\mathbf{M}$. The eigenvalues of $\mathbf{A}_\Theta$ are given by

$$\lambda_l = \frac{1 - 4(1 - \Theta)\Delta t h^{-2} \sin^2\left(\frac{l\pi}{2(N+1)}\right)}{1 + 4\Theta\Delta t h^{-2} \sin^2\left(\frac{l\pi}{2(N+1)}\right)}. \tag{3.103}$$

The convergence condition (3.101) is satisfied if

$$\forall l = 1, \ldots, N, \quad |\lambda_l| \leq 1. \tag{3.104}$$

---

[16] Basically the consistency error is defined by the orders of the finite difference schemes used for discretization.

Denoting

$$x_l = 4\Delta t h^{-2} \sin^2\left(\frac{l\pi}{2(N+1)}\right) \geq 0,$$

we can write

$$\lambda_l = 1 - \frac{x_l}{1 + \Theta x_l} \leq 1. \tag{3.105}$$

We leave it for the reader to check that

$$\lambda_l \geq -1, \tag{3.106}$$

which shows that for

$$\frac{1}{2} \leq \Theta \leq 1$$

the Θ-scheme is stable for all h and Δt. For

$$0 \leq \Theta < \frac{1}{2},$$

the Θ-scheme is stable if the Courant-Friedrichs-Levy (CFL) condition,

$$\frac{\Delta t}{h^2} \leq \frac{1}{2(1 - 2\Theta)}, \tag{3.107}$$

holds. We can conclude that if the scheme is consistent and stable, then it is convergent with the same order the consistency error shows.

Mean Reversion and Trinomial Trees

In the previous chapters, we have dealt with the basic Black-Scholes model (and its discrete tree versions) for describing the stock price movement of an equity. In this chapter, we introduce several *interest rate instruments* (also named *fixed income instruments*) and a number of basic models, the so-called one-factor *short rate models*. These describe the stochastic behavior of the short rate, the fictitious underlying which is, by construction, the interest rate paid for an incremental time.

Fixed income instruments are of huge importance in financial markets. According to the Bank of International Settlement, the outstanding notional volume of *over-the-counter*[1] (OTC) derivatives was 600 (American) trillion USD by the end of 2010. The portion of OTC interest rate derivatives among these was 465 trillion, more than three quarters in terms of notional amount. (Source: http://www.bis.org/statistics/otcder/dt1920a.pdf).

4.1 SOME FIXED INCOME TERMS

Governments (or banks or corporations) issue *bonds* when they need money to fulfill their obligations and the income from taxes (revenues) does not suffice or when it can be foreseen that there will be a liquidity bottleneck in the near future. The investor in the bond pays a sum that is to be invested, say, 10 000 EUR to the German Republic, and obtains the fixed income of the annual interest rate on her investment. At the maturity of the bond, the invested sum is paid back to the investor. This scenario of course describes the ideal case and neglects the possibility of credit events such as defaults. The level of interest rates the issuer of the bond needs to pay depends, obviously, on the market's view of the credit quality of the issuer of the bond, on the time to maturity and on the market level of interest rates on issuance. Bonds are typically exchange-traded and thus have a market price which fluctuates with their attractivity.

4.1.1 Interest Rates and Compounding

When a government pays, as described above, an interest rate of c_a ("annual coupon") for a one year bond, a capital of 1 EUR will have grown to $(1 + c_a)$ after this year. If this amount is again reinvested at a rate c_a, one obtains with *annual compounding*

$$C(t_0 + n) = C(t_0) \cdot (1 + c_a)^n. \tag{4.1}$$

After n years, the capital $C(.)$ has grown by a factor $(1 + c_a)^n$. If coupons are paid semi-annually or quarterly, we obtain the growth factor $(1 + c_s/2)^{2n}$ for *semi-annual compounding* based on a semi-annual rate $c_s/2$ for half a year and the factor $(1 + c_q/4)^{4n}$ for *quarterly compounding* in a similar way.

---

[1] Meaning: not exchange-traded.

In the limit where time slices become infinitesimally small, one obtains continuous compounding at a continuous rate r,

$$B(t_0 + \Delta t) = B(t_0)e^{r\Delta t}, \tag{4.2}$$

or, in equivalent differential formulation

$$dB(t) = r \cdot B(t)dt. \tag{4.3}$$

The formulation (4.2) describes the growth of an account continuously compounded by the interest rate r. Alternatively, one might ask for the size of an investment at time t_0 that will have a value of 1 at time $t_0 + \Delta t$. With the notation of (4.2), $e^{-r\Delta t}$ is then called the *discount factor* for the tenor Δt. To emphasize that the continuous interest rate r depends on t_0 and on $t_1 = t_0 + \Delta t$, we write

$$DF(t_0, t_1) = e^{-r(t_0,t_1)(t_1 - t_0)} \tag{4.4}$$

for the discount factor from time t_1 to $t_0 < t_1$.

When we neglect day-count conventions,[2] the *present value* $P(t_0)$ of a family of n cashflows $C_i(t_i)$ (paying C_i at time t_i) is then given by

$$P(t_0) = \sum_{i=1}^{n} e^{-r(t_0,t_i)(t_i - t_0)} C_i(t_i). \tag{4.5}$$

4.1.2   Libor Rates and Vanilla Interest Rate Swaps

For certain tenors (e.g., 3 months, 6 months, 12 months) in the most liquid currencies, major banks report their cost (i.e., interest rates) of borrowing unsecured funds (from other banks) to the British bankers association. The contributor banks answer the question: "At what rate could you borrow funds, were you to do so by asking for and then accepting inter-bank offers in a reasonable market size just prior to 11 am?". The respective Libor (London interbank offering rate), say, the EUR 6 month rate (or Euribor6m), is calculated by removing the top and bottom quartiles of these answers and then averaging the results.[3] Libor rates in the original meaning are paid at the end of the respective period and are therefore discretely compounded.

Instead of equipping a bond with a fixed coupon, a *floating rate note* pays a variable coupon, e.g., a Libor rate. In a *vanilla floater*, the length of a coupon period corresponds to the tenor of the Libor rate, so the semi-annual floater pays Libor6M (times 1/2 because the coupon is paid only for half a year), the annual floater pays Libor12M. Each coupon rate is set at the beginning of the respective coupon period and paid at its end.[4] So if the bank obtains (1+Libor · (year fraction of the Libor rate)) at the end of a Libor interval, then the present value of the cashflow at the beginning of the interval is exactly 1. This follows from the definition of Libor rates. We can propagate backwards through time and obtain the following

---

[2] Day-count conventions formulate how many days are counted between two calendar dates. E.g., the convention "30/360" counts each calendar month with 30 days. Therefore, under "30/360", there are three days counted from February 28 to March 1, but also from March 28 to April 1.

[3] For details see http://www.bbalibor.com/bbalibor-explained/the-basics.

[4] Again, there are nasty details such as day count conventions, business day conventions and settlement conventions meaning that there is typically a delay of two business days before cashflows are executed.

identity: Assume a vanilla floater with nominal amount Z pays the following cashflows at the dates $t_i = t_0 + i \cdot \Delta t$, $(i = 1, \dots, n)$ with the Libor rates set in advance

$$\text{Libor}(t_{i-1}, t_{i-1} + \Delta t) \cdot \Delta t \cdot Z, i = 1, \dots, n - 1 (\text{coupons})$$

and

$$\text{Libor}(t_{n-1}, t_{n-1} + \Delta t) \cdot \Delta t \cdot Z + Z, (\text{final coupon plus redemption of nominal}),$$

then, disregarding day-count, business day and settlement conventions, its present value at any coupon date t_i equals Z.

Vanilla Interest Rate Swaps and Bootstrapping

In general, *swaps* are OTC instruments between two parties (let's call them A and B) which have agreed on a notional amount and on rules for payments at certain dates from A to B and vice versa. In a *vanilla interest rate swap*, one party pays fixed rates on the notional, the other one floating rates. Vanilla interest rate swaps are highly standardized by the International Swaps and Derivatives Association (www.isda.org). For the EUR, such a swap agreement contains the following key elements (the right hand column contains specific examples):

Legal names of counterparties A and B	
Maturity date	Oct. 15, 2015
Trade date	Oct. 15, 2012
Notional amount	18 mio EUR
A pays to B	2.66 percent, annual, 30/360
B pays to A	Euribor6m, semiannual, ACT/365
Fixing of Euribor6m	in advance

The cashflows between the counterparties are schematically drawn in Figure 4.1.

Again, we have neglected a number of details such as settlement rules and the details of Euribor fixing. The fixing of Euribor in advance means that the floating rate is, like in the vanilla floater example above, fixed at the beginning of each coupon period. In a typical swap, there is no exchange of notionals but the fixed rate is chosen in such a way that at the trade date, the swap has a value of zero for both parties. If this is not the case, there may be upfront payments at the trade date. It can be easily shown that a vanilla interest rate swap can be replicated by the difference of a fixed rate bond and a vanilla floating rate note. The unique

A pays (fixed)   B pays (floating)

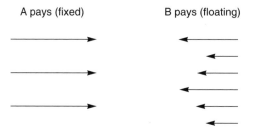

Figure 4.1   Schematic cashflows of a vanilla interest rate swap. A annually pays fixed coupons, B semi-annually pays floating coupons (Euribor6m). Maturity is at the top.

fixed rate in a swap that yields an initial swap value of zero is then denoted as *constant maturity swap rate* or *CMS rate*. It depends on the time to maturity when entering the swap. Obviously, "10y EUR CMS" is the EUR fixed rate for a swap with a maturity of 10 years, "18m USD CMS" is the 18 month USD rate.

In the above example, A pays fixed coupons. For the counterparty A, the example swap is (by convention) named a *payer swap*, for B a *receiver swap*. A pays the *fixed leg*, B pays the *floating leg*. Although theoretically the floating leg plus notional at maturity can be replicated by a vanilla floater and therefore has a deterministic present value of the notional at the trade date, in practice – due to credit or liquidity considerations – it makes a difference in the swap rate (the fixed rate) whether it is paid against Euribor6m (semi-annually) or Euribor3m (quarterly).

If one wants to valuate a swap that has been entered in the past, one has to valuate the bond that corresponds to the fixed leg. Assuming all discount factors for the dates on which fixed payments occur are known, the present value of the bond is obtained by formula (4.5). On the other hand, if swap rates for all (say, annual) maturities are quoted, can we then derive the discount factors? The answer is obviously "yes" and can be obtained by induction: If we already know the discount factors for years $1, \dots, n$ and if we are quoted the $(n+1)$-years swap rate $CMS(n+1)$, then (4.5) leads to

$$1 = \sum_{i=1}^{n} e^{-r(t_0, t_0+i) \cdot i} CMS(n+1) + e^{-r(t_0, t_0+n+1) \cdot (n+1)} (1 + CMS(n+1)). \qquad (4.6)$$

This recursive algorithm is called *bootstrapping of zero rates* $r(t_0, t_0 + i)$ from swap rates. For long-dated swaps, quotations are not available for every year (e.g., there might be no quotation for the rates between 45y and 50y available). In such a case, to obtain unique discount factors, one could either interpolate the swap rates linearly, or require that the zero rates for 46, 47, 48 and 49 years are the same as the 50y zero rate.

Exercise: Write down conditions on the swap rates that guarantee that discount factors are between 0 and 1.

Forward Rates

Assume that, at time t_0, you know that you are entitled to get a cashflow C at time t_2. What is the fair value X of this cashflow at time $t_1 \in (t_0, t_2)$? A fair swap would obviously consist of the cashflows C at time t_2 and $-X$ at time t_1, therefore, if we know the zero rates $r(t_0, t_i)$,

$$X \cdot e^{-r(t_0, t_1)(t_1 - t_0)} = C \cdot e^{-r(t_0, t_2)(t_2 - t_0)} \qquad (4.7)$$

must hold. Therefore,

$$\log(X/C) = -\frac{r(t_0, t_2)(t_2 - t_0) - r(t_0, t_1)(t_1 - t_0)}{t_2 - t_1} \cdot (t_2 - t_1) \qquad (4.8)$$

is the discount factor to be used to obtain X from C. The rate

$$f(t0, t1, t2) := \frac{r(t_0, t_2)(t_2 - t_0) - r(t_0, t_1)(t_1 - t_0)}{t_2 - t_1} \qquad (4.9)$$

is named the continuously compounded forward rate from t_1 to t_2 implied at t_0.

Forward Start Swap Rates

By utilizing the forward rates as in (4.9), one can obviously calculate fair CMS rates for vanilla interest rate swaps starting in the future.

4.2 BLACK76 FOR CAPS AND SWAPTIONS

If the zero rate curve $r(t_0, t)$ at a time t_0 is given (or has been interpolated or extrapolated) for all t, the fair forward rates (either forward zero rates with continuous compounding, forward Libor rates with discrete compounding or forward CMS rates) can be calculated following (4.9) and its Libor and CMS modifications.

Like equity shares, the rates that are traded in the markets fluctuate and therefore derivatives on interest rates may be attractive investments in order to reduce fixed income risk or to take risky positions.

A *cap* is a contract that allows the holder of the cap to limit floating payments by the strike rate of the cap. To be more specific, a vanilla cap (cap on a Libor rate) generates at each coupon day the cashflow $\max(r_L - r_C, 0) \cdot X$ ($\times$year fraction)[5] for the owner of the cap, with r_L being the Libor rate set at the beginning of the coupon interval, r_C being the strike rate, and X the notional of the cap. Therefore, a 5 year cap on Euribor6m with a strike rate of 4.5 percent produces zero cashflows if the Euribor6m at the beginning of the coupon interval is below 4.5 percent, and pays the difference to the strike rate otherwise. So, in combination with a Euribor payment obligation, the combined payment is then, at each coupon day, $\max(r_L, r_C) \cdot X \cdot 1/2$.

In the above example, the 5 year cap consists of 10 possible payments (every 6 months). The individual option $\max(r_L - r_C, 0)$ for one coupon period (set in advance, paid at the end) is called a *caplet*. Similarly, a *floorlet* bounds floating payments from below with a payoff $\max(r_F - r_L, 0)$, and a *floor* consists of consecutive floorlets. An investor in a floating rate note can therefore obtain a coupon of at least r_F by buying the respective floor.

Caps and floors are liquidly traded for the most liquid currencies for different lifetimes and different strike rates. Market convention for the Euribor is that caps/floors with maturities of up to 2 years refer to the Euribor3m, longer maturities refer to the 6 month rate. Note that these conventions depend on the respective currency. A 3 year cap would therefore consist of 6 caplets with the floating rate for the first caplet set immediately. As the value of this first caplet is known at the beginning, market convention ignores possible payments from the first caplet/floorlet in the valuation of cap/floor premia.

Cap–Floor–Parity

Combining a long position in a caplet and a short position in a floorlet with the same strike rate r_C and neglecting the constant factors X($\times$year fraction) yields

$$\max(r_L - r_C, 0) - \max(r_C - r_L, 0) = r_L - r_C, \qquad (4.10)$$

which, on the right hand side shows one cashflow of a vanilla swap. Combining the different coupon dates then yields

$$\text{cap} - \text{floor} = \text{swap}, \qquad (4.11)$$

which holds independent of the model used for cap/floor valuation. It therefore suffices to derive prices for caps.

---

[5] Which is calculated by the currency-specific day count convention.

Black76 Pricing of Caplets

Assume the caplet to be valuated at time t_0 starts at t_k (meaning that the Libor rate is set at t_k) and pays the caplet payoff at t_{k+1}. The Black76 model assumes that the Libor rate set at t_k is lognormally distributed with an expected value of F_k, the forward Libor rate observed at t_0, and has an annualized volatility of σ_k. As the caplet payment occurs at time t_{k+1}, the rate $r(t_0, t_{k+1})$ must be used for discounting.

Let $DCF(t_k, t_{k+1})$ denote the day count fraction between t_k and t_{k+1}.[6] Then one obtains (see, e.g., Hull (2002); Wilmott (1998); Haug (1998))

$$\text{caplet value} = X \cdot DCF(t_k, t_{k+1}) \cdot e^{-r(t_0, t_{k+1})(t_{k+1} - t_0)}[F_k N(d_1) - r_C N(d_2)], \qquad (4.12)$$

with

$$d_1 = \frac{\log(F_k/r_C) + \sigma_k^2(t_k - t_0)/2}{\sigma_k \sqrt{t_k - t_0}},$$

$$d_2 = \frac{\log(F_k/r_C) - \sigma_k^2(t_k - t_0)/2}{\sigma_k \sqrt{t_k - t_0}},$$

where N is the standard cumulative normal distribution function.

Vanilla Interest Rate Swaptions and Their Black76 Pricing

A *payer swaption* is the optional right to become the payer (see page 42) in a vanilla interest rate swap starting at a future date. Thus, a 3×5 payer swaption with a strike rate of 3.95 percent allows the owner of the swaption to pay a fixed rate of 3.95 percent in a 5 year swap starting in 3 years. The swaption holder decides in 3 years whether to exercise or not. If market rates for the CMS5y are below 3.95 percent then, she will not exercise.

Like in the formula for the caps, the Black76 model for swaptions assumes that the forward rate of the swap is lognormally distributed with a known or quoted volatility. Let c denote the value of the European $T \times T_1$ payer swaption (if exercised at time $t_0 + T$, a T_1 year swap would start), p the value of the respective European receiver swaption, F the fair forward swap rate, X the strike rate (=fixed rate) of the swaption, σ the volatility of the forward rate F, m the payment frequency of the fixed leg. Then (Wilmott, 1998),

$$c = \left[\frac{1 - \frac{1}{(1+(F/m))^{T_1 \cdot m}}}{F} \right] e^{-rT} \left(F N(d_1) - X N(d_2) \right), \qquad (4.13)$$

$$p = \left[\frac{1 - \frac{1}{(1+(F/m))^{T_1 \cdot m}}}{F} \right] e^{-rT} \left(X N(-d_2) - F N(-d_1) \right), \qquad (4.14)$$

with $d_1 = \frac{\log(F/X) + (\sigma^2/2)T}{\sigma\sqrt{T}}$, $d_2 = d_1 - \sigma\sqrt{T}$.

At the money swaptions: A swaption is called "at the money" if the strike price X and the forward rate F coincide. These at the money swaptions are typically much more liquid than swaptions which are far *in the money* or far *out of the money*. Depending on the

---

[6] For the EUR, the day count convention for caps is ACT/360. Thus, if there are 182 days between t_k and t_{k+1}, then $DCF(t_k, t_{k+1}) = 182/360$.

sophistication of the model, for the calibration of (non-Black) interest rate models, at-the-money (ATM) swaption matrices or swaption cubes are required. ATM swaption matrices contain the volatilities for various $i \times j$ ATM swaptions, swaption cubes add various strike rates (or, more popular, the signed distance to the ATM rate) as a third dimension.

4.3 ONE-FACTOR SHORT RATE MODELS

When using the Black76 model for caps or swaptions, the stochastic underlying is the Libor rate of the caplet or the CMS rate, each observed at a fixed time. In this sense, Black76 models forward rates. It does not answer how, e.g., the Libor spot rate develops in the course of time. In (4.3), we have formulated the growth of an account B by the incremental growth rate r. With non-constant r, we can write

$$dB_t = B_t r_t dt \quad \text{or} \quad B_t = B_0 e^{\int_0^t r_s ds}. \tag{4.15}$$

We call r_t the *short rate*, as it is the growth rate in the time interval $(t, t + dt)$, which is regarded as infinitesimally short. One could imagine r_t to be simply a deterministic function of time. However, experience tells us that interest rates behave in a non-deterministic way. One-factor short rate models then depend on one stochastic process, typically a Wiener process,

$$dr_t = g(r_t, t)dt + h(r_t, t)dW_t. \tag{4.16}$$

The functions g and h determine the qualitative and quantitative behavior of the short rate. Analogously to the derivation of the Black-Scholes equation by Itô's Lemma and no arbitrage arguments, we will derive a partial differential equation for financial instruments whose underlying is the short rate in Chapter 5. The main difference to the Black-Scholes case is that the underlying itself is (unlike the equity) not a tradable quantity, and the hedging argument requires two different financial instruments, e.g., two bonds with different maturities.

4.3.1 Prominent Short Rate Models

Historically, interest rate models were developed after Black-Scholes. In this subsection, we present some named one factor models and try to work out the main differences between them. For the Hull-White model, analytic formulae are available for bonds and European bond options. These will be quoted in section 4.4 and used as reference solutions for trinomial trees in section 4.5.

Vasicek: The Vasicek model reads

$$dr_t = (a - br_t)dt + \sigma dW_t, \tag{4.17}$$

with constants a, $b > 0$, and σ.

Ho-Lee: The Ho-Lee model comes with a time-dependent $a(t)$ and constant σ,

$$dr_t = a(t)dt + \sigma dW_t. \tag{4.18}$$

Hull-White: The one-factor Hull-White model in its most general form has time-dependencies in all parameters

$$dr_t = (a(t) - b(t)r_t)dt + \sigma(t)dW_t. \tag{4.19}$$

When comparing these models, the Hull-White model obviously is the most general one, with Vasicek and Ho-Lee being special cases. It can be shown that in the Hull-White model the short rate is normally distributed at any time, and therefore negative interest rates can and will occur.[7] For the Hull-White model, it is possible (see also Chapter 16) to fit the function $a(t)$ in such a way that bond prices for all maturities can be matched, which is not the case for the Vasicek model due to its constant parameters. That said, the Vasicek model does have its merits for instructive purposes, but not for actual valuation. The Ho-Lee model, on the other hand, does not contain the mean-reverting term $-br$.[8] Although interest rate curves can be matched with the Ho-Lee model (due to the time-dependence of $a(t)$), the variance of future short rates grows linearly with the time horizon. This makes the Ho-Lee model unsuitable for long-dated instruments. The original paper used binomial trees as the numerical method, which would not have worked with a mean-reverting model.

Cox-Ingersoll-Ross: The Cox-Ingersoll-Ross model is mean reverting like the Vasicek model, but uses a different stochastic component,

$$dr_t = (a - br_t)dt + \sigma \sqrt{r}dW_t, \tag{4.20}$$

with constants a, $b > 0$, and σ.

For $2ab > \sigma^2$, the short rate process remains positive. We will rediscover this condition (under the name "Feller condition") when discussing the Heston model in Chapter 13. The Cox-Ingersoll-Ross model provides an analytic formula for the bond price but no explicit solution for the distribution of the short rate. For more details see Shreve (2008); Wilmott (1998).

Black-Karasinski: The Black-Karasinski model can be seen as a Hull-White model for the logarithm of the short rate

$$d(\log r_t) = (a - b\log(r_t))dt + \sigma dW_t. \tag{4.21}$$

Short rates are lognormally distributed under the Black-Karasinksi model; for the valuation of bonds and bond options, numerical methods must be applied.

4.4 THE HULL-WHITE MODEL IN MORE DETAIL

Following Shreve (2008), and a more detailed account in Shreve (1997), for the one factor Hull-White model (4.19) the following fair value (at time t) $B(t, T)$ of the zero coupon bond which pays 1 at time $T > t$ is obtained:

$$B(t, T) = \exp\{-r(t)C(t, T) - A(t, T)\}. \tag{4.22}$$

Here, the short rate at time t is $r(t)$, and we have used the notation (according to Shreve (1997))

$$K(t) = \int_0^t b(u)du,$$

$$A(t, T) = \int_t^T \left[e^{K(v)}a(v) \left(\int_v^T e^{-K(y)}dy \right) - \frac{1}{2}e^{2K(v)}\sigma^2(v) \left(\int_v^T e^{-K(y)}dy \right)^2 \right] dv,$$

$$C(t, T) = e^{K(t)} \int_t^T e^{-K(y)}dy.$$

---

[7] This is, in the authors' opinion not necessarily a disadvantage: In the turbulent times of 2011/2012, we noticed cases of negative rates, e.g., for German government bonds.

[8] This mean-reverting term is responsible for reverting realizations of short rates that are "far away" from the equilibrium rate $a(t)/b(t)$. Low rates tend to go up, high rates tend to go down.

Short rates in the future (at time T) are normally distributed with mean $\mu_2(t, T)$ and variance $\sigma_2^2(t, T)$ if the short rate equals $r(t)$ at time t. In addition, the integrals $\int_t^T r(\tau)d\tau$ appearing in the discounting formulae are normally distributed with mean $\mu_1(t, T)$ and variance $\sigma_1^2(t, T)$,

$$\mu_1(t, T) = \int_t^T \left[r(t)e^{-K(v)+K(t)} + e^{-K(v)} \int_t^v e^{K(u)}a(u)du \right] dv,$$

$$\sigma_1^2(t, T) = \int_t^T e^{2K(v)}\sigma^2(v) \left(\int_v^T e^{-K(y)}dy \right)^2 dv,$$

$$\mu_2(t, T) = r(t)e^{-K(T)+K(t)} + e^{-K(T)} \int_t^T e^{K(u)}a(u)du,$$

$$\sigma_2^2(t, T) = e^{-2K(T)} \int_t^T e^{K(u)}\sigma^2(u)du,$$

$$\rho(t, T)\sigma_1(t, T)\sigma_2(t, T) = \int_t^T e^{-K(u)-K(T)} \int_t^u e^{2K(v)}\sigma^2(v)dvdu.$$

Any fixed income derivative whose payoff depends on the short rate r at the future time T, $V = V(r(T), T)$ can, under the Hull-White one-factor model, be valuated as

$$V(r(t), t) = \int_{-\infty}^{\infty} \int_{-\infty}^{\infty} e^{-x} \frac{1}{2\pi\sigma_1(t, T)\sigma_2(t, T)\sqrt{1 - \rho(t, T)^2}} \cdot$$

$$\exp\left[-\frac{1}{2(1 - \rho(t, T)^2)} \left(\frac{(x - \mu_1(t, T))^2}{\sigma_1^2(t, T)} \right. \right. \tag{4.23}$$

$$\left. \left. + \frac{2\rho(t, T)(x - \mu_1(t, T))(y - \mu_2(t, T))}{\sigma_1(t, T)\sigma_2(t, T)} + \frac{(y - \mu_2(t, T))^2}{\sigma_2^2(t, T)} \right) \right]$$

$$V(y, T)dxdy.$$

Under fairly weak conditions on $V(y, T)$, it can be written outside the inner integral, which can then be evaluated analytically. Thus, in fact, the double integral (4.23) can be simplified to a single one. This leads to analytic solutions for, e.g., European swaptions under the Hull-White model.

4.5 TRINOMIAL TREES

Due to the convection term,[9] mean-reverting short-rate models cannot be easily implemented with recombining binomial trees.

The basic branching of a trinomial tree offers three possibilities in each node. Similar to the construction of binomial trees in section 2.4, the weights for each branch must be chosen in such a way that the discrete distribution of the trinomial tree converges to the continuous

---

[9] In section 5.1, the partial differential equation for short rate models is derived. The term $(a(t) - b(t)r)\frac{\partial V}{\partial r}$ arises from mean reversion. In fluid dynamic problems, first order derivatives relate to transport by convection.

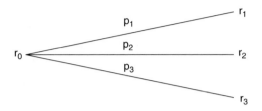

Figure 4.2   Symmetric branching in a trinomial tree.

distribution of the short rate model. Hull (2002) describes a general tree building procedure which can, at least in theory, be used for all short rate models we have described in the previous section.

To simplify demonstration, we start with a Vasicek model, formulated as

$$d\tilde{r}(t) = b \cdot (\theta - \tilde{r}(t))dt + \sigma dW_t. \tag{4.24}$$

Substituting $r = \tilde{r} - \theta$, we obtain

$$dr(t) = -br(t)dt + \sigma dW_t. \tag{4.25}$$

Hull starts from Equation (4.25) for the basic tree. More general drift terms θ are then obtained by deforming the basic tree to match a specific yield curve.

At one node of a trinomial tree, we start in a state r_0 at time t and have three (given) possible states r_1, r_2, r_3 at time $t + \Delta t$, as indicated in Figure 4.2. Following Hull, in the basic tree with symmetric branching , Δt is chosen as T/n, with T being the lifetime of the financial instrument to be valuated, the middle point r_2 is chosen to equal r_0, and $\Delta r = r_1 - r_2 = r_2 - r_3$ is chosen as $\Delta r = \sigma\sqrt{3\Delta t}$.

When $r_0 = j\Delta r$ with $j \in \{j_{min}, j_{max}\}$ (with j_{min} typically being negative), the branch probabilities p_1, p_2, p_3 are chosen in such a way that they sum up to 1 and match mean and variance. This yields

$$
\begin{aligned}
p_1 &= 1/6 + (b^2 j^2 (\Delta t)^2 - bj\Delta t)/2, \\
p_2 &= 2/3 - b^2 j^2 (\Delta t)^2, \\
p_3 &= 1/6 + (b^2 j^2 (\Delta t)^2 + bj\Delta t)/2.
\end{aligned}
\tag{4.26}
$$

If $|bj\Delta t| > \sqrt{2/3}$, meaning that r_0 is "far away" from the equilibrium level 0, then p_2 becomes negative, and a numerical scheme ignoring that fact would run into severe stability problems (due to $|p_1| + |p_2| + |p_3| > 1$ in that case).

Therefore, up-branching and down-branching nodes are introduced into trinomial trees as shown in Figure 4.3.

The probability weights in these two cases are then

$$
\begin{aligned}
p_1 &= 1/6 + (b^2 j^2 (\Delta t)^2 + bj\Delta t)/2, \\
p_2 &= -1/3 - b^2 j^2 (\Delta t)^2 - 2bj\Delta t, \\
p_3 &= 7/6 + (b^2 j^2 (\Delta t)^2 + 3bj\Delta t)/2,
\end{aligned}
\tag{4.27}
$$

Weights for up-branching

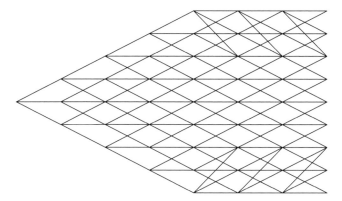

Figure 4.3   Trinomial tree with up-branches at the bottom and down-branches at the top.

and

$$p_1 = 7/6 + (b^2 j^2 (\Delta t)^2 - 3bj\Delta t)/2,$$

$$p_2 = -1/3 - b^2 j^2 (\Delta t)^2 + 2bj\Delta t,$$

$$p_3 = 1/6 + (b^2 j^2 (\Delta t)^2 - bj\Delta t)/2.$$

(4.28)

Weights for down-branching

Again, $p_2 \geq 0$ imposes conditions on $bj\Delta t$. For down-branching and up-branching, the respective nodes must be sufficiently far away from the equilibrium to yield a numerically stable scheme: $|bj\Delta t| > 1 - \sqrt{2/3}$.

Remarks

In Chapter 3, it turned out that the timestep must satisfy a condition similar to (3.71) to obtain a stable scheme for an explicit time-stepping algorithm. At first glance, one might think that this condition would not be imposed on trinomial trees. But in fact, the choice of $\Delta r = \sigma\sqrt{3\Delta t}$ is of exactly the same order. With typical market volatilities for the Hull-White model of 1 percent per year (understood in absolute terms of short rate changes), this means that in order to obtain a resolution of 10 basis points for the interest rates, the maximal time step would be one day! Thus, the valuation of a 30 year instrument would need 10 000 time steps.

On the other hand, if one wants to limit the number of time steps, the resolution of interest rates becomes poor. In the above example, using 100 time steps would lead to interest rate nodes at a distance of 1 percent.

Hull recommends to switch to the down-branching/up-branching scheme at the first possible node for computational efficiency, see footnote on page 695 of Hull (2002). If the reversion speed is high, which is observed for mean reverting models in electricity spot markets,[10] only very few grid points for the underlying are generated when using this suggestion.

---

[10] In 2011, typical reversion speeds for the EUR short rate have been between 0.01 and 0.1 per year in the Hull-White model. In electricity spot markets, reversion speeds can be of the order 1000/year. This reflects the fact that, on the time scale of days, there is almost no autocorrelation in electricity spot markets.

Example Code

The following piece of Mathematica code valuates a European call option on a zero coupon bond with face amount 1 on the basis tree for (4.25) with an initial short rate $r_0 = 0$. The maturity of the bond is at time T, and the call option (with a strike price `strike`) may be exercised at $T \cdot (n_{ex}/n)$. In total, n time levels are used. For discounting, the average value of interest rates in each branch is used. It should be fairly obvious how the code must be modified to price a put option on the bond or how to price the bond itself.

```
TrinomialBondOption[b_, sigma_, T_, n_, nex_, strike_] :=
Module[{dt, dr, value, node, level, branchmid, branchup, branchdown,
   jmax, i, TrinomTree, TrinomTreeOld},
 dt = T/n;
 dr = sigma *Sqrt[3*dt];
 branchmid[x_] := {1/6 + (x*x - x)/2, 2/3 - x^2, 1/6 + (x*x + x)/2};
 branchup[x_] := {1/6 + (x*x + x)/2, -1/3 - x^2 - 2*x,
   7/6 + (x*x + 3*x)/2};
 branchdown[x_] := {7/6 + (x*x - 3*x)/2, -1/3 - x^2 + 2*x,
   1/6 + 1/2 (x*x - x)};
 jmax = Min[Ceiling[0.184/(b*dt)], n];
 TrinomTree = Table[1., {node, -jmax, jmax}];
 TrinomTreeOld = TrinomTree;
 Do[TrinomTree =
   Table[Which[node > level, 0, node < -level, 0, node == jmax,
     branchdown[
       b*node*dt] . {Exp[-dt*node*dr] *
       TrinomTreeOld[[jmax + 1 + node]],
       Exp[-dt*(node - 1/2)*dr]*TrinomTreeOld[[jmax + 1 + node - 1]],
        Exp[-dt*(-1) node*dr]*TrinomTreeOld[[jmax + 1 + node - 2]]},
     node == -jmax,
     branchup[
       b*node*dt] . Exp[-dt*(node + 1)*dr]*
       TrinomTreeOld[[jmax + 1 + node + 2]],
       Exp[-dt*(node + 1/2)*dr]*TrinomTreeOld[[jmax + 1 + node + 1]],
        Exp[-dt*node*dr]*TrinomTreeOld[[jmax + 1 + node]], -jmax <
     node && node < jmax,
     branchmid[
       b*node*dt] . {Exp[-dt*(node + 1/2)*dr]*
       TrinomTreeOld[[jmax + 1 + node + 1]],
       Exp[-dt*node*dr]*TrinomTreeOld[[jmax + 1 + node]],
       Exp[-dt*(node - 1/2)*dr] TrinomTreeOld[[
         jmax + 1 + node - 1]]}],
     {node, -jmax, jmax}];
  If[level == nex,
   TrinomTreeOld =
    Table[Max[TrinomTree[[i]] - strike, 0], {i, 1,
      Length[TrinomTree]}], TrinomTreeOld = TrinomTree], {level,
   n - 1, 0, -1}];
 value = TrinomTree[[jmax + 1]];
 Clear[TrinomTree]; Clear[TrinomTreeOld]; value]
```

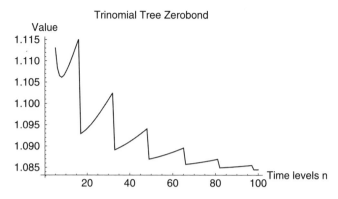

Figure 4.4   Value of the 30 year zero coupon bond under the Vasicek model ($a = 0$, $b = 0.1$, $r(0) = 0$, $\sigma = 0.01$), as a function of the number of time levels. The analytic value is 1.0832, indicated by the n-axis.

Examples and Results

As a first example, we valuate a 30 year zero coupon bond under the Vasicek model, see Figure 4.4. Similar to binomial trees, the numerical bond value obtained by the trinomial tree depends strongly on the discretization used.

This is even more true for instruments exhibiting a more option-like behavior. The next example deals with 15 year European call options with various strikes on a (then starting) 15 year zero bond. Again, we use a Vasicek model and use $n = 30, \dots, 100$ for the 15 year option and $n = 30, \dots, 100$ for the 15 year bond in the trinomial trees. The values for the options again depend strongly on the time discretization used (see Figure 4.5).

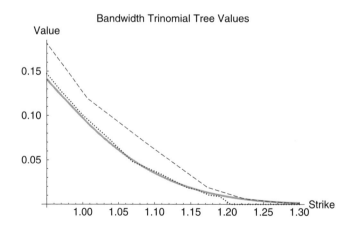

Figure 4.5   Value of the 15 year call option on a 15 year zero coupon bond under the Vasicek model($a = 0$, $b = 0.5$, $r(0) = 0$, $\sigma = 0.05$) as a function of the strike price of the option. Thick gray line: analytic value, dotted line: (pointwise) minimum value achieved for n-values between 60 and 200 for the 30 years time range, dashed line: corresponding (pointwise) maximum value.

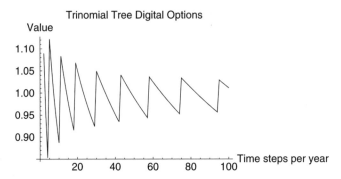

Figure 4.6 Value of the 10 year digital range accrual under the Vasicek model ($a = 0$, $b = 0.1$, $r(0) = 0$, $\sigma = 0.01$) as a function of the number of time steps per year. An annual coupon of 0.15 is paid if and only if the short rate lies in the interval $(-0.016, 0.016)$.

Now consider the following exotic instrument, which can be interpreted as a prototype of a *digital range accrual*: For a lifetime of, in our example, 10 years, a coupon is paid at the end of each year, provided that a trigger interest rate lies within a certain range.

Here, we use the short rate as the trigger rate, and require that it lies in the interval $(-1.6\%,$ $1.6\%)$ to obtain a coupon of 15%. Our instrument pays coupons only, no redemption. Again, we use a Vasicek model with mean reverting level 0. Figure 4.6 shows the valuation results for different time discretizations.

Trinomial trees are not only used for one-factor short rate models but also for higher-dimensional models, e.g., the two-factor Hull-White model, which will be introduced in Chapter 7. Binder and Schatz (2006) report that 30 year discount factors for a two-factor Hull-White model valuated by two-dimensional trinomial trees may carry relative errors of 5% compared to the analytic solution, when time steps of 50 days are used (see Table 4.1). The typical tree building procedure overcomes these errors by modifying the nodes and/or weights of the tree. However, by doing so, the parameters of the model are changed and analytic solutions for, say, swap rates are no longer available.

Concluding Remarks on Trinomial Trees

From our point of view, trinomial trees deliver reasonable indicative results only for financial instruments which have comparably short lifetimes and whose payoffs do not exhibit too

Table 4.1 Trinomial tree results for the two factor Hull-White model with parameters $\theta = 0.012$, $a = 0.2$, $b = 0.1$, $\sigma_1 = 0.01$, $\sigma_2 = 0.001$, $\rho = 0.3$. Time step was 50 days.

Maturity (years)	Trinomial tree value	Analytic solution
1	0.950341	0.950353
2	0.901665	0.901756
4	0.808564	0.809135
10	0.572741	0.576645
20	0.315969	0.324704
30	0.17375	0.18328

exotic behaviors. The only advantage we can see is that trinomial trees are explicit schemes and therefore it is not necessary to solve a linear system in the valuation procedure. This explicitness also leads to severe restrictions on the time step if the user desires a high resolution in the interest rate domain. Trinomial trees with down-branching and up-branching regimes allow to treat models with significant convection (such as mean-reverting models). This approach introduces artificial boundaries where the model is cut off, thus implicitly changing the model.

We will see in the next chapter that there is no need to rely on trees. From the numerical analyst's point of view, there are much superior numerical methods available.

Upwinding Techniques for Short Rate Models

5.1 DERIVATION OF A PDE FOR SHORT RATE MODELS

Assume the short rate r_t (see Chapter 4) is modeled by an Itô process,

$$dr_t = \mu(r,t)dt + \sigma(r,t)dW_t,$$

where we again use the notation $r(t) = r_t$, W_t is a Brownian motion, and μ and σ are functions to be defined later.

We are interested in the change dV of the value of an interest rate instrument $V(r_t,t)$ in an infinitesimally short time interval dt. Again, we utilize Itô's Lemma and try to use the same kind of analysis that has been successful in deriving the Black-Scholes PDE (PS-PDE), where we got rid of the stochastic terms in the BS-PDE by Δ-hedging.

We set up a self-replicating portfolio π containing two interest rate instruments[1] with different maturities T_1 and T_2 and corresponding values V_1 and V_2 (Hull, 2002). By applying the Itô Lemma for an infinitesimal change $d\pi_t = dV_1 - \Delta dV_2$, we obtain

$$d\pi_t = \left(\frac{\partial V_1}{\partial r}\mu(r,t) + \frac{\partial V_1}{\partial t} + \frac{1}{2}\sigma^2(r,t)\frac{\partial^2 V_1}{\partial r^2} \right) dt + \frac{\partial V_1}{\partial r}\sigma(r,t)dW_t \tag{5.1}$$

$$- \Delta \left[\left(\frac{\partial V_2}{\partial r}\mu(r,t) + \frac{\partial V_2}{\partial t} + \frac{1}{2}\sigma^2(r,t)\frac{\partial^2 V_2}{\partial r^2} \right) dt + \frac{\partial V_2}{\partial r}\sigma(r,t)dW_t \right].$$

Choosing $\Delta := \frac{\partial V_1}{\partial r} / \frac{\partial V_2}{\partial r}$, the stochastic terms in the equation above can be eliminated. To avoid arbitrage, we have to use the risk-free rate,

$$d\pi_t = \left(\frac{\partial V_1}{\partial t} + \frac{1}{2}\sigma^2(r,t)\frac{\partial^2 V_1}{\partial r^2} - \left(\frac{\partial V_1}{\partial r} / \frac{\partial V_2}{\partial r} \right) \right.$$

$$\left. \cdot \left(\frac{\partial V_2}{\partial t} + \frac{1}{2}\sigma^2(r,t)\frac{\partial^2 V_2}{\partial r^2} \right) \right) dt$$

$$= r\,\pi_t\,dt = r\left(V_1 - V_2 \cdot \frac{\partial V_1}{\partial r} / \frac{\partial V_2}{\partial r} \right) dt. \tag{5.2}$$

Rearranging equations (5.3)–(5.5) yields

$$\frac{\frac{\partial V_1}{\partial t} + \frac{1}{2}\sigma^2(r,t)\frac{\partial^2 V_1}{\partial r^2} - rV_1}{\frac{\partial V_1}{\partial r}} = \frac{\frac{\partial V_2}{\partial t} + \frac{1}{2}\sigma^2(r,t)\frac{\partial^2 V_2}{\partial r^2} - rV_2}{\frac{\partial V_2}{\partial r}}.$$

---

[1] In contrast to the Black-Scholes self-replicating portfolio, where the option and the underlying are tradable quantities, the interest rate (short rate) is a non-tradable quantity. To circumvent this problem, two different maturities are used to set up the portfolio.

This equality only holds when both sides of the equation solely depend on r and t and not on product specific quantities, thus

$$\frac{\partial V}{\partial t} + \underbrace{\frac{1}{2}\sigma^2(r,t)\frac{\partial^2 V}{\partial r^2}}_{\text{Diffusion}} - \underbrace{\omega(r,t)\frac{\partial V}{\partial r}}_{\text{Convection}} - \underbrace{rV}_{\text{Reaction}} = 0 \qquad \text{for } r \in \mathbb{R}. \qquad (5.3)$$

The function $\omega(r,t)$ is determined by the market price of the short rate risk. In the case of the Hull-White model, we have $-\omega(r,t) = a(t) - b(t)r$, and thus

$$\frac{\partial V}{\partial t} + \frac{1}{2}\sigma(t)^2\frac{\partial^2 V}{\partial r^2} + \left(a(t) - b(t)r\right)\frac{\partial V}{\partial r} - rV = 0 \qquad (r \in \mathbb{R}). \qquad (5.4)$$

To model the individual properties of a particular instrument, specific terminal conditions, such as boundary conditions or interface conditions, have to be set. For instance, consider the simple case of a zero bond with a nominal of 1 and maturity T. To calculate the current price V_0 under the assumption that $r(0) = r_0$, one needs to solve the partial differential equation with the terminal condition

$$V(r,T) = 1. \qquad (5.5)$$

The partial differential equations obtained by using (one or more factor) short rate models can be interpreted as convection-diffusion-reaction equations (Anderson, Tannehill and Pletchter, 1997). This type of equation can, e.g., be found in heat transfer applications.[2] The numerical solution using standard discretization methods entails severe problems, resulting in strong oscillations in the computed values. The drift term (first derivative) is chiefly responsible for these difficulties and forces us to use specifically developed methods with so-called upwind strategies (Quarteroni, Sacco and Saleri, 2002; LeVeque, 1992) in order to obtain a stable solution. Very roughly speaking, it is mandatory to "follow the direction of information flow", and to use information only from those points where the information came from. In trinomial tree methods, the up-branching and down-branching takes into account the upwinding and leads to non-negative weights which correspond to stability.

5.2 UPWIND SCHEMES

Originating from the field of computational fluid dynamics, upwind schemes denote a class of numerical discretization methods for solving hyperbolic partial differential equations. In our case, they are used to cure the oscillations induced by using standard discretization techniques in convection dominated domains of combined diffusion-convection-reaction equations. Upwind schemes use an adaptive or solution-sensitive finite difference stencil to numerically simulate the direction of propagation of information in a flow field in a proper way.

---

[2] Transport phenomena such as heat transfer can be described by a generic scalar transport equation which in its general form reads

$$\frac{\partial \Phi}{\partial t} + \nabla \cdot f(t, x, \Phi, \nabla\Phi) = g(t, x, \Phi).$$

Here, f denotes the flux and g the source. Different physical processes like conduction (diffusion), convection and reaction can occur in heat transfer problems.

Figure 5.1 Set of discrete points with indices $\{i - 1, i, i + 1\}$. The formulation of the first derivative by finite differences depends on the sign of a. Upwinding schemes consider the "flow"-direction of the information and only take the corresponding points (marked with dots) into account. The left hand figure shows the points used for a first order upwinding scheme for $a > 0$. The right hand figure shows the same for $a < 0$.

5.2.1 Model Equation

To illustrate the method, let us consider the hyperbolic linear advection equation

$$\frac{\partial u}{\partial t} + a \frac{\partial u}{\partial x} = 0. \tag{5.6}$$

Discretizing the spatial computational domain yields a discrete set of grid points x_i. The grid point with index i has only two neighboring points, x_{i-1} and x_{i+1}. If a is positive, the left side is called upwind side and the right side is called downwind side[3] (and vice versa if a is negative). Depending on the sign of a it is possible to construct finite difference schemes containing more points in the upwind direction. These schemes are therefore called upwind-biased or upwinding schemes.

First Order Upwind Scheme

A discretized version of (5.6) using a first order upwind scheme ($\mathcal{O}(h)$) and explicit time discretization is[4]

$$\begin{aligned}
\frac{u_i^{n+1} - u_i^n}{\Delta t} + a \frac{u_i^n - u_{i-1}^n}{\Delta x} &= 0 \quad \text{for} \quad a > 0, \\
\frac{u_i^{n+1} - u_i^n}{\Delta t} + a \frac{u_{i+1}^n - u_i^n}{\Delta x} &= 0 \quad \text{for} \quad a < 0.
\end{aligned} \tag{5.7}$$

The grid points of the space domain used for the formulation of the derivative with respect to the "flow"-direction of the information are displayed in Figure 5.1.

Severe numerical diffusion[5] is introduced in the solution in spatial regions where large gradients exist. The scheme can be derived starting with the fact that the solution u of (5.6) is constant along characteristic curves,[6] and therefore

$$u_i^{n+1} = u(x_i - a\Delta t, t_n). \tag{5.8}$$

---

[3] Think of a river and its flow direction – the water comes from the upwind side.

[4] This scheme is also called Courant-Isaacson-Rees method.

[5] When discretizing the continuous equations of motion by dividing time and space into a grid, the resulting discrete finite difference equations are in general more diffusive than the original differential equations. Therefore, the simulated system behaves differently from the system described by the continuous equation.

[6] Characteristics are a key concept in the analysis of partial differential equations. In an equation such as (5.6), the characteristics describe the propagation direction of the wave.

Since in general $x_i - a\Delta t$ is not a grid point, the value of the solution at this point is approximated by a linear interpolation of the values at the neighboring grid points,

$$u(x_i - a\Delta t, t_n) \approx \begin{cases} \frac{a\Delta t}{\Delta X} u_{i-1}^n + \left(1 - \frac{a\Delta t}{\Delta x}\right) u_i^n & \text{for} \quad a > 0 \\ \left(1 + \frac{a\Delta t}{\Delta x}\right) u_i^n - \frac{a\Delta t}{\Delta X} u_{i+1}^n & \text{for} \quad a > 0 \end{cases}. \tag{5.9}$$

By inspection it is easy to see that the previous equation is equivalent to (5.7).

An Example

To illustrate the effect of upwinding schemes, we will solve (5.6) using the discretization in space and time given by (5.7). The computational domain (space × time) is given by

$$[0, 3] \times [0, 1].$$

Let us specify the initial condition

$$u(x, 0) = \exp\left\{-\left(\frac{x - 1.0}{0.1}\right)^2\right\},$$

the Dirichlet boundary condition

$$u(0, t) = 0$$

and the parameter $a = 1.0$. The number of discretization points for the spatial and the time dimensions are chosen to be $n_x = 301$ and $n_t = 201$. Therefore, as the Courant-Friedrichs-Lewy (CFL) condition

$$\left|\frac{a\Delta t}{\Delta x}\right| \leq 1 \tag{5.10}$$

is satisfied, the explicit Euler time-stepping scheme yields stable results. Figure 5.2 shows $u(x, t)$ for $t = 0, 0.25, 0.5, 0.75$ and $t = 1.0$. The same problem calculated with the central difference quotient for approximating the first derivative (3.51) defined in Chapter 3 is shown in Figures 5.3 and 5.4. Using this discretization scheme, the solution blows up, and oscillations start to occur that destroy the solution. In the next subsection, we will show that using the central difference quotient in place of the upwinding scheme makes the propagation unconditionally unstable (Jacobson, 1999).

Some Theoretical Results

To examine the reason for the instability in the solution of (5.6) when using a central difference quotient, we start with

$$\frac{u_i^{n+1} - u_i^n}{\Delta t} + a \frac{u_{i+1}^n - u_{i-1}^n}{2\Delta x} = 0. \tag{5.11}$$

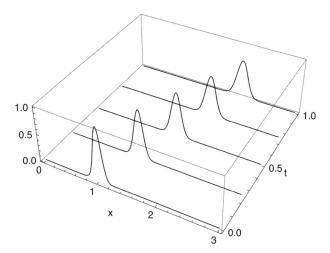

Figure 5.2   Solution of (5.6) for several points in time between $t = 0$ and $t = 1.0$. The analytical solution would be a peak with identical shape at $t = 0$, but rigidly shifted from 1.0 to 2.0 in x-direction. Obviously, an additional diffusive term leads to the dispersion of the solution.

Replacing u_i^{n+1}, u_{i+1}^n and u_{i-1}^n using the Taylor expansions,

$$u_i^{n+1} = u_i^n + \Delta t \frac{\partial u}{\partial t} + \frac{(\Delta t)^2}{2} \frac{\partial^2 u}{\partial t^2} + \mathcal{O}((\Delta t)^3),$$

$$u_{i+1}^n = u_i^n + \Delta x \frac{\partial u}{\partial x} + \frac{(\Delta x)^2}{2} \frac{\partial^2 u}{\partial x^2} + \mathcal{O}((\Delta x)^3),$$

$$u_{i-1}^n = u_i^n - \Delta x \frac{\partial u}{\partial x} + \frac{(\Delta x)^2}{2} \frac{\partial^2 u}{\partial x^2} + \mathcal{O}((\Delta x)^3),$$

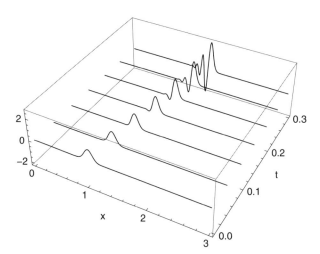

Figure 5.3   Solution of (5.6) for $t = 0$ to $t = 0.5$ using the second order central difference quotient (3.51) together with explicit time stepping.

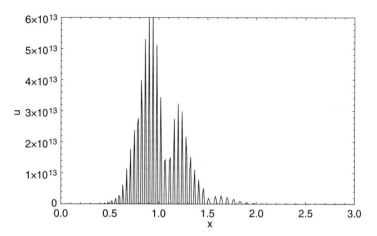

Figure 5.4   Solution of (5.6) at $t = 1.0$ using the second order central difference quotient defined in (3.51) together with explicit time stepping.

yields

$$\frac{\partial u}{\partial t} + a\frac{\partial u}{\partial x} = -\frac{\Delta t}{2}\frac{\partial^2 u}{\partial t^2} + \mathcal{O}((\Delta x)^2 + (\Delta t)^2). \tag{5.12}$$

Using[7]

$$\frac{\partial^2 u}{\partial t^2} = a^2\frac{\partial^2 u}{\partial x^2}, \tag{5.13}$$

we obtain

$$\frac{\partial u}{\partial t} + a\frac{\partial u}{\partial x} = -a^2\frac{\Delta t}{2}\frac{\partial^2 u}{\partial x^2} + \mathcal{O}((\Delta x)^2 + (\Delta t)^2). \tag{5.14}$$

Numerical diffusion is introduced due to the discretization scheme used – the negative diffusion coefficient in the leading error term makes the scheme unconditionally unstable. Performing the same type of analysis for the upwinding scheme defined in (5.7) for $a > 0$, we end up with

$$\frac{\partial u}{\partial t} + a\frac{\partial u}{\partial x} = -\frac{\Delta t}{2}\frac{\partial^2 u}{\partial t^2} + a\frac{\Delta x}{2}\frac{\partial^2 u}{\partial x^2} + \mathcal{O}((\Delta x)^2 + (\Delta t)^2). \tag{5.15}$$

Again using the identity (5.13) and defining

$$C := \left|\frac{a\Delta t}{\Delta x}\right|, \tag{5.16}$$

we obtain

$$\frac{\partial u}{\partial t} + a\frac{\partial u}{\partial x} = +a\frac{\Delta x}{2}(1 - C)\frac{\partial^2 u}{\partial x^2} + \mathcal{O}((\Delta x)^2 + (\Delta t)^2). \tag{5.17}$$

---

[7] Assuming everything is smooth enough we change the order of differentiation and obtain

$$\frac{\partial u}{\partial t} = -a\frac{\partial u}{\partial x} \rightarrow \frac{\partial}{\partial t}\frac{\partial u}{\partial t} = -a\frac{\partial}{\partial t}\frac{\partial u}{\partial x} \rightarrow \frac{\partial^2 u}{\partial t^2} = -a\frac{\partial}{\partial x}\frac{\partial u}{\partial t} \rightarrow \frac{\partial^2 u}{\partial t^2} = a^2\frac{\partial^2 u}{\partial x^2}.$$

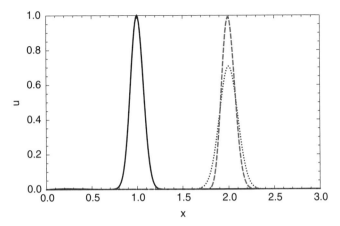

Figure 5.5   Solution of (5.6) at $t = 0.0$ (solid) and $t = 1.0$ using the first order upwinding scheme (5.7) (dotted) and the Lax-Wendroff scheme (5.18) (dashed). Obviously, the diffusive behavior of the first order upwinding scheme is reduced by the anti-diffusion term introduced by the Lax-Wendroff scheme.

Therefore, the scheme is stable for $C \leq 1$ and of order one.

Higher Order Upwinding Schemes

The Lax-Wendroff scheme (Quarteroni, Sacco and Saleri, 2002)[8] can be derived using a Taylor expansion of u_i^{n+1} (first equation in section 5.2.1). For the linear advection Equation (5.6), the Lax-Wendroff scheme yields

$$u_i^{n+1} = u_i^n - \frac{a\Delta t}{2\Delta x}\left(u_{i+1}^n - u_{i-1}^n\right) + \frac{a^2(\Delta t)^2}{2(\Delta x)^2}\left(u_{i+1}^n - 2u_i^n + u_{i-1}^n\right). \qquad (5.18)$$

The second term on the right-hand side can be interpreted as a diffusion term that stabilizes the method (remember that when using the central difference quotient for the discretization of the first derivative, we obtained an unconditionally unstable algorithm). Rewriting (5.21) for the case $a > 0$,

$$u_i^{n+1} = u_i^n - C\left(u_i^n - u_{i-1}^n\right) - (1 - C)\frac{C}{2}\left(u_{i+1}^n - 2u_i^n + u_{i-1}^n\right), \qquad (5.19)$$

allows for a different interpretation. Now, the second term on the right hand side can be seen as an anti-diffusion term that reduces the diffusive behavior of the first order upwinding scheme described in (5.7). Figure 5.5 shows the effect of this anti-diffusion term.

Numerical experiments reveal an oscillatory behavior in the neighborhood of discontinuities, which can occur in finance due to discontinuous payoffs. This shows that in certain situations the anti-diffusive term of the Lax-Wendroff method is too high and therefore needs to be corrected. We will in the following derive such a correction using the total variation diminishing

---

[8] The Lax-Wendroff method consists of two steps – a step for calculating auxiliary points for half step size in the spatial and in the time dimension, and a second step performing the time integration using a Leapfrog-like method. All spatial derivatives are performed using second order finite differences, therefore the scheme is second order in space and time.

framework (TVD) (Harten, 1983).[9,10] We start with an attempt to control the anti-diffusive term by introducing suitable parameters Φ_i and Φ_{i-1},

$$u_i^{n+1} = u_i^n - C\left(u_i^n - u_{i-1}^n\right) - \frac{(1-C)C}{2}\left(\Phi_i\left(u_{i+1}^n - u_i^n\right) - \Phi_{i-1}\left(u_i^n - u_{i-1}^n\right)\right). \quad (5.24)$$

Setting

$$\Phi_i = \Phi(r_i) \quad \text{with} \quad r_i = \frac{u_i - u_{i-1}}{u_{i+1} - u_i},$$

we obtain

$$
\begin{aligned}
u_i^{n+1} &= u_i^n - C\left(u_i^n - u_{i-1}^n\right) - \frac{(1-C)C}{2}\left(\Phi(r_i)\left(u_{i+1}^n - u_i^n\right) - \Phi(r_{i-1})\left(u_i^n - u_{i-1}^n\right)\right) \\
&= u_i^n - C\left\{1 + \frac{1}{2}(1-C)\left[\frac{\Phi(r_i)}{r_i} - \Phi(r_{i-1})\right]\right\}\left(u_i^n - u_{i-1}^n\right) \qquad (5.25) \\
&= u_i^n - A^n\left(u_i^n - u_{i-1}^n\right) + B^n\left(u_{i+1}^n - u_i^n\right),
\end{aligned}
$$

with

$$A^n = C\left\{1 + \frac{1}{2}(1-C)\left[\frac{\Phi(r_i)}{r_i} - \Phi(r_{i-1})\right]\right\} \quad B^n = 0. \qquad (5.26)$$

The conditions (5.23) reduce to

$$0 \le A^n \le 1. \qquad (5.27)$$

A comparison of results obtained using the first order upwinding scheme, the Lax-Wendroff scheme and a TVD scheme is shown in Figure 5.6.

---

[9] If it exists, the total variation of a function u mapping from $[a, b] \to \mathcal{R}$ is given by

$$TV_{[a,b]}(u) = \sup_{a=x_0 < \ldots < x_n = b} \sum_{i=0}^{n-1} |u(x_{i+1} - u(x_i)| \qquad (5.20)$$

and a method is called total variation diminishing if

$$TV(u^{n+1}) \le TV(u^n). \qquad (5.21)$$

It can be shown, that a method of the form

$$u_i^{n+1} = u_i^n - A^n\left(u_i^n - u_{i-1}^n\right) + B^n\left(u_{i+1}^n - u_i^n\right), \qquad (5.22)$$

where the coefficients A^n and B^n may depend on the approximate solutions

$$A^n = A\left(\ldots, u_{i-1}^n, u_i^n\right), \quad B^n = B\left(\ldots, u_i^n, u_{i+1}^n\right),$$

is TVD if the following criteria are fulfilled

$$A^n \ge 0, \quad B^n \ge 0, \quad A^n + B^n \le 1. \qquad (5.23)$$

[10] Intuitively, a system is said to be monotonicity preserving if no new local extrema can be created within the solution's spatial domain as a function of time and if the value of a local minimum is non-decreasing, and the value of a local maximum is non-increasing as a function of time. Harten proved that a monotone scheme is TVD and on the other hand a TVD scheme is monotonicity preserving. Godunov's theorem proves that only first order linear schemes preserve monotonicity and are therefore TVD. Higher order linear schemes, although more accurate for smooth solutions, are not TVD and tend to introduce spurious oscillations (wiggles) where discontinuities or shocks arise. To overcome these drawbacks, various high-resolution, nonlinear techniques have been developed, often using flux/slope limiters.

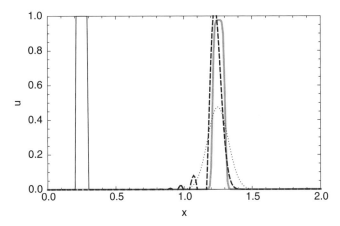

Figure 5.6   Solution of (5.6) at $t = 0.0$ (continuous black) and $t = 1.0$ using the first order upwinding scheme (5.7) (dotted), the Lax-Wendroff scheme (5.18) (dashed) and the TVD scheme with the "super-bee" limiter (continuous gray). The first order upwinding scheme is TVD but introduces severe numerical diffusion. The Lax-Wendroff scheme starts to develop oscillations when applied to non-smooth functions. The second order TVD scheme reduces the diffusion of the first order algorithm and does not show oscillations in the solution.

Condition (5.27) is satisfied for all $C \in \,]0; 1]$ if

$$\left| \frac{\Phi(r_i)}{r_i} - \Phi(s) \right| \le 2 \quad \text{for all} \quad r \ne 0, s \tag{5.28}$$

Each setting of the form

$$\Phi(r) = \Theta(r) + (1 - \Theta(r))r \tag{5.29}$$

leads to methods of order two.[11] To obtain TVD methods, $\Phi(r)$ must lie between the "super-bee" limiter by Roe (1986),

$$\Phi(r) = \max(0, \min(1, 2r), \min(r, 2)), \tag{5.30}$$

and the "min-mod" limiter

$$\Phi(r) = \max(0, \min(r, 1)). \tag{5.31}$$

5.3   A PUTTABLE FIXED RATE BOND UNDER THE HULL-WHITE ONE FACTOR MODEL

A fixed rate bond is a type of debt instrument bond with a fixed coupon rate. The coupon rate is payable at specified dates before bond maturity. A bond is puttable (also called retractable) if the holder of the bond has the right, but not the obligation, to demand early repayment of the principal at specified date(s) before the bond reaches the date of maturity. A bond is callable (also called redeemable) if the issuer of the bond is allowed to redeem the bond at specified date(s) before the bond reaches the date of maturity. In other words, on the call date(s), the

---

[11] To obtain second order methods, Θ must be Lipschitz continuous.

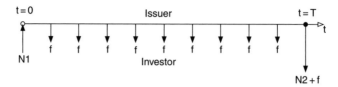

Figure 5.7 The figure shows the time line plus the cashflows of a fixed rate bond. The time line is marked using an open arrow. All cashflows are marked using filled arrows. At time $t = 0$, the bond investor pays the face value of the bond to the bond issuer (open circle). Each coupon period, the issuer of the bond pays the coupon f to the investor. At the end of the contract period ($t = T$, marked with a filled black circle) the issuer of the bond pays the last coupon plus the face value to the bond investor. Possible call/put dates are fixed by the term sheet. Typically they coincide with the coupon dates, but this need not to be the case.

issuer has the right, but not the obligation, to buy back the bond from the bond holders at a defined call price. Figure 5.7 shows the main properties of such an instrument.

5.3.1 Bond Details

For the remainder of this section, we consider a bond with the following details as an example:

- Contract period of bond: $T = 10y$
- Coupon frequency: Annually
- Coupon rate: 5% fixed.
- Put dates: Annually starting one year after the issuing of the bond until one year before maturity.

5.3.2 Model Details

We valuate the bond under a one-factor Hull-White model (4.19). Model parameters are assumed to be piecewise constant functions of time (see Figure 5.8).

- We assume today's spot rate $r(0) = 0.03$,
- The mean reversion speed parameter $b(t)$ remains constant within $[0, T]$ and $b(t) = 0.1$,

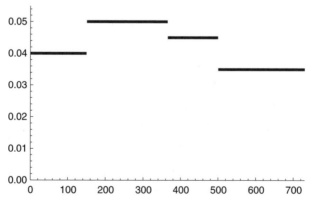

Figure 5.8 The figure shows model parameters as a function of time (in days). All time-dependent model parameters are assumed to be piecewise constant, changing their values only on model term dates.

- The long-term drift level $\Theta(t)$ is set to 0.05 in $[0, T/2]$ and to 0.045 in $[T/2; T]$ and therefore we have $a(t) = \Theta(t)b(t)$,[12]
- The volatility $\sigma(t) = 0.005$ is constant.

5.3.3   Numerical Method

Below, we summarize details of the algorithms used for the valuation of the bond:

- The theoretical domain for the spatial dimension $r \in]-\infty; \infty[$ is restricted to $r \in [a, b]$, and Neumann boundary conditions of the form

$$\frac{\partial V}{\partial r}\Big|_{r=a} = 0, \quad \frac{\partial V}{\partial r}\Big|_{r=b} = 0 \tag{5.32}$$

are applied. The question of how to find appropriate cut off values a and b remains. Defining $\sigma_{max} = \max(\sigma(t)), t \in [0, T]$ we choose

$$a = r(0) + \sqrt{T}K\sigma_{max} \quad \text{and} \quad b = r(0) - \sqrt{T}K\sigma_{max} \tag{5.33}$$

for the cut-off points. From experience we know that $K \approx 7$ is a sufficiently good choice leading to cut off values $a = -0.09$ and $b = 0.15$ (for a detailed discussion of boundary conditions, see Chapter 6). The number of equidistantly spaced grid points is N, yielding a set of points $\{r_0, r_1 \ldots r_{N-1}\}$.
- A finite difference discretization in the spatial dimension using second order finite difference formulae for the diffusion part and the simple upwinding scheme for the discretization of the convection term is used. Rewriting (5.4) in the form

$$\frac{\partial V}{\partial t} + L(t)V(t) = 0, \tag{5.34}$$

and specifying the discrete operator $L(j)$, where the index j denotes the time point at which the operator is evaluated, yields

$$L(j)V_i^j = \begin{cases} \frac{1}{2}\sigma(j)^2 \dfrac{V_{i+1}^j - 2V_i^j + V_{i-1}^j}{h^2} + \left(a(j) - b(j)r_i\right) \dfrac{V_i^j - V_{i-1}^j}{h} - r_i V_i^j \\ \text{if } \left(a(j) - b(j)r_i\right) > 0 \\ \frac{1}{2}\sigma(j)^2 \dfrac{V_{i+1}^j - 2V_i^j + V_{i-1}^j}{h^2} + \left(a(j) - b(j)r_i\right) \dfrac{V_{i+1}^j - V_i^j}{h} - r_i V_i^j \\ \text{if } \left(a(j) - b(j)r_i\right) < 0. \end{cases} \tag{5.35}$$

---

[12] There is another commonly used notation for the general Hull-White model:

$$dr_t = b(t)(\Theta(t) - r_t)dt + \sigma(t)dW_t.$$

In this notation, $\Theta(t)$ is the long-term drift level.

• A second order semi-implicit time discretization using the Crank-Nicholson scheme is used. The time interval $[0, 10]$ (in years) is split into $M - 1$ time intervals (M points in time resulting in a set of time points TP that are measured in days starting from $t = 0^{13}$). Starting to derive an equation similar to (3.70),[14]

$$\frac{V(t) - V(t - \Delta t)}{\Delta t} + (1 - \Theta)(L(t)V(t)) + \Theta(L(t - \Delta t)V(t - \Delta t)) = 0, \qquad (5.36)$$

we obtain for $\Theta = 1/2$

$$\underbrace{\left(1 - \frac{\Delta t}{2}L(t - \Delta t)\right)}_{A_{HW}} V(t - \Delta t) = \underbrace{\left(1 + \frac{\Delta t}{2}L(t)\right)}_{B_{HW}} V(t). \qquad (5.37)$$

With the definition of the following matrices,

$$A = \begin{pmatrix} -2 & 1 & 0 & \cdots & 0 \\ 1 & -2 & 1 & \ddots & \vdots \\ 0 & 1 & \ddots & \ddots & 0 \\ \vdots & \ddots & \ddots & \ddots & 1 \\ 0 & \cdots & 0 & 1 & -2 \end{pmatrix},$$

$$B^- = \begin{pmatrix} 1 & 0 & 0 & \cdots & 0 \\ -1 & 1 & 0 & \ddots & \vdots \\ 0 & -1 & \ddots & \ddots & 0 \\ \vdots & \ddots & \ddots & \ddots & 0 \\ 0 & \cdots & 0 & -1 & 1 \end{pmatrix},$$

$$B^+ = \begin{pmatrix} 1 & -1 & 0 & \cdots & 0 \\ 0 & 1 & -1 & \ddots & \vdots \\ 0 & 0 & \ddots & \ddots & 0 \\ \vdots & \ddots & \ddots & \ddots & -1 \\ 0 & \cdots & 0 & 0 & 1 \end{pmatrix},$$

$$D^+ = \begin{pmatrix} \max(a_j - b_j r_0) & 0 & 0 & \cdots & 0 \\ 0 & \max(a_j - b_j r_1) & 0 & \ddots & \vdots \\ 0 & 0 & \ddots & \ddots & 0 \\ \vdots & \ddots & \ddots & \ddots & 0 \\ 0 & \cdots & 0 & 0 & \max(a_j - b_j r_{N-1}) \end{pmatrix},$$

---

[13] Without loss of generality, we assume the starting point in time to be 0. Usually, a reference date is chosen and all relevant dates in a system are calculated relative to this reference date.

[14] In contrast to the classical heat equation, we are going backwards in time and are therefore using a backward finite difference quotient for the discretization of the time derivative.

$$\mathbf{D^-} = \begin{pmatrix} \min(a_j - b_j r_0) & 0 & 0 & \cdots & 0 \\ 0 & \min(a_j - b_j r_1) & 0 & \ddots & \vdots \\ 0 & 0 & \ddots & \ddots & 0 \\ \vdots & & \ddots & \ddots & 0 \\ 0 & & \cdots & 0 & 0 & \min(a_j - b_j r_{N-1}) \end{pmatrix},$$

$$\mathbf{R} = \begin{pmatrix} r_0 & 0 & 0 & \cdots & 0 \\ 0 & r_1 & 0 & \ddots & \vdots \\ 0 & 0 & \ddots & \ddots & 0 \\ \vdots & \ddots & \ddots & \ddots & 0 \\ 0 & \cdots & 0 & 0 & r_{N-1} \end{pmatrix},$$

we obtain

$$\mathbf{A_{HW}} = \mathbf{I} - \frac{s_{j-1}^2 \Delta t}{2h^2} \mathbf{A} - \frac{\Delta t}{2h} (\mathbf{D^+ B^-} + \mathbf{D^- B^+}) + \mathbf{R} \tag{5.38}$$

and

$$\mathbf{B_{HW}} = \mathbf{I} + \frac{s_{j-1}^2 \Delta t}{2h^2} \mathbf{A} + \frac{\Delta t}{2h} (\mathbf{D^+ B^-} + \mathbf{D^- B^+}) - \mathbf{R}. \tag{5.39}$$

The boundary conditions (5.32) can be incorporated by updating the first and the last row vector $\mathbf{a_0}$ and $\mathbf{a_{N-1}}$ of the coefficient matrix $\mathbf{A_{HW}}$ as well as by setting the first and the last element of the right hand side vector $\mathbf{B_{HW}} \mathbf{v}^j$ to 0. Using first order finite differences for the discretization of (5.32) yields

$$\mathbf{a_0} = (-1, 1, 0, \ldots, 0), \quad \mathbf{a_{N-1}} = (0, \ldots, 0, 1, -1). \tag{5.40}$$

For convenience, we assume the time discretization to be consistent with the time line of the instrument (all relevant instrument dates, such as coupon dates and put dates as well as model term dates, are contained in the set of time points).

• Starting at $t = T$ ($V(T)$ is known by the payoff function at maturity), in each time step a system of linear equations,

$$\mathbf{A_{HW}} \mathbf{v}^{j-1} = \mathbf{B_{HW}} \mathbf{v}^j, \tag{5.41}$$

must be solved[15] by utilizing algorithms for tridiagonal matrices.

• If a coupon date is reached, the value on the grid point r_i is updated according to

$$v_i^j = v_i^j + f, \tag{5.42}$$

where f is the coupon rate of the fixed rate bond.

---

[15] Note that $\mathbf{v}^j$ is the vector of instrument values of length N indexed by $0, 1, \ldots, N-1$ on the grid points. At a certain point in time j the instrument values at time point $j-1$ are unknown. These unknown values are the solution of the system of linear equations (5.41).

- If a put date is reached, the value on the grid point r_i is updated according to

$$v_i^j = \max\left(p, v_i^j\right), \tag{5.43}$$

where p is the put rate. In order to calculate the value of the puttable as well as the non-puttable instrument, in each time step the system of equations is solved for two different right hand sides.
- If $t = 0$ is reached after $M - 1$ steps, the product value v is obtained by interpolation from $\mathbf{v}^0$.

5.3.4   An Algorithm in Pseudocode

$V(i,T) \leftarrow FV+f \quad \forall i \in \{0, N - 1\}$
for $j = M - 2 \rightarrow 0$ **do**
$\quad \Delta t \leftarrow TP(j+1) - TP(j)$
$\quad$ SOLVE (5.41)
$\quad$ **if** $j == putdate$ **then**
$\quad\quad v(i) \leftarrow MAX(v(i), p) \quad \forall i \in \{0, N - 1\}$
$\quad$ **end if**
$\quad$ **if** $j == coupondate$ **then**
$\quad\quad v(i) \leftarrow v(i)+f \quad \forall i \in \{0, N - 1\}$
$\quad$ **end if**
$\quad$ **if** $j == modeltermdate$ **then**
$\quad\quad$ UPDATE $\mathbf{A}_{HW}$ and $\mathbf{B}_{HW}$
$\quad$ **end if**
$\quad j \leftarrow j - 1$
end for
$v \leftarrow$ INTERPOLATE$(\mathbf{v}^0)$

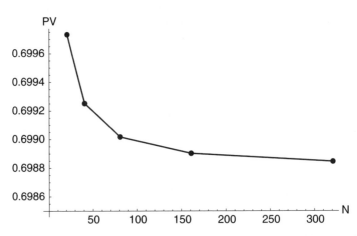

Figure 5.9   The figure shows the present value of a non-puttable zero bond with a maturity of 10 years and a nominal value of 1 as a function of discretization points N in the spatial dimension. For time discretization $\Delta t = 1$ is used.

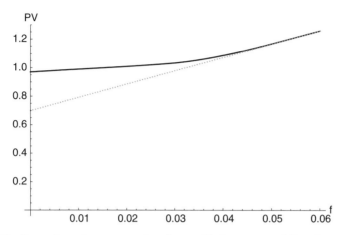

Figure 5.10   The figure shows the present value of a puttable (put rate $p = 1.0$) and a non-puttable fixed rate bond with a maturity of 10 years and a nominal value of 1 as a function of the coupon rate f.

5.3.5   Results

The number of days (equal to the number of intervals) until maturity is assumed to be 3650 with $\Delta t = 1$ (interval length). As a first step, the number of grid points needed for the spatial dimension is determined by calculating the value for a non-puttable zero bond ($f = 0$) with identical maturity using the model and numerical methods described above. From Figure 5.9, we see that $N = 161$ grid points are sufficient (the difference in the present value of the zero bond for $N = 321$ and $N = 161$ is smaller than one basis point).

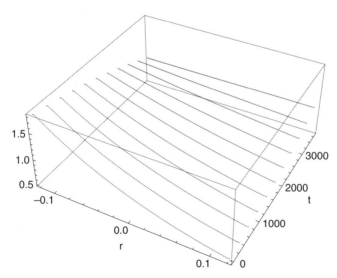

Figure 5.11   The figure shows the present value of a non-puttable fixed rate bond with $f = 0.025$ as a function of t and r.

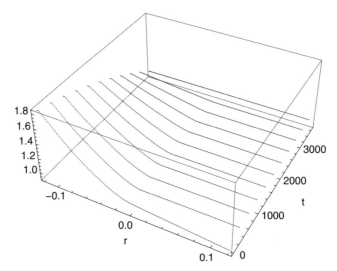

Figure 5.12   The figure shows the present value of a puttable fixed rate bond with $f = 0.025$ and $p = 1.0$ as a function of t and r.

Next, we examine the present value of the puttable and the non-puttable bond as a function of the coupon rate f for a fixed put rate $p = 1.0$. As expected, in the limit of high coupon rates the present values for the puttable and the non-puttable product are equal, since no puts will take place, a fact that can also be seen in Figure 5.10. The bond value as a function of r and t for fixed $f = 0.025$ can be seen in Figures 5.11 (non-puttable) and 5.12 (puttable with $p = 1.0$).

Boundary, Terminal and Interface Conditions and their Influence

In Chapters 3 and 4, we have learnt about the Black-Scholes differential equation and the differential equations of a number of short rate models. These differential equations describe (in the PDE equivalent of the risk-free measure) the model for the movement of the underlying, which is, in the case of Black-Scholes, the equity, and in the case of the interest rate models of Chapter 4, the short rate. The differential equation itself is not sufficient to valuate a financial instrument; in oder to do so, we additionally need final conditions, boundary conditions and sometimes also interface conditions. All of these depend on the term sheet of the specific instrument. In this chapter, we deal with the formulation of such conditions for specific examples. There are quite a few financial instruments with more or less heavily path-dependent payoffs available, and this path-dependence may be arbitrarily complicated. Therefore, we will concentrate on specific aspects that are fundamental from our point of view. It may be a reasonable advice to avoid instruments for which the formulation of the, say, interface conditions, already cause a headache.

6.1 TERMINAL CONDITIONS FOR EQUITY OPTIONS

In Chapter 2, we have introduced call and put options and their payoffs. Digital options (other names: binary options, cash-or-nothing options) pay a certain amount of cash c if, at expiry T, the underlying S is above the strike price K (digital call) or below the strike price (digital put), see Figure 6.1,

$$V_{DigCall}(S,T) = \begin{cases} c & \text{if } S \geq K \\ 0 & \text{if } S < K \end{cases}. \tag{6.1}$$

A *compound option* is an option on an option. As an example, a call option (expiry T_1) on a put option (expiry T_2) on the equity S gives the owner (of the call) the right to buy (at T_1) the put option for a fixed price $K_{compound}$ (the strike price of the compound option). Therefore, if we know the value $P(S,T_1)$ of the put option at T_1 (by, e.g., applying the Black-Scholes formula for the put), we can formulate the terminal condition for the compound option,

$$V(S,T_1) = \max(P(S,T_1) - K, 0). \tag{6.2}$$

A (mathematically) similar instrument is a *chooser option* which allows the owner at T_1 to choose between a call option and a put option on the same underlying with typically the same strike prices, both expiring at T_2. In Figure 6.2, the value of such a chooser option is plotted as a function of the underlying and time, when the underlying pays significant discrete dividends. We will discuss discrete dividends in section 6.4.

Asian options The attribute "Asian" refers to a wide variety of derivatives, for which the payoff depends on some average of the underlying. These averages may be arithmetic or geometric averages, either taken discretely or continuously. For instance, a continuous

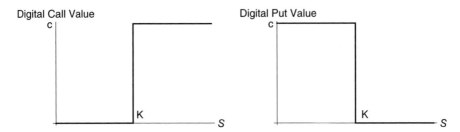

Figure 6.1 Payoff of a digital call and a digital put option at expiry as functions of the equity price S. Both options have a strike price K.

arithmetic average would be the time integral over the realized stock price path, divided by the length of the time interval. For certain geometric and/or continuous average samplings, (semi-)closed form solutions are available (Wilmott, 1998; Elshegmani et al., 2011). From our experience, the only relevant averages for the practitioner are discrete arithmetic averages, e.g., the arithmetic average of the closing prices on the last business day of each month.

If the final average relevant for the payoff is taken over the n realized stock prices at times $T_1, \ldots, T_n$, let $A_n := (S(T_1) + \cdots + S(T_n))/n$, then, obviously, $A_i = \frac{i-1}{i} A_{i-1} + \frac{1}{i} S(T_i)$. We denote by $V(S, A, t)$ the value of an Asian option at time t, when the stock price is S at time t and A is the discrete arithmetic average taken over all $T_j < t$. At an observation time T_i, the following condition must hold (Wilmott, 1998),

$$V(S, A, T_i^-) = V\left(S, \frac{i-1}{i} A + \frac{1}{i} S, T_i^+\right), \tag{6.3}$$

with the notation $f(\tau^-) = \lim_{\tau \to \tau^-} f(\tau)$ and $f(\tau^+) = \lim_{\tau \to \tau^+} f(\tau)$ for the one-sided limits. The differential equation for the value of the discrete arithmetic Asian is still the Black-Scholes equation (3.19), but with V depending on the additional parameter A,

$$\frac{\partial V}{\partial t}(S, A, t) + \frac{\sigma^2 S^2}{2} \frac{\partial^2 V}{\partial S^2}(S, A, t) + rS \frac{\partial V}{\partial S}(S, A, t) - rV(S, A, t) = 0. \tag{6.4}$$

If one wants to apply finite differences or finite elements to solve (6.4), one needs to solve the classical Black-Scholes equation for a range of reasonable parameter values of A. To obtain the values at T_i^-, one needs to know V for an average $A + \frac{1}{i} S(T_i)$ at T_i^+ (see (6.3)). In general, this average at T_i^+ will not be a point of the A-grid, therefore interpolation techniques have to be used.

The pricing of Asian options by finite differences or finite elements may become quite time consuming due to the additional parameter for the average. In practice, (Quasi) Monte Carlo techniques (Chapter 9 and Chapter 11) seem to be much more efficient for Asian-style options.

6.2 TERMINAL CONDITIONS FOR FIXED INCOME INSTRUMENTS

Terminal conditions for bonds with coupon rates that are known in advance are most easily formulated. If the bond pays a single cashflow of c at time T, then $V(r, T) = c$. When an instrument is made up of several cashflows c_i at T_i (like it is the case for coupon-paying bonds), then obviously

$$V(r, T_i) = c_i + V(r, T_i^+). \tag{6.5}$$

Due to this jump in the *dirty value*,[1] one should try to have a point of the time grid on coupon days when applying a time-stepping scheme.

To calculate present values of fixed cashflows in the future, solving the differential equation typically is an overkill if the yield curve is known, because one simply needs to discount the future cashflows. However, this procedure of solving the PDE makes sense when floating rates come into play. A constant maturity floater with caps/floors pays the redemption at maturity (redemption rates of 100 percent of the face value of the bond are quite common) and pays coupons which depend on some floating rate, e.g., the 10 year swap rate (CMS10y). If the floating rate which determines the coupon paid at the i-th coupon date T_i is observed at T_{i-1}, then the coupons are set *in advance*, if it is observed at T_i, then the setting rule is called *in arrears*. Setting in advance allows the calculation of accrued interest without having to argue about the height of the future coupon.

A *reverse*[2] *floater* may, for example, pay annual coupon rates of

$$\min(7\%, \max(2\%, 10\% - 2 \cdot \text{CMS10y})),$$

with the CMS10y set in advance (at the beginning of each coupon period). The minimum coupon of 2 percent is the floor, the maximum of 7 percent is the cap of this floating coupon. To valuate such a floating coupon, we observe:

1. On the set date, the reference rate (in our example: 10 year swap rate CMS10y) can be obtained from the zero yield rates by solving (4.6) for the swap rate.
2. In one-factor short rate models, the zero yield rates are determined by the short rate r, the parameters of the model, the respective set dates and the tenor of the reference rate. For Hull-White or for Cox-Ingersoll-Ross, these rates can be obtained from the analytic formulae for the zero coupon bonds. For Black-Karasinski, PDEs have to be solved numerically to obtain the yield rates.
3. The height of the future coupon is known on the set date and is not changed anymore between the set date and the coupon date. Therefore, the present value PV of the future coupon $c_i(T_i)$ (paid on T_i) valuated on the set date T_{i-1} at a short rate value of r is obtained by multiplying the coupon rate by the discount factor DF (for the discounting from T_i to T_{i-1}), which again depends only on the short rate at the set date. Schematically:

$$PV(c_i(T_i))(r, T_{i-1}) = c_i(r, T_{i-1}) \cdot DF(r, T_{i-1}, T_i). \tag{6.6}$$

4. The present value of this coupon at a grid point (r, t) for $t < T_{i-1}$ is then obtained by solving the corresponding short rate PDE with (6.6) as a terminal condition at T_{i-1}.

Exercise: How do the steps from above change for a coupon set in arrears?

---

[1] If a coupon-paying bond is traded between coupon days, then the new owner gets the coupon paid for the complete coupon interval. To take into account this possible imbalance between seller and buyer, the buyer has to pay *accrued interest* (proportion of the coupon) for the elapsed time between the previous coupon day and the settlement date of the trade. The dirty value of a bond is the present value of future cashflows, the *clean value* is the dirty value minus the accrued interest.

[2] The term "reverse" reflects the construction that coupons decrease when the underlying floating rates (here the CMS10y) increase and vice versa.

6.3 CALLABILITY AND BERMUDAN OPTIONS

The reverse floater from the previous section would in reality be typically equipped with an early redemption option for the issuer of the floating rate note, meaning that the issuer may, at certain dates, redeem the floater for a price (that may depend on the redemption date) fixed in the term sheet. In the above example, the term sheet might state that, after an initial period of several years, the issuer has the right to buy back (to call) the reverse floater for a fixed price of 100 percent of the nominal value. A *Bermudan callable* instrument has more than one of these call possibilities at discrete points in time.

If there is only one call date (or only one call date left) and if buy and sell price are identical, then a rational issuer will call the bond if and only if she cannot buy the remaining cashflows for a cheaper price than the call price, or, equivalently, if she can resell the remaining cashflows for a price that is higher than the call price. This is exactly the same argument we used for the exercise strategy of call options on equity. Let T be the maturity of the bond and let $T_1, \ldots, T_n < T$ denote the call dates of a Bermudan callable instrument (for call prices $K_1, \ldots, K_N$). Then

1. For T_n, the issuer must decide whether to call the bond or not, by comparing the keep value and the exercise price (stated in the term sheet). The keep value $KV(r, T_n)$ is obtained by the procedure (6.6) from above. For any r, the value of the callable bond $CV(r, T_n)$ is then the cheaper one of the keep value and the call price

$$CV(r, T_n) = \min(K_n, KV(r, T_n)). \qquad (6.7)$$

2. Propagate backwards in time: At time T_{i-1} the keep value $KV(r, t_{i-1})$ of the callable bond consists of several components:
   (a) The keep value (at T_{i-1}) of either the call price K_i or the cashflows after T_i. This is obtained by solving the short rate PDE for KV with the terminal condition (6.7) and T_n replaced by T_i.
   (b) Add possible coupon payments (paid at time t) for $T_{i-1} < t \leq T_i$ by applying (6.6).

6.4 DIVIDENDS

When companies pay dividends to their shareholders, there is a drop in the value of the share after the dividend payment, because one is entitled to receive the dividend only if one owns the share before the ex-dividend date. For derivatives on an equity that pays a discrete dividend D at time t_D, this means that

$$V(S_{t_D}, t_D^+) = V(S_{t_D} - D, t_D^-), \qquad (6.8)$$

because the equity value drops by D. Veiga and Wystup (2009) formulate additional conditions when the dividend is not paid for sure but depends on a dividend policy.

Treating discrete dividends by a drop in the share price has the disadvantage that closed form solutions cease to exist because a shifted log-normally distributed variable (the share price) is not log-normally distributed any more. If dividend rates are fairly low, it may make sense to discount a dividend, which is assumed to be paid between the valuation day of an option and its expiry, to the valuation date and subtract the result from the current share price. This anticipates the dividend payment and may lead to closed form solutions. Note that volatilities have to be adjusted to justify such an approach. See Hull (2002) for more details.

Chooser Option on Dividend Paying Stock

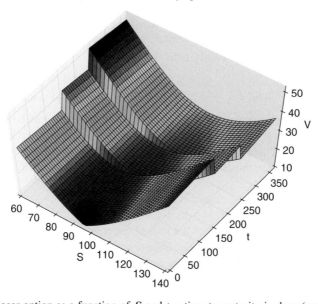

Figure 6.2   Chooser option as a function of S and t = time to maturity in days (expiry in the front). The equity pays two large dividends of 10 currency units each visible by the steps ($K = 100$, $r = 0.05$, $\sigma = 0.25$). For the same value of S, the value of the put part of the option (low values of S) is higher before the dividend date, because S will drop and make the put more valuable. A similar argument holds for the call part.

If the underlying of a derivative instrument is an equity index, its movement is frequently modeled by using a continuous equity yield,

$$dS = S(r - y)dt + \sigma S dW. \tag{6.9}$$

The equity yield y is then the weighted average of the dividend returns of the equities composing the index.

Figure 6.2 shows the value of a chooser option as a function of the stock price and of time to expiry. The dividends lead to significant steps.

6.5 SNOWBALLS AND TARNS

In this section, we deal with the interface conditions of two groups of exotic instruments with a strong path dependence. In a snowball floater, the coupon at time T_i depends on the coupon paid at time T_{i-1} and some reference rate. The following example should illustrate this:

A Snowball Example

Lifetime of the bond: 10 years.

Semiannual coupons (20 coupons in total). The rates in the following lines are the corresponding annual rates.

Coupon rates 1 and 2: 7.5%

Coupon rate (T_i) $(i \geq 3)$ = coupon rate (T_{i-1}) + 7% $-$ 2 $\cdot$ Euribor6m at T_i, set in arrears with a floor at 0.

This example exhibits extreme leverage. Small changes in the Euribor can change the coupons quite strongly. To reduce the issuer's risk, snowball floaters are typically callable, thus giving the issuer the right of early redemption.

A TARN Example

TARN stands for target redemption note. With these instruments, the bond has a maximum lifetime (say, 15 years). If the sum of the coupons paid so far reaches a certain level (the *target*), the bond is redeemed. There is no optionality for issuer or investor, but an external trigger (the sum of coupons) that determines the redemption date. For example, a typical termsheet of a TARN is:

Maximum lifetime: 15 years, annual coupons

Coupons 1 to 7: 4%. Coupon T_i $(i \geq 8)$ = 6%-CMS10y.

Target redemption occurs as soon as the sum of coupons reaches 35%.

The term sheets of TARNs typically also have to specify if a) the difference between the sum of coupons and the target level is paid in the case of target redemption, and b) if the difference between the target level and the sum of coupons is paid when this sum is not reached until maturity. The underlying (in our example: CMS10y) need not be an interest rate but could be something completely different, such as an exchange rate.

Like in the case of discrete Asian options, the path dependence of future cashflows of snowballs and TARNs leads us to introducing an additional state variable as a parameter. In the case of snowballs, this is the previous coupon rate, in the case of TARNs we use the sum of coupons so far.

The Snowball Case

Let, for $t \in (T_{i-1}, T_i)$, $V(r, t, a)$ be the value of the (non-callable) snowball floater for which the coupon paid at T_{i-1} was a. Then, under the short rate models of Chapter 4, for any parameter a, V has to fulfill the short rate PDE between T_{i-1} and T_i. If coupons are set in arrears, then the following interface condition must hold,

$$V(r, T_i, a) = V(r, T_i^+, f(r, T_i, a)) + f(r, T_i, a) \cdot \text{nominal value}, \qquad (6.10)$$

where $f(r, T_i, a)$ decribes the new snowball coupon. In our example, this was a + 7% $-$ 2$\cdot$ Euribor6m(r, T_i). A similar interface condition can be found when the coupons are not set in arrears, but in advance. For a range of parameters a, the PDE must be solved. Information between Vs for different a values is exchanged only at coupon dates via $f(r, T_i, a)$. If the snowball floater is callable at certain dates, V has to be, like in section 6.3, replaced by the pointwise minimum of the keep value and the call price.

The TARN Case

For the TARN case, the parameter a stands for the sum of coupons so far. Again, between coupon dates, $V(r, t, a)$ has to fulfill the respective differential equation for the interest rate model. At the coupon dates, we have

$$V(r, T_i, a) = V(r, T_i^+, f(r, T_i, a)) + \text{Cashflow}(r, T_i, a), \qquad (6.11)$$

with $f(r, T_i, a) = a + \text{coupon}(r, T_i)$. There are two possibilities: If $f(r, T_i, a)$ is higher than the target level (pointwise in r), than $V(r, T_i^+, f(r, T_i, a)) = 0$ (because the instrument ceases to exist after redemption), and the cashflow at (r, T_i, a) consists of the redemption and the final coupon. Otherwise, if the target level is not reached yet, the pointwise cashflow is the coupon, and the parameter transformation between a and $f(r, T_i, a)$ is carried out.

6.6 BOUNDARY CONDITIONS

In the previous chapters, we have presented examples of models for the stochastic behavior of underlyings for which the domain of interest is, in principle, unbounded: There is no intrinsic limit for stock prices or for interest rates. When we want to apply finite difference or finite element methods to the valuation of instruments, we have to introduce artificial boundaries and artificial boundary conditions in order to obtain a finite calculation domain.[3] For some examples, these boundary conditions are quite obvious, but frequently this is not the case. However, it turns out that, provided the calculation domain is large enough, the specific shape of boundary conditions typically has only very small impact on the value of the instrument to be valuated.

6.6.1 Double Barrier Options and Dirichlet Boundary Conditions

We introduced up-and-out call options in Chapter 2. A double knock-out call option becomes worthless if the underlying ever leaves the interval (B_L, B_U). Under the Black-Scholes model, the problem to be solved consists of the Black-Scholes differential equation (see (3.19)),

$$\frac{\partial V}{\partial t} + \frac{\sigma^2 S^2}{2} \frac{\partial^2 V}{\partial S^2} + rS \frac{\partial V}{\partial S} - rV = 0,$$

the end condition (payoff for the call),

$$V(S, T) = \max(S - K, 0) \qquad \text{for } S \in [B_L, B_U], \tag{6.12}$$

and the boundary conditions at $S = B_L$ and at $S = B_U$. If S reaches the barriers B_L or B_U, the option is knocked out, and therefore $V(B, t)$ has to vanish for $B = B_L, B = B_U$,

$$V(B_L, t) = V(B_U, t) = 0 \qquad \text{for } t \in [0, T]. \tag{6.13}$$

If the option has not been knocked out, then, at expiry, its value is the same as that of a vanilla option. If B_U approaches infinity and B_L approaches 0, then the likelihood to hit the barrier tends to zero. Intuitively, it is clear that for fixed S_0, the value $V(S_0, 0)$ of the double barrier call option from above converges to the the vanilla call value with $B_U \to \infty$ and $B_L \to 0$. This can be proved rigorously by a series expansion for the double barrier option.

In practice, one could set $B_U = S_0 \exp\{(r - \sigma^2/2)T + j\sigma\sqrt{(T)}\}$ and $B_L = S_0 \exp\{(r - \sigma^2/2)T - j\sigma\sqrt{(T)}\}$. With $j = 5$, the likelihood to hit the barrier is lower than 10^{-6}, with $j = 7$, it is around 10^{-12}. This follows from the decay of the probability density of the normal distribution. If, say, $r = 0.045$, $\sigma = 0.3$, $T = 1$, then the 5σ artificial boundaries would be at

---

[3] To be more specific, this is only true when implicit schemes are used. If an explicit time-stepping scheme is used and if there are enough grid points in the direction of the underlying, one could, in a tree-wise manner, reduce the number of grid-points linearly when propagating backwards and therefore get along without boundary conditions. Nevertheless, as pointed out in the previous chapters, we strongly recommend implicit schemes for stability reasons.

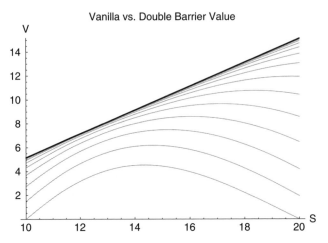

Figure 6.3   For $K = 5$, $\sigma = 0.3$, $r = 0.03$, $T = 1$ year, the thick curve is the value of the European vanilla call. The thin curves give the values of the double barrier knock-out options with $B_L = 10 \cdot \exp(-\sigma\sqrt{T} * j/4)$, $B_U = 20 \cdot \exp(\sigma\sqrt{T} \cdot * j/4)$, $j = 0, \dots, 28$. Boundary conditions which are far away do not influence the option value.

$B_U = e^{1.5}S_0$ and $B = e^{-1.5}S_0$. Figure 6.3 shows the convergence of these barrier option values (with widening barrier ranges) towards the vanilla option value.

6.6.2   Artificial Boundary Conditions and the Neumann Case

In practice, there are only few cases for which the boundary conditions can be obtained in a straightforward way from the term sheet. But, as indicated by the previous example, when the artificial boundaries are reasonably far away (say, $5\sigma\sqrt{T}$) from the points for which the instrument values should be calculated, the specific shape of the boundary condition only plays a minor role. Typically, so-called Neumann boundary conditions, which formulate conditions on the normal derivative of the value of the instrument, lead to numerical solutions exhibiting artificial boundary layers which are less pronounced than for Dirichlet conditions. Note that these boundary layers do not arise from the specific numerical method which is applied but would appear also if the analytic solution could be calculated exactly. Estimates for the error introduced by the artificial boundary conditions can be obtained by applying the maximum principle for parabolic equations (Binder, 2013; Protter and Weinberger, 1967).

Figures 6.4 and 6.5 show the results for the values of zero coupon bonds under a Vasicek model with mean reversion level $a = 0$, reversion speed $b = 0.1$ and $\sigma = 0.01$. We cut off the calculation domain at $r = \pm 0.2$ and prescribe either Dirichlet conditions $V = 1$ or homogeneous Neumann conditions $\frac{\partial v}{\partial r} = 0$ there. As negative interest rates are possible in the Vasicek model, the bond assumes also values significantly greater than 1. The boundary layers for the Dirichlet conditions are much more pronounced but their influence is, similar to the Neumann conditions, only a local one.

Binder and Schatz (2006) study various combinations of finite elements (with and without streamline diffusion techniques) and Dirichlet/Neumann boundary conditions for two-factor Hull-White models. It turns out that for such a (spatially) two-dimensional mean-reverting

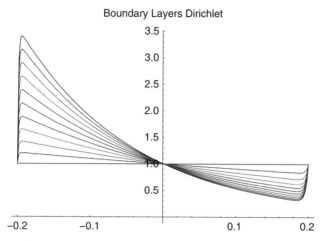

Figure 6.4   Values of zero bonds maturing in $0, 1, \ldots, 10$ years under a Vasicek model with artificial Dirichlet conditions.

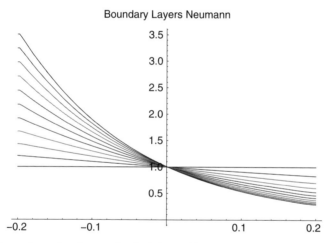

Figure 6.5   Values of zero bonds maturing in $0, 1, \ldots, 10$ years under a Vasicek model with artificial Neumann conditions.

model, the combination of an appropriate treatment of the convection (streamline diffusion or other upwinding methods) and homogeneous Neumann boundary conditions deliver the best results, not only for the value of the instrument but also for the sensitivities of the value with respect to the interest rate state variables. We will deal with the two factor Hull-White model in more detail in Chapter 7.

Finite Element Methods

7.1 INTRODUCTION

The finite element method is a numerical method for solving partial differential equations (PDEs), and has become particularly popular in engineering and physics. More recently, it has also gained interest in the quantitative finance community as a valuable tool to solve PDEs that arise in modeling financial instruments. The basic strategy of the finite element method is to divide the region of interest into smaller parts (finite elements), and to approximate the solution in each element by a simple function. The method can thus be seen as a piecewise approximation. Polynomial-type interpolation functions are most widely used for the element solutions (also called approximating functions or interpolation functions), due to

1. the ease of formulating and computing the finite element equations,
2. the possibility to obtain higher accuracy by increasing the order of the polynomial.

Although other types of interpolation functions, such as trigonometric functions, can be used, we restrict ourselves to polynomial functions in this book. The interested reader is referred to (Zienkiewicz and Taylor, 2000a) and (Segerlind, 1984) and the references therein.

7.1.1 Weighted Residual Methods

If an approximate solution (trial function) is substituted into a differential equation a residual remains, since the approximate solution does not satisfy the equation. Consider, as an example, the one-dimensional second order partial differential equation

$$A\frac{d^2y}{dx^2} + Q = 0, \quad \text{with } y(0) = y_0 \text{ and } y(\mathbf{H}) = y_{\mathbf{H}}. \tag{7.1}$$

Substituting $y(x)$ by the approximative solution $h(x)$,

$$A\frac{d^2h(x)}{dx^2} + Q = R(x) \neq 0, \tag{7.2}$$

yields a non-zero residual $R(x)$ since $h(x)$ does not satisfy the equation exactly. The weighted residual method demands

$$\int_0^H W_i(x)R(x)dx = 0, \tag{7.3}$$

where the number of weighting functions $W_i(x)$ is determined by the number of unknown coefficients in the trial function. Different choices for the weighting functions – which are sometimes also called testing functions – are available. We list some of the more popular choices here:

- Collocation method: Dirac-delta functions are used as weighting functions, $W_i(x) = \delta(x - X_i)$. The residual will thus vanish at the points X_i if (7.3) is fulfilled.

- Subdomain method: the idea is to force the weighted residual to be zero not just at fixed points in the domain, but over various subsections of the domain. To accomplish this, the weight functions are set to unity ($W(x) = 1$), and the integral over the entire domain is broken into a number of subdomains sufficient to evaluate all unknown parameters.
- Galerkin method: if we consider a trial function of the form

$$h(x) = \sum_i a_i N_i(x) \tag{7.4}$$

the Galerkin method uses the same functions $N_i(x)$ for $W_i(x)$ that are used for the approximate solutions. Under the assumption that we are looking for a function y in a function space U, also the testing functions W are element of the function space U (for example polynomials of order one). This is the most popular method and is used for solving problems with first derivative terms. The Galerkin method will be used exclusively throughout this chapter.
- Least squares method: the residual is used as a weighting function and a new error term is defined which is then minimized with respect to the unknown coefficients of the trial functions.[1]

7.1.2 Basic Steps

The practical application of the finite element method can be broken down into the following series of basic steps:

1. Discretization of the region of interest: The most important concepts used for grid generation, such as refinement strategies and adaptivity, will be presented later in this chapter. This step also includes numbering the nodes and specifying their corresponding coordinate values.
2. The trial function $h(x)$ is specified (for instance, the order of a polynomial approximation) and for each element, the partial differential equation is written in terms of the unknown nodal values.
3. Using the Galerkin method for each element a system of equations is developed. These equations are then assembled into the global system of equations that covers the whole domain.

---

[1] The new residual S in the least squares method is given by

$$S = \int_\Omega R(x)R(x)dx = \int_\Omega R^2(x)dx.$$

In order to achieve a minimum of this scalar function, the derivatives of S with respect to all the unknown parameters must be zero,

$$\frac{\partial S}{\partial a_i} = 0 = 2\int_\Omega R(x)\frac{\partial R(x)}{\partial a_i}dx.$$

By comparison, we can identify the weight function (the factor 2 can be dropped – it cancels out in the equation) to be

$$W_i(x) = \frac{\partial R(x)}{\partial a_i}.$$

Note that the Galerkin method may be viewed as a modification of the Least Squares method. Rather than using the derivative of the residual with respect to the unknown a_j, the derivative of the approximating function $h(x)$ is used. Then,

$$W_i(x) = \frac{\partial h(x)}{\partial a_i} = N_i(x).$$

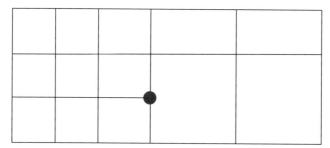

Figure 7.1   The figure shows a mesh with a dangling node (round point). If a partial differential equation would be solved on this domain, additional effort is necessary to treat dangling nodes in the resulting system of equations.

4. Add the boundary/terminal/interface conditions.
5. Solve the system of equations (see Chapter 8 for different methods to solve linear systems of equations).

Each of the steps described above will be worked out in detail in the following sections of this chapter.

7.2   GRID GENERATION

In contrast to physics and engineering, where the optimal element type and approximation order is often determined by the nature of the problem, the situation is not equally clear when applying the finite element method to financial problems. Two key questions need to be asked in advance of tackling a problem:

1. Is it desirable to refine the mesh, by locally adding additional elements, during the simulation process?
2. Are higher order derivatives of the (approximate) solution required?

The first question is only crucial in two or more dimensions and gives a hint regarding the type of preferred element. Triangular and tetrahedral elements allow for local mesh refinement without the danger of generating dangling nodes (see Figure 7.1).

The answer to the second question indicates the required order of approximation: If the calculation of Greeks or similar quantities connected with higher-order derivatives is of relevance, higher order approximations should be used.[2] Mesh generation algorithms for technical applications, generally involve complex iterative smoothing techniques that attempt to align elements with boundaries or physical domains. In financial engineering, on the other hand, structured rectangular or hexahedral meshes can be easily generated using tensor products (cartesian grids) that lead to structured meshes. Strictly speaking, a structured mesh (see Figure 7.2) can be identified by all interior nodes of the mesh having an equal number of adjacent elements. Rectangular or hexahedral structured meshes may also serve as starting points for structured triangular or tetrahedral meshes.

---

[2] Consider the calculation of the gamma of an option: When linear elements are used, the first derivative of the option value with respect to the underlying would be constant inside an element, and the second derivative would therefore be zero, but a Dirac-Delta would occur across element boundaries.

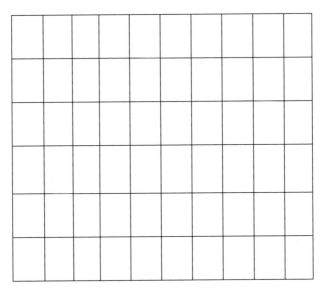

Figure 7.2   The figure shows a structured mesh formed by rectangular elements. All interior nodes have an equal number of adjacent elements.

Unstructured meshes (see Figure 7.3), on the other hand, drop the node valence requirement and allow any number of elements to meet at a single node. Triangular and tetrahedral meshes are by far the most common forms used here. Most mesh generation techniques for unstructured meshes currently used fall into one of three categories, namely the Quad/Octree technique, Delauny triangulation and the advancing front algorithm, which are briefly summarized in the following.

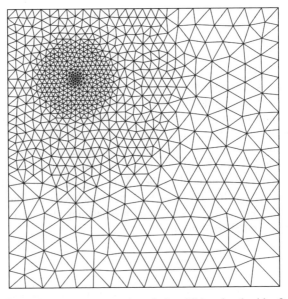

Figure 7.3   The figure shows a unstructured mesh. In addition, local grid refinement is applied.

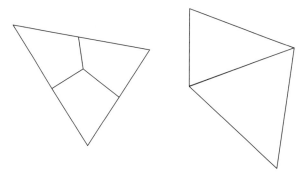

Figure 7.4   The figure shows two ways to generate quadrilaterals meshes starting from triangles – on the left hand side a triangle is split into three quadrilaterals and on the right hand side two triangles are merged to a quadrilateral.

The Octree technique recursively subdivides cubes or quads containing the computational domain until the desired resolution is achieved. Due to local refinements, dangling nodes will occur. Methods based on the Delauny criterion are by far the most popular ones for triangular and tetrahedral meshing today. Put simply, the Delaunay criterion states that any node must not be contained inside the circumsphere/circumcircle of any tetrahedra/triangle in the mesh.

Typically, the boundary of the computational domain is meshed first to provide an initial set of nodes. After triangulating the boundary nodes according to the Delaunay criterion, nodes are inserted incrementally into the existing mesh. This leads to a local reshaping of the triangles or tetrahedra as each new node is inserted to maintain the Delaunay criterion. Depending on the method chosen for inserting the points into the existing mesh one distinguishes between the so-called point insertion technique and the boundary constrained triangulation.

Another popular family of triangular and tetrahedral mesh generation algorithms is the advancing (or moving) front method. Tetrahedra are progressively built from the triangulated surface of the computational domain inward. An active front is maintained where new tetrahedra/triangles are formed.

To obtain unstructured quadrilateral or hexahedral meshes, unstructured triangular or tetrahedral meshes often serve as starting points. Such an indirect method is demonstrated in Figure 7.4, where a quad mesh is generated by splitting each triangle into three quads or by combining two triangles into a quad.

7.3 ELEMENTS

The shape functions (basis functions $N_i(x)$ used for generating the trial function $h(x)$) for one-, two- and three-dimensional elements are derived in this section and the appendix of this chapter. We first list a number of general properties valid for all shape functions used in this book, independent of the dimension:

1. A shape function is always equal to one at its designated node (same nodal index) and zero at the other nodes of the element (see, for instance, Figure 7.6).
2. At any point inside the element (including the boundaries), the sum over all shape functions is equal to one.

We focus on linear shape functions in this chapter. As solutions in quantitative finance are smooth if no barriers, caps, floors,... occur, using higher order elements allows to reduce the number of elements used for discretization.

We will show later in this chapter that all finite element solutions require the evaluation of integrals, which, depending on the order and type of the interpolation function, may not be analytically tractable. A common method to simplify integrations is to perform a variable transformation (see the Appendix of this chapter), i.e., to rewrite the integral in an alternative coordinate system.

7.3.1   1D Elements

Many problems in computational finance can be described by one-dimensional models, e.g., instruments under one factor short rate models or all options with only one underlying. The one-dimensional region is then a line and the division into elements or subregions is very straightforward. We introduce the superscript e to mark quantities and values determined for a certain element.

1D linear element

A line segment with two end nodes $X_i^{(e)}$ and $X_j^{(e)}$ has the length $L^{(e)} = X_j^{(e)} - X_i^{(e)}$ (assuming $X_j^{(e)} < X_i^{(e)}$) and corresponding nodal values $\Phi_i^{(e)}$ and $\Phi_j^{(e)}$. We start with a linear approximation, such that the unknown function $\Phi^{(e)}(x)$ varies linearly between these nodes inside the current element (see Figure 7.5),

$$\Phi^{(e)}(x) = \alpha_1^{(e)} + \alpha_2^{(e)} x. \tag{7.5}$$

The coefficients α_1 and α_2 can be determined from the nodal values by solving

$$\Phi_i^{(e)} = \alpha_1^{(e)} + \alpha_2^{(e)} X_i, \tag{7.6}$$

$$\Phi_j^{(e)} = \alpha_1^{(e)} + \alpha_2^{(e)} X_j, \tag{7.7}$$

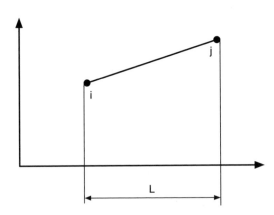

Figure 7.5   The figure shows the function $\Phi^{(e)}(x)$ varying linearly between the nodes indexed by i and j.

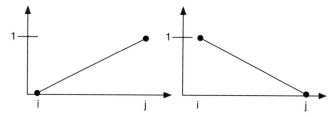

Figure 7.6   The figure shows the shape functions N_i and N_j for the linear 1D element.

which yields

$$\alpha_1^{(e)} = \frac{\Phi_i^{(e)} X_j^{(e)} - \Phi_j^{(e)} X_i^{(e)}}{X_j^{(e)} - X_i^{(e)}}, \tag{7.8}$$

$$\alpha_2^{(e)} = \frac{\Phi_j^{(e)} - \Phi_i^{(e)}}{X_j^{(e)} - X_i^{(e)}}. \tag{7.9}$$

Substituting L and rearranging leads to

$$\Phi^{(e)}(x) = \frac{X_j^{(e)} - x}{L^{(e)}} \Phi_i^{(e)} + \frac{x - X_i^{(e)}}{L^{(e)}} \Phi_j^{(e)}. \tag{7.10}$$

Such equations, where the nodal values are multiplied by affine linear functions of x, are typical for the finite element formalism. The linear functions appearing in Equation (7.10) are called shape functions or interpolation functions. In the literature, the variable N with a subscript that indicates the node of the element is frequently used to denote shape functions (see Figure 7.6),

$$\Phi^{(e)}(x) = N_i^{(e)} \Phi_i^{(e)} + N_j^{(e)} \Phi_j^{(e)}, \tag{7.11}$$

$$N_i^{(e)} = \frac{X_j^{(e)} - x}{L^{(e)}}, \tag{7.12}$$

$$N_j^{(e)} = \frac{x - X_i^{(e)}}{L^{(e)}}. \tag{7.13}$$

Using vector notation, we can write

$$\Phi^{(e)}(x) = \mathbf{N}^{(e)} \mathbf{\Phi}^{(e)T}, \tag{7.14}$$

where

$$\mathbf{N}^{(e)} = \left(N_i^{(e)}, N_j^{(e)} \right) \tag{7.15}$$

is called the shape function vector and

$$\mathbf{\Phi}^{(e)T} = \begin{pmatrix} \Phi_i^{(e)} \\ \Phi_j^{(e)} \end{pmatrix} \tag{7.16}$$

is the vector of the unknown nodal values.

Example

Consider the value of a bond that is worth 80 at a yield of 0.05 and worth 95 at a yield of 0.025. Assume the variation of the bond value to be linear in between. From Equation (7.11), the distribution of the bond value over an element can be written as

$$V = N_i V_i + N_j V_j.$$

To obtain the value of the bond at a yield of 0.045, we start with the calculation of the shape functions,

$$N_i = \frac{r_j - r}{r_j - r_i} = \frac{0.02}{0.025} = \frac{4}{5},$$

$$N_j = \frac{r - r_i}{r_j - r_i} = \frac{0.005}{0.025} = \frac{1}{5}.$$

Substitution of N_i and N_j gives a bond price of 83 for a yield of 0.045. Note that $N_i + N_j = 1$.

7.3.2   2D Elements

For 2D problems we introduce two different geometries: the triangular and rectangular element families. In both cases we focus on linear and quadratic shape functions, which we consider sufficient for financial modeling.

2D Triangular Linear Element

The two-dimensional linear element is also known as simplex element and is represented by a linear polynomial in x and y,

$$\Phi^{(e)}(x, y) = \alpha_1^{(e)} + \alpha_2^{(e)} x + \alpha_3^{(e)} y. \tag{7.17}$$

Figure 7.7 shows such an element. The nodal values can again be used to determine α_1, α_2 and α_3 by solving the linear system

$$\Phi_i^{(e)} = \alpha_1^{(e)} + \alpha_2^{(e)} X_i + \alpha_3^{(e)} Y_i,$$

$$\Phi_j^{(e)} = \alpha_1^{(e)} + \alpha_2^{(e)} X_j + \alpha_3^{(e)} Y_j,$$

$$\Phi_k^{(e)} = \alpha_1^{(e)} + \alpha_2^{(e)} X_k + \alpha_3^{(e)} Y_k,$$

which yields

$$\alpha_1^{(e)} = \frac{1}{2A} \left((X_j Y_k - X_k Y_j) \Phi_i^{(e)} + (X_k Y_i - X_i Y_k) \Phi_j^{(e)} + (X_i Y_j - X_j Y_i) \Phi_k^{(e)} \right),$$

$$\alpha_2^{(e)} = \frac{1}{2A} \left((Y_j - Y_k) \Phi_i^{(e)} + (Y_k - Y_i) \Phi_j^{(e)} + (Y_i - Y_j) \Phi_k^{(e)} \right),$$

$$\alpha_3^{(e)} = \frac{1}{2A} \left((X_k - X_j) \Phi_i^{(e)} + (X_i - X_k) \Phi_j^{(e)} + (X_j - X_i) \Phi_k^{(e)} \right).$$

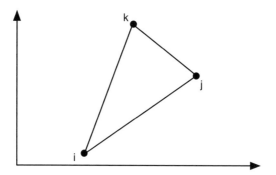

Figure 7.7   The figure shows the linear triangular element with the node numbering i and j and k.

Here, A is the area of the element which can be easily calculated by

$$2A = \det \begin{pmatrix} 1 & X_i & Y_i \\ 1 & X_j & Y_j \\ 1 & X_k & Y_k \end{pmatrix}. \tag{7.18}$$

Again, the shape functions can be obtained by substituting the values for α_1, α_2 and α_3 into equation (7.17). The unknown quantity can then be expressed as

$$\Phi^{(e)}(x, y) = N_i^{(e)} \Phi_i^{(e)} + N_j^{(e)} \Phi_j^{(e)} + N_k^{(e)} \Phi_k^{(e)}, \tag{7.19}$$

with the shape functions

$$N_i^{(e)} = \frac{1}{2A}(a_i + b_i x + c_i y),$$

$$N_j^{(e)} = \frac{1}{2A}(a_j + b_j x + c_j y),$$

$$N_k^{(e)} = \frac{1}{2A}(a_k + b_k x + c_k y).$$

Omitting the superscript e, the coefficients a, b, c in the above equation are

$$
\begin{aligned}
a_i &= (X_j Y_k - X_k Y_j), & b_i &= (Y_j - Y_k), & c_i &= (X_k - X_j), \\
a_j &= (X_k Y_i - X_i Y_k), & b_j &= (Y_k - Y_i), & c_j &= (Y_i - Y_j), \\
a_k &= (X_i Y_j - X_j Y_i), & b_k &= (X_i - X_k), & c_k &= (X_j - X_i).
\end{aligned}
\tag{7.20}
$$

Note that these shape functions satisfy the properties discussed for the one dimensional case: Each shape function has a value of one at its designated node and a value of zero at the other two. Summing up all three functions always amounts to one. The shape functions vary linearly along the edges between its node and the other two nodes, and the shape function is zero along the edge opposite its node. Also note that derivatives with respect to the spatial coordinates are constant inside an element.

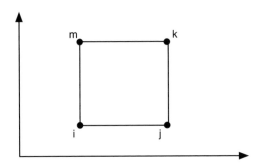

Figure 7.8   The figure shows the linear rectangular element with the node numbering i, j, k and m.

2D Rectangular Linear Element

A quadrilateral element has four nodes as shown in Figure 7.8. A mesh built from rectangular quadrilaterals is identical to the finite difference mesh treated in Chapter 3. We choose the origin of the coordinate system to be in the center of the rectangle with side lengths $2a$ and $2b$, respectively,

$$\Phi^{(e)}(x) = \alpha_1^{(e)} + \alpha_2^{(e)}x + \alpha_3^{(e)}y + \alpha_4^{(e)}xy. \tag{7.21}$$

Note that the gradient inside an element varies linearly. Again, one can derive an equation for the unknown value inside an element of the form

$$\Phi^{(e)} = N_i^{(e)}\Phi_i^{(e)} + N_j^{(e)}\Phi_j^{(e)} + N_k^{(e)}\Phi_k^{(e)} + N_l^{(e)}\Phi_l^{(e)}, \tag{7.22}$$

with the shape functions of the rectangular element,

$$N_i = \frac{1}{4ab}(b-x)(a-y),$$

$$N_j = \frac{1}{4ab}(b+x)(a-y),$$

$$N_k = \frac{1}{4ab}(b-x)(a+y),$$

$$N_l = \frac{1}{4ab}(b+x)(a+y). \tag{7.23}$$

7.4 THE ASSEMBLING PROCESS

We now proceed to the next of the steps outlined in section 7.1.2, namely the assembling of a linear system of equations using the discrete finite elements. We show this procedure in a step-by-step manner by applying the finite element method to a two-dimensional static diffusion-reaction equation,

$$\nabla(\lambda\nabla)\Phi(x, y) - G\Phi(x, y) + Q = 0. \tag{7.24}$$

With the definition

$$\lambda = \begin{pmatrix} \lambda_x & 0 \\ 0 & \lambda_y \end{pmatrix}, \tag{7.25}$$

this is equivalent to

$$\lambda_x \frac{\partial^2 \Phi(x, y)}{\partial x^2} + \lambda_y \frac{\partial^2 \Phi(x, y)}{\partial y^2} - G\Phi(x, y) + Q = 0, \tag{7.26}$$

when λ is independent of the spatial coordinates.[3] In a first step, we derive the integral equations that define the element matrices. An element's contribution[4] to the system of equations is given by

$$R^{(e)} = -\int_A \mathbf{N}^T \left(\lambda_x \frac{\partial^2 \Phi(x, y)}{\partial x^2} + \lambda_y \frac{\partial^2 \Phi(x, y)}{\partial y^2} - G\Phi(x, y) + Q \right) dA, \tag{7.27}$$

where A denotes the element's area and $\mathbf{N}$ is the row vector containing the element's shape functions. By applying the product rule of differentiation, the second derivative terms can be replaced by first order derivatives: Substituting

$$\frac{\partial}{\partial x} \left(\mathbf{N}^T \frac{\partial \Phi}{\partial x} \right) = \mathbf{N}^T \frac{\partial^2 \Phi}{\partial x^2} + \frac{\partial \mathbf{N}^T}{\partial x} \frac{\partial \Phi}{\partial x} \tag{7.28}$$

into Equation (7.27) and rearranging yields

$$-\int_A \mathbf{N}^T \lambda_x \frac{\partial^2 \Phi}{\partial x^2} dA = -\int_A \lambda_x \frac{\partial}{\partial x} \left(\mathbf{N}^T \frac{\partial \Phi}{\partial x} \right) dA + \int_A \lambda_x \frac{\partial \mathbf{N}^T}{\partial x} \frac{\partial \Phi}{\partial x} dA. \tag{7.29}$$

The first integral on the right hand side can be replaced by an integral over the boundary of the computational domain, $\Gamma = \partial A$, using Green's theorem,

$$\int_A \frac{\partial}{\partial x} \left(\mathbf{N}^T \frac{\partial \Phi}{\partial x} \right) dA = \int_\Gamma \mathbf{N}^T \frac{\partial \Phi}{\partial x} \cos(\Psi) d\Gamma, \tag{7.30}$$

where the angle between the outward normal and the element boundary Γ is denoted by Ψ. Inserting Equation (7.30) into Equation (7.29) leads to

$$-\int_A \lambda_x \mathbf{N}^T \frac{\partial^2 \Phi}{\partial x^2} dA = -\int_\Gamma \lambda_x \mathbf{N}^T \frac{\partial \Phi}{\partial x} \cos(\Psi) d\Gamma + \int_A \lambda_x \frac{\partial \mathbf{N}^T}{\partial x} \frac{\partial \Phi}{\partial x} dA. \tag{7.31}$$

Performing equivalent operations with the derivatives by y,

$$\frac{\partial}{\partial y} \left(\mathbf{N}^T \frac{\partial \Phi}{\partial y} \right), \tag{7.32}$$

produces

$$-\int_A \lambda_y \mathbf{N}^T \frac{\partial^2 \Phi}{\partial y^2} dA = -\int_\Gamma \lambda_y \mathbf{N}^T \frac{\partial \Phi}{\partial y} \sin(\Psi) d\Gamma + \int_A \lambda_y \frac{\partial \mathbf{N}^T}{\partial y} \frac{\partial \Phi}{\partial y} dA. \tag{7.33}$$

---

[3] If λ *shows a more complicated structure* the divergence used in Equation (7.24) is more suitable for mathematical analysis.
[4] To simplify notation, we now drop the superscript (e), and will only add it where appropriate.

Inserting these results into the residual Equation (7.27) gives

$$R^{(e)} = - \int_\Gamma \mathbf{N}^T \left(\lambda_x \frac{\partial \Phi}{\partial x} \cos(\Psi) + \lambda_y \frac{\partial \Phi}{\partial y} \sin(\Psi) \right) d\Gamma$$

$$+ \int_A \left(\lambda_x \frac{\partial \mathbf{N}}{\partial x} \frac{\partial \Phi}{\partial x} + \lambda_y \frac{\partial \mathbf{N}}{\partial y} \frac{\partial \phi}{\partial y} \right) dA \qquad (7.34)$$

$$+ \int_A G \mathbf{N}^T \Phi dA - \int_A Q \mathbf{N}^T dA.$$

In the Galerkin formulation, the unknown quantity $\Phi(x, y)$ is expressed by

$$\Phi(x, y)^{(e)} = \mathbf{N}^{(e)} \mathbf{\Phi}^{(e)}. \qquad (7.35)$$

Substitution and rearranging yields

$$R^{(e)} = - \int_\Gamma \mathbf{N}^T \left(\lambda_x \frac{\partial \Phi}{\partial x} \cos(\Psi) + \lambda_y \frac{\partial \Phi}{\partial y} \sin(\Psi) \right) d\Gamma \qquad (7.36)$$

$$+ \underbrace{\left(\int_A \left(\lambda_x \frac{\partial \mathbf{N}^T}{\partial x} \frac{\partial \mathbf{N}}{\partial x} + \lambda_y \frac{\partial \mathbf{N}^T}{\partial y} \frac{\partial \mathbf{N}}{\partial y} \right) \right) dA}_{\mathbf{K}^{(e)}} \mathbf{\Phi}^{(e)}$$

$$+ \underbrace{\left(\int_A G \mathbf{N}^T \mathbf{N} dA \right)}_{\mathbf{M}^{(e)}} \mathbf{\Phi}^{(e)} - \underbrace{\int_A Q \mathbf{N}^T dA}_{\mathbf{f}^{(e)}}.$$

In a first step, we neglect the integral over Γ (the boundary of the element),[5] and write this equation in a more compact form,

$$R^{(e)} = \mathbf{K}^{(e)} \mathbf{\Phi}^{(e)} + \mathbf{M}^{(e)} \mathbf{\Phi}^{(e)} - \mathbf{f}^{(e)}. \qquad (7.37)$$

In the finite element world, $\mathbf{K}^{(e)}$ is named element stiffness matrix, $\mathbf{M}^{(e)}$ is named element mass matrix and $\mathbf{f}^{(e)}$ is called the element load vector. For a deeper analysis of the element stiffness matrix we calculate the gradient vector of

$$\Phi(x, y)^{(e)} = \mathbf{N}^{(e)} \mathbf{\Phi}^{(e)}, \qquad (7.38)$$

and obtain

$$\begin{pmatrix} \dfrac{\partial \Phi(x, y)^{(e)}}{\partial x} \\ \dfrac{\partial \Phi(x, y)^{(e)}}{\partial y} \end{pmatrix} = \begin{pmatrix} \dfrac{\partial \mathbf{N}^{(e)}}{\partial x} \\ \dfrac{\partial \mathbf{N}^{(e)}}{\partial y} \end{pmatrix} \mathbf{\Phi}^{(e)} =: \mathbf{B} \mathbf{\Phi}^{(e)}. \qquad (7.39)$$

[5] Note that this term is only relevant at the boundaries of the whole computational domain or at interfaces inside the computational domain (e.g., two different materials with two different heat conduction coefficients) and does not contribute otherwise. The incorporation of boundary conditions will be discussed later in this chapter.

Therefore we end up with

$$\int_A \left(\lambda_x \frac{\partial \mathbf{N}^T}{\partial x} \frac{\partial \mathbf{N}}{\partial x} + \lambda_y \frac{\partial \mathbf{N}^T}{\partial y} \frac{\partial \mathbf{N}}{\partial y} \right) = \int_A \mathbf{B}^T \lambda \mathbf{B} dA. \tag{7.40}$$

7.4.1 Element Matrices

To obtain the element matrices, it is necessary to evaluate the integrals derived in the last subsection. Restricting ourselves to the two-dimensional case, we will now show that this can be done analytically for simple linear elements. For the linear triangular element the element shape functions are given by Equation (7.20) and thus we have

$$\mathbf{B} = \frac{1}{2A} \begin{pmatrix} b_i & b_j & b_k \\ c_i & c_j & c_k \end{pmatrix}. \tag{7.41}$$

Since $\mathbf{B}$ is independent of any coordinates, the element stiffness matrix can be simplified to

$$\mathbf{K}^{(e)} = \mathbf{B}^T \lambda \mathbf{B} A. \tag{7.42}$$

Expanding the matrix products yields

$$\mathbf{K}^{(e)} = \frac{\lambda_x}{4A} \begin{pmatrix} b_i^2 & b_i b_j & b_i b_k \\ b_i b_j & b_j^2 & b_j b_k \\ b_i b_k & b_j b_k & b_k^2 \end{pmatrix} + \frac{\lambda_y}{4A} \begin{pmatrix} c_i^2 & c_i c_j & c_i c_k \\ c_i c_j & c_j^2 & c_j c_k \\ c_i c_k & c_j c_k & c_k^2 \end{pmatrix}. \tag{7.43}$$

As long as G is constant inside the element, the element mass matrix can be easily evaluated using the factorial integration formula (7.138),

$$\mathbf{M}^{(e)} = G \int_A \mathbf{N}^T \mathbf{N} dA = G \int_A \begin{pmatrix} N_i^2 & N_i N_j & N_i N_k \\ N_i N_j & N_j^2 & N_j N_k \\ N_i N_k & N_j N_k & N_k^2 \end{pmatrix} dA = \frac{GA}{12} \begin{pmatrix} 2 & 1 & 1 \\ 1 & 2 & 1 \\ 1 & 1 & 2 \end{pmatrix}. \tag{7.44}$$

The evaluation of the force vector is also based on the application of the integration formula (7.138). Assuming Q to be constant within the element yields

$$\mathbf{f}^{(e)} = \int_A Q \mathbf{N}^T dA = Q \int_A \begin{pmatrix} N_i \\ N_j \\ N_k \end{pmatrix} dA = \frac{QA}{3} \begin{pmatrix} 1 \\ 1 \\ 1 \end{pmatrix}. \tag{7.45}$$

We leave it to the reader to derive the corresponding results for the linear quadrilateral element (see for example Segerlind) and will only show the final results here,

$$\mathbf{K}^{(e)} = \frac{\lambda_x a}{6b} \begin{pmatrix} 2 & -2 & -1 & 1 \\ -2 & 2 & 1 & -1 \\ -1 & 1 & 2 & -2 \\ 1 & -1 & -2 & 2 \end{pmatrix} + \frac{\lambda_y b}{6a} \begin{pmatrix} 2 & 1 & -1 & -2 \\ 1 & 2 & -2 & -1 \\ -1 & -2 & 2 & 1 \\ -2 & -1 & 1 & 2 \end{pmatrix}, \tag{7.46}$$

$$
\mathbf{M}^{(e)} = \frac{GA}{36} \begin{pmatrix} 4 & 2 & 1 & 2 \\ 2 & 4 & 2 & 1 \\ 1 & 2 & 4 & 2 \\ 2 & 1 & 2 & 4 \end{pmatrix},
\tag{7.47}
$$

$$
\mathbf{f}^{(e)} = \frac{QA}{4} \begin{pmatrix} 1 \\ 1 \\ 1 \\ 1 \end{pmatrix}.
\tag{7.48}
$$

Transforming the Integration Variables

For higher order elements numerical integration methods are applied. Inspecting Equation (7.129) reveals that we have used the determinant of the Jacobian matrix in the transformation equation

$$
\int_{X_i}^{X_m} f(x)dx = \int_{-1}^{1} g(\xi) \left(\frac{d(x(\xi))}{d\xi} \right) d\xi,
\tag{7.49}
$$

where

$$
x = \sum_{n=1}^{m} N_n(\xi) X_n.
\tag{7.50}
$$

The X_n are the global coordinates of the local node numbers $1, 2, \ldots, m$. It can be easily verified that the Jacobian of the transformation equation of the linear element with two nodes is $L/2$, where L is the element length.

Likewise, in the two-dimensional case the change of variables to area coordinates requires the Jacobian determinant in the double integral,

$$
\int_A f(x, y)dA = \int_0^1 \int_0^{1-L_1} g(L_1, L_2)|det[J]|dL_2 dL_1.
\tag{7.51}
$$

As an example, we derive the determinant of the linear triangular element: We start with

$$
x(L_1, L_2) = N_1(L_1, L_2)X_1 + N_2(L_1, L_2)X_2 + N_3(L_1, L_2)X_3,
$$
$$
y(L_1, L_2) = N_1(L_1, L_2)Y_1 + N_2(L_1, L_2)Y_2 + N_3(L_1, L_2)Y_3,
\tag{7.52}
$$

where X_i and Y_i denote the global coordinates of the element nodes. Using Equation (7.135) and the fact that the area coordinates for the linear triangular element are identical to the shape functions allows us to rewrite these equations as

$$
x(L_1, L_2) = L_1 X_1 + L_2 X_2 + (1 - L_1 - L_2)X_3,
$$
$$
y(L_1, L_2) = L_1 Y_1 + L_2 Y_2 + (1 - L_1 - L_2)Y_3.
\tag{7.53}
$$

It is now straightforward to calculate the entries of the Jacobian matrix,

$$
\begin{pmatrix}
\dfrac{\partial x}{\partial L_1} & \dfrac{\partial y}{\partial L_1} \\[2mm]
\dfrac{\partial x}{\partial L_2} & \dfrac{\partial y}{\partial L_2}
\end{pmatrix}
=
\begin{pmatrix}
X_1 - X_3 & Y_1 - Y_3 \\
X_2 - X_3 & Y_2 - Y_3
\end{pmatrix}.
\tag{7.54}
$$

It is easy to verify that the determinant of this matrix is equal to $2A$, where A is the area of the element. For the linear quadrilateral element the Jacobian matrix can be calculated by following the same steps, leading to the general equation

$$
\mathbf{J} =
\begin{pmatrix}
\dfrac{\partial N_1}{\partial \xi} & \dfrac{\partial N_2}{\partial \xi} & \dfrac{\partial N_3}{\partial \xi} & \dfrac{\partial N_4}{\partial \xi} \\[2mm]
\dfrac{\partial N_1}{\partial \eta} & \dfrac{\partial N_2}{\partial \eta} & \dfrac{\partial N_3}{\partial \eta} & \dfrac{\partial N_4}{\partial \eta}
\end{pmatrix}
\begin{pmatrix}
X_1 & Y_1 \\
X_2 & Y_2 \\
X_3 & Y_3 \\
X_4 & Y_4
\end{pmatrix}.
\tag{7.55}
$$

Inserting the shape functions of Equation (7.23) and carrying out the derivatives yields

$$
\mathbf{J} = \frac{1}{4}
\begin{pmatrix}
-(1-\eta) & (1-\eta) & (1+\eta) & -(1+\eta) \\
-(1-\xi) & -(1+\xi) & (1+\xi) & (1-\xi)
\end{pmatrix}
\begin{pmatrix}
X_1 & Y_1 \\
X_2 & Y_2 \\
X_3 & Y_3 \\
X_4 & Y_4
\end{pmatrix}.
\tag{7.56}
$$

For these natural and global coordinates the matrix and its determinant can be easily calculated. The calculation and evaluation of the Jacobian matrix becomes more involved as the shape functions become more complicated with an increasing number of nodes per element.

Numerical Integration Techniques

Gauss-Legendre quadrature is typically used to evaluate the element matrices in the natural coordinate systems. For the one-dimensional integral of a function $g(x)$ the method reads

$$
\frac{L}{2} \int_{-1}^{1} g(\xi)d\xi = \frac{L}{2} \sum_{i=1}^{n} g(\xi_i)w_i.
\tag{7.57}
$$

where the w_i are weights. With this formula, the integral over a polynomial of degree $2n - 1$ can be calculated exactly with n sampling points. The sampling points ξ are located in a way to achieve the optimal accuracy, and the corresponding weights up to $n = 3$ can be found in Table 7.1. For two-dimensional integrals in quadrilateral regions the general form of the integral is

$$
\int_{-1}^{1} \int_{-1}^{1} g(\xi, \eta)d\xi d\eta.
\tag{7.58}
$$

This integral can be calculated by first evaluating the inner integral and keeping ξ constant and subsequently evaluating the outer integral, ending up with

$$
\int_{-1}^{1} \int_{-1}^{1} g(\xi, \eta)d\xi d\eta = \sum_{i=1}^{n} \sum_{j=1}^{m} w_i w_j g(\xi_i, \eta_j).
\tag{7.59}
$$

Table 7.1 Sampling points ξ_i and the corresponding weights w_i for the Gauss-Legendre quadrature in one dimension and up to $n = 3$ sampling points.

n	ξ_i	w_i
1	0.0	2.0
2	±0.577350	1.0
3	0.0	8/9
	±0.774597	5/9

Here, n is set such that $2n - 1$ is the highest power of the polynomial in ξ and m is set such that $2m - 1$ is equal to the highest power of the polynomial in η. As a consequence, the implementation of Equation (7.59) amounts to a sum over $n \times m$ points, where the values for ξ_k, η_k and w_k with $k \in \{i, j\}$ are taken from Table 7.1. The introduction of area coordinates leads to integrals of the form

$$\int_A f(L_1, L_2, L_3)dA = \sum_{i=1}^{n} f(L_{1i}, L_{2i}, L_{3i})w_i \tag{7.60}$$

for the integration over triangular areas. Table 7.2 shows coordinates and weights up to quadratic order. Analogously to the two-dimensional case, where the double integral can be reduced to a single sum over integration points and their corresponding weights, we use

$$\int_{-1}^{1} \int_{-1}^{1} \int_{-1}^{1} g(\xi, \eta, \rho)d\xi d\eta d\rho = \sum_{i=1}^{n}\sum_{j=1}^{m}\sum_{k=1}^{l} w_i w_j w_k g(\xi_i, \eta_j, \rho_k) \tag{7.61}$$

for integration in hexahedron meshes. Volume coordinates can be used to evaluate integrals over a tetrahedron

$$\int_V f(L_1, L_2, L_3, L_4)dV = \sum_{i=1}^{n} w_i f(L_{1i}, L_{2i}, L_{3i}, L_{4i}). \tag{7.62}$$

The coordinates in the local coordinate system and the weights up to quadratic order are given in Table 7.3.

Table 7.2 Sampling points L_1, L_2 and L_3 and the corresponding weights w_i for the area coordinates used to perform integrations over triangular regions. For $n = 1$, the sampling point corresponds to the center of mass. For $n = 3$, the sampling points represent the mid points of the three lines confining the triangle.

n	L_1	L_2	L_3	w_i	Type
1	1/3	1/3	1/3	1	linear triangle
3	1/2	1/2	0	1/3	quadratic triangle
	0	1/2	1/2	1/3	
	1/2	0	0	1/3	

Table 7.3 Sampling points L_1, L_2, L_3 and L_4 and corresponding weights W_i for volume coordinates to perform integrations over tetrahedral regions. Note that $a = 0.58541020$ and $b = 0.13819669$.

n	L_1	L_2	L_3	L_4	w_i	Type
1	1/4	1/4	1/4	1/4	1	linear tetrahedron
4	a	b	b	b	1/4	quadratic tetrahedron
	b	a	b	b	1/4	
	b	b	a	b	1/4	
	b	b	b	a	1/4	

7.4.2 Time Discretization

A time-dependent diffusion-reaction equation for a scalar quantity,

$$\frac{\partial \Phi}{\partial t} = L\Phi, \tag{7.63}$$

where L is the differential operator defined in Equation (7.26), can be written in a semi-discretized form as

$$\frac{\partial \Phi}{\partial t} = \mathbf{f} - \mathbf{K}\Phi - \mathbf{M}\Phi. \tag{7.64}$$

The variation of the time derivative on the left-hand side within an element can be stated as

$$\frac{\partial \Phi}{\partial t} = \mathbf{N}\dot{\Phi}^{(e)}. \tag{7.65}$$

In Galerkin formulation, the residual integral for this term is

$$\mathbf{R}^{(e)} = \int_A \mathbf{N}^T \mathbf{N}\dot{\Phi}^{(e)} dA = \mathbf{C}^{(e)}\dot{\Phi}^{(e)}, \tag{7.66}$$

where $\mathbf{C}^{(e)}$ is called the element's capacitance matrix.[6] We can use the finite difference method introduced in Chapter 3 for discretizing the transient terms. Using the time-stepping schemes in Table 3.1 and recalling Equation (3.64), we obtain

$$\mathbf{C}\frac{\Phi^{n+1} - \Phi^n}{\Delta t} = \mathbf{f}^{n+\Theta} - \mathbf{K}\Phi^{n+\Theta} - \mathbf{M}\Phi^{n+\Theta}, \tag{7.67}$$

$$\mathbf{C}\frac{\Phi^{n+1} - \Phi^n}{\Delta t} = \Theta\mathbf{f}^{n+1} - (1-\Theta)\mathbf{f}^n - (\mathbf{K} - \mathbf{M})(\Theta\Phi^{n+1} - (1-\Theta)\Phi^n).$$

Rearranging this equation yields an equation of the form $\mathbf{U}\Phi = \mathbf{b}$ for the nodal values of the unknown quantity Φ,

$$(\mathbf{C} + \Theta\Delta t(\mathbf{K} + \mathbf{M}))\Phi^{n+1} = (\mathbf{C} - (1-\Theta)\Delta t(\mathbf{K} + \mathbf{M})\Phi^n + \Delta t(\Theta\mathbf{f}^{n+1} + (1-\Theta)\mathbf{f}^n). \tag{7.68}$$

Note that the values for the load vectors must be known at time $n + 1$ as well as at time n.

---

[6] It can be immediately seen that the matrix elements of the capacitance matrix and the mass matrix are equal.

The Capacitance Matrix for Different Elements

The integral defining the capacitance matrix,

$$\mathbf{C}^{(e)} = \int_A \mathbf{N}^T \mathbf{N} dA, \tag{7.69}$$

can be evaluated analytically for specific types of elements. For the one-dimensional linear element, the capacitance matrix is given by

$$\mathbf{C}^{(e)} = \frac{1}{6} \begin{pmatrix} 2 & 1 \\ 1 & 2 \end{pmatrix}, \tag{7.70}$$

for the two-dimensional linear triangular element by

$$\mathbf{C}^{(e)} = \frac{A}{12} \begin{pmatrix} 2 & 1 & 1 \\ 1 & 2 & 1 \\ 1 & 1 & 2 \end{pmatrix}, \tag{7.71}$$

and for the three-dimensional linear rectangular element by

$$\mathbf{C}^{(e)} = \frac{A}{36} \begin{pmatrix} 4 & 2 & 1 & 2 \\ 2 & 4 & 2 & 1 \\ 1 & 2 & 4 & 2 \\ 2 & 1 & 2 & 4 \end{pmatrix}. \tag{7.72}$$

This formulation of the problem is called consistent formulation, because the linear variation of $\partial \Phi / \partial t$ with respect to x within an element is consistent with the linear variation assumed for $\Phi(x)$. For both integrals, the same set of weighting functions are used. An alternative formulation that assumes that the variation of $\partial \Phi / \partial t$ with respect to x is constant between the midpoints of adjacent elements is called the lumped formulation. The lumped formulation leads to diagonal capacitance matrices.

7.4.3   Global Matrices

An equation of the form (7.68) can be derived for each element. Irrespective of the type of the partial differential equation (diffusion, reaction-diffusion, reaction-convection-diffusion), for a time-dependent problem with a time discretization $\Theta \neq 0$ a system of linear equations

$$\mathbf{U} \Phi^{n+1} = \mathbf{b} \tag{7.73}$$

must be solved in each time step. For instance, for a single triangular element (with nodes i, j, k) with linear test functions and a fully implicit time-stepping scheme ($\Theta = 1$), the resulting coefficient matrix $[U]$ of the system of linear equations of a diffusion-reaction equation is

$$\mathbf{U} = \begin{pmatrix} U_{ii} & U_{ij} & U_{ik} \\ U_{ji} & U_{jj} & U_{jk} \\ U_{ki} & U_{kj} & U_{kk} \end{pmatrix} = \frac{A}{12} \begin{pmatrix} 2 & 1 & 1 \\ 1 & 2 & 1 \\ 1 & 1 & 2 \end{pmatrix} + \Delta t \left[\frac{\lambda_x}{4A} \begin{pmatrix} b_i^2 & b_i b_j & b_i b_k \\ b_i b_j & b_j^2 & b_j b_k \\ b_i b_k & b_j b_k & b_k^2 \end{pmatrix} \right.$$

$$\left. + \frac{\lambda_y}{4A} \begin{pmatrix} c_i^2 & c_i c_j & c_i c_k \\ c_i c_j & c_j^2 & c_j c_k \\ c_i c_k & c_j c_k & c_k^2 \end{pmatrix} + \frac{A}{12} \begin{pmatrix} 2 & 1 & 1 \\ 1 & 2 & 1 \\ 1 & 1 & 2 \end{pmatrix} \right], \tag{7.74}$$

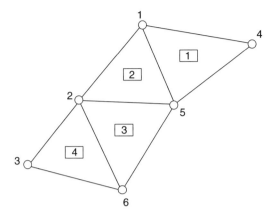

Figure 7.9 The figure shows the simple mesh used for explaining the global matrix assembling process. Numbers in frames denote element numbers, numbers without frames are the node numbers. Table 7.4 associates global node numbers with the local element numbers i, j, k.

where the corresponding right-hand-side vector is given by

$$\mathbf{b} = \begin{pmatrix} b_i \\ b_j \\ b_k \end{pmatrix} = \frac{A}{12} \begin{pmatrix} 2 & 1 & 1 \\ 1 & 2 & 1 \\ 1 & 1 & 2 \end{pmatrix} \mathbf{\Phi^n} + \Delta t \mathbf{f}^{n+1}. \tag{7.75}$$

To obtain a solution, terminal/initial and boundary conditions must be specified. If the computational domain is divided into N elements, the global coefficient matrix of the whole system must be assembled from the coefficient matrices of the single elements. The procedure to incorporate the element matrices into a global system of equations is called direct stiffness method. We will illustrate the procedure using a simple triangular mesh (see Figure 7.9) consisting of 6 nodes and 4 elements. The dimension of the coefficient matrix is 6×6 (6 unknowns). We will now loop through the elements and add their contributions to the global coefficient matrix – this assembling process is shown step by step in Table 7.5. The positions for the entries of a single element (3×3 matrix) are determined by the global node numbers of the element's node. Table 7.4 summarizes the connections between elements, local and global node numbering. An identical procedure is performed for the assembling of the right-hand-side vector $\mathbf{b}$ as shown in Table 7.6.

Table 7.4 The table explains the relation between the local node numbering i, j, k, the global node numbers 1–6 and the elements 1–4.

	i	j	k
Element 1	1	5	4
Element 2	1	2	5
Element 3	6	5	2
Element 4	2	3	6

Table 7.5 Form of the global matrix after assembling the first element (first table), the first and the second (second table) elements and all (third table) elements. All empty entries are zero.

	1	2	3	4	5	6
1	$U_{ii}^{(1)}$			$U_{ik}^{(1)}$	$U_{ij}^{(1)}$	
2						
3						
4	$U_{ki}^{(1)}$			$U_{kk}^{(1)}$	$U_{kj}^{(1)}$	
5	$U_{ji}^{(1)}$			$U_{jk}^{(1)}$	$U_{jj}^{(1)}$	
6						

	1	2	3	4	5	6
1	$U_{ii}^{(1)} + U_{ii}^{(2)}$	$U_{ij}^{(2)}$		$U_{ik}^{(1)}$	$U_{ij}^{(1)} + U_{ik}^{(2)}$	
2	$U_{ji}^{(2)}$	$U_{jj}^{(2)}$			$U_{jk}^{(2)}$	
3						
4	$U_{ki}^{(1)}$			$U_{kk}^{(1)}$	$U_{kj}^{(1)}$	
5	$U_{ji}^{(1)} + U_{ki}^{(2)}$	$U_{kj}^{(2)}$		$U_{jk}^{(1)}$	$U_{jj}^{(1)} + U_{kk}^{(2)}$	
6						

	1	2	3	4	5	6
1	$U_{ii}^{(1)} + U_{ii}^{(2)}$	$U_{ij}^{(2)}$		$U_{ik}^{(1)}$	$U_{ij}^{(1)} + U_{ik}^{(2)}$	
2	$U_{ji}^{(2)}$	$U_{jj}^{(2)} + U_{kk}^{(3)} + U_{ii}^{(4)}$	$U_{ij}^{(4)}$		$U_{jk}^{(2)} + U_{kj}^{(3)}$	$U_{ki}^{(3)} + U_{ik}^{(4)}$
3		$U_{ji}^{(4)}$	$U_{jj}^{(4)}$			$U_{jk}^{(4)}$
4	$U_{ki}^{(1)}$			$U_{kk}^{(1)}$	$U_{kj}^{(1)}$	
5	$U_{ji}^{(1)} + U_{ki}^{(2)}$	$U_{kj}^{(2)} + U_{jk}^{(3)}$		$U_{jk}^{(1)}$	$U_{jj}^{(1)} + U_{kk}^{(2)} + U_{jj}^{(3)}$	$U_{ji}^{(3)}$
6		$U_{ik}^{(3)} + U_{ki}^{(4)}$	$U_{kj}^{(4)}$		$U_{ij}^{(3)}$	$U_{ii}^{(3)} + U_{kk}^{(4)}$

Table 7.6 Form of the right-hand-side vector after assembling all elements.

1	$b_i^{(1)} + b_i^{(2)}$
2	$b_j^{(2)} + b_k^{(3)} + b_i^{(4)}$
3	$b_j^{(4)}$
4	$b_k^{(1)}$
5	$b_j^{(1)} + b_k^{(2)} + b_j^{(3)}$
6	$b_i^{(3)} + b_k^{(4)}$

7.4.4   Boundary Conditions

In this book, we focus on Dirichlet and Neumann boundary conditions (for a discussion of their usage, see Chapter 6):

- Dirichlet boundary condition: $\Phi(x, y)$ is known on some parts of the boundary

$$\Phi(x, y) = g \quad \text{on } \Gamma_1. \tag{7.76}$$

In quantitative finance this situation occurs, for instance, in the valuation of barrier options.

- Neumann boundary condition: The value of the normal derivative is known

$$\lambda_x \frac{\partial \Phi}{\partial x} \cos(\Psi) + \lambda_y \frac{\partial \Phi}{\partial y} \sin(\Psi) = h. \tag{7.77}$$

For $\lambda_x = \lambda_y$, this expression reduces to

$$\lambda_x \frac{\partial \Phi}{\partial \mathbf{n}} = h \quad \text{on } \Gamma_2, \tag{7.78}$$

where $\partial \Phi / \partial \mathbf{n}$ is the derivative normal to the boundary and $\Gamma_1 \cup \Gamma_2 = \Gamma$. For most applications in quantitative finance h can be chosen equal to zero.

Dirichlet Boundary Conditions

Dirichlet boundary conditions are straightforward to implement; we will present two different methods.[7] The simplest way is to keep the equations in the assembled matrix and to set the diagonal matrix entries for each known nodal value equal to 1 and all other entries in this row to 0.

Assume that the value of Φ at node 3 in the above example is known, $\Phi(x_6, y_6) = g_6$. The matrix and the right-hand side vector would in this case have the form shown in Table 7.7. While this method is straightforward and easy to implement, it has two drawbacks: first, known values are kept in the set of equations as unknown values, and second, the method destroys the symmetry of the coefficient matrix.[8]

The second method – which is only a slight modification of the first one – accomplishes the same goal but preserves the symmetry of the matrix. Again, we keep the equations in the assembled matrix, but now multiply the diagonal matrix entry for each known nodal value with l, where l is a number several orders of magnitude larger than any other term in the matrix. The corresponding right-hand side value is replaced by the known nodal value multiplied by the new diagonal entry – see matrix and vector in Table 7.8. The method is easy to understand by dividing all entries of the row corresponding to the known value by its diagonal entry (including the right-hand side vector). This yields a diagonal entry equal to unity and very small off-diagonal values (order $1/l$) in the matrix, and the known nodal value in the right-hand-side vector. This is essentially the same result as the one obtained with method one.

---

[7] An additional way to incorporate Dirichlet boundaries that we do not discuss here is to simply remove the equations associated with the boundary condition and rearrange the others. For large 2D and 3D problems this can significantly reduce the number of equations and in turn the size of the matrix. The disadvantage of the approach is that the rearranging can be cumbersome and complicated.

[8] The disadvantage of destroying the symmetry may have consequences for the type of solver (see Chapter 8) that can be applied to solve the system of linear equations. In quantitative finance, many models lead to antisymmetric coefficient matrices; thus this drawback may not be as severe as for example in structural mechanics, where symmetric coefficient matrices occur by default.

Table 7.7 Form of the coefficient matrix and the right-hand-side vector after incorporating a Dirichlet boundary condition at node 3 into the fully assembled matrix.

	1	2	3	4	5	6
1	$U_{ii}^{(1)}+U_{ii}^{(2)}$	$U_{ij}^{(2)}$		$U_{ik}^{(1)}$	$U_{ij}^{(1)}+U_{ik}^{(2)}$	
2	$U_{ji}^{(2)}$	$U_{jj}^{(2)}+U_{kk}^{(3)}+U_{ii}^{(4)}$	$U_{ij}^{(4)}$		$U_{jk}^{(2)}+U_{kj}^{(3)}$	$U_{ki}^{(3)}+U_{ik}^{(4)}$
3			1			
4	$U_{ki}^{(1)}$			$U_{kk}^{(1)}$	$U_{kj}^{(1)}$	
5	$U_{ji}^{(1)}+U_{ki}^{(2)}$	$U_{kj}^{(2)}+U_{jk}^{(3)}$		$U_{jk}^{(1)}$	$U_{jj}^{(1)}+U_{kk}^{(2)}+U_{jj}^{(3)}$	$U_{ji}^{(3)}$
6		$U_{ik}^{(3)}+U_{ki}^{(4)}$	$U_{kj}^{(4)}$		$U_{ij}^{(3)}$	$U_{ii}^{(3)}+U_{kk}^{(4)}$

1	$b_i^{(1)}+b_i^{(2)}$
2	$b_j^{(2)}+b_k^{(3)}+b_i^{(4)}$
3	g_3
4	$b_k^{(1)}$
5	$b_j^{(1)}+b_k^{(2)}+b_j^{(3)}$
6	$b_i^{(3)}+b_k^{(4)}$

Table 7.8 Form of the coefficient matrix and the right-hand-side vector after incorporating a Dirichlet boundary condition at node 3 into the fully assembled matrix preserving the matrix symmetry.

	1	2	3	4	5	6
1	$U_{ii}^{(1)}+U_{ii}^{(2)}$	$U_{ij}^{(2)}$		$U_{ik}^{(1)}$	$U_{ij}^{(1)}+U_{ik}^{(2)}$	
2	$U_{ji}^{(2)}$	$U_{jj}^{(2)}+U_{kk}^{(3)}+U_{ii}^{(4)}$	$U_{ij}^{(4)}$		$U_{jk}^{(2)}+U_{kj}^{(3)}$	$U_{ki}^{(3)}+U_{ik}^{(4)}$
3		$U_{ji}^{(4)}$	$lU_{jj}^{(4)}$			$U_{jk}^{(4)}$
4	$U_{ki}^{(1)}$			$U_{kk}^{(1)}$	$U_{kj}^{(1)}$	
5	$U_{ji}^{(1)}+U_{ki}^{(2)}$	$U_{kj}^{(2)}+U_{jk}^{(3)}$		$U_{jk}^{(1)}$	$U_{jj}^{(1)}+U_{kk}^{(2)}+U_{jj}^{(3)}$	$U_{ji}^{(3)}$
6		$U_{ik}^{(3)}+U_{ki}^{(4)}$	$U_{kj}^{(4)}$		$U_{ij}^{(3)}$	$U_{ii}^{(3)}+U_{kk}^{(4)}$

1	$b_i^{(1)}+b_i^{(2)}$
2	$b_j^{(2)}+b_k^{(3)}+b_i^{(4)}$
3	$g_3 lU_{jj}^{(4)}$
4	$b_k^{(1)}$
5	$b_j^{(1)}+b_k^{(2)}+b_j^{(3)}$
6	$b_i^{(3)}+b_k^{(4)}$

Neumann Boundary Conditions

The inclusion of boundary conditions of the Neumann type is accomplished by using the surface integral of Equation (7.36),

$$\int_\Gamma \mathbf{N}^T \left(\lambda_x \frac{\partial \Phi}{\partial x} \cos(\Psi) + \lambda_y \frac{\partial \Phi}{\partial y} \sin(\Psi) \right) d\Gamma = \int_\Gamma \mathbf{N}^T \frac{\partial \Phi}{\partial \mathbf{n}} d\Gamma = \int_\Gamma \mathbf{N}^T h \, d\Gamma. \quad (7.79)$$

This integral is added to the element load vector $\mathbf{f}^{(e)}$ and will be denoted $\mathbf{f}_S^{(e)}$ (S for surface). It can be evaluated once the element shape functions are known. Here, we demonstrate the calculation for the linear triangular and the bilinear rectangular element. Depending on the side of the triangle where the Neumann boundary condition is specified, we obtain the results

$$\mathbf{f}_S^{(e)} = \frac{hL_{ij}}{2} \begin{pmatrix} 1 \\ 1 \\ 0 \end{pmatrix}, \quad \mathbf{f}_S^{(e)} = \frac{hL_{jk}}{2} \begin{pmatrix} 0 \\ 1 \\ 1 \end{pmatrix}, \quad \mathbf{f}_S^{(e)} = \frac{hL_{ik}}{2} \begin{pmatrix} 1 \\ 0 \\ 1 \end{pmatrix}, \quad (7.80)$$

for sides ij, jk, ik, respectively. The quantities L_{ij}, L_{jk} and L_{ik} are the lengths of the sides. For the bilinear rectangular element we obtain

$$\mathbf{f}_S^{(e)} = \frac{hL_{ij}}{2} \begin{pmatrix} 1 \\ 1 \\ 0 \\ 0 \end{pmatrix}, \quad \mathbf{f}_S^{(e)} = \frac{hL_{jk}}{2} \begin{pmatrix} 0 \\ 1 \\ 1 \\ 0 \end{pmatrix},$$

$$(7.81)$$

$$\mathbf{f}_S^{(e)} = \frac{hL_{km}}{2} \begin{pmatrix} 0 \\ 0 \\ 1 \\ 1 \end{pmatrix}, \quad \mathbf{f}_S^{(e)} = \frac{hL_{im}}{2} \begin{pmatrix} 1 \\ 0 \\ 0 \\ 1 \end{pmatrix},$$

for sides ij, jk, km, im, respectively. The quantities L_{ij}, L_{jk}, L_{km} and L_{im} are the lengths of the sides. If the boundary value h is specified on more than one side of an element, the vectors $\mathbf{f}_S^{(e)}$ of the appropriate sides need to be summed up.

7.4.5 Application of the Finite Element Method to Convection-Diffusion-Reaction Problems

For a large part of the models used in this book, the corresponding differential equations are of the convection-diffusion-reaction type,

$$\lambda_x \frac{\partial^2 \Phi(x, y)}{\partial x^2} + \lambda_y \frac{\partial^2 \Phi(x, y)}{\partial y^2} + \mathbf{v}\nabla\Phi(x, y) - G\Phi(x, y) + Q = 0. \quad (7.82)$$

Here, $\mathbf{v} = (v_x, v_y)$ is the velocity vector. In such equations, the Galerkin-type approximation, which we have used exclusively up to now, would result in solutions with spurious oscillations in space in convection dominated regions. As pointed out in Chapter 6, this problem is not

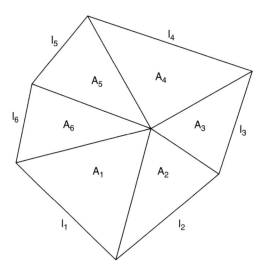

Figure 7.10   The figure shows a part of the mesh used for calculating the local element size. Here the A_i are the areas of elements connected to the central node and the l_i the lengths of the respective opposite sides.

specific to the finite element method, all other discretization techniques do have the same difficulties. There are several stabilization techniques available for the finite element method, for example the Streamline-Diffusion (SD)/Streamline-Upwind-Petrov-Galerkin (SUPG) method, the Galerkin Least Squares (GLS) and the Subgrid Scale method (SGS) [Zienkiewicz and Taylor, 2000b; Lewis, Nethariasu and Seetharamu, 2004]. The fundamental idea of the SUPG technique is to add extra diffusion in the direction of the streamline by replacing the weighting function W with

$$W + \delta_i \mathbf{v} \nabla W, \tag{7.83}$$

where δ_i is an element dependent/$\mathbf{v}$-dependent factor,[9]

$$\delta_i = \frac{h_i}{2|\mathbf{v}|}. \tag{7.84}$$

The characteristic element size h_i can be easily calculated in two dimensions (see, for instance, Figure 7.10),

$$h_i = \min\left(\left\{\frac{2A_i}{l_i}\right\}\right), \tag{7.85}$$

with A_i denoting the areas of elements connected to the central node and the l_i denoting the length of the respective opposite sides, where i goes from 1 to the number of elements connected to the node. In three dimensions, $2A_i$ is replaced by $3V_i$ and l_i is replaced by the area opposite the node in question.

---

[9] Different choices for δ_i are available. The interested reader can consult [Zienkiewicz and Taylor, 2000b; Lewis, Nethariasu and Seetharamu, 2004].

7.5   A ZERO COUPON BOND UNDER THE TWO FACTOR HULL-WHITE MODEL

In the following we compare the numerical results for the price of a zero coupon bond with face amount 1 and different life times obtained by the use of standard finite elements, finite elements with streamline diffusion, and the analytical solution under the two factor Hull-White interest rate model with constant model parameters. The two-factor Hull-White model extends the one-factor Hull-White model (4.19) by adding a stochastic disturbance to the long-term drift term. This second stochastic factor is modeled by a mean-reverting process with a mean reversion level of zero,

$$
\begin{aligned}
dr_t &= (\theta(t) + u_t - \alpha(t)r_t)dt + \sigma_r(t)dW_t^1, \\
du_t &= -bu_t + \sigma_u dW_t^2.
\end{aligned}
\tag{7.86}
$$

No-arbitrage arguments lead to the fundamental Hull-White equation:

$$
0 = \frac{V^{n+1} - V^n}{\Delta t} + \frac{1}{2}\left(\sigma_1^{n+1}\right)^2 \frac{\partial^2 V^{n+1}}{\partial r^2} + \rho^{n+1}\sigma_1^{n+1}\sigma_2^{n+1}\frac{\partial^2 V^{n+1}}{\partial r \partial u} + \frac{1}{2}\left(\sigma_1^{n+1}\right)^2 \frac{\partial^2 V^{n+1}}{\partial u^2}
$$
$$
\left(\theta^{n+1} + u - \alpha^{n+1}r\right)\frac{\partial V^{n+1}}{\partial r} - b^{n+1}u\frac{\partial V^{n+1}}{\partial u} - rV^{n+1}.
\tag{7.87}
$$

Omitting the time indices of the model parameters, the weak formulation of the implicitly time-discretized problem reads for any test function W

$$
\int_\Omega W \frac{V^{n+1} - V^n}{\Delta t} \, drdu + \int_\Omega W \left(\frac{\partial}{\partial r}\left(\frac{1}{2}\sigma_1^2 \frac{\partial V^{n+1}}{\partial r} + \frac{1}{2}\rho\sigma_1\sigma_2 \frac{\partial V^{n+1}}{\partial u} \right) \right.
$$
$$
\left. + \frac{\partial}{\partial u}\left(\frac{1}{2}\sigma_2^2 \frac{\partial V^{n+1}}{\partial u} + \frac{1}{2}\rho\sigma_1\sigma_2 \frac{\partial V^{n+1}}{\partial r} \right) \right) drdu
\tag{7.88}
$$
$$
+ \int_\Omega W \left((\theta + u - \alpha r)\frac{\partial V^{n+1}}{\partial r} - bu\frac{\partial V^{n+1}}{\partial u} \right) drdu - \int_\Omega W \left(rV^{n+1} \right) drdu = 0.
$$

Note that in the Galerkin setup, W is taken from the set of functions used for the approximation of the solution. Applying integration by parts in the second order terms yields

$$
\int_\Omega W \frac{V^{n+1} - V^n}{\Delta t} \, drdu - \int_\Omega \left(\frac{\partial W}{\partial r}\left(\frac{1}{2}\sigma_1^2 \frac{\partial V^{n+1}}{\partial r} + \frac{1}{2}\rho\sigma_1\sigma_2 \frac{\partial V^{n+1}}{\partial u} \right) \right.
$$
$$
\left. + \frac{\partial W}{\partial u}\left(\frac{1}{2}\sigma_2^2 \frac{\partial V^{n+1}}{\partial u} + \frac{1}{2}\rho\sigma_1\sigma_2 \frac{\partial V^{n+1}}{\partial r} \right) \right) drdu
$$
$$
+ \int_\Gamma W \left(\frac{1}{2}\sigma_1^2 \frac{\partial V^{n+1}}{\partial r} + \frac{1}{2}\rho\sigma_1\sigma_2 \frac{\partial V^{n+1}}{\partial u} \right) \mathbf{n}_r \, ds
\tag{7.89}
$$
$$
+ \int_\Gamma W \left(\frac{1}{2}\sigma_2^2 \frac{\partial V^{n+1}}{\partial u} + \frac{1}{2}\rho\sigma_1\sigma_2 \frac{\partial V^{n+1}}{\partial r} \right) \mathbf{n}_u \, ds
$$
$$
+ \int_\Omega W \left((\theta + u - \alpha r)\frac{\partial V^{n+1}}{\partial r} - bu\frac{\partial V^{n+1}}{\partial u} \right) drdu - \int_\Omega W \left(rV^{n+1} \right) drdu = 0,
$$

where the problem is to find $V^{n+1} \in U$ such that for all $W \in U$ Equation (7.89) holds. To overcome the instabilities occurring due to convection domination we use the SD/SUPG method. We remember that the fundamental idea of this method is to add extra diffusion in the direction of the streamline by replacing the test function W with $W + \delta_i \mathbf{v} \nabla W$ (with $\mathbf{v} = (\theta + u - \alpha r, -bu)^T$). With this additional term we obtain

$$
\int_\Omega W \frac{V^{n+1} - V^n}{\Delta t} \, dr du - \int_\Omega \left(\frac{\partial W}{\partial r} \left(\frac{1}{2} \sigma_1^2 \frac{\partial V^{n+1}}{\partial r} + \frac{1}{2} \rho \sigma_1 \sigma_2 \frac{\partial V^{n+1}}{\partial u} \right) \right.
$$
$$
\left. + \frac{\partial W}{\partial u} \left(\frac{1}{2} \sigma_2^2 \frac{\partial V^{n+1}}{\partial u} + \frac{1}{2} \rho \sigma_1 \sigma_2 \frac{\partial V^{n+1}}{\partial r} \right) \right) \, dr du
$$
$$
+ \int_\Gamma W \left(\frac{1}{2} \sigma_1^2 \frac{\partial V^{n+1}}{\partial r} + \frac{1}{2} \rho \sigma_1 \sigma_2 \frac{\partial V^{n+1}}{\partial u} \right) \mathbf{n}_r \, ds
$$
$$
+ \int_\Gamma W \left(\frac{1}{2} \sigma_2^2 \frac{\partial V^{n+1}}{\partial u} + \frac{1}{2} \rho \sigma_1 \sigma_2 \frac{\partial V^{n+1}}{\partial r} \right) \mathbf{n}_u \, ds
$$
$$
+ \int_\Omega W \left((\theta + u - \alpha r) \frac{\partial V^{n+1}}{\partial r} - bu \frac{\partial V^{n+1}}{\partial u} \right) \, dr du - \int_\Omega W \left(r V^{n+1} \right) \, dr du
$$
$$
+ \sum_{i=1}^N \int_{\Omega_i} \delta_i \mathbf{v} \nabla W \frac{V^{n+1} - V^n}{\Delta t} \, dr du \tag{7.90}
$$
$$
+ \sum_{i=1}^N \int_{\Omega_i} \delta_i \mathbf{v} \nabla W \left(\frac{\partial}{\partial r} \left(\frac{1}{2} \sigma_1^2 \frac{\partial V^{n+1}}{\partial r} + \frac{1}{2} \rho \sigma_1 \sigma_2 \frac{\partial V^{n+1}}{\partial u} \right) \right.
$$
$$
\left. + \frac{\partial}{\partial u} \left(\frac{1}{2} \sigma_2^2 \frac{\partial V^{n+1}}{\partial u} + \frac{1}{2} \rho \sigma_1 \sigma_2 \frac{\partial V^{n+1}}{\partial r} \right) \right) \, dr du
$$
$$
+ \sum_{i=1}^N \int_{\Omega_i} \delta_i \mathbf{v} \nabla W \left((\theta + u - \alpha r) \frac{\partial V^{n+1}}{\partial r} - bu \frac{\partial V^{n+1}}{\partial u} \right) \, dr du
$$
$$
+ \sum_{i=1}^N \int_\Omega \delta_i \mathbf{v} \nabla W \left(r V^{n+1} \right) \, dr du = 0.
$$

The additional term in the convective part is

$$
\sum_{i=1}^N \int_{\Omega_i} \delta_i \mathbf{v} \nabla W \left((\theta + u - \alpha r) \frac{\partial V^{n+1}}{\partial r} - bu \frac{\partial V^{n+1}}{\partial u} \right) \, dr du, \tag{7.91}
$$

which has the typical form of a diffusion term. The parameters δ_i depend on the size of the finite elements and on the convection-diffusion ratio, so the artificial diffusion is higher in convection dominated regions and smaller in regions where diffusion dominates. Again, although the size of the computational domain is, in principle, unbounded, calculations can only be performed on a bounded domain in practice. We choose the size of the computational domain in a way such that the information of the prescribed boundary condition does, during the considered time interval, not propagate through to the center. The center of the domain is determined by the current short rates, and the choice of the boundary thus has no influence on the solution. This may also be interpreted as the probability of very high or low, maybe even negative, interest rates being very small. Choosing homogeneous Neumann boundary conditions forces all surface integrals to vanish. For our calculations we have chosen a structured, two-dimensional, quadrilateral grid with graded higher resolution in both directions near the values of interest of

Table 7.9 The table shows values obtained for a zero coupon bond under the two-factor Hull-White model for different life times. The analytical solution is compared to solutions obtained numerically using the standard Galerkin finite element method or the Galerkin finite element method with streamline diffusion stabilization. A discretization with a time step of 20 days and a space discretization of 30 × 30 points has been used for these calculations.

Life times	Analytical solution	Standard FEM	FEM with SD
1 year	0.954581	0.95458	0.95458
10 years	0.661886	0.661777	0.661855
20 years	0.461421	0.460902	0.461405
40 years	0.268027	0.265955	0.268311

Table 7.10 Same as Table 7.9, but with a space discretization of 10 × 10 points.

Life times	Analytical solution	Standard FEM	FEM with SD
1 year	0.954581	0.954592	0.954582
10 years	0.661886	0.663975	0.661414
20 years	0.461421	0.472521	0.459271
40 years	0.268027	0.464601	0.262467

the factors r and u. We have used fully implicit ($\Theta = 1$) time stepping, therefore discretizations in time and space (r-u-plane) can be chosen independently. The resulting system of linear equations is solved using BiCGStab (see Chapter 8 for further details).

For the comparison of different numerical methods, we have used the following parameters for the two factor Hull-White model:

$$\alpha = 1.2 \quad b = 0.03 \quad \theta = 0.05 \quad \sigma_1 = 0.02 \quad \sigma_2 = 0.01 \quad \rho = 0.5. \tag{7.92}$$

We have used a discretization with a time step of 20 days and a space discretization of 30 × 30 points (note that these are quite few points for instruments with relatively long lifetimes). The solutions obtained by the different methods are displayed in Table 7.9. If we use an obviously too coarse space discretization, namely 10 × 10, we still obtain realistic results in the streamline diffusion case, but unacceptable results for long life times in the standard finite element case (Table 7.10).

7.6 APPENDIX: HIGHER ORDER ELEMENTS

In this appendix a number of additional elements are described and local and natural coordinates are explained.

1D Quadratic Element

Instead of using linear segments, parabolic functions can be used to approximate the unknown within an element,

$$\Phi^{(e)}(x) = \alpha_1^{(e)} + \alpha_2^{(e)}x + \alpha_3^{(e)}x^2. \tag{7.93}$$

In order to determine the parameters, one additional point is now required. We choose the mid point of the line segment in addition to the end points. As a result, we obtain the following equations for the unknowns at these locations,

$$\Phi_i^{(e)} = \alpha_1^{(e)} + \alpha_2^{(e)} X_i + \alpha_3^{(e)} X_i^2, \tag{7.94}$$

$$\Phi_j^{(e)} = \alpha_1^{(e)} + \alpha_2^{(e)} X_j + \alpha_3^{(e)} X_j^2, \tag{7.95}$$

$$\Phi_k^{(e)} = \alpha_1^{(e)} + \alpha_2^{(e)} X_k + \alpha_3^{(e)} X_k^2. \tag{7.96}$$

Without loss of generality, we can set $X_i = 0$, $X_j = L/2$ and $X_k = L$, where L is the length of the element under consideration. With this transformation, we obtain

$$\Phi_i^{(e)} = \alpha_1^{(e)}, \tag{7.97}$$

$$\Phi_j^{(e)} = \alpha_1^{(e)} + \alpha_2^{(e)} \frac{L}{2} + \alpha_3^{(e)} \left(\frac{L}{2}\right)^2, \tag{7.98}$$

$$\Phi_k^{(e)} = \alpha_1^{(e)} + \alpha_2^{(e)} L + \alpha_3^{(e)} L^2. \tag{7.99}$$

Again, the three constants $\alpha_1, \alpha_2, \alpha_3$ can be determined from these equations,

$$\alpha_1^{(e)} = \Phi_i^{(e)}, \tag{7.100}$$

$$\alpha_2^{(e)} = \frac{1}{L} \left(-3\Phi_i^{(e)} + 4\Phi_j^{(e)} - \Phi_k^{(e)}\right), \tag{7.101}$$

$$\alpha_3^{(e)} = \frac{2}{L^2} \left(\Phi_i^{(e)} - 2\Phi_j^{(e)} + \Phi_k^{(e)}\right). \tag{7.102}$$

Substitution into (7.93) and rearranging yields

$$\Phi^{(e)} = \Phi_i^{(e)} \left(1 - \frac{3x}{L} + \frac{2x^2}{L^2}\right) + \Phi_j^{(e)} \left(\frac{4x}{L} - \frac{4x^2}{L^2}\right) + \Phi_k^{(e)} \left(-\frac{x}{L} + \frac{2x^2}{L^2}\right). \tag{7.103}$$

From this equation, we can read off the shape functions of a one-dimensional quadratic element,

$$\Phi^{(e)}(x) = N_i^{(e)} \Phi_i^{(e)} + N_j^{(e)} \Phi_j^{(e)}, \tag{7.104}$$

$$N_i^{(e)} = 1 - \frac{3x}{L} + \frac{2x^2}{L^2}, \tag{7.105}$$

$$N_j^{(e)} = \frac{4x}{L} - \frac{4x^2}{L^2}, \tag{7.106}$$

$$N_k^{(e)} = \frac{2x^2}{L^2} - \frac{x}{L}. \tag{7.107}$$

Note that although the derivatives of the quadratic shape functions depend on x, they are not continuous at the inter-element nodes. Elements exhibiting this behavior belong to the C^0 element family, where the superscript 0 denotes that only zero order derivatives are continuous. Readers familiar with polynomial interpolation may have noticed that the type of interpolation used here is known as Lagrangian interpolation. To generate functions of the C^1 element family, Hermite polynomials can be used.

2D Quadratic Elements

The quadratic approximation over a triangular element has the form

$$\Phi^{(e)}(x) = \alpha_1^{(e)} + \alpha_2^{(e)}x + \alpha_3^{(e)}y + \alpha_4^{(e)}x^2 + \alpha_5^{(e)}y^2 + \alpha_6^{(e)}xy. \tag{7.108}$$

In order to calculate the six constants, the quadratic shape function needs six nodes. Similarly, a quadratic approximation over a rectangular element is given by

$$\Phi^{(e)}(x) = \alpha_1^{(e)} + \alpha_2^{(e)}x + \alpha_3^{(e)}y + \alpha_4^{(e)}x^2 + \alpha_5^{(e)}y^2 + \alpha_6^{(e)}xy + \alpha_7^{(e)}x^2y + \alpha_8^{(e)}xy^2. \tag{7.109}$$

This so-called biquadratic element does not belong to the family of Lagrangian interpolation elements since we have avoided interior nodes.[10] For both the triangular and the rectangular case the shape functions can be derived in the same manner as in the linear case, but the process becomes somewhat tedious. We will present a more elegant way of deriving such shape functions after having introduced natural coordinates later in the Appendix.

7.6.1   3D Elements

In the three-dimensional case, we will restrict ourselves to linear approximation functions in tetrahedral and hexahedral geometries. Both are extensions of the linear triangular and rectangular elements derived above. Note that the amount of data required to describe the computational domain and the boundary conditions in three dimensions is significantly larger than in two dimensions. An example of a financial product that requires a three-dimensional partial differential equation is a cross-currency swap, where the three spatial coordinates are the domestic rate, the foreign rate and the exchange rate.

3D Tetrahedral Linear Element

The approximation function for a tetrahedral linear element is a linear polynomial in x, y and z,

$$\Phi^{(e)}(x) = \alpha_1^{(e)} + \alpha_2^{(e)}x + \alpha_3^{(e)}y + \alpha_4^e z. \tag{7.110}$$

The nodes of the tetrahedron are labeled by i, j, k and l. A variable within the element is determined by

$$\Phi^{(e)}(x, y, z) = N_i^{(e)}\Phi_i^{(e)} + N_j^{(e)}\Phi_j^{(e)} + N_k^{(e)}\Phi_k^{(e)} + N_l^{(e)}\Phi_l^{(e)}, \tag{7.111}$$

with the shape functions

$$N_\beta = \frac{1}{6V}(a_\beta + b_\beta x + c_\beta y + d_\beta z), \quad \beta \in \{i, j, k, l\}. \tag{7.112}$$

---

[10] A Lagrangian element yielding a quadratic approximation over a rectangular geometry needs nine nodes. In contrast to the biquadratic element this additional node is located in the center of the rectangle.

Here, we have used the following abbreviations:

$$6V = \begin{vmatrix} 1 & X_i & Y_i & Z_i \\ 1 & X_j & Y_j & Z_j \\ 1 & X_k & Y_k & Z_k \\ 1 & X_l & Y_l & Z_l \end{vmatrix}, \tag{7.113}$$

$$a_i = \begin{vmatrix} X_j & Y_j & Z_j \\ X_k & Y_k & Z_k \\ X_l & Y_l & Z_l \end{vmatrix}, \tag{7.114}$$

$$b_i = \begin{vmatrix} 1 & Y_j & Z_j \\ 1 & Y_k & Z_k \\ 1 & Y_l & Z_l \end{vmatrix}, \tag{7.115}$$

$$c_i = \begin{vmatrix} X_j & 1 & Z_j \\ X_k & 1 & Z_k \\ X_l & 1 & Z_l \end{vmatrix}, \tag{7.116}$$

$$d_i = \begin{vmatrix} X_j & Y_j & 1 \\ X_k & Y_k & 1 \\ X_l & Y_l & 1 \end{vmatrix}. \tag{7.117}$$

All other constants are defined by a cyclic interchange of the indices i, j, k and l. Note that the ordering of the nodes follows a right hand rule: the first three nodes are ordered in an anti-clockwise manner. The process of determining the shape functions is identical to the two-dimensional case.

3D Hexahedral Linear Element

The linear hexahedral element has eight corner nodes and the lowest order polynomial with eight unknown coefficients has the form

$$\Phi^{(e)}(x) = \alpha_1^{(e)} + \alpha_2^{(e)}x + \alpha_3^{(e)}y + \alpha_4^{(e)}z + \alpha_5^{(e)}xy + \alpha_6^{(e)}xz + \alpha_7^{(e)}yz + \alpha_8^{(e)}xyz. \tag{7.118}$$

The corresponding shape functions will be derived using natural coordinates later in this chapter. Note that for cubic elements the mesh is again identical to a standard finite difference mesh in three dimensions.

7.6.2 Local and Natural Coordinates

The derivation of element matrices and vectors involves integrating the shape functions and their derivatives over the element. The evaluation of these integrals can be considerably simplified by switching to new shape functions defined in a local coordinate system within each element. In the following, we derive so-called natural coordinates, a particular set of local coordinate systems, for one, two and three dimensions. In general, natural coordinates allow to specify any point inside an element by a set of dimensionless numbers between 0 and 1 or between -1 and 1.

1D Local Coordinates

Equations for N_i and N_j in (7.12) and (7.13) correspond to an element where the origin of the coordinate system is to the left of node i. A possible natural coordinate system can be introduced by identifying two coordinates L_i and L_j defined by

$$L_i = \frac{l}{L} = \frac{X_j - x}{L} \tag{7.119}$$

$$L_j = \frac{\hat{l}}{L} = \frac{x - X_i}{L}. \tag{7.120}$$

Note that L_i and L_j are not independent but are related by

$$L_i + L_j = 1. \tag{7.121}$$

Comparing Equations (7.120) and (7.12) as well as equations (7.120) and (7.13) reveals that these natural coordinates are identical to the shape functions of the one-dimensional linear element ($L_i = N_i$ and $L_j = N_j$). Each point inside the element can thus be conveniently expressed by the element's nodal coordinates,

$$x = X_i L_i + X_j L_j. \tag{7.122}$$

An appealing feature of this kind of coordinates is the fact that the integral over products of linear shape functions can be evaluated analytically,

$$\int_{X_i}^{X_j} L_i^\alpha L_j^\beta dx = \frac{\alpha! \beta!}{(\alpha + \beta + 1)!} L. \tag{7.123}$$

Since the analytical integration is not possible for higher order shape functions, we now develop an alternative coordinate system that is better suited for fast numerical integration. We start with a local coordinate system q with the origin located at the center of the element. The corresponding coordinate transformation is (keep in mind that $L = X_i - X_j$)

$$x(q) = X_i + \frac{L}{2} + q \quad \text{with} \quad q \in \left[-\frac{L}{2}; \frac{L}{2} \right], \tag{7.124}$$

and the shape functions are

$$N_i(q) = \left(\frac{1}{2} - \frac{q}{L} \right), \tag{7.125}$$

$$N_j(q) = \left(\frac{1}{2} + \frac{q}{L} \right). \tag{7.126}$$

Next, we transform to a system ξ with natural coordinates running from -1 to $+1$, i.e., $\xi_i = -1$ and $\xi_j = 1$. This particular choice allows to perform numerical integration with the Gauss-Legendre method which has its sampling points and weighting coefficients defined on this interval. Using the ratio $2q/L = \xi$ we rewrite the shape functions (7.125, 7.126),

$$N_i(\xi) = \frac{1}{2}(1 - \xi), \tag{7.127}$$

$$N_j(\xi) = \frac{1}{2}(1 + \xi). \tag{7.128}$$

The effect of our subsequent transformations on the integration is

$$\int_{X_i}^{X_j} f(x)dx = \int_{-L/2}^{L/2} r(q)dq = \int_{-1}^{1} g(\xi)d\xi, \tag{7.129}$$

where $r(q)$ is $f(x)$ written in terms of q and $g(\xi)$ is $r(q)$ written in terms of ξ.

For the quadratic one-dimensional element, the shape functions in the ξ-system are

$$N_i(\xi) = \frac{\xi}{2}(\xi - 1), \tag{7.130}$$

$$N_j(\xi) = -(\xi + 1)(\xi - 1), \tag{7.131}$$

$$N_k(\xi) = \frac{\xi}{2}(e\xi + 1). \tag{7.132}$$

2D Natural Coordinates

A natural coordinate system for triangular elements can be built by introducing area coordinates. Let us consider a point P located inside a triangle. The local coordinates L_i, L_j and L_k of this point can be defined by using appropriate dimensionless areas. L_i, for instance, can be defined as the ratio between the area of the triangle spanned by points P, j, k and the total area of the element, and analogously for the other coordinates,

$$L_\beta = \frac{A_\beta}{A} \quad \text{with} \quad \beta \in i, j, k. \tag{7.133}$$

It is obvious that

$$A_i + A_j + A_k = A, \tag{7.134}$$

and therefore we have

$$\frac{A_i}{A} + \frac{A_j}{A} + \frac{A_k}{A} = L_i + L_j + L_k = 1. \tag{7.135}$$

Since the relationship between the natural coordinates and the cartesian coordinates (x, y) is

$$L_iX_i + L_jX_j + L_kX_k = x,$$
$$L_iY_i + L_jY_j + L_kY_k = y, \tag{7.136}$$

it can be concluded from Equation (7.135) that the natural coordinates are identical to the shape functions of the linear triangular element in (7.20),

$$L_i = N_i, \quad L_j = N_j, \quad L_k = N_k. \tag{7.137}$$

Note that the local (natural) coordinates and shape functions are identical for all linear elements irrespective of whether they are derived for one, two or three dimensions. As in the one-dimensional case, an analytical formula for the integration over the triangle area can be found,

$$\int_A N_i^\alpha N_j^\beta N_k^\gamma dA = \frac{\alpha!\beta!\gamma!}{(\alpha + \beta + \gamma + 2)!} 2A. \tag{7.138}$$

Incorporating derivative boundary conditions requires the solution of integrals along the element edges. Since the shape function of the opposite point is equal to zero when considering a particular side of the triangle, this case can be mapped to the evaluation of a one-dimensional integral through Equation (7.123).

In the case of a quadratic approximation on a triangular element, the shape functions can also be expressed using the natural coordinate system (area coordinates). With the additional nodes located at the midpoints of the boundaries the shape functions are

$$N_1 = L_i(2L_i - 1),$$

$$N_2 = 4L_i L_j,$$

$$N_3 = L_j(2L_j - 1),$$

$$N_4 = 4L_j L_k, \tag{7.139}$$

$$N_5 = L_k(2L_k - 1),$$

$$N_6 = 4L_k L_i.$$

For the quadrilateral elements dimensionless coordinates exist, too, and allow the deformation of a rectangle into a general quadrilateral. The shape function for the linear rectangular element defined in (7.23) can be expressed in terms of length ratios $\xi = x/b$ and $\eta = y/a$, leading to the shape functions

$$N_i = \frac{1}{4}(1 - \xi)(1 - \eta),$$

$$N_j = \frac{1}{4}(1 + \xi)(1 - \eta),$$

$$N_k = \frac{1}{4}(1 + \xi)(1 + \eta), \tag{7.140}$$

$$N_l = \frac{1}{4}(1 - \xi)(1 + \eta)$$

where

$$-1 \le \xi \le 1,$$

$$-1 \le \eta \le 1. \tag{7.141}$$

Again, these natural coordinates can also be used for the quadratic element, yielding the shape functions

$$N_1 = -\frac{1}{4}(1-\xi)(1-\eta)(1+\xi+\eta),$$

$$N_2 = \frac{1}{2}(1-\xi^2)(1-\eta),$$

$$N_3 = \frac{1}{4}(1+\xi)(1-\eta)(\xi-\eta-1),$$

$$N_4 = \frac{1}{2}(1+\xi)(1-\eta^2),$$

$$N_5 = \frac{1}{4}(1+\xi)(1+\eta)(\xi+\eta-1),$$ \hfill (7.142)

$$N_6 = \frac{1}{2}(1-\xi^2)(1+\eta),$$

$$N_7 = -\frac{1}{4}(1-\xi)(1+\eta)(\xi-\eta+1),$$

$$N_8 = \frac{1}{2}(1-\xi)(1-\eta^2).$$

3D Natural Coordinates

Analogously to the two dimensional case, natural coordinates for the three dimensional case can be established using volume ratios. For tetrahedrons we assume a point P, located inside the element, to be a corner node of four new tetrahedra. The natural coordinates are then the volume ratios between these new tetrahedra and the volume of the original element,

$$L_\beta = \frac{V_\beta}{V} \quad \beta \in \{i, j, k, l\}. \tag{7.143}$$

Again, these coordinates fulfill the well-known property

$$L_i + L_j + L_k + L_l = 1. \tag{7.144}$$

Note that in the case of linear shape functions we again have

$$N_\beta = L_\beta, \quad \beta \in \{i, j, k, l\}, \tag{7.145}$$

where the N_β are defined in (7.112). As usual, an analytic integration formula is available in the linear case,

$$\int_V N_i^\alpha N_j^\beta N_k^\gamma N_l^\delta dV = \frac{\alpha! \beta! \gamma! \delta!}{(\alpha+\beta+\gamma+\delta+3)!} 6V. \tag{7.146}$$

A natural coordinate system for the general hexahedron element can be established along the same lines as for the general quadrilateral element by using the length ratios. Adding

$$\rho = z/c$$

to the previously defined variables η and ξ, we end up with

$$N_1 = \frac{1}{8}(1 - \xi)(1 - \eta)(1 - \rho),$$

$$N_2 = \frac{1}{8}(1 - \xi)(1 + \eta)(1 - \rho),$$

$$N_3 = \frac{1}{8}(1 + \xi)(1 + \eta)(1 - \rho),$$

$$N_4 = \frac{1}{8}(1 + \xi)(1 - \eta)(1 - \rho),$$

$$N_5 = \frac{1}{8}(1 - \xi)(1 - \eta)(1 + \rho),$$

$$N_6 = \frac{1}{8}(1 - \xi)(1 + \eta)(1 + \rho),$$

$$N_7 = \frac{1}{8}(1 + \xi)(1 + \eta)(1 + \rho),$$

$$N_8 = \frac{1}{8}(1 + \xi)(1 - \eta)(1 + \rho),$$

(7.147)

for the eight shape functions.

8
Solving Systems of Linear Equations

As pointed out in the previous chapters, the discretization of partial differential equations with finite difference or finite element methods in connection with implicit or semi-implicit time-stepping schemes results in large systems of linear equations,

$$
\begin{aligned}
a_{11}x_1 + a_{12}x_2 + \cdots + a_{1n}x_n &= b_1 \\
a_{21}x_1 + a_{22}x_2 + \cdots + a_{2n}x_n &= b_2 \\
&\vdots \\
a_{n1}x_1 + a_{n2}x_2 + \cdots + a_{nn}x_n &= b_n
\end{aligned}
\tag{8.1}
$$

or, in matrix-vector form,

$$
\mathbf{A}\mathbf{x} = \mathbf{b}.
\tag{8.2}
$$

The matrix $\mathbf{A}$ is called the coefficient matrix, $\mathbf{x}$ is the vector of unknowns and $\mathbf{b}$ the right-hand side. We will restrict ourselves to systems with quadratic coefficient matrices:[1] for a number of n unknowns (the length of the vector $\mathbf{x}$), the dimension of $\mathbf{A}$ is $n \times n$. Furthermore, we will assume that the coefficient matrix is regular (rank of $\mathbf{A} = n$).

Depending on the financial model chosen and the desired accuracy of the discretization scheme, the sparsity of the coefficient matrix $\mathbf{A}$ can range from tridiagonal[2] to dense.[3] There are many different algorithms available for solving linear systems. In order to choose the optimal algorithm for a given problem, a number of factors must be considered:

- System size: for large n, direct methods become inefficient in terms of speed and memory usage, and iterative solvers should be preferred.
- Sparsity: if the number of zero matrix entries $a_{ij} = 0$ in the matrix is large (which is typically the case in banded matrices), methods where only the action of the coefficient matrix on a given vector needs to be calculated should be preferred. Furthermore, the storage space of the matrices is reduced considerably when only the non-zero entries are stored.
- Properties of the coefficient matrix: certain properties of the coefficient matrix, such as definiteness, allow to select tailor-made algorithms which are more effective/stable than general purpose algorithms. For example, for systems with positive definite coefficient matrices, Cholesky factorization can be used instead of Gaussian elimination.

---

[1] A linear system with an $m \times n$ coefficient matrix A can be transformed in to a quadratic system by multiplying with its transpose from the left,

$$
\mathbf{A}^T \mathbf{A}\mathbf{x} = \mathbf{A}^T \mathbf{b}.
$$

If $\mathbf{A}$ is regular, $\mathbf{A}^T\mathbf{A}$ will become symmetric and positive semidefinite – if $\mathbf{A}$ is non-quadratic, $\mathbf{A}^T\mathbf{A}\mathbf{x} = \mathbf{A}^T\mathbf{b}$ is the so-called normal equation.

[2] In the case of a PDE representation of a one-dimensional model (Black-Scholes, one factor Hull-White), a discretization with a second order finite difference operator or a linear finite element scheme would result in a simple tridiagonal matrix.

[3] Some processes used in modeling financial instruments add an integral term to the partial differential equation, leading to a partial-integro-differential equation; for example the Bates equity model. A straightforward discretization of such an equation would lead to a dense matrix.

Further information concerning the methods covered in this section can be found in (Stoer and Bulirsch, 2002; Saad, 2003). An especially good reference for the multigrid method is Hackbusch (2003).

8.1 DIRECT METHODS

Direct methods for solving linear systems $\mathbf{Ax} = \mathbf{b}$ involve at least the explicit factorization of the coefficient matrix $\mathbf{A}$ (or, in most cases, a permutation of the rows and columns of $\mathbf{A}$) into the product of lower and upper triangular matrices $\mathbf{L}$ and $\mathbf{U}$. The solution process is completed for a given right hand side $\mathbf{b}$ by back substitution. A number of methods used for the LU factorization process are described in the following: Gaussian elimination can be used for all kinds of coefficient matrices, whereas other methods, such as Cholesky factorization, gain a speed advantage by exploiting specific properties of $\mathbf{A}$, such as positive definiteness. In recent years, a number of solvers for the direct solution of large sparse, symmetric linear systems of equations has been developed; we refer the interested reader to the survey of Gould and coworkers (Gould, Hu and Scott 2005).

8.1.1 Gaussian Elimination

The Gaussian elimination algorithm can be used to solve systems of linear equations, to determine the rank of a matrix, to calculate the determinant of a matrix, or to calculate the inverse of an invertible matrix. Elementary row operations (multiplying rows, swapping rows, and adding multiples of rows to other rows) are used to reduce the coefficient matrix $\mathbf{A}$ to a triangular form.[4] In a second step, back-substitution is applied to obtain the solution of the system of linear equations. In principle, Gaussian elimination computes a matrix decomposition – the elementary row operations are equivalent to multiplying the original matrix with its inverse from the left. The number of operations for a coefficient matrix of $n \times n$ is of order n^3. The basic algorithm for a system of n unknowns consists of the following steps:

1. Change the order of equations to assure that $a_{11} \neq 0$.
2. Add multiples of the first equation to the remaining $n - 1$ equations in order to obtain zeros in the first column starting from the second equation, resulting in the linear system

$$a_{11}x_1 + a_{12}x_2 + \cdots + a_{1n}x_n = b_1$$
$$a'_{22}x_2 + \cdots + a'_{2n}x_n = b'_2$$
$$\vdots \quad \vdots$$
$$a'_{n2}x_2 + \cdots + a'_{nn}x_n = b'_n.$$

Here, $'$ indicates that the coefficient has been altered.

---

[4] The row operations may also result in a degenerate equation, indicating the system has no unique solution but may have multiple solutions (this case will not be examined further).

3. Repeat steps (1) and (2) for the block starting with the appropriate equation until no more equations are left. This results in the following form of the linear system:

$$\bar{a}_{11}x_1 + \bar{a}_{12}x_2 + \cdots + \bar{a}_{1r}x_r + \bar{a}_{1r+1}x_{r+1} + \cdots + \bar{a}_{1n}x_n = \bar{b}_1$$

$$\bar{a}_{22}x_2 + \cdots + \bar{a}_{2r}x_r + \bar{a}_{2r+1}x_{r+1} + \cdots + \bar{a}_{2n}x_n = \bar{b}_2$$

$$\vdots \quad \vdots$$

$$\bar{a}_{rr}x_r + \bar{a}_{rr+1}x_{r+1} + \cdots + \bar{a}_{rn}x_n = \bar{b}_r$$

$$\bar{a}_{r+1r+1}x_{r+1} + \cdots + \bar{a}_{r+1n}x_n = \bar{b}_{r+1}$$

$$\vdots \quad \vdots$$

$$\bar{a}_{nn}x_n = \bar{b}_n$$

The values $\bar{a}_{i,j}$ are the final matrix entries after the procedure has completed and the matrix has been reduced to triangular form. If $\mathbf{A}$ is regular, it can be guaranteed that $\bar{a}_{ii} \neq 0$ by appropriate reordering of the equations.

4. Starting with x_n, the solutions x_i can be calculated by back-substitution.

Gaussian elimination is numerically stable for diagonally dominant or positive definite matrices, but can be prone to rounding errors that lead to numerical instabilities in other cases. For general matrices, pivoting is used to stabilize the algorithm. A pivot or pivot element is a specific element of the coefficient matrix that is selected by the Gaussian elimination algorithm (step (1) in the algorithm above is a kind of pivoting). To improve numerical stability, it is in general desirable to choose a pivot element with a large absolute value and interchange columns and rows to place the pivot element in the upper left position of the current block. One distinguishes between partial and total pivoting: Partial pivoting restricts the search for the pivot element to the current column, whereas total pivoting searches the whole coefficient matrix. Total pivoting thus interchanges rows *and* columns and achieves increased numerical stability. Pivoting can be thought of as swapping or sorting rows or columns in a matrix, and can therefore be represented as a multiplication by permutation matrices. However, practical implementations do not really move rows and columns but only keep track of the permutations for efficiency reasons.

8.1.2   Thomas Algorithm

The Thomas algorithm (tridiagonal matrix algorithm), see Algorithm 1, is a simplified version of Gaussian elimination for the efficient solution of linear systems of equations with a *tridiagonal* coefficient matrix $\mathbf{A}$. It reduces the number of operations required to compute the solution to order n. The discretization of one-dimensional convection-diffusion-reaction PDEs with second order finite difference or finite element schemes results in tridiagonal coefficient matrices.

Algorithm 1   Pseudocode for the Thomas algorithm. The Thomas algorithm solves (8.2) for tridiagonal coefficient matrices $\mathbf{A}$. Note that this version of the algorithm overwrites the input diagonal and the input right-hand side vector. $diag(\mathbf{A})$ denotes the diagonal, $supdiag(A)$ the upper diagonal and $subdiag(A)$ the lower diagonal of the coefficient matrix.

Require: let d be $diag(A)$ indexed $1, n$
Require: let u be $supdiag(A)$ indexed $1, n - 1$
Require: let l be $subdiag(A)$ indexed $1, n - 1$
Require: let b be the right hand side of (8.2) indexed $1, n$
  for $i = 2, \dots, n$ **do**
    $m = l[i - 1]/d[i - 1]$
    $d[i] = d[i] - m * u[i - 1]$
    $b[i] = b[i] - m * b[i - 1]$
  end for
  $x[n] = v[n]/b[n]$
  for $i = n - 1, \dots, 1, i - -$ **do**
    $x[i] = (b[i] - u[i] * x[i + 1])/d[i]$
  end for

8.1.3 LU Decomposition

LU decomposition (also called LU factorization) factorizes a matrix into the product of a lower triangular matrix **L** and an upper triangular matrix **U**. In some cases, an additional permutation matrix is included in the factorization. LU decomposition can be interpreted as the matrix form of Gaussian elimination. The LU decomposition of a square matrix **A** of dimension $n \times n$ is

$$\mathbf{A} = \mathbf{LU}. \tag{8.3}$$

For some non-singular coefficient matrices **A** an LU decomposition is not always possible. In these cases, an LU decomposition with partial pivoting is commonly used,

$$\mathbf{PA} = \mathbf{LU}, \tag{8.4}$$

where **P** a permutation matrix. All square matrices can be factorized in this form in a numerically stable way (depending on the condition number of **A**). Again, the number of operations is of order n^3. The big advantage of LU decomposition compared to Gaussian elimination is its efficiency in repeatedly solving a linear system of equations for different right-hand sides, as the factorization only needs to be performed once.[5] For an LU decomposition $\mathbf{PA} = \mathbf{LU}$ with permutation matrix **P** $(\mathbf{P} = \mathbf{P}^{-1})$, the linear system (8.2) becomes

$$\mathbf{LUx} = \mathbf{Pb}. \tag{8.5}$$

This system can be solved by performing two steps,

- solve $\mathbf{Ly} = \mathbf{Pb}$ for **y**,
- solve $\mathbf{Ux} = \mathbf{y}$ for **x**.

Both steps can be performed by simple forward or backward substitution, respectively.

---

[5] This situation occurs very frequently in quantitative finance: In the case of time-dependent model parameters, the equations change only at specific points in time, but are constant in the intermediate time intervals.

Algorithm 2   Pseudocode of the LUP algorithm. The matrices **U** and **L** are stored in place of the matrix **A**. The permutation matrix **P** is dynamically maintained as an array p, where $p[i] = j$ indicates that the i-th row of **P** contains a 1 in column j.

Require: let p be an array of size n
  for $i = 1, \ldots, n$ **do**
    $p[i] = i$
  end for
  for $k = 1, \ldots, n$ **do**
    $q = 0$
    for $i = k, \ldots, n$ **do**
      if $a_{ik} > q$ **then**
        $q = |a[i, k]|0$
        $r = i$
      end if
    end for
    if $q == 0$ **then**
      Error - Matrix Singular
    end if
    exchange $p[k]$ with $p[r]$
    for $i = 1, \ldots, n$ **do**
      exchange $a[k, i]$ with $a[r, i]$
    end for
    for $i = k + 1, \ldots, n$ **do**
      $a[i, k] = a[i, k]/a[k, k]$
      for $j = k + 1, \ldots, n$ **do**
        $a[i, j] = a[i, j] - a[i, k]a[k, j]$
      end for
    end for
  end for
  $a[i, j] = l_{ij}$ if i > j
  $a[i, j] = u_{ij}$ if i $\leq$ j

8.1.4 Cholesky Decomposition

The Cholesky decomposition is a fast method for the LU decomposition of symmetric and positive definite coefficient matrices **A**, where the upper triangular matrix is the transpose of the lower triangular matrix,

$$\mathbf{A} = \mathbf{LL}^T. \tag{8.6}$$

The Cholesky algorithm to calculate the decomposition matrix **L** is given in Algorithm 3.

Algorithm 3   Pseudocode of a basic version of the Cholesky algorithm. The matrix **L** is computed and stored in place of the lower triangle of matrix **A**. Since the square-root operation is time consuming standard implementations perform an $\mathbf{A} = \mathbf{LDL}^T$ decomposition where $diag(\mathbf{L}) = 1$ instead.

```
for i = 1, ... , n do
  for j = 1, ... , i − 1 do
    x = a[i, j]
    for k = 1, ... , j − 1 do
      x = x − a[i, k] ∗ a[j, k]
    end for
    a[i, j] = x/a[j, j]
  end for
  x=a[i,i]
  for k = 1, ... , i − 1 do
    x = x − a[i, k] ∗ a[i, k]
  end for
  if x > 0 then
    a[i, i] = SQRT(x)
  else
    Error - Matrix Singular
  end if
end for
```

8.2 ITERATIVE SOLVERS

For large and/or sparse systems of equations of the form (8.2), direct solvers are time-consuming and might, for a very large number of unknowns n, not be applicable at all. Iterative solvers are typically used to overcome this problem: starting from an initial vector x_0, an iterative method generates a sequence of consecutive vectors $x_0 \rightarrow x_1 \rightarrow x_2 \rightarrow \cdots$ that converges towards the solution. The computational effort for a single iteration step $x_i \rightarrow x_{i+1}$ is comparable to the effort of multiplying the vector x by the matrix A. For sparse matrices, in particular, this is possible at comparatively little cost. The classical iterative methods – Jacobi, Gauss Seidel and Successive Overrelaxation – are simple to derive, implement, and analyze, but convergence is usually slow, only guaranteed for a limited class of matrices and often depends on the choice of additional parameters that are hard to estimate. Krylov subspace methods, on the other hand, have no additional parameters that influence convergence. The iterative process is stopped after a predefined error estimate[6] is smaller than a chosen ε (for instance $\varepsilon = 10^{-8}$). These error estimates can be of the form

$$\varepsilon_1 := \gamma ||x_{i+1} - x_i||_2, \tag{8.7}$$

where i is the iteration index and γ is a discretization- and dimension-dependent factor – for example, $\sqrt{h^d}$ for a d-dimensional finite difference discretization with equidistant grid spacings for all spatial dimensions. Another estimate that asserts the correctness of the solution can be defined by

$$\varepsilon_2 := \gamma ||Ax_i - b||_2, \tag{8.8}$$

but depending on the matrix A the calculation of ε_2 can be costly.

---

[6] Specific algorithms often favor specific error estimates that are calculated as a side-effect of the algorithm at no extra cost.

8.2.1 Matrix Decomposition

For a linear system of equations defined as in (8.2), the exact solution can, in theory, always be calculated using the inverse of the matrix, $\mathbf{x} := \mathbf{A}^{-1}\mathbf{b}$. In general, an iterative procedure for obtaining the solution $\mathbf{x}$ can be written as

$$\mathbf{x}^{(i+1)} = \Phi(\mathbf{x}^{(i)}), \quad i = 0, 1, \dots, \tag{8.9}$$

where Φ (depends at least on $\mathbf{A}$ and $\mathbf{b}$) specifies the iteration. With a non-singular $n \times n$ matrix $\mathbf{B}$, the linear system (8.2) can be expanded

$$\mathbf{B}\mathbf{x} + (\mathbf{A} - \mathbf{B})\mathbf{x} = \mathbf{b} \tag{8.10}$$

in order to obtain a family of iterative methods,

$$\mathbf{B}\mathbf{x}^{(i+1)} + (\mathbf{A} - \mathbf{B})\mathbf{x}^{(i)} = \mathbf{b}, \tag{8.11}$$

or, explicitly solving Equation (8.11) for $\mathbf{x}^{(i+1)}$,

$$\mathbf{x}^{(i+1)} = \mathbf{x}^{(i)} - \mathbf{B}^{-1}(\mathbf{A}\mathbf{x}^{(i)} - \mathbf{b}) = (\mathbf{I} - \mathbf{B}^{-1}\mathbf{A})\mathbf{x}^{(i)} + \mathbf{B}^{-1}\mathbf{b}. \tag{8.12}$$

Different choices of $\mathbf{B}$ lead to different iterative methods; in making this choice, two considerations should be taken into account:

1. Equation (8.11) should be easy to solve for $\mathbf{x}^{(i+1)}$.
2. The absolute values of the eigenvalues of $\mathbf{I} - \mathbf{B}^{-1}\mathbf{A}$ should be small. Note that if $\mathbf{B} = \mathbf{A}$, all eigenvalues of this matrix will be 0, so this condition amounts to trying to choose $\mathbf{B}$ similar to the matrix $\mathbf{A}$.

To find matrices $\mathbf{B}$ that obey this condition, we start with a standard decomposition of the matrix $\mathbf{A}$,

$$\mathbf{A} = \mathbf{D} - \mathbf{E} - \mathbf{F}, \tag{8.13}$$

where

$$\mathbf{D} = \begin{pmatrix} a_{11} & & 0 \\ & \ddots & \\ 0 & & a_{nn} \end{pmatrix},$$

$$\mathbf{E} = -\begin{pmatrix} 0 & & & 0 \\ a_{21} & 0 & & \\ \vdots & \ddots & \ddots & \\ a_{n1} & \cdots & a_{n,n-1} & 0 \end{pmatrix}, \tag{8.14}$$

$$\mathbf{F} = -\begin{pmatrix} 0 & a_{12} & \cdots & a_{1n} \\ & 0 & \ddots & \\ & & \ddots & a_{n-1,n} \\ 0 & & & 0 \end{pmatrix}.$$

If $a_{jj} \neq 0$ for $j = 1, 2, \dots, n$ we further introduce

$$
\begin{aligned}
\mathbf{L} &:= \mathbf{D}^{-1}\mathbf{E}, \\
\mathbf{U} &:= \mathbf{D}^{-1}\mathbf{F}, \\
\mathbf{J} &:= \mathbf{L} + \mathbf{U}, \\
\mathbf{H} &:= (\mathbf{I} - \mathbf{L})^{-1}\mathbf{U}.
\end{aligned}
\tag{8.15}
$$

The standard convergence condition for all iterative methods is

$$
\rho(\mathbf{I} - \mathbf{B}^{-1}\mathbf{A}) < 1,
\tag{8.16}
$$

where ρ is the spectral radius of the iteration matrix, $\rho(\mathbf{X}) = \max(|\lambda_j|)$ for $j = 1, \dots, n$. The smaller the spectral radius is, the higher the rate of convergence of the iterative method. This motivates us to regard the matrix $\mathbf{B}$ as parameter-dependent, $\mathbf{B} \to \mathbf{B}(\omega)$, where the parameter ω is chosen in order to make $\rho(\mathbf{I} - \mathbf{B}(\omega)^{-1}\mathbf{A})$ as small as possible.

Jacobi Iterative Method

The Jacobi method is defined by the choice

$$
\mathbf{B} = \mathbf{D}, \qquad \mathbf{I} - \mathbf{B}^{-1}\mathbf{A} = \mathbf{J},
\tag{8.17}
$$

which leads to the following update rule for each iteration:

$$
x_j^{(i+1)} = \frac{1}{a_{jj}} \left(b_j - \sum_{k \neq j} a_{jk} x_k^{(i)} \right), \quad j = 1, 2, \dots, n, \quad i = 0, 1, \dots .
\tag{8.18}
$$

After each iteration step, error estimates, such as ϵ_1 or ϵ_2 defined above, can be checked whether the desired accuracy is reached. The ω-Jacobi method is a simple extension of the above Jacobi iteration with $\mathbf{B} = \omega\mathbf{D}$,

$$
x_j^{(i+1)} = \frac{\omega}{a_{jj}} \left(b_j - \sum_{k \neq j} a_{jk} x_k^{(i)} \right), \quad j = 1, 2, \dots, n, \quad i = 0, 1, \dots .
\tag{8.19}
$$

Gauss-Seidel Iterative Method

For the Gauss-Seidel method we choose

$$
\mathbf{B} = \mathbf{D} - \mathbf{E}, \qquad \mathbf{I} - \mathbf{B}^{-1}\mathbf{A} = (\mathbf{I} - \mathbf{L})^{-1}\mathbf{U} = \mathbf{H},
\tag{8.20}
$$

which leads to the update rule

$$
x_j^{(i+1)} = \frac{1}{a_{jj}} \left(b_j - \sum_{k > j} a_{jk} x_k^{(i)} - \sum_{k < j} a_{jk} x_k^{(i+1)} \right), \quad j = 1, 2, \dots, n, \quad i = 0, 1, \dots .
\tag{8.21}
$$

Again, error estimates can be checked after each iteration step whether the desired accuracy is reached.

Although the element-wise formulation of the Gauss-Seidel method is extremely similar to that of the Jacobi method, there are important differences: The computation of $\mathbf{x}^{(i+1)}$ uses only those elements of $\mathbf{x}^{(i+1)}$ that have been computed previously in the iteration, and only those elements of $\mathbf{x}^{(i)}$ that have not yet been touched in the current iteration update. Therefore, unlike in the Jacobi method, only one storage vector is required, as elements can be overwritten while they are computed. This can be advantageous for very large problems. However, for the very same reason, the computation of the elements cannot be performed in parallel, in contrast to the Jacobi method. Furthermore, the values obtained in each iteration step are dependent on the order of the original equations.

Successive Over-Relaxation

The successive over-relaxation (SOR) method is a variant of the Gauss-Seidel method that improves the convergence. The iteration update rule is

$$x_j^{(i+1)} = (1 - \omega)x_j^{(i)} + \frac{\omega}{a_{jj}} \left(b_j - \sum_{k>j} a_{jk}x_k^{(i)} - \sum_{k<j} a_{jk}x_k^{(i+1)} \right), \tag{8.22}$$

where $j = 1, 2, \ldots, n$ and $i = 0, 1, \ldots$. The choice of the relaxation parameter ω determines the improvement of the convergence. The optimal relaxation parameter depends on the properties of the coefficient matrix $\mathbf{A}$.

8.2.2 Krylov Methods

Krylov subspace methods form a basis comprised of the sequence of successive matrix powers times an initial residual (the Krylov sequence). The residual is then minimized within this subspace, resulting in an approximation to the solution. Since Krylov subspace methods form a basis, it can be shown that the method always converges after n iterations, where n is the size of the linear system. In practice, this statement does not hold due to rounding errors; however, the iterative process typically reaches the desired accuracy after considerably fewer iterations.

Conjugate Gradient Method

The conjugate gradient method can be applied for solving a system of linear equations $\mathbf{A}x = b$, with a symmetric positive definite $n \times n$ matrix $\mathbf{A}$. Starting from an initial vector $\mathbf{x}_0$, the sequence of consecutive vectors $\mathbf{x}_0 \to \mathbf{x}_1 \to \mathbf{x}_2 \to \cdots \mathbf{x}_n$ converges towards the solution in at least n steps, when applying exact operations (i.e., no rounding errors). The computational costs per step $\mathbf{x}_k \to \mathbf{x}_{k+1}$ amounts to the multiplication of the coefficient matrix by a vector and six additional vector-vector multiplications. The algorithm proceeds as follows (bold notation is omitted here):

1. Start with a vector $x_0 \in \mathbb{R}^n$ and set $p_0 := r_0 := b - Ax_0$
2. For each iteration k:

$$a_k := \frac{r_k^T r_k}{p_k^T A p_k}$$

$$x_{k+1} := x_k + a_k p_k$$

$$r_{k+1} := r_k - a_k A p_k \tag{8.23}$$

$$b_k := \frac{r_{k+1}^T r_{k+1}}{r_k^T r_k}$$

$$p_{k+1} := r_{k+1} + b_k p_k$$

3. Check convergence.

If the coefficient matrix $\mathbf{A}$ is non-symmetric but regular, it is possible to solve $\mathbf{A}^T \mathbf{A} \mathbf{x} = \mathbf{A}^T \mathbf{b}$ instead, since $\mathbf{A}^T \mathbf{A}$ is then symmetric and positive. One should note, however, that the condition number of the coefficient matrix is squared in this case, which can deteriorate the convergence rate of the algorithm.

Stabilized Bi-Conjugate Gradient Method

The stabilized bi-conjugate gradient method is a Krylov subspace method for solving (8.2) with a non-symmetric coefficient matrix $\mathbf{A}$. The algorithm proceeds as follows (note that bold notation is omitted here):

1. Start with a vector $x_0 \in \mathbb{R}^n$ and set $p_0 := \tilde{r}_0 := r_0 := b - Ax_0$ and calculate $\rho_0 = r_0^T \tilde{r}_0$.
2. For each iteration k:

$$s_k := Ap_k$$

$$\sigma_k := s_k^T \tilde{r}_0$$

$$\alpha_k := \frac{\rho_k}{\sigma_k}$$

$$w_k := r_k - \alpha_k s_k$$

$$v_k := Aw_k$$

$$\omega_k := \frac{v_k^T w_k}{v_k^T v_k} \tag{8.24}$$

$$x_{k+1} := x_k - \alpha_k p_k - \omega_k w_k$$

$$r_{k+1} := r_k - \alpha_k s_k - \omega_k v_k$$

$$\rho_{k+1} := r_{k+1}^T \tilde{r}_0$$

$$\beta_k := \frac{\rho_{k+1}}{\rho_k} \frac{\alpha_k}{\omega_k}$$

$$p_{k+1} := r_{k+1} + \beta_k (p_k - \omega_k s_k)$$

3. Check convergence.

The algorithm should be stopped before reaching the maximum number of iterations if $||r_{k+1}|| < \epsilon$, where ϵ is the desired accuracy.

8.2.3 Multigrid Solvers

The first multigrid scheme for the solution of the Poisson equation in a unit square was developed in the 1960s. In the following decades, the theory behind multigrid solvers has advanced considerably; nowadays, the method is applied to a wide range of problems, in particular to linear and nonlinear boundary value problems. Recent developments of solvers in this field rely on algebraic multigrid (AMG) methods that resemble the geometric multigrid (grid-based) process, but utilize only information contained in the algebraic system to be solved. All multigrid methods use a hierarchy of discretizations. The characteristic feature of

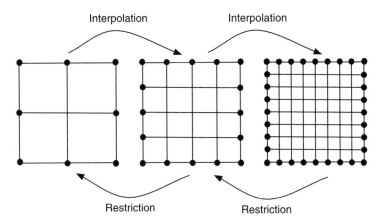

Figure 8.1   Hierarchical grid levels. The restriction operator is used to go from the fine grid to the coarse grid, the interpolation (prolongation) operator is used to go from the coarse grid to the fine grid. Black dots indicate boundary nodes.

the algorithm is its fast convergence for boundary-value problems: While classical iterative methods typically slow down when the grid spacing is decreased (number of grid points for a given geometry is increased), the convergence rate of the multigrid method is not deteriorated.

To analyze the multigrid method, we recall two of the standard iterative techniques: the Jacobi and Gauss-Seidel schemes. Both methods usually exhibit poor convergence, compare Figure 8.2. However, if one decomposes the errors into their frequency components, one observes that errors with a length scale comparable to the grid size are damped rapidly, and iterations leave behind smooth, longer wave-length errors.[7] The idea of multigrid is to employ grids of different mesh size to cover different wavelengths. The high-frequency components of the error are reduced by applying iterative methods (smoothers) such as ω-Jacobi or Gauss-Seidel. Low-frequency error components are effectively reduced by a coarse grid correction procedure. The solution of the coarse grid problem is then interpolated back to the fine grid in order to correct the fine grid approximation for its low-frequency errors. To exemplify the concept, we apply the multigrid method to the two-dimensional Poisson equation,

$$\nabla^2 \Phi = f. \tag{8.25}$$

We discretize the equation using the finite difference method with an equal number of discretization points for both spatial dimensions, and choose homogenous Dirichlet boundary conditions. Now consider a hierarchical number of grids G_l with grid spacings h_l, where l denotes the level index ranging from $l = sl$ for the coarsest grid up to $maxl$ for the finest grid (compare Figure 8.1). The level $l = sl$ is called the "solution level" where the defect system (residual system) is solved exactly. For each level l, we can define the grid spacing to be $h_{l-1} = 2h_l$, starting with $h_{maxl} = h$, where h denotes the grid spacing of the discretized PDE at the level of the finest level. Correspondingly, the number of grid points for each level and each spatial coordinate is defined as $n_{l-1} = 2^{-1} n_l$, again starting with $l = maxl$ and $n_{maxl} = n$,

---

[7] These smooth components are responsible for the slow global convergence of the classical iterative methods.

where n denotes the number of points used for the discretization of the PDE at the level of the desired solution. In the following, A_{h_l} is the discretized left-hand side operator and b_{h_l} the discretized right-hand side of (8.2) at grid level l. With these definitions, the multigrid algorithm is described as follows (note that bold notation is omitted here):

1. Start with a vector $x_{0,h_{maxl}}$, for example $x_{0,h_{maxl}}^{i,j} = 0$ with $i, j \in \mathcal{G}_{maxl}$.
2. For each iteration k start with $l = maxl$:
   (a) Pre-smoothing: $\hat{x}_{k,h_l} = G_{h_l}^{Pr,v} x_{k,h_l}$

   $G_{h_l}^{Pr,v}$ is the pre-smoothing operator (superscript Pr) for a certain grid level (subscript h_l) and v denotes the number of pre-smoothing steps. For the smoothing operator $G_{h_l}^{Pr,v}$ different choices are possible (Gauss-Seidel, ω-Jacobi,...).
   (b) Calculation of the defect: $d_{k,h_l} = b_{h_l} - A_{h_l}\hat{x}_{k,h_l}$
   (c) Coarse-grid approximation: $d_{k,h_{l-1}} = I_{h_l}^{h_{l-1}} d_{k,h_l}$

   $I_{h_l}^{h_{l-1}}$ is the restriction operator, where we use the *nine-point restriction* here,

$$I_{h_l}^{h_{l-1}} = \begin{pmatrix} \frac{1}{16} & \frac{1}{8} & \frac{1}{16} \\ \frac{1}{8} & \frac{1}{4} & \frac{1}{8} \\ \frac{1}{16} & \frac{1}{8} & \frac{1}{16} \end{pmatrix}. \tag{8.26}$$

   (d) Solution of the defect system: $A_{h_{l-1}}\omega_{k,h_{l-1}} = d_{k,h_{l-1}}$
   The defect system is solved recursively by starting over at point (a), until the solution level sl is reached, where the defect system $A_{h_{sl}}\omega_{k,h_{sl}} = d_{k,h_{sl}}$ is solved exactly. This recursive call is repeated γ times. Here, we choose $\gamma = 1$ for all calculations, which corresponds to a so-called V-cycle.
   (e) Prolongation: $\omega_{k,h_l} = I_{h_{l-1}}^{h_l} \omega_{k,h_{l-1}}$

   For the prolongation operator $I_{h_{l-1}}^{h_l}$, we use a piecewise linear interpolation called *nine-point prolongation*, which is the adjoint of the restriction operator $I_{h_l}^{h_{l-1}}$,

$$I_{h_{l-1}}^{h_l} = \begin{pmatrix} \frac{1}{4} & \frac{1}{2} & \frac{1}{4} \\ \frac{1}{2} & 1 & \frac{1}{2} \\ \frac{1}{4} & \frac{1}{2} & \frac{1}{4} \end{pmatrix}. \tag{8.27}$$

   (f) Correction: $\hat{x}_{k+1,h_l} = \hat{x}_{k,h_l} + \omega_{k,h_l}$
   Correction of the smoothed approximation $\hat{x}_{k+1,h_l}$ by the coarse grid approximation ω_{k,h_l}.
   (g) Post-smoothing: $x_{k+1,h_l} = G_{h_l}^{Po,\mu} \hat{x}_{k+1,h_l}$

   $G_{h_l}^{Po,\mu}$ is the post-smoothing operator (superscript Po) for a certain grid level (subscript h_l) and μ denotes the number of post-smoothing steps, where we choose $\mu = v = 1$ for our calculations.

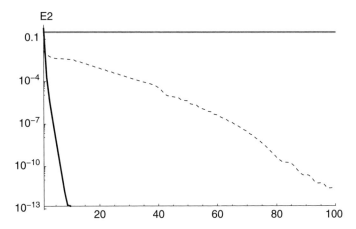

Figure 8.2 A comparison of the convergence rates, measured in terms of ϵ_1, for the multigrid method (black), the conjugate gradient method (black dashed) and the Jacobi iterative method (gray) for the solution of a 2D-Poisson equation on a 65×65 grid using a second order finite difference approximation for the Laplace operator.

A comparison of the convergence rates, measured in terms of ϵ_1 for the multigrid method, the conjugate gradient method and the Jacobi iterative method for the solution of a 2D-Poisson equation on a 65×65 grid using a second order finite difference approximation for the Laplace operator can be seen in Figure 8.2.

We conclude this example by noting that the multigrid method is not restricted to simple discretizations as the one shown here, but can be applied to arbitrarily complex meshes, such as adaptive meshes or mixed finite element meshes.

8.2.4 Preconditioning

Preconditioning refers to the procedure of transforming a problem (by applying the so-called preconditioner) in order to make it more suitable for numerical treatment. More specifically, the rate of convergence for most iterative linear solvers depends on the condition number of the coefficient matrix $\mathbf{A}$. For the matrices considered in this chapter, the condition number c can be computed from their maximum ($\lambda_{\max}(\mathbf{A})$) and minimum ($\lambda_{\min}(\mathbf{A})$) eigenvalues/singular values (depending on whether $\mathbf{A}^T\mathbf{A} = \mathbf{A}\mathbf{A}^T$),

$$c = \left| \frac{\lambda_{\max}(\mathbf{A})}{\lambda_{\min}(\mathbf{A})} \right|. \tag{8.28}$$

Applying a preconditioner reduces the condition number of $\mathbf{A}$, resulting in increased convergence speed of the corresponding iterative method. In place of the linear system (8.2), the preconditioned system

$$\mathbf{B}^{-1}\mathbf{A}\mathbf{x} = \mathbf{B}^{-1}\mathbf{b} \tag{8.29}$$

is then solved. The preconditioned matrix $B^{-1}A$ is hardly ever formed explicitly, typically only the action of B^{-1} on a given vector is needed. Since this operation must be performed in each iteration, its computational cost should be small.[8] Some popular choices for the matrix B are

- Jacobi or diagonal preconditioner $B = \text{diag}(A)$
- Incomplete LU decomposition of A
- Incomplete Cholesky factorization of A
- Multigrid preconditioning.

Preconditioned Conjugate Gradient Method

The conjugate gradient algorithm with a preconditioner B proceeds as follows (note that bold notation is omitted here):

1. Start with a vector $x_0 \in \mathbb{R}^n$ and set $r_0 := b - Ax_0$, $q_0 := B^{-1}r_0$ and $p_0 := q_0$
2. For each iteration k, compute:

$$
\begin{aligned}
a_k &:= \frac{r_k^T q_k}{p_k^T A p_k} \\
x_{k+1} &:= x_k + a_k p_k \\
r_{k+1} &:= r_k - a_k A p_k \\
q_{k+1} &:= B^{-1} r_{k+1} \\
b_k &:= \frac{r_{k+1}^T q_{k+1}}{r_k^T q_k} \\
p_{k+1} &:= q_{k+1} + b_k p_k
\end{aligned}
\tag{8.30}
$$

3. Check convergence.

Depending on the matrix B used for preconditioning, an additional system of linear equations $q_{k+1} := B^{-1}r_{k+1}$ must be solved in each iteration step.

Preconditioned Stabilized Bi-Conjugate Gradient Method

Assuming a preconditioner of the form $B = B_1 B_2$, the algorithm proceeds as follows (bold notation is omitted here)

1. Start with a vector $x_0 \in \mathbb{R}^n$ and set $p_0 := \tilde{r}_0 := r_0 := b - Ax_0$ and calculate $\rho_0 = r_0^T \tilde{r}_0$.

---

[8] The cheapest choice for the preconditioner matrix B is the identity matrix I, resulting in zero reduction of the condition number. The other extreme is $B = A$, resulting in $c = 1$, but the computational cost would be identical to solving the system $Ax = b$ directly.

2. For each iteration k, compute:

$$y_k := B^{-1} p_k$$

$$s_k := A y_k$$

$$\sigma_k := s_k^T \tilde{r}_0$$

$$\alpha_k := \frac{\rho_k}{\sigma_k}$$

$$w_k := r_k - \alpha_k s_k$$

$$z_k := B^{-1} w_k$$

$$v_k := A z_k$$

$$\omega_k := \frac{B_1^{-1} v_k^T B_1^{-1} w_k}{B_1^{-1} v_k^T B_1^{-1} v_k}$$

$$x_{k+1} := x_k - \alpha_k p_k - \omega_k w_k$$

$$r_{k+1} := r_k - \alpha_k s_k - \omega_k v_k$$

$$\rho_{k+1} := r_{k+1}^T \tilde{r}_0$$

$$\beta_k := \frac{\rho_{k+1}}{\rho_k} \frac{\alpha_k}{\omega_k}$$

$$p_{k+1} := r_{k+1} + \beta_k (p_k - \omega_k s_k)$$

(8.31)

3. Check convergence. The algorithm should be stopped before reaching the maximum number of iterations if $||r_{k+1}|| < \varepsilon$, where ε is the desired accuracy.

9

Monte Carlo Simulation

The objective of this chapter is to convey an understanding of the basic principles of Monte Carlo methods, with a particular focus on integration[1] problems. Monte Carlo methods are a class of computational algorithms that rely on stochastic sampling of a (usually high-dimensional) parameter space to achieve an approximation of the desired result. In finance, these methods are used, for instance, in valuating and analyzing instruments, portfolios or investments. The various sources of uncertainty (e.g., the interest rate of a floating rate bond) that affect the result are simulated, a value for each of the simulation paths[2] is computed (e.g., the value of the floating rate bond in each interest rate scenario), and the final value is determined by averaging over the range of outcomes. From a more mathematical viewpoint, each source of uncertainty can be interpreted as a random variable. In probability theory, the expectation (expected value, first moment) of such a random variable is the weighted average of all possible values that this random variable can assume.[3]

9.1 THE PRINCIPLES OF MONTE CARLO INTEGRATION

The integral of a function f can be expressed by a mean value,

$$I = \int_a^b f(x)dx = (b - a)M[f], \tag{9.1}$$

where a and b are the integration limits and $M[f]$ is the mean value of the function over this interval. The basic idea of the Monte Carlo method is to use the sample mean for $M[f]$,

$$M[f] \approx \frac{1}{N} \sum_{i=1}^N f(x_i), \tag{9.2}$$

with N sampling points x_i drawn from a distribution D. With regard to (9.2), the laws of statistics[4] ensure that one would achieve exact results (neglecting rounding errors) in the case $N \to \infty$. As an example, consider the integral of a function f over the unit interval,

$$I = \int_0^1 f(x)dx. \tag{9.3}$$

---

[1] We emphasize that integration in this context also means the solution of an SDE.
[2] Note that in our notation one path can consist of a set of underlying processes describing the aforementioned sources of uncertainty.
[3] The expected value is the integral of the random variable x with respect to its probability measure $v(x)$,

$$E[x] = \int_{-\infty}^\infty x\, v(x)dx.$$

[4] The law of large numbers ensures that this estimate converges to the correct result and the central limit theorem provides information about the likely magnitude of the error in the estimate after a finite number of draws.

We can try to approximate the integral by evaluating f at N uniformly distributed random numbers u_i in the interval $[0; 1]$,

$$\hat{I}_N = \frac{1}{N} \sum_{i=1}^{N} f(u_i). \tag{9.4}$$

Under weak assumptions on f in the unit interval, the law of large numbers mentioned above states that $\hat{I}_N \to I$ with probability 1 if $N \to \infty$ (Glasserman, 2003). If f is also square integrable, we can also calculate

$$\sigma_f^2 = \int_0^1 (f(x) - I)^2 dx, \tag{9.5}$$

and the error $\hat{I}_N - I$ is normally distributed with mean 0 and standard deviation

$$\sigma_f / \sqrt{N}. \tag{9.6}$$

Therefore we obtain for the $\alpha_\%$-confidence interval $[c_-, c_+]$

$$c_\pm = \hat{I}_N \pm \frac{z\sigma_f}{\sqrt{N}}, \tag{9.7}$$

where z is the corresponding value of the standard normal distribution for which the cumulative distribution function is $\Phi(z) = 1 - \alpha/2$ ($\alpha = \alpha_\%/100$; for example $z = 1.96$ for the 95% confidence interval). As σ_f is unknown, we replace it by the sample standard deviation s_f

$$s_f = \sqrt{\frac{1}{N-1} \sum_{i=1}^{N} (f(u_i) - \hat{I}_N)^2}. \tag{9.8}$$

Examining (9.6), we immediately notice that the convergence is worse than the simple trapezoidal rule [$\mathcal{O}(N^{-1/2})$ compared to $\mathcal{O}(N^{-2})$ for differentiable functions]. However, while the convergence rate of the Monte Carlo method is independent of the dimension d of f, the convergence rate of the trapezoidal rule for a d-dimensional function is of order $\mathcal{O}(N^{-2/d})$. This degradation of the convergence rate with an increasing number of dimensions is characteristic for all deterministic integration schemes, and favors the Monte Carlo method for higher-dimensional problems (Glasserman, 2003). Figure 9.1 shows the result of applying the Monte Carlo method to integrate the function $f(x) = x^2$ in $[0; 1]$. Equations (9.4)–(9.8) have been used to calculate the Monte Carlo estimator and the corresponding 95% confidence interval.

9.2 PRICING DERIVATIVES WITH MONTE CARLO METHODS

As discussed in Chapters 2–4, the price of a financial derivative can be obtained by calculating the expectation value of a function depending on a random variate,

$$V = E[g(Z)] = \int_{\mathbb{R}^d} g(z) \, dF_Z(z), \tag{9.9}$$

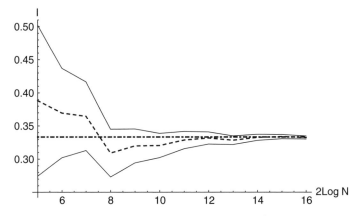

Figure 9.1   The figure shows the result for the integral of $f(x) = x^2$ over the unit interval. The black dashed line indicates the Monte Carlo estimator, the black dot-dashed line marks the exact solution of the problem and the black lines indicate the 95% confidence interval. The number of paths varies between 2^5 and 2^{16}.

where Z is a random variate in $\mathbb{R}^d$ with distribution function F_Z and g a function mapping from $\mathbb{R}^d$ to $\mathbb{R}$.[5] If this expectation value is not analytically available we need numerical values for approximating it.

9.2.1   Discretizing the Stochastic Differential Equation

We recall that the stochastic process X_t is the solution of a stochastic differential equation of the type

$$dX_t = \mu(X_t, t)dt + \sigma(X_t, t)dW_t \quad \text{for} \quad 0 \leq t \leq \text{T}. \tag{9.10}$$

In Chapter 3 we have developed a framework for transforming the SDE into a PDE and solved this PDE by applying different discretization techniques. Now we want to apply discretization schemes to the SDE itself starting with the Euler discretization.[6] Approximations y_j for X_{t_j} are calculated by

$$\Delta W = W_{t_{j+1}} - W_{t_j} = Z\sqrt{\Delta t}, \tag{9.11}$$

$$y_{j+1} = y_j + \mu(y_j, t_j)\Delta t + \sigma(y_j, t_j)\Delta W, \tag{9.12}$$

where we need to specify the initial conditions t_0, $y_0 = X_0$ and $W_0 = 0$, as well as the time increment $\Delta t = T/m$ (m a suitable integer).[7] We call the solution X_t for a given realization of the Wiener process a path or trajectory. The Euler discretization in Equation (9.12) is of order Δt meaning

$$X_t - y_t = \mathcal{O}(h). \tag{9.13}$$

---

[5] In the case of European options, $g(Z)$ would be the payoff of the option and F_Z the risk neutral distribution function of the underlying.

[6] This discretization is the equivalent of the Euler discretization used for ordinary differential equations.

[7] For practical simulations Δt will not be constant, but a time grid will be generated taking into account all relevant dates for the instrument under consideration and a maximal time step length.

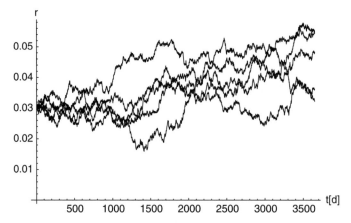

Figure 9.2   The figure shows five different paths for a time discretization ($\Delta t = 1$) of a Vasicek model with $\Theta = 0.005$, $\alpha = 0.1$ and $\sigma = 0.005$.

The algorithm is an explicit method as μ and σ are evaluated at time t_j when calculating the quantities for t_{j+1}. An example of paths for the Vasicek model (one factor Hull-White model with constant parameters), discretized with the Euler scheme is given in Figure 9.2. Higher-order algorithms can again be obtained by using the concept of stochastic Taylor expansions. Using Itô's lemma we state that

$$d\sigma(X_t) = \left(\sigma'(X_t)\, \mu(X_t) + \frac{1}{2}\sigma''(X_t)\, \sigma^2(X_t) \right) dt + \sigma'(X_t)\, \sigma(X_t)\, dW_t.$$

Now we discretize this equation for $s > t$,

$$\sigma(X_s) - \sigma(X_t) = \left(\sigma'(X_t)\, \mu(X_t) + \frac{1}{2}\sigma''(X_t)\, \sigma^2(X_t) \right) (s - t) + \sigma'(X_t)\, \sigma(X_t)\, (W_s - W_t),$$

where we again evaluate the coefficients at the left side t of the time interval $[t, s]$. Since $W_s - W_t$ is of order $\sqrt{s - t}$ for sufficiently small interval length $s - t$, we can approximate

$$\sigma(X_s) \approx \sigma(X_t) + \sigma'(X_t)\, \sigma(X_t)\, (W_s - W_t).$$

Therefore we obtain for $X_{t+\Delta t}$

$$X_{t+\Delta t} \approx X_t + \int_t^{t+\Delta t} \mu(X_s)\, ds + \int_t^{t+\Delta t} \sigma(X_t)\, dW_s + \sigma'(X_t)\, \sigma(X_t) \int_t^{t+\Delta t} (W_s - W_t)\, dW_s.$$

Using

$$\int_0^T W_t\, dW_t = \frac{1}{2} W_T^2 - \frac{T}{2},$$

$$\int_t^{t+\Delta t} (W_s - W_t)\, dW_s = \frac{1}{2}(W_{t+\Delta t} - W_t)^2 - \frac{1}{2}\Delta t = \frac{1}{2}(\Delta W_t)^2 - \frac{1}{2}\Delta t,$$

we obtain the faster converging *Milstein Scheme*.

$$X_{t+\Delta t} \approx X_t + \mu(X_t)\, \Delta t + \sigma(X_t)\, \Delta W_t + \frac{\sigma'(X_t)\, \sigma(X_t)}{2}\, ((\Delta W_t)^2 - \Delta t). \qquad (9.14)$$

9.2.2 Pricing Formalism

The pricing of non-callable instruments with Monte Carlo methods can be implemented in a straight-forward manner:

- Create a time grid with a maximum time step Δt_{max} that includes all relevant dates of the instrument. This step yields a time discretization with $N_{\Delta t}$ points in time and a vector Δt of $(N_{\Delta t} - 1)$ time intervals.
- Start by simulating N independent sample paths, where a single path can be a set of stochastic factors. The rate used for discounting has to be part of the path.[8]
- For each path calculate all M cashflows at the corresponding cashflow dates (maturity date, coupon dates).
- Calculate the discount factors approximating the integral with a simple trapezoidal rule.

$$DF_{i,j} = \exp\left\{ -\int_{T_0}^{T_{C_j}} r(s)ds \right\}$$

$$\approx \Pi_{k=\text{IND}(T_0)}^{\text{IND}(T_{C_j})-1} \exp\left\{ -\frac{1}{2}(r[k] + r[k+1])\Delta t[k] \right\},$$

(9.15)

where T_0 is the valuation date and T_{C_j} is the jth cashflow date. Index i indicates the ith-path. The function IND(.) calculates the index on the time grid for a given point in time.

- Discount each cashflow $CF_{i,j}$[9] with the correct path-dependent discount factor (note that the superscript $\hat{}$ denotes a discounted value).

$$\hat{C}F_{ij} = CF_{ij}DF_{ij}.$$

(9.16)

- Calculate the Monte Carlo estimator V by summing over all discounted cashflows and dividing by the number of sample paths.

$$V = \frac{1}{N}\sum_{i=1}^{N}\sum_{j=1}^{M}\hat{C}F_{ij}.$$

(9.17)

9.2.3 Valuation of a Steepener under a Two Factor Hull-White Model

Instrument Description

A Steepener is a structured financial instrument where the cashflows depend on—often leveraged—differences in the evolution of reference rates with different tenors in one currency. For the example in this section a Steepener instrument with the following properties has been used (again, we ignore nasty details such as coupon basis, business day conventions, ...)

- Coupon: $10 \times 5Y$ EURCMS $- 10 \times 2Y$ EURCMS floored with 0, the first coupon is fixed to 3.5%.
- Coupon fixing: One year in advance
- Coupon frequency: Annually

---

[8] Considering a cross-currency derivative like an FX linked bond one path would consist of a sample of the domestic currency r_d, a sample of the foreign currency r_f and a sample of the corresponding foreign exchange rate f.

[9] Here we assume that the cashflows have the same currency as our spot rate r.

- Instrument start date: 2007-01-01
- Instrument maturity date: 2013-01-01

Path Generation for a Two-Factor Hull-White Model

The two stochastic factors of the two-factor Hull-White model (7.86) are correlated with correlation $\rho = \rho_{ru}$. Applying the formalism for multivariate normals, a Cholesky decomposition of the correlation matrix Ω (note that the volatilities can be pulled out as constant factors),

$$\Omega = \begin{pmatrix} 1 & \rho \\ \rho & 1 \end{pmatrix}, \tag{9.18}$$

is calculated yielding

$$A = \begin{pmatrix} 1 & 0 \\ \rho & \sqrt{1 - \rho^2} \end{pmatrix} \tag{9.19}$$

for the Cholesky factor A. The stochastic differential equations are discretized using the Euler scheme. For a given time discretization ($N_{\Delta t}$ points in time and a vector Δt containing the $N_{\Delta t} - 1$ time intervals) and a given initial value for the spot rate r_0, the path generation for a single path is given in Algorithm 4.

Algorithm 4 Euler discretization of a two-factor Hull-White model (see Chapter 4) using an Euler discretization scheme. The initial value for the spot rate r_0 and a time discretization have to be provided.

$r[0] = r_0$
$u[0] = 0$
for $i = 1 \rightarrow N_{\Delta t} - 1$ **do**
  $X_0 \sim N(0, 1)$
  $X_1 \sim N(0, 1)$
  $Z_0 = X_0$
  $Z_1 = \rho X_0 + \sqrt{1 - \rho^2} X_1$
  $u[i] = u[i - 1] - b\,u[i - 1]\Delta t[i - 1] + \sigma_u[i]\sqrt{\Delta t[i - 1]}Z_1$
  $r[i] = r[i - 1] + (\Theta[i] + u[i] - r[i - 1]\alpha[i])\Delta t[i - 1] + \sigma_r[i]\sqrt{\Delta t[i - 1]}Z_0$
end for

Instrument Valuation

The valuation date for the Steepener is 2007-12-05. The model has been calibrated to a market data set with the yield curve shown in Figure 9.3, the cap data for different maturities and strikes X shown in Figure 9.4, and swaption data displayed in Figure 9.5. The calibration yields a two factor Hull-White model with $b = 0.0461952$, $\alpha = 1.32293$, $\rho = 0.162613$ and σ_r, σ_u and Θ as shown in Figure 9.6. In Figure 9.10, the value of the Steepener as a function of the number of paths used for the Monte Carlo simulation is displayed. As a reference value the

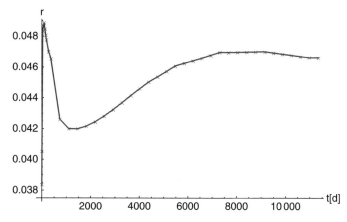

Figure 9.3 Yield curve used for calibration of the Hull-White 2D and the LMM model for the valuation of the Steepener.

solution obtained by solving the PDE with a corresponding terminal condition and Neumann boundaries using the finite element method with streamlined diffusion is given by $V = 101.53$.

9.3 AN INTRODUCTION TO THE LIBOR MARKET MODEL

One of the most widely used interest rate models is the Libor market model (LMM). Unlike the short rate models discussed so far, it captures the dynamics of the entire curve of interest rates by using dynamic Libor forwards as its building blocks. In this section we closely follow

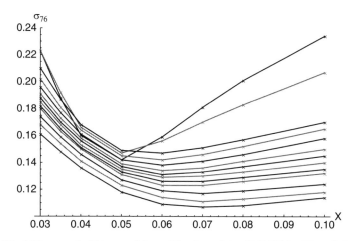

Figure 9.4 Black76 cap volatilities used for calibration of the Hull-White 2D and the LMM model for the valuation of the Steepener. Cap maturities are $1, 2, 3, 4, 5, 6, 7, 8, 9, 10, 12, 15, 20$ years, coupon basis is $30/360$ and the coupon frequency is quarterly for the caps with maturities 1 and 2 years and semi-annual for the rest. Subsequent maturities are presented by alternating black and gray lines with the 1-year cap data starting with the highest value of the Black76 volatility.

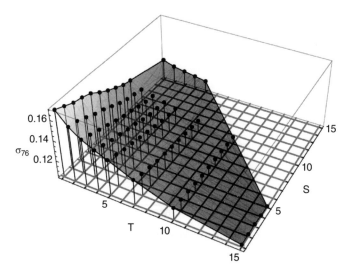

Figure 9.5 Black76 swaption volatilities used for calibration of the Hull-White 2D and the LMM models, for the valuation of the Steepener. Black dots indicate available market data points – T is the expiry date of the swaption and S is the lifetime of the underlying swap with an annual frequency and an $ACT/360$ basis.

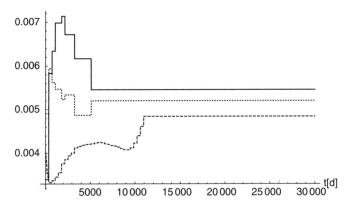

Figure 9.6 Time-dependent model parameters σ_r (black line), σ_u (black dotted line) and Θ (black dashed line) of the calibrated two factor Hull-White model, where Θ is scaled by a factor of $1/10$.

Rebonato's formulation of the LMM (Rebonato, 2009). He introduces the LMM as a set of no-arbitrage conditions among forward rates (or discount bonds) where the precise form of the no-arbitrage conditions depends on the chosen unit of account – the numeraire. It can be shown that these no-arbitrage conditions are functions of the volatilities of, and of the correlations among the forward rates alone. The reason is that the physical origin of the no-arbitrage condition is the covariance between the payoff and the discounting.[10] The stochastic

---

[10] Cashflows can be discounted in several different ways (i.e. we can use several different stochastic numeraires to relate a future payoff to its values today). These different stochastic numeraires will in general co-vary (positively or negatively) with the same payoff in different ways.

discounting may be high when the payoff is high, thus reducing the value today, or vice versa. It is important to stress, however, that the value of a payoff must be independent of the way one chooses to discount it. Therefore, the dynamics of the forward rates must be adjusted to compensate the co-variation in order to obtain a numeraire-independent price.

Libor Market Model Setup

When considering a discrete set of default-free discount bonds, $P_t^i = P(t, T_i)$ a possible choice for the numeraire is the discount bond P_t^i. A generic instantaneous forward rate at time t resetting at time T and paying at time $S = T + \tau$ can be denoted by $f(t, T, T + \tau)$. The N reset times are indexed and numbered from 1 to N: $T_1, T_2, \ldots, T_N$. The payment time for the i-th forward rate coincides with the reset time for the $(i + 1)$-st forward rate yielding

$$F(t, T_i, T_{i+1}) = f_t^i, \quad i = 1, 2, \ldots, N. \tag{9.20}$$

The instantaneous volatilities of the forward rates are denoted by

$$\sigma(t, T_i) = \sigma_t^i, \quad i = 1, 2, \ldots, N. \tag{9.21}$$

and the instantaneous correlation between forward rate i and forward rate j is denoted by

$$\rho(t, T_i, T_j) = \rho_{i,j}^t, \quad i, j = 1, 2, \ldots, N. \tag{9.22}$$

Forward rates and discount bonds are linked via

$$f_t^i = \left(\frac{P_t^i}{P_t^{i+1}} - 1 \right) \frac{1}{\tau_i}, \tag{9.23}$$

with

$$\tau_i = T_{i+1} - T_i, \tag{9.24}$$

where τ_i is the tenor of the forward rate. The description of the (discrete) yield curve is completed by providing the value of the spot rate, i.e., the rate for lending or borrowing from spot time to T_1,

$$r_0 = \left(\frac{1}{P_0^1} - 1 \right) \frac{1}{\tau_1}. \tag{9.25}$$

This setup provides a description of a discrete set of forward rates indexed by a continuous time index. In the deterministic volatility LMM the evolution of the forward rates is described by equations of motion of the form

$$\frac{df_t^i}{f_t^i} = \mu^i(\{\mathbf{f}_t\}, \{\sigma_t\}, \rho, t)dt + \sigma^i(t, T_i)dz_t^i, \tag{9.26}$$

with

$$\mathbb{E}\left[dz_t^i dz_t^j \right] = \rho(t, T_i, T_j)dt. \tag{9.27}$$

Here, $\mathbf{f}_t$ is the vector of spanning forward rates that constitute the yield curve, σ_t is the vector of the associated volatilities and ρ the matrix of the associated correlations. The functions $\sigma^i(t, T_i)$ do not need to be the same for different forward rates, we therefore we use a superscript to

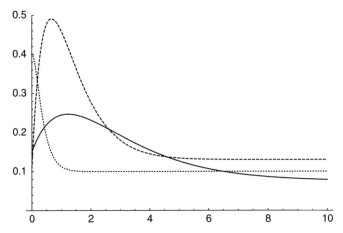

Figure 9.7 The figure shows different possible shapes of the volatility function (9.29) for the LMM. Normal trading periods (humped, black continuous line with parameter set $a = 0.075$, $b = 0.25$, $c = 0.65$, $d = 0.075$ and black dashed line with parameter set $a = -0.02$, $b = 1.5$, $c = 1.5$, $d = 0.13$) as well as a scenario for an excited trading period (monotonically decaying, black dotted line with parameter set $a = 0.3$, $b = 1.6$, $c = 5.0$, $d = 0.1$) are included.

identify the different volatility functions. An LMM is said to be time homogeneous if these functions are identical for all forward rates and if this common function can be expressed in the form

$$\sigma(t, T_i) = \sigma(T_i - t) = \sigma_t^i. \tag{9.28}$$

The superscript i now denotes the dependence on the expiry of the forward rate T_i of the same volatility function for all forward rates. In the time homogeneous formulation, at a given time t the volatilities of two forward rates differ only because they have different times to expiry – i.e., they are at different times of their otherwise identical life, making the smile surface time invariant.[11]

The Volatility Function in the LMM

Among a number of different financially plausible functions satisfying Equation (9.28),

$$\sigma_t^T = [a + b(T - t)] \exp[-c(T - t)] + d = [a + b(\tau)] \exp[-c(\tau)] + d \quad \tau = T - t \tag{9.29}$$

provides a good choice (Rebonato, 2009). Depending on the parameters, humped forms (normal trading periods, see Figure 9.7 black continuous and dashed lines) as well as monotonically decaying (excited trading periods, see Figure 9.7 black dotted line) forms for the volatility are possible. Another desired property is the functions' square integrability,[12] since this type of integral is linked to the pricing of plain vanilla and complex instruments. The different parameters appearing in the above function do have intuitive interpretations: $a + d$ is the value of the instantaneous volatility of any forward rate as its expiry approaches zero and d is the

---

[11] Considering hedging this feature is desirable.
[12] Closed form solutions of the integrals of its square are available.

value of the instantaneous volatility for very long maturities. The maximum of the hump, if the choice of the parameters allows for one, is given by $\bar{\tau} = \frac{1}{c} - \frac{a}{b}$.

Correlation in the LMM

Equation (9.26) can be written in the form

$$\frac{df_t^i}{f_t^i} = \mu^i(\{\mathbf{f}_t\}, \{\sigma_t\}, t)dt + \sum_{k=1}^m \sigma_{ik}dz_k, \tag{9.30}$$

assuming that we are dealing with m ($m \leq N$) factors and that the Brownian increments are independent,

$$\mathbb{E}\left[dz_j dz_k\right] = \delta_{jk}dt, \tag{9.31}$$

with δ_{jk} being the Kronecker delta. Because of the independence,

$$\sigma_i(t) = \sqrt{\sum_{k=1}^m \sigma_{ik}^2(t)}. \tag{9.32}$$

As pointed out above, $\sigma_i(t)$ is up to choice. If it is chosen in such a way that

$$\int_0^{T_i} \sigma_i(t)^2 dt = \hat{\sigma}_i^2 T_i \tag{9.33}$$

holds true, then the market caplets ($\hat{\sigma}$ represents the Black implied volatility) will be correctly priced.[13] By multiplying and dividing each σ_{ik} by the volatility σ_i of the i-th forward rate,

$$\frac{df_t^i}{f_t^i} = \mu^i(\{\mathbf{f}_t\}, \{\sigma_t\}, t)dt + \sigma_i \sum_{k=1}^m \frac{\sigma_{ik}}{\sigma_i}dz_k, \tag{9.34}$$

and using Equation (9.33) to replace σ_i in the denominator,

$$\frac{df_t^i}{f_t^i} = \mu^i(\{\mathbf{f}_t\}, \{\sigma_t\}, t)dt + \sigma_i \sum_{k=1}^m \frac{\sigma_{ik}}{\sqrt{\sum_{k=1}^m \sigma_{ik}^2}}dz_k \tag{9.35}$$

is obtained. Defining the quantity b_{ik} as

$$b_{ik} = \frac{\sigma_{ik}}{\sqrt{\sum_{k=1}^m \sigma_{ik}^2}}, \tag{9.36}$$

the last equation can be expressed in a more succinct way,

$$\frac{df_t^i}{f_t^i} = \mu^i(\{\mathbf{f}_t\}, \{\sigma_t\}, t)dt + \sigma_i \sum_{k=1}^m b_{ik}dz_k. \tag{9.37}$$

A closer look at this equation shows that the stochastic part of the evolution of the forward rate can be decomposed into a component σ_i that only depends on the volatility and the $[N \times m]$

---

[13] This is often referred to as the caplet pricing condition.

matrix $\mathbf{B}$ of elements b_{jk} that only affects the correlation. The corresponding correlation matrix can be written as

$$\mathbf{B}\mathbf{B}^T = \rho. \tag{9.38}$$

For each forward rate and for a given parametrization of the volatility function (such as the one shown in Equation (9.29)), it can be checked whether the integral of the square of the instantaneous volatility does coincide with the total Black variance,[14]

$$\hat{\sigma}_{T_i}^2 T_i = \int_0^T ([a + b(\tau)] \exp[-c(\tau)] + d)^2 d\tau. \tag{9.39}$$

In order to exactly reproduce the prices of all of today's caplets, a different scaling factor is assigned to each forward rate defined by

$$k_{T_i}^2 = \frac{\hat{\sigma}_{T_i}^2 T_i}{\int_0^T ([a + b(\tau)] \exp[-c(\tau)] + d)^2 d\tau}. \tag{9.40}$$

Therefore, the volatility function becomes

$$\sigma_t^i = k_{T_i} \{([a + b(\tau)] \exp[-c(\tau)] + d)\}. \tag{9.41}$$

By introducing this forward-specific scaling factor, the caplet condition is fulfilled by construction along the whole curve.

It remains to find functional forms for the correlation function. The following properties can be observed from market data:

Observation (i) The further apart two forward rates are, the more decorrelated they are.
Observation (ii) The forward curve tends to flatten and correlation increases with large maturities. $\rho_{i,i+p}$ with p constant increases with increasing i.

A very simple form provided by Rebonato (2004) is given by

$$\rho(t, T_i, T_j) = \exp[-\beta|T_i - T_j|], \qquad \beta > 0, \quad t \leq \min(T_i, T_j), \tag{9.42}$$

where expiries of the i-th and j-th forward rate are denoted by T_i and T_j. This equation shows that the further apart two forward rates are, the more de-correlated they are. Parameter β is called the de-correlation factor or the rate of de-correlation. Furthermore, for any positive β, the resulting matrix is real and positive definite. The disadvantage of the form above is that the decorrelation of forward rates only depends on the time span $T_i - T_j$ and is independent of the expiry of the first forward rate (therefore not fulfilling observation (ii)) as can be seen in Figure 9.8. Although empirical results show that this is a very poor approximation, it is widely used because it has a number of computational advantages. In the Libor market model the quantities

$$C(i, j, k) = \int_{T_k}^{T_{k+1}} \sigma_u^i \sigma_u^j \rho(u, T_i, T_j) du \tag{9.43}$$

---

[14] Generally this condition can only be fulfilled for each forward rate if the number of forward rates coincides with the number of parameters chosen for the parametrization of the volatility function. Therefore even in a world without smiles not all Black caplet prices of all the forward rates can be recovered exactly by the model.

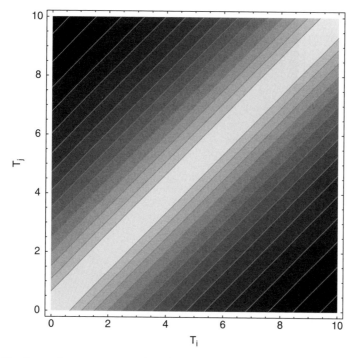

Figure 9.8 The figure shows a contour plot of the one-parameter correlation function (9.42) with $\beta = 0.1$. Whereas correlation decreases for increasing maturity intervals, the correlation of forward rates, separated by the same time span is constant irrespective of the expiry of the first.

play an essential role, as they enter the drift of the forward rates and must be calculated, either implicitly or explicitly, to evaluate any complex payoff. If we do not use explicit time-dependence in our ansatz for the correlation ρ_{ij} and a simple functional form for the instantaneous volatility (which is not possible for forms other than linear) this integral can be pre-calculated, considerably decreasing the computational effort.

Several ways to improve the correlation matrix given in (9.42) exist (Schoenmakers and Coffey, 2000; Doust, 2007). For calibration purposes it is advantageous to keep the number of parameters used for constructing the correlation matrix as low as possible. The classical two-parameter parameterization of the correlation functional is given by,

$$\rho_{i,j} = \rho_\infty + (1 - \rho_\infty)\exp\{-\beta|T_i - T_j|\}, \tag{9.44}$$

where $-1 \le \rho_\infty \le 1$ and $\beta \ge 0$. De-correlation of forward rates with increasing distance does not tend towards zero, but towards ρ_∞ instead. ρ_∞ represents the asymptotic correlation between the rates with highest distance. Requirement (ii) above is still not fulfilled in this setup. To also fulfill condition (ii), Rebonato (2004) suggested the following three parameter correlation functional,

$$\rho_{i,j} = \rho_\infty + (1 - \rho_\infty)\exp\left\{-\beta_0 \exp\{-\beta_1 \min(T_1, T_j)\}|T_i - T_j|\right\}, \tag{9.45}$$

Where $-1 \le \rho_\infty \le 1$ and $\beta_0 \ge 0$ and $\beta_1 \in \mathbb{R}$. Again the minimum correlation asymptotically tends towards ρ_∞ and the expression $-\beta_1 \min(T_1, T_j)$ controls the rate of decay. Figure 9.9

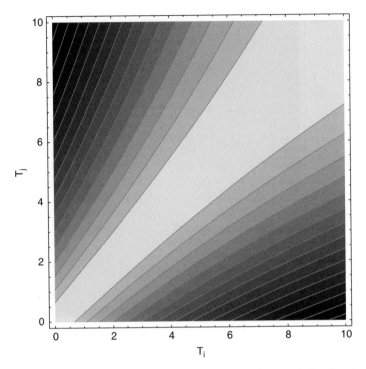

Figure 9.9 The figure shows a contour plot of the three parameter correlation function (9.45) with $\beta_0 = 0.1$, $\beta_1 = 0.2$ and $\rho_\infty = 0$. Correlation decreases for increasing maturity intervals and the correlation of forward rates, separated by the same time span, is increasing with an extension of the expiry date of the first.

shows that the correlation between forward rates with identical time span depends on the expiry of the first forward rate.

A Steepener Under the Libor Market Model

The Steepener instrument described in section 9.2.3 is valuated under a Libor market model calibrated to the same market data as the two-factor Hull-White model before, obtaining the parameters $a = 2.72067$, $b = 0.871985$, $c = 1.21931$ and $d = 4.94402$ for the volatility function (9.29) and $\beta_0 = 0.01$ and $\beta_1 = 0.01$ for the correlation function (9.45) (note that $\rho_\infty = 0$). Figure 9.10 shows the Steepener values obtained under the two-factor Hull-White model (gray squares) and the Libor market model (black circles).

9.4 RANDOM NUMBER GENERATION

As can be concluded from the previous section, the evaluation of an integral with the Monte Carlo method requires sets of numbers with specific distributions.[15] Optimally, these numbers

---

[15] Random number generation is the core of a Monte Carlo simulation. Usually, uniformly distributed random numbers are generated and then transformed to the desired distribution.

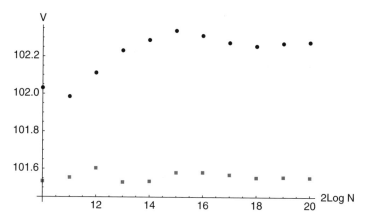

Figure 9.10   The figure shows the values of the Steepener instrument described in section 9.2.3 obtained under the two factor Hull-White model (gray squares) and the Libor market model (black circles) using Monte Carlo simulation. N is the number of paths used for the simulation.

should be drawn randomly, a task that is impossible with computers. The generation of "random numbers" on computers is performed in an entirely deterministic and predictable way – therefore they are often called pseudo-random numbers. Nevertheless, we will use the term "random numbers" for these computer-generated numbers and will treat them as if they were genuinely random. This assumption allows us to use tools from the field of statistics and probability theory to analyze the Monte Carlo computations. We define the *process of the generation of genuinely uniformly distributed random numbers* as a mechanism that produces a sequence of "random" numbers x_i that obey the following properties:

(i) the x_i are uniformly distributed in the unit interval,
(ii) the x_i are mutually independent.

While (i) can be achieved by normalization, (ii) means that all pairs of numbers must be uncorrelated such that it is not possible to predict the value of x_i from the values of $x_1, \dots, x_{i-1}$.

There is a vast amount of literature covering uniform and nonuniform random variate generation in detail, see, for example, Gentle (2003). In the following, we will give a short overview of the most important methods.

9.4.1   Properties of a Random Number Generator

In most cases, the reader of this book will not have to implement a random number generator herself, but will be able to use existing routines and libraries. Here, we list a number of key points that should be kept in mind when deciding which algorithm to use for random number generation:

- Periodicity: All random number generators will eventually repeat themselves. Therefore, all else being equal, algorithms with a longer periodicity are preferred.
- Reproducibility: Often, simulations have to be rerun, or different simulations have to be run using exactly the same samples.

- Speed: Since random number generators are regularly called several millions of times in a single simulation, execution speed must be fast.
- Portability: All else being equal, a random number generator should give identical samples (within machine precision and neglecting rounding errors) on different computing platforms. Since many implementations of random number generators rely on machine specific number representations, for example on the way overflows are handled by the system, this task can be hard to achieve.
- Randomness: As pointed out above, the computer implementation of a random number generator follows a strictly deterministic way. Therefore, differences in the quality of mimicking randomness arise for different random number generators. Theoretical aspects as well as statistical properties of the generated random numbers should be taken into account for comparison.

9.4.2   Uniform Variates

Linear congruental generators, first proposed by Lehmer (1951), form the standard approach for calculating uniform variates.

Algorithm 5   The number N_0 is called the seed. The algorithm ensures that $x_i \in [0; 1)$ and the x_i will be taken as uniform variates. Whether they are suitable in the sense of the properties listed above depends on a, b and M.

Require: Choose M
Require: Choose a $\in 1, \ldots, M-1$
Require: Choose b $\in 0, \ldots, M-1$
Require: Choose $N_0 \in 0, \ldots, M-1$
  for $i = 1, 2, \ldots$ **do**
    $N_i = \mathrm{mod}(aN_{i-1} + b, M)$
    $x_i = N_i/M$
  end for

Obviously, the numbers N_i defined in Algorithm 5 are periodic with a period $p \leq M$. It is important to note that a number of settings for the parameters a, b and the seed N_0 need to be excluded: For instance, $b = 0$ in combination with $N_0 = 0$ would lead to a sequence of zeros, or the case $a = 1$ would produce the easy to predict sequence $N_n = \mathrm{mod}(N_0 + nb, M)$. A set of simple conditions is available that ensures the generator has full period ($p = M - 1$). Following Knuth (1998), these conditions are (assuming $b \neq 0$):

(i) b and M are relatively prime,
(ii) every prime number that divides M divides $a - 1$,
(iii) $a - 1$ is divisible by 4 if M is.

To examine the properties of a linear congruental generator, we use the following one-liner in Mathematica:

```
LCG[N0_, n_, a_, M_]:=Module[{t, s = N0},For[A ={N0};i = 1, i <= n, i++,
t = Mod[a*s, M]; A = Append[A, t];s = t]]
```

Depending on the starting value N_0, we obtain the following sequences A_{N_0} with parameters $a = 6$, $b = 0$ and $M = 11$:

$$A_1 = \{1, 6, 3, 7, 9, 10, 5, 8, 4, 2, 1\}$$
$$A_2 = \{2, 1, 6, 3, 7, 9, 10, 5, 8, 4, 2\}$$
$$A_3 = \{3, 7, 9, 10, 5, 8, 4, 2, 1, 6, 3\}$$
$$A_4 = \{4, 2, 1, 6, 3, 7, 9, 10, 5, 8, 4\}$$
$$A_5 = \{5, 8, 4, 2, 1, 6, 3, 7, 9, 10, 5\}$$
$$A_6 = \{6, 3, 7, 9, 10, 5, 8, 4, 2, 1, 6\}$$
$$A_7 = \{7, 9, 10, 5, 8, 4, 2, 1, 6, 3, 7\}$$
$$A_8 = \{8, 4, 2, 1, 6, 3, 7, 9, 10, 5, 8\}$$
$$A_9 = \{9, 10, 5, 8, 4, 2, 1, 6, 3, 7, 9\}$$
$$A_{10} = \{10, 5, 8, 4, 2, 1, 6, 3, 7, 9, 10\}.$$

Once a value is repeated, of course the whole sequence will repeat. Independent of the choice of N_0, $M - 1 = 10$ distinct numbers are generated. If we set the multiplier $a = 3$ we obtain

$$A_1 = \{1, 3, 9, 5, 4, 1, 3, 9, 5, 4, 1\}$$
$$A_2 = \{2, 6, 7, 10, 8, 2, 6, 7, 10, 8, 2\}$$
$$A_3 = \{3, 9, 5, 4, 1, 3, 9, 5, 4, 1, 3\}$$
$$A_4 = \{4, 1, 3, 9, 5, 4, 1, 3, 9, 5, 4\}$$
$$A_5 = \{5, 4, 1, 3, 9, 5, 4, 1, 3, 9, 5\}$$
$$A_6 = \{6, 7, 10, 8, 2, 6, 7, 10, 8, 2, 6\}$$
$$A_7 = \{7, 10, 8, 2, 6, 7, 10, 8, 2, 6, 7\}$$
$$A_8 = \{8, 2, 6, 7, 10, 8, 2, 6, 7, 10, 8\}$$
$$A_9 = \{9, 5, 4, 1, 3, 9, 5, 4, 1, 3, 9\}$$
$$A_{10} = \{10, 8, 2, 6, 7, 10, 8, 2, 6, 7, 10\}.$$

Now two cycles are generated independent of the seed N_0. It has been shown by Marsaglia (see Marsaglia (1972) and references therein), that no additional generality is achieved by applying the condition $b \neq 0$, but on the other hand, choosing $b \neq 0$ slows the execution speed. Therefore, most modern generators set $b = 0$ and M prime. As we have seen in the example above, these settings do not ensure that the resulting sequence of random numbers has full period. Full period for $b = 0$, $M = 11$ and $N_0 \neq 0$ can only be achieved if

- $a^{M-1} - 1$ is a multiple of M and
- $a^j - 1$ is not a multiple of M for $j = 1, \ldots, M - 2$.

A common choice for 32-bit computers is $M = 2^{31} - 1$, $a = 16807$ and $b = 0$. Several statistical tests can be performed to assess the quality of the generated random numbers. The most basic test is to compare the known moments of the desired distribution with the moments evaluated from the sample. Another simple test is to check for correlations, e.g., whether small numbers are likely to be followed by other small numbers. A histogram allows us to

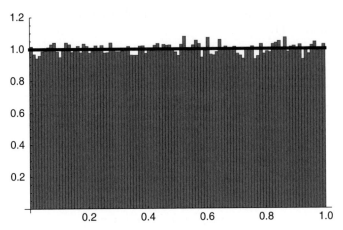

Figure 9.11   The histogram shows the relative frequency of 100 000 uniformly distributed random numbers. The bin width is 0.01. The thick line indicates the theoretical distribution function.

check how well the probability distribution function is approximated. An example is provided in Figure 9.11 for the uniform distribution. To complement these basic tests, Marsaglia has published the so-called "Diehard" tests, a battery of statistical tests for measuring the quality of a random number generator (http://www.stat.fsu.edu/pub/diehard/). A different test suite has been implemented by the National Institute of Standards and Technology (NIST) of the USA (Rukhin et al. 2001). The most recently published test environment for uniform random number generators is the TestU01 software library (L'Ecuyer and Simard, 2007), which offers several different random number generators and a collection of utilities for their empirical statistical testing.

9.4.3   Random Vectors

Uniformly distributed random numbers x_1, x_2, ... can be used to form d-dimensional tuples $(x_i, x_{i+1}, \ldots, x_{i+d-1})$, which can be analyzed with respect to their correlation and distribution. One can, for instance, measure how uniformly the tuples fill $[0, 1]^d$, a process we illustrate here using a simple 2D example. Figure 9.12 shows consecutive overlapping pairs (x_1, x_2), $(x_2, x_3) \ldots$, (x_{10}, x_{11}) produced by the linear congruental algorithm (Algorithm 5) with parameters $a = 6$, $b = 0$, $M = 11$ and seed $N_0 = 1$. They obviously form a regular pattern, where the ten distinct points obtained from the full period of the random number generator lie on just two lines through the unit square. This behavior is inherent to all linear congruental random number generators. Marsaglia showed (1968) that overlapping d-tuples formed from the consecutive output of a linear congruental random number generator with parameter M lie on at most $(d!M)^{1/d}$ hyperplanes in the d-dimensional unit cube. For $d = 3$ and $M = 2^{31} - 1$ this yields approximately 108 planes, a number that drops to below 39 for $d = 10$. As a consequence, for higher dimensions the lattice structure of random numbers generated by linear congruental generators clearly distinguishes them from genuinely random numbers, even for optimal parameter settings.

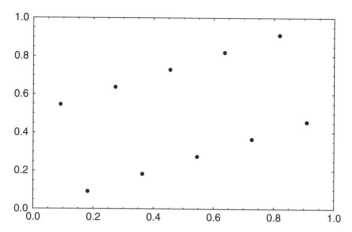

Figure 9.12   Plot of consecutive overlapping pairs (x_i, x_{i+1}). A regular pattern, which is inherent in all linear congruental generators, can be clearly identified.

9.4.4   Recent Developments in Random Number Generation

Compared to modern random number generators, the linear congruental method shows poor randomness if huge amounts of random numbers or higher dimensional random vectors are needed. A very popular modern algorithm for uniformly distributed random number generation is the Mersenne Twister, a pseudo-random number generator developed by Matsumoto and Nishimura (1998), which is based on a matrix linear recurrence over a finite binary field. The period of the commonly used variant of the Mersenne Twister[16] is $p = 2^{19937} - 1$, which is a Mersenne prime number and has given the algorithm its name. The random numbers produced with the Mersenne Twister pass numerous tests for statistical randomness, including the Diehard tests. They also pass most, but not all, of the more stringent TestU01 Crush randomness tests (L'Ecuyer and Simard, 2007). It is worth noting that the Mersenne Twister uses either linear congruental or Fibonacci-based random number generators for the seeding process.

Though widely used, the Mersenne Twister has been criticized as being too complex and too sensitive to poor initialization. Marsaglia has provided several alternatives, which are less complex and provide significantly larger periods. For instance, a simple complementary multiply-with-carry generator has been reported to have a period 10^{33000} times as long, while being significantly faster and achieving better or equal randomness (Marsaglia, 2003).

A different group of algorithms is based on Controllable Cellular Automata which evolve a state vector of 0s and 1s according to a deterministic rule. For a given cellular automaton, an element (or cell) at a given position in the new state vector is determined by specific neighbouring cells of that cell in the old state vector. A subset of cells of the state vectors is then output as random bits from which the pseudo-random numbers are generated (see, for example, the Mathematica Documentation).

Readers interested in further details of random number generation are referred to L'Ecuyer and Simard (2007) as a good starting point. There are more than 200 different random number

---

[16] The commonly used variant of the Mersenne Twister is named MT19937, with 32-bit word length. There is also a variant with 64-bit word length, MT19937-64, which generates a different sequence.

generators included in TestU01, and the documentation contains a wealth of information as well as important references for the various methods.

9.4.5 Transforming Variables

Simulation algorithms regularly need random numbers or random vectors drawn from a specific distribution. These can be generated by transforming samples from the uniform distribution to samples from the desired distribution. A vast amount of literature is available on general purpose methods as well as on algorithms for specific special cases.

Inversion

Suppose we want a random sample x from the cumulative distribution function F. Let us draw a random number from the uniform distribution,

$$u \sim U[0, 1], \tag{9.46}$$

and use the inverse of F to calculate

$$x = F^{-1}(u), \tag{9.47}$$

where x is now distributed according to the probability density f of the cumulative distribution F. The inverse of F is well-defined if F is monotonically increasing.[17] Otherwise, a unique definition of the inverse can be accomplished by applying a rule like

$$F^{-1}(u) = \inf\{x : F(x) \geq u\}. \tag{9.48}$$

Although the inverse transform method is hardly ever the fastest method to obtain samples from a certain distribution, a desirable feature is the monotonicity and – in the case of a strictly increasing distribution function – continuous mapping of the input u to the output x (see for example Figure 9.13 for the application of the inversion method to sample from the standard normal distribution). This can be important when increasing the efficiency of the Monte Carlo simulation using variance reduction techniques (Glasserman, 2003).

Transformation Methods

As indicated by their name, transformation methods use transformations between random variables. Assume X is a random variable with known density $f(x)$ and distribution $F_X(x)$, and $h : A \rightarrow B$ is a strictly monotonous function, where A, $B \subseteq \mathbb{R}$ and h is zero outside of A. Then, we can state that

(a) $Y = h(X)$ is a random variable. If $h' > 0$, its distribution is

$$F_Y(y) = F_X(h^{-1}(y)).$$

---

[17] The assumption that F is even strictly monotonically increasing would allow a transformation in both directions. Obviously, if we start from the uniform distribution [0; 1] it is also possible to generate discrete random numbers like $1, 2, 3, 4, 5, 6$ by dividing the unit interval into six parts.

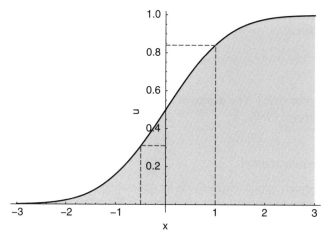

Figure 9.13   The application of the inverse transform method to the normal distribution. The continuous line shows the cumulative distribution function of the normal distribution. $u = 0.84$ maps to $x = 1$ and $u = 0.31$ maps to $x = -0.5$ (dashed).

(b) If h^{-1} is absolutely continuous, then for almost all y the density of $h(X)$ is

$$h(X) = f(h^{-1}(y)) \left| \frac{dh^{-1}(y)}{dy} \right|. \tag{9.49}$$

Considering the uniform distribution for F_X, the density function is

$$f(x) = \begin{cases} 1 & x \in [0; 1] \\ 0 & \text{else} \end{cases}. \tag{9.50}$$

To find random numbers Y for a pre-specified density $g(y)$ we need to find a transformation h such that $g(y)$ is identical to the density in (9.49).

As an example, consider the exponential distribution with parameter $\lambda > 0$, whose density is given by

$$g(y) = \begin{cases} \lambda \exp\{-\lambda y\} & \text{for} \quad y \geq 0 \\ 0 & \text{for} \quad y < 0 \end{cases}. \tag{9.51}$$

We now seek to generate an exponentially distributed random variable Y out of a uniformly distributed one. The transformation from the unit interval to $\mathbb{R}^+$,

$$y = h(x) = -\frac{1}{\lambda} \ln(x), \tag{9.52}$$

with its inverse function,

$$h^{-1}(y) = \exp\{-\lambda y\} \quad \text{for} \quad y > 0, \tag{9.53}$$

is inserted into (9.49) resulting in

$$f(h^{-1}(y)) \left| \frac{dh^{-1}(y)}{dy} \right| = 1 \cdot \left| \frac{dh^{-1}(y)}{dy} \right| = \lambda \exp\{-\lambda y\} = g(y) \tag{9.54}$$

for the density of $h(X)$; $(h(X)$ is therefore distributed exponentially). Then, if U_i is a nonuniform random variate,

$$-\frac{1}{\lambda} \ln(U_i)$$

is exponentially distributed. The theory of transformation methods in higher dimensions is examined in (Devroye, 1986).

Acceptance-Rejection Method

One of the most widely applicable methods for generating random samples is the acceptance-rejection method (see Algorithm 6) introduced by von Neumann (Knuth, 1998). In this method, two different distributions are used – the target distribution $\mathcal{F}$ with density function $f(x)$, and a second distribution $\mathcal{G}$ with density function $g(x)$ for which the generation of random numbers is more convienient.[18] Furthermore, we assume that

$$\sup_x \left\{ \frac{f(x)}{g(x)} \right\} \leq c \tag{9.55}$$

where $c > 0$ is a constant. In a concrete implementation, we would like c to be as close to 1 as possible. A deficiency of most acceptance-rejection methods is the fact that there is no upper bound on the number of uniforms required to get a specific random variable of the desired distribution. This prohibits their use in Quasi Monte Carlo simulations – where the number of variates to generate is an input to the algorithm calculating the low discrepancy sequences.

Algorithm 6   Acceptance-rejection algorithm for continuous random variables. In a first step, random numbers for the convenient distribution are generated. Then, random subsets of the generated candidates are rejected. The rejection mechanism is designed in a way that the remaining accepted samples are indeed distributed according to the target distribution. The probability of acceptance on each attempt is $1/c$. This technique is not restricted to univariate distributions.

Require: Generate a random variate $X \sim \mathcal{G}$
Require: Generate a random variate $U \sim [0, 1]$ independent of X
  if $U \leq \frac{f(X)}{cg(X)}$ **then**
    return X (accept)
  else
    reject
  end if

---

[18] We assume that we already have an efficient algorithm for generating random variates from $\mathcal{G}$, for example the inverse transform method.

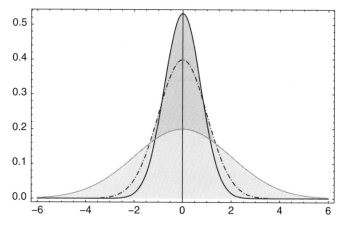

Figure 9.14   The probability density function for the normal distribution for three different settings of the standard deviation σ (dark gray: $\sigma = 0.75$, hatched: $\sigma = 1$ (standard normal distribution), pale gray: $\sigma = 2$) for $\mu = 0$.

9.4.6   Random Number Generation for Commonly Used Distributions

Normal Random Numbers

For many financial applications, normally distributed random variates are required. We use the notation $X \sim N(\mu, \sigma^2)$ to indicate that the random variable X is normally distributed with mean μ and variance σ^2. Such a sample is connected to the standard normal distribution $Z \sim N(0, 1)$ (see Figure 9.14) by

$$\mu + \sigma Z \sim N(\mu, \sigma^2). \tag{9.56}$$

A very simple method to generate normally distributed random numbers is the Box-Muller algorithm. It generates a sample from the bivariate standard normal distribution where each component can therefore be considered as a random number drawn from a univariate standard normal distribution.

Suppose U_1 and U_2 are independent uniformly distributed random variables in the interval $[0; 1]$ and

$$R^2 = -2 \log(U_1), \tag{9.57}$$
$$\Theta = 2\pi U_2. \tag{9.58}$$

Then,[19]

$$Z_1 = R \cos(\Theta), \tag{9.59}$$
$$Z_2 = R \sin(\Theta), \tag{9.60}$$

are independent random variables drawn from a standard normal distribution. A major drawback of this basic algorithm is the use of trigonometric functions, which are comparatively expensive in many computing environments. Several alternatives have been proposed, for

---

[19] R^2 is the square of the norm of the standard bivariate normal variable, and is therefore chi-squared distributed with two degrees of freedom. In the special case of two degrees of freedom, the chi-squared distribution coincides with the exponential distribution.

instance the implementation of the algorithm in the so-called polar form (Marsaglia and Bray, 1964; Bell, 1968) using acceptance-rejection techniques to sample points in the unit disc, which are then transformed to normal variables. For example the algorithm of Marsaglia and Bray (1964) (Algorithm 7) generates U_1 and U_2 uniformly distributed over the square $[-1; 1] \times [-1; 1]$ by applying the transformation

$$U_1 = 2\hat{U}_1 - 1, \tag{9.61}$$
$$U_2 = 2\hat{U}_2 - 1 \tag{9.62}$$

where $\hat{U}_1 \sim U[0, 1]$ and $\hat{U}_2 \sim U[0, 1]$. Then, with

$$R^2 = U_1^2 + U_2^2, \tag{9.63}$$

only points for which $R^2 \leq 1$ are accepted, producing points uniformly distributed over a disk with radius 1 centered at the origin. The pairs (U_1, U_2) can be projected from the unit disk to the unit circle by division through R. Following the argumentation of the Box-Muller algorithm we end up with Algorithm 7.

Algorithm 7   Marsaglia-Bray algorithm for generating normal random variables.

---

while $(R > 1)$ **do**
  Generate $U_1\,U_2 \sim$ Uniform $[0; 1]$
  $U_1 = 2U_1 - 1$
  $U_2 = 2U_2 - 1$
  $R^2 = U_1^2 + U_2^2$
end while
$X = \sqrt{-2 \log R^2 / R^2}$
$Z_1 = U_1 X$
$Z_2 = U_2 X$

The most widely used method for sampling from a standard normal distribution is to approximate the inverse normal. Different numerical implementations with different degrees of accuracy and efficiency are available. A recently published paper by Shaw, Luu and Brickman (2011) presents the differential equations and solution methods for approximating inverse functions of the form (9.47). According to Jäckel (2002), the most accurate whilst still highly efficient implementation for single precision is provided by Peter Acklam. Another widely used implementation is the improved version of the Beasley and Springer method (1977) by Moro (1995). For double precision implementations, we suggest to use the algorithm provided by Wichura (1988). In Table 9.1, a number of different implementations of inversion algorithms for single as well as double precision are compared. Details of the implementation can be found in (Shaw, Luu and Brickman, 2011). All accuracy comparisons are made against the algorithm provided by the Boost library ("www.boost.org") – their implementations of the inverse of the cumulative normal distribution guarantee an accuracy of 10^{-19} at the cost of low execution speed.

Table 9.1   The table shows different properties of several methods implementing an approximation for the inverse of the cumulative normal distribution function. All accuracy comparisons are made against the algorithm provided by the Boost library (www.boost.org). The first row indicates the different algorithms – gsl (gnu scientific library), acklam (a highly efficient implementation for single precision provided by Peter Acklam), bsm (Moro's improvement of the Beasley and Springer algorithm (Moro, 1995)), Giles and Shaw different variants for approximating the inverse cumulative function (Shaw, Luu and Brickman, 2011, Giles, 2010), wichura (implementations presented by Wichura (1988) for single and double precision). The overall sample size for the numerical experiment has been $5 \cdot 10^7$ – time needed for generation is given by T measured in ms. x is the speed factor comparing each implementation with the implementation of Acklam (the fastest of the algorithms tested), without taking into account the accuracy. The remaining rows show the fractions (in %) of the sample which have an error (absolute of the difference to the corresponding value obtained with the Boost algorithm) in the indicated range. This serves as an indicator for the quality of the algorithm used. All algorithms with a fraction of 100% in the last row are suited to use in a double precision implementation of a Monte Carlo algorithm.

Method	gsl	acklam	bsm	giles1	giles2	shaw1	shaw3	wichura1	wichura2
T	2183	814.1	1191	4486	2464	3904	2892	1545	982.7
x	2.7	1	1.5	5.5	3	4.8	3.6	1.9	1.2
$10^{-7} \geq e > 10^{-8}$	0.00	0.00	0.00	0.00	14.37	0.00	0.01	0.00	10.07
$10^{-8} \geq e > 10^{-9}$	0.00	0.00	0.00	0.00	61.88	0.00	50.74	0.00	56.31
$10^{-9} \geq e > 10^{-10}$	0.00	18.82	38.65	0.00	20.58	0.00	40.99	0.00	28.34
$10^{-10} \geq e > 10^{-11}$	0.00	60.65	42.67	0.00	2.86	0.00	6.22	0.00	4.76
$10^{-11} \geq e > 10^{-12}$	0.00	18.34	16.02	0.00	0.28	0.00	1.88	0.00	0.47
$10^{-12} \geq e > 10^{-13}$	0.00	1.98	2.40	0.00	0.03	0.00	0.13	0.00	0.05
$10^{-13} \geq e > 10^{-14}$	0.00	0.20	0.23	0.00	0.00	0.00	0.01	0.00	0.00
$10^{-14} \geq e$	100.00	0.02	0.03	100.00	0.00	100.00	0.00	100.00	0.00

Multivariate Normals

A d-dimensional normal distribution $N(\mu, \Sigma)$ is characterized by a vector μ with dimension d and the covariance matrix Σ with dimension $d \times d$. The covariance matrix must be symmetric and positive semi-definite.[20] The entries of the covariance matrix are connected to the correlation between two random variables X_i and X_j via the marginal standard deviations

$$\Sigma_{ij} = \sigma_i \sigma_j \rho_{ij}, \tag{9.64}$$

or, in matrix form,

$$\Sigma = \begin{pmatrix} \sigma_1 & & \\ & \sigma_2 & \\ & & \ddots \\ & & & \sigma_d \end{pmatrix} \begin{pmatrix} \rho_{11} & \rho_{12} & \cdots & \rho_{1d} \\ \rho_{21} & \rho_{22} & & \rho_{2d} \\ \vdots & & \ddots & \vdots \\ \rho_{d1} & \rho_{d2} & \cdots & \rho_{dd} \end{pmatrix} \begin{pmatrix} \sigma_1 & & \\ & \sigma_2 & \\ & & \ddots \\ & & & \sigma_d \end{pmatrix}. \tag{9.65}$$

Using the linear transformation property,[21] we know that if $Z \sim N(0, I)$ and $X = \mu + AZ$ then $X \sim N(\mu, AA^T)$. The problem of finding X drawn from the multivariate normal $N(\mu, \Sigma)$

---

[20] A real matrix M is symmetric if $M = M^T$ and positive semi-definite if $x^T M x \geq 0$ for all $x \in \mathbb{R}$.
[21] Any linear transformation of a normal vector is again normal

$$X \sim N(\mu, \Sigma) \rightarrow AX \sim N(A\mu, A\Sigma A^T),$$

where μ is a d-dimensional vector, A is a $d \times d$ matrix and A is a $n \times d$ matrix.

Table 9.2 The table shows different properties of several methods implementing an approximation for the inverse of the gamma distribution function for a shape parameter $\alpha = 0.8$. All comparisons are made against the algorithm provided by the BOOST library (DiDonato and Alfred, 1986) (www.boost.org). The first row indicates the different algorithms – gsl (gnu scientific library), power sum100 (Steinbrecher and Shaw, 2007) (the inverse function is approximated by a polynomial approximation – the number of summands used for approximation is 100), power sum40 (the same algorithm like before but the number of summands is reduced to 40), halley it2 (inversion is performed using Halley's cubic convergence method for root finding – two iterations have been performed), nr it5 (implementation of the inversion using a Newton Raphson method with five iterations). The overall sample size for the numerical experiment has been $5 \cdot 10^7$ – time needed for generation is given by T measured in *ms*. x is the speed factor comparing each implementation with the power sum 100 implementation, without taking into account the accuracy. The remaining rows show the fractions (in %) of the sample which have an error (absolute of the difference to the corresponding value obtained with the Boost algorithm) in the indicated range. This serves as an indicator for the quality of the algorithm used.

Method	gsl	power sum100	power sum40	halley it2	nr it5
t	11.5	0.331	0.182	1.16	2.887
T	575903	16534.4	9124.91	57988.2	144030
x	35	1	0.55	3.5	8.7
$10^{-0} \geq e > 10^{-1}$	0.00	0.20	0.50	0.24	3.04
$10^{-1} \geq e > 10^{-2}$	0.00	0.97	2.37	1.33	0.66
$10^{-2} \geq e > 10^{-3}$	0.00	1.33	3.22	2.29	2.74
$10^{-3} \geq e > 10^{-4}$	0.00	1.47	3.47	3.05	5.50
$10^{-4} \geq e > 10^{-5}$	0.00	1.53	3.52	3.61	4.93
$10^{-5} \geq e > 10^{-6}$	0.00	1.55	3.48	4.00	4.03
$10^{-6} \geq e > 10^{-7}$	0.00	1.55	3.40	4.23	5.37
$10^{-7} \geq e > 10^{-8}$	0.00	1.55	3.31	4.30	6.09
$10^{-8} \geq e > 10^{-9}$	0.00	1.54	3.21	4.24	3.99
$10^{-9} \geq e > 10^{-10}$	0.00	1.52	3.09	4.05	4.56
$10^{-10} \geq e > 10^{-11}$	0.00	1.50	2.98	3.75	4.84
$10^{-11} \geq e > 10^{-12}$	0.00	1.48	2.86	3.36	4.87
$10^{-12} \geq e > 10^{-13}$	0.00	1.46	2.76	2.88	4.73
$10^{-13} \geq e > 10^{-14}$	0.03	1.44	2.65	2.33	4.49
$10^{-14} \geq e$	99.97	80.93	59.18	56.33	40.14

is reduced to the problem of finding an appropriate matrix A for which $AA^T = \Sigma$, since the vector of independent standard normal random variables Z can be generated using any of the methods discussed above. The Cholesky factorization discussed in Chapter 8 provides such a factorization of Σ with A being lower triangular. Note that a Cholesky factorization of Σ exists only if the matrix is positive definite. The fact that A is lower triangular is convenient because it reduces the effort of calculating $\mu + AZ$ to

$$
\begin{aligned}
X_1 &= \mu_1 + A_{11}Z_1, \\
X_2 &= \mu_2 + A_{21}Z_1 + A_{22}Z_2, \\
&\vdots \\
X_d &= \mu_d + A_{d1}Z_1 + A_{d2}Z_2 + \cdots + A_{dd}Z_d.
\end{aligned}
\tag{9.66}
$$

Table 9.3 The table shows different properties of several methods implementing an approximation for the inverse of the gamma distribution function for a shape parameter $\alpha = 0.08$. All comparisons are made against the algorithm provided by the BOOST library (DiDonato and Alfred, 1986) (www.boost.org). The first row indicates the different algorithms – the gsl (gnu scientific library) could not handle the inversion therefore it has not been included in the comparison of the algorithms for $\alpha = 0.08$, power sum100 (Steinbrecher and Shaw, 2007) (the inverse function is approximated by a polynomial approximation – the number of summands used for approximation is 100), power sum40 (the same algorithm as before but the number of summands is reduced to 40), halley it2 (inversion is performed using Halley's cubic convergence method for root finding – two iterations have been performed), nr it5 (implementation of the inversion using a Newton Raphson method with five iterations). t gives the time needed to obtain a single normally distributed random number from a uniformly distributed one – time is measured μs. The overall sample size for the numerical experiment has been $5 \cdot 10^7$ – time needed for generation is given by T measured in ms. x is the speed factor comparing each implementation with the power sum 100 implementation, without taking into account the accuracy. The remaining rows show the fractions (in %) of the sample which have an error (absolute of the difference to the corresponding value obtained with the Boost algorithm) in the indicated range. This serves as an indicator for the quality of the algorithm used.

Method	power sum100	power sum40	halley it2	nr it5
t	0.623	0.266	0.687	1.07
T	31126.7	13285.9	34354.9	53361.1
x	1	0.43	1.1	1.7
$10^{-0} \geq e > 10^{-1}$	0.02	0.04	0.02	7.24
$10^{-1} \geq e > 10^{-2}$	0.09	0.23	0.12	3.65
$10^{-2} \geq e > 10^{-3}$	0.13	0.33	0.21	0.98
$10^{-3} \geq e > 10^{-4}$	0.15	0.37	0.28	0.11
$10^{-4} \geq e > 10^{-5}$	0.16	0.39	0.34	0.01
$10^{-5} \geq e > 10^{-6}$	0.16	0.40	0.38	0.00
$10^{-6} \geq e > 10^{-7}$	0.17	0.41	0.40	0.00
$10^{-7} \geq e > 10^{-8}$	0.17	0.41	0.40	0.00
$10^{-8} \geq e > 10^{-9}$	0.17	0.42	0.38	0.00
$10^{-9} \geq e > 10^{-10}$	0.17	0.42	0.33	0.00
$10^{-10} \geq e > 10^{-11}$	0.17	0.42	0.268	0.00
$10^{-11} \geq e > 10^{-12}$	0.17	0.42	0.68	0.00
$10^{-12} \geq e > 10^{-13}$	0.17	0.42	4.25	0.00
$10^{-13} \geq e > 10^{-14}$	0.17	0.42	2.25	0.00
$10^{-14} \geq e$	97.92	94.92	89.70	88.01

Other Important Distributions

In addition to the normal distribution, the Gamma and exponential distributions are frequently used in quantitative finance. The Gamma distribution has the form

$$f_{\alpha,\beta}(x) = \frac{1}{\Gamma(\alpha)\beta^\alpha} x^{\alpha-1} e^{-\frac{x}{\beta}} \quad x \geq 0, \tag{9.67}$$

where α is the shape parameter and β the scale parameter.[22] The scale parameter β can be fixed at 1 when sampling for the Gamma distribution: if X has the Gamma distribution with

---

[22] The Chi-Squared distribution, important when using square root diffusion processes (Cox-Ingersoll-Ross model, Heston 1993) is a special case of the Gamma distribution with scale parameter $\beta = 2$ and shape parameter $\alpha = v/2$.

Table 9.4   The table shows the computation time T for a sample of $5 \cdot 10^7$ pseudo-random numbers drawn from the gamma distribution using different rejection methods. Implementation and algorithmic details can be found in the literature – johnk (Jöhnk, 1964) ahrens (Ahrens, Dieter and Greenberg, 1982), best (Best, 1983), kundu (Kundu and Gupta, 2007), marsaglia (Marsaglia and Tsang, 2000).

Method	johnk	ahrens	best	kundu	marsaglia
$\alpha = 0.8(T)$	12664.75	8467.53	9458.12	32807.15	3530.28
$\alpha = 0.08(T)$	10971.77	5626.55	8086.19	37344.54	7697.93

parameters $(\alpha, 1)$, then βX is Gamma distributed with parameters (α, β). Different implementations for sampling from the Gamma distribution using the inversion method are compared in Tables 9.2 and 9.3. An important conclusion to be drawn from this data is that the accuracy (and, as a consequence, computation speed) of the methods depend on the shape parameter α.

Rejection sampling can also be used to generate pseudo-random numbers that obey a gamma distribution. Table 9.4 compares the overall time required for generating a sample of $5 \cdot 10^7$ gamma distributed random variables. These algorithms tend to be more efficient than the inversion algorithms presented above, however, they do have a number of drawbacks when being used in parallel environments.[23]

The exponential distribution is a family of continuous probability distributions describing the time between events in a Poisson process, i.e., a process in which events occur continuously and independently at a constant average rate. The probability density function of an exponential distribution is given by

$$f_\lambda(x) = \begin{cases} \lambda e^{-\lambda x}, & x \geq 0 \\ 0, & x < 0 \end{cases} \tag{9.68}$$

where λ is called the rate parameter. The exponential distribution can be sampled by using a simple transformation from the uniform distribution,

$$Y = -\frac{1}{\lambda} \ln(U), \tag{9.69}$$

where U is sampled from the uniform distribution $U \sim \text{Unif}\,]0; 1]$. The exponential distribution can be used for generating paths in jump models by simulating the wait times between jumps (the wait times need then be mapped to the underlying time grid used for the simulation). Random numbers connected with the jump (for example, normal random numbers for a Merton Jump Diffusion model) need to be simulated in addition to that.

---

[23] The inversion algorithm guarantees that for each uniform random number, a corresponding random number of the desired distribution is generated. In a parallel computation, one can simply pass blocks of (sequentially produced) uniform random numbers to the inversion algorithm, which can be executed in parallel. On the other hand, parallel random number generators must be used with the rejection algorithm since the number of uniform random numbers required to produce a fixed-size sample of the desired distribution is not known in advance.

10

Advanced Monte Carlo Techniques

In this chapter, we present two classes of methods to improve the speed and efficiency of Monte Carlo simulations. First, we discuss tools that reduce the variance of the estimators while preserving other qualities, such as unbiasedness, at the same time. An alternative approach is the so-called Quasi Monte Carlo (QMC) method, which uses low-discrepancy sequences in place of sequences of pseudo-random numbers.

10.1 VARIANCE REDUCTION TECHNIQUES

Variance reduction techniques try to obtain statistically efficient estimators by reducing their variance. The common underlying principle is the utilization of additional information about the problem in order to reduce the effect of random sampling on the variance of the observations. The accomplishable efficiency gain often depends on the contract parameters of the instrument to be valuated, for instance, on the strike price. For practical implementations, the most important consideration is thus the efficiency trade-off: Simple and easy to implement techniques, such as the control variate technique, often provide already significant variance reduction. More sophisticated methods usually also entail a higher computational cost, and it depends on the specific problem whether this additional cost can be compensated by still higher variance reduction.

10.1.1 Antithetic Variates

Suppose we would like to estimate $\mu = E[f(Z)] = E[Y]$, where $f(Z)$ is, for instance, a function used for the valuation of an instrument and Z a set of random variables, and that we have generated two samples (paths) Y_1 and Y_2. We can then calculate an unbiased estimate for μ,

$$\tilde{\mu} = \frac{Y_1 + Y_2}{2}, \tag{10.1}$$

where the variance of this estimator is

$$\text{Var}(\tilde{\mu}) = \frac{\text{Var}(Y_1) + \text{Var}(Y_2) + 2\text{Cov}(Y_1, Y_2)}{4}. \tag{10.2}$$

If Y_1 and Y_2 are independent and identically distributed, the covariance cancels,

$$\text{Var}(\tilde{\mu}) = \frac{\text{Var}(Y_1)}{2} = \frac{\text{Var}(Y_2)}{2}. \tag{10.3}$$

The overall variance $\text{Var}(\tilde{\mu})$ can be reduced by choosing Y_2 in such a way that Y_1 and Y_2 are no longer independent and identically distributed and $\text{Cov}(Y_1, Y_2) < 0$. Figure 10.1 shows results of applying the Monte Carlo method with antithetic variates to the toy problem of integrating the function $f(x) = x^2$ in $[0; 1]$. Equations (9.3)–(9.8) have been used to calculate the Monte Carlo estimators and the corresponding 95% confidence intervals.

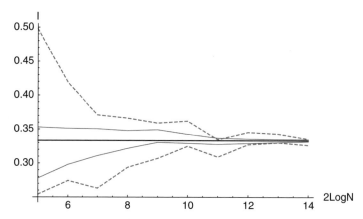

Figure 10.1   The figure shows the results of calculating the integral of $f(x) = x^2$ over the unit interval. The thin gray lines indicate the confidence interval of the estimator using antithetic variates (for each random variable z the antithetic variable $1 - z$ is used). Gray dashed lines indicate the confidence interval of the Monte Carlo estimator without antithetic variates and the thick black line indicates the exact solution of the problem. The number of paths varies between 2^5 and 2^{14}. For 2^{14} paths the variance is reduced from 0.0887127 to 0.00547148 using the antithetic variates.

In general, antithetic variates only result in a small variance reduction – note that they can, however, also lead to an increase. If the function $h(U_1, \ldots U_m)$ is a monotonic function of its arguments on $[0, 1]^m$, then for the set $U = (U_1, \ldots, U_m)$ of independent, identically distributed random variates ($U_i \in [0, 1]$) it can be proven (Ross, 2006) that

$$\mathrm{Cov}(h(U), h(1 - U)) < 0, \tag{10.4}$$

where

$$\mathrm{Cov}(h(U), h(1 - U)) := \mathrm{Cov}(h(U_1, \ldots, U_m), h(1 - U_1, \ldots, 1 - U_m)).$$

The above statement is a sufficient, but not a necessary condition for variance reduction. Antithetic variate techniques can also be applied in simulations including non-uniform variates as long as the inverse method is used to generate random variates of the desired distribution.[1] If variance reduction by antithetic variates is used for simulations with normally distributed random variables a considerable amount of computation time can be saved. Only half of the sample has to be generated using a random number generator and the application of the inverse cumulative distribution function since if $X \sim N(\mu, \sigma^2)$, also $\tilde{X} \sim N(\mu, \sigma^2)$ with $\tilde{X} = 2\mu - X$. Obviously X and $\tilde{X}$ are negatively correlated assuring a variance reduction.

Variance Reduction for Zero-coupon Valuation Under the Vasicek Model

To demonstrate the effect of path generation with antithetic normal variates, two sample paths (Euler discretization with $\Delta t = 1$) for a Vasicek model with $\Theta = 0.05$, $\alpha = 0.1$ and $\sigma = 0.005$ are shown in Figure 10.2. We calculated the value of a 10y zero coupon bond using $N = 1000$

---

[1] A rigorous argumentation takes the monotonicity of the cumulative distribution function into account.

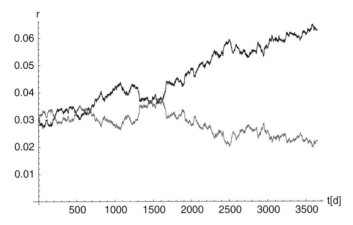

Figure 10.2   The figure shows two different paths with a time discretization ($\Delta t = 1$) for a Vasicek model with $\Theta = 0.05$, $\alpha = 0.1$ and $\sigma = 0.005$. Set X was used for the black path, the corresponding antithetic set $\tilde{X}$ for the gray path.

sample paths, yielding the estimator $\mu = 0.690367$ and $\sigma^2 = 0.00215847$. In the next step, we used the first 500 paths of the original sample, and generated another 500 paths using the antithetic normal variates. This calculation results in the estimator $\mu = 0.68973$ and a significantly reduced variance of $\sigma^2 = 0.000860689$. The histogram plot of $x_i = V_i - \mu$ for both variants is shown in Figure 10.3, and reveals that the points generated from the antithetic paths feature a higher concentration around the origin, i.e., a lower variance.

10.1.2   Control Variates

The control variate method uses information on the errors of known quantities, which are often obtained from the analytic solution of a similar but simpler problem, to reduce the variance

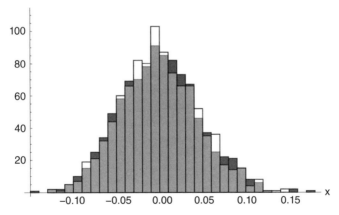

Figure 10.3   An overlay (light gray) of the histograms of $x_i = V_i - \mu$, where V_i are the bond values of a 10y zero coupon bond, calculated using $N = 1000$ paths for both normal (dark gray) and antithetic (white) sampling. The histograms show that the points generated from the antithetic paths feature a higher concentration around the origin, i.e., a lower variance.

of an unknown estimator. Suppose $\mu = E[X]$ is to be estimated. Then, Y is called a control variate of X if

(i) the mean $\Theta = E[Y]$ is known, and
(ii) Y is correlated with X.

Then,

$$Z = X + \beta(Y - \Theta) \tag{10.5}$$

is a control variate estimator of μ. The estimator Z is unbiased, since

$$E[Z] = E[X + \beta(Y - \Theta)] = E[X] = \mu. \tag{10.6}$$

Var[Z] is reduced compared to Var[X] if, and only if,

$$\beta^2 \text{Var}[Y] + 2\beta \text{Cov}[X, Y] < 0, \tag{10.7}$$

and in addition, Var[Z] is minimized (Ross, 2006) at

$$\beta^\star = -\frac{\text{Cov}[X, Y]}{\text{Var}[Y]}. \tag{10.8}$$

For $\beta^\star$ the variance is given by

$$\text{Var}[Z] = \text{Var}[X] - \frac{\text{Cov}[X, Y]^2}{\text{Var}[Y]} = \left(1 - \rho_{X,Y}^2\right) \text{Var}[X], \tag{10.9}$$

where $\rho_{X,Y}$ is the correlation between X and Y.[2] Typically, neither Var[Y] nor Cov[X, Y] are known and $\beta^\star$ needs to be estimated using the unbiased sample covariance and sample variance formula,

$$\hat{\beta}^\star = -\frac{\sum_{i=1}^{N}(X_i - \overline{X})(Y_i - \overline{Y})}{\sum_{i=1}^{N}(Y_i - \overline{Y})^2}. \tag{10.10}$$

The control variate method can be generalized to the case of multiple controls (Glasserman, 2003).

Estimating the Price of an Arithmetic Average Rate Call Option

When compared to a plain vanilla option, the key distinctive feature of an Asian option is the averaging of the stock price over the life-span of the option that replaces the terminal stock price $S(T)$ (Average Rate Option: ARO) or the strike price X_S (Average Strike Option: ASO) in the payoff. The type of averaging can either be arithmetic ($A(T)$, arithmetic Asian option) or geometric ($G(T)$, geometric Asian option – this type of option is not found in practice but is used here to improve the simulation efficiency), where

$$A(T) = \frac{1}{M} \sum_{i=1}^{M} S(t_i),$$

$$G(T) = \left(\Pi_{i=1}^{M} S(t_i)\right)^{\frac{1}{M}}. \tag{10.11}$$

---

[2] The second statement in the definition of a control variate, point (ii) above, states that Y must be correlated with X. Equation (10.9) shows the more strongly X and Y are correlated (positively or negatively), the greater the reduction in variance is.

While analytic formulae for geometric Asian options exist for various models of the underlying, there is no closed-form price formula for arithmetic Asian options due to the lack of an explicit representation of the distribution of the sum of lognormal prices. A control variate Monte Carlo method can be used to valuate an ARO under the Black-Scholes model, where the corresponding geometric Asian option is used as the control variate. The payoffs of the Asian options with arithmetic and geometric averaging are highly correlated. The risk neutral prices for the ARO can be expressed as expected discounted payoffs,

$$\mu = E[X] = E[e^{-rT}(A(T) - X_S(T))^+],$$
$$\Theta = E[Y] = E[e^{-rT}(G(T) - X_S(T))^+],$$

(10.12)

and the control variate estimator is thus given by

$$Z = e^{-rT}(A(T) - X_S(T))^+ + \beta(e^{-rT}(G(T) - X_S(T))^+ - \Theta).$$

(10.13)

In the Black-Scholes world, the price V_0 for the geometric Asian option (continuous case) at time $t = 0$ can be calculated analytically (Kemna and Vorst, 1990),

$$V_{0,G} = \Theta = S(0)e^{(b-r)T}\Phi(d_1) - X_S e^{-rT}\Phi(d_2),$$

(10.14)

where

$$b = \frac{1}{2}\left(r - \frac{\sigma^2}{6}\right),$$

$$\sigma_A = \frac{\sigma}{\sqrt{3}},$$

$$d_1 = \frac{\log\left(\frac{S(0)}{X_S}\right) + \left(b + \frac{\sigma_A^2}{2}\right)T}{\sigma_A\sqrt{T}},$$

(10.15)

$$d_2 = d_1 - \sigma_A\sqrt{T}.$$

The price of the corresponding arithmetic Asian option can therefore be calculated using $\mu = E[Z]$ and the analytically known value Θ,

$$V_{0,A} = \mu = E[e^{-rT}(A(T) - X_S(T))^+] =$$
$$= E[e^{-rT}(A(T) - X_S(T))^+ + \beta(e^{-rT}(G(T) - X_S(T))^+ - \Theta)],$$

(10.16)

where the mean value $E[Z]$ is again calculated by averaging over N paths. Figure 10.4 shows the 95% confidence intervals for the value of an arithmetic average rate European call option with $\sigma = 0.2$, $r = 0.05$, $S(0) = 100$, $X_S = 100$, $T = 1.0$ as a function of the number of paths N. Under the Black-Scholes model, the corresponding option with geometric averaging is analytically tractable (flat yield curve and flat volatility) with a result of $V_0 = 5.547$ and is used as the control variate with $\beta = -1$.[3] We have used an Euler discretization of the SDE with $\Delta T = 1/365$ for the simulation. Figure 10.4 shows that the control variate Monte Carlo method considerably reduces the variance of the estimator. The method can be extended to more advanced equity models: In Levy models, for instance, the pricing problem for geometrically

---

[3] The value for β can be further improved using regression analysis (Glasserman, 2003).

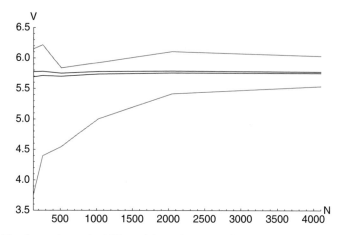

Figure 10.4   The figure shows the 95% confidence intervals of the value of an average rate European call option with $\sigma = 0.2$, $r = 0.05$, $S(0) = 100$, $X_S = 100$, $T = 1.0$ as a function of the number of paths N for standard Monte Carlo (gray) and a Monte Carlo simulation where the corresponding option with geometric averaging has been used as a control variate (black). The value obtained using Monte Carlo with control variate and $N = 2^{16}$ sample paths is 5.76. The control variate technique considerably reduces the variance.

averaged Asian options can still be solved (Fusai and Meucci, 2008) (semi)-analytically, while for the arithmetic average option numerical methods must be applied.

10.1.3   Conditioning

Similar to the control variate method, conditional Monte Carlo tries to reduce the variance of the estimator $\mu = E[X]$ by exploiting knowledge about the simulated system. Suppose X and Z are two random vectors, and let $Y = h(X)$ be a random variable. The conditional expectation value

$$V = E[Y \mid Z] \tag{10.17}$$

can then be regarded as a random variable that depends on Z. The law of iterated conditional expectations assures us that

$$E[V] = E[E[Y \mid Z]] = E[Y], \tag{10.18}$$

thus one can just as well simulate random paths of random variables V in place of random variables Y in order to estimate μ. The conditional variance formula

$$\text{Var}(Y) = E[\text{Var}(Y \mid Z)] + \text{Var}(E[Y \mid Z]) \tag{10.19}$$

implies that[4]

$$\text{Var}(Y) \geq \text{Var}(E[Y \mid Z]). \tag{10.20}$$

---

[4] Also $\text{Var}(Y \mid Z)$ is a random variable depending on Z and since a variance is always non-negative, $E[\text{Var}(Y \mid Z)] \geq 0$.

Therefore using V instead of Y leads to a better estimator for μ. Boyle, Broadie and Glasserman (1997) note that replacing an estimator by its conditional expectation reduces the variance because parts of the integration are performed analytically, and thus less is left to be done by Monte Carlo simulation.[5]

A Down-and-In European Call Option Under the Black-Scholes Model

The risk neutral pricing formula for a down-and-in European call option is

$$V_0 = E[e^{-rT} 1_{t_\tau < T}(S_T - X_S)^+], \tag{10.21}$$

where T is the time to maturity, X_S is the strike price of the option, r is the risk-free rate and $(S_T - X_S)^+$ denotes the maximum of $S_T - X_S$ and 0. The symbol $1_{t_\tau < T}$ denotes the indicator function with hitting time t_τ, where τ is a non-negative random variable. To reduce the variance of the estimation of V_0, the simulation is stopped as soon as the barrier is hit at the hitting time t_τ. The value of a European call option is then calculated using the Black-Scholes formula, replacing the actual price of the underlying S with $S(t_\tau) = S_{t_\tau}$. Using the conditional expectation this can be expressed by

$$
\begin{aligned}
V_0 &= E[e^{-rT}(S(T) - X_S)^+] \\
&= E[e^{-rT} E[(S(T) - X_S)^+ \mid t_\tau, S(t_\tau)]] \\
&= E[e^{-rT} e^{r(T-t_\tau)} E[e^{-r(T-t_\tau)}(S(T) - X_S)^+ \mid t_\tau, S(t_\tau)]] \\
&= E[e^{-rt_\tau} BS(S(t_\tau), t_\tau, T, X_S)].
\end{aligned}
\tag{10.22}
$$

Note that the inner expectation is replaced by the Black-Scholes formula (closed form expression),

$$
\begin{aligned}
BS(S(t_i), t_i, T, X_S)] &= E\left[e^{-r(T-t_i)}(S(T) - X_S)\right] \\
&= S(t_i)\Phi(d_1) - X_S e^{-r(T-t_i)}\Phi(d_2),
\end{aligned}
\tag{10.23}
$$

with

$$d_1 = \frac{\log\left(\dfrac{S(t_i)}{X_S}\right) + \left(r + \dfrac{\sigma^2}{2}\right)(T - t_i)}{\sigma(T - t_i)}, \tag{10.24}$$

$$d_2 = d_1 - \sqrt{T - t_i}.$$

We now replace the subscript τ by i to indicate that the hitting time is path-dependent. If the price of the underlying does not hit the barrier, the option value is 0. Therefore, in path i the down-and-in call option has the value

$$V_0 = \begin{cases} e^{-rt_i} BS(S(t_i), t_i, T, X_S)] & \text{if} \quad t_i < T \\ 0 & \text{else.} \end{cases} \tag{10.25}$$

We now consider a down-and-in European call option with $\sigma = 0.3$, $r = 0.1$, $S(0) = 100$, $X_S = 100$, $T = 0.2$ and a barrier $b = 95$ as a showcase for the method. This barrier option

---

[5] Note that Y and Z need to depend on each other in order to obtain satisfactory results. If Y and Z are independent, then simulated runs of Z have no influence on the expected value of Y.

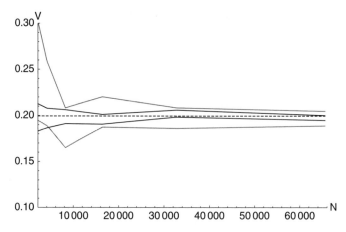

Figure 10.5   The figure shows the 95% confidence intervals for the value of a down-and-in European call option with $\sigma = 0.3$, $r = 0.1$, $S(0) = 100$, $X_S = 100$, $T = 0.2$ and a barrier $b = 95$ as a function of the number of paths N for a standard Monte Carlo (gray) and a conditional Monte Carlo (black) simulation. The black dashed line indicates the option value obtained from a conditional Monte Carlo calculation with $N = 2^{19}$ sample paths. The conditional Monte Carlo method considerably reduces the variance. A time step of $\Delta t = 0.1$ has been used for the simulations.

is analytically tractable under the Black-Scholes model (flat yield curve and flat volatility), with a result of $V_0 = 1.94693$. As soon as the interest rate and/or the volatility are no longer constant no analytical solution is available and therefore numerical simulation (PDE or MC) must be applied. A Monte Carlo calculation with Euler discretization of the SDE requires a very small time step $\Delta t \leq 0.1$ to come close to the analytical solution.[6] Figure 10.5 shows that the conditional Monte Carlo method considerably reduces the variance of the estimator. In general, the method is also applicable for situations that involve more complex models with time-dependent parameters, as long as analytical formulae or efficient numerical methods are available for the valuation of the European option.

10.1.4   Additional Techniques for Variance Reduction

Several additional techniques for variance reduction exist, but many of them are not as easy to apply as the three methods presented in the previous sections. Furthermore, they rely on more elaborate mathematics – therefore the interested reader should take a look at Glasserman (2003) and the references therein.

Methods constraining the fraction of observations drawn from specific subsets of the sample space are subsumed under the term "stratified sampling".[7] To calculate $\mu = E[X]$ via random sampling, independent $X_1, \ldots, X_n$ with the same distribution as X are generated. Furthermore, the real line is partitioned into disjoint subsets $A_1, \ldots, A_m$ for which $P(X \in \cup A_i) = 1$ and $p_i = P(X \in A_i)$. In general, for finite sample size the fraction of the samples that falls into A_i is not equal to p_i. In the stratified sampling method, the decision on which fraction of the

---

[6] For a given discretization, the option value converges (by increasing the number of paths) to a slightly different value than the analytical one due to the discretization error.

[7] These subsets are also called *strata*, hence the name *stratified sampling*.

sample is to be drawn from each of the subsets is made in advance – each observation from A_I is therefore constrained to have the distribution of Y conditional on $Y \in A_i$.

The importance sampling method tries to reduce the variance of a Monte Carlo estimator by changing the probability measure from which paths are generated. This way, more weight can be given to "important" outcomes, increasing the sample efficiency. This method has the highest potential of variance reduction, sometimes even by orders of magnitude. However, if the importance sampling distribution is not chosen carefully, it can also increase the variance, and can even produce infinite variance.

10.2 QUASI MONTE CARLO METHOD

A *low-discrepancy sequence* is a sequence of tuples that fills a d-dimensional hypercube more uniformly than uncorrelated random points. Such quasi-random sequences improve the performance of Monte Carlo simulations, offering shorter computation times and/or higher accuracy in a number of cases. It is important to stress that low-discrepancy sequences are fully deterministic. The mathematical tools used in Quasi Monte Carlo simulations originate in number theory and are quite demanding – discrepancy replaces the concept of variance for measuring dispersion. Changing the bases of numbers, using different prime number properties, and the use coefficients of primitive polynomials form the number theoretic toolkit used for developing low-discrepancy sequences. For the interested reader, we recommend the book of Niederreiter (1992) for a rigorous review of the mathematical foundations. QMC methods were made popular in finance mainly by the work of Paskov and Traub (1995), who used an improved Sobol algorithm for calculating derivatives.

An error analysis of the Monte Carlo method shows that increasing the number of paths N increases the accuracy of the estimator with a convergence rate $\mathcal{O}(N^{-1/2})$. As pointed out in the previous chapter, this convergence rate is independent of the dimensionality of the problem. For a Quasi Monte Carlo setup, the convergence rate[8] lies between $\mathcal{O}(N^{-1})$ and $\mathcal{O}(\ln^d N/N)$ (Niederreiter, 1992), depending on the application.

10.2.1 Low-Discrepancy Sequences

The basic idea of low-discrepancy sequences is to add successive points in such a way that each point is repelled from the others, thus filling the "gaps" in the sequence and avoiding clustering. To measure the uniformity of the distribution of a sequence of N points $\{X_1, \ldots, X_N\}$ in a d-dimensional space (note that X_i is a d-dimensional vector[9]) the discrepancy is

$$D_N(X_1, \ldots, X_N) = \sup_{\beta \in [0,1]^d} \left| \frac{1}{N} \sum_{n=1}^{N} 1_{[0,\beta[}(X_n) - \beta_1 \cdot \ldots \cdot \beta_d \right|, \qquad (10.26)$$

where $[0, \beta[= [0, \beta_1[\times \ldots \times [0, \beta_d[$ and 1_A is the characteristic function of set A.[10] A sequence of numbers $X = \{X_i\}_{i=1}^{\infty}$ is called uniformly distributed if

$$\lim_{N \to \infty} D_N(X) = 0. \qquad (10.27)$$

---

[8] Theoretical upper bound rate of convergence (or maximum error) for the multi-dimensional low-discrepancy sequences.

[9] The dimension of the vector corresponds to the number of discretization steps used for the time-discretization of the underlying SDE.

[10] The characteristic function of a set A is 1 for all members of A and 0 otherwise.

Table 10.1   The table shows the first 16 numbers of the van der Corput
sequence in base 2. Each additional number is used for filling the gap.

x	0	1/16	2/16	3/16	4/16	5/16	6/16	7/16
n	0	8	4	12	2	10	6	14
x	8/16	9/16	10/16	11/16	12/16	13/16	14/16	15/16
n	1	9	5	13	3	11	7	15

It can be shown that, if the uniformly distributed sequence of numbers X is used for calculating the Monte Carlo estimator $\hat{I}$ (the sample mean in 9.2), I_N goes to I for $N \to \infty$.
The approximation error directly depends on $D_N(X)$. The behavior of filling the gap can be
illustrated by taking the van der Corput sequence (Niederreiter, 1992) in base 2 which is a
building block for several other low-discrepancy sequences. The van der Corput sequence
yields numbers in the interval $[0; 1[$; 1 is never reached but approximated for large n.
Table 10.1 shows the first 16 numbers of the van der Corput sequence in base 2 calculated
with Algorithm 8 setting $b = 2$ and n varying between 0 and 15. In practice the first numbers
in the sequence are discarded (especially $n = 0$ yielding 0 can not be used for inversion).

For practical applications, multi-dimensional low-discrepancy sequences need to be constructed. The dimensionality of the problem is given by the number of discretization steps in
the time dimension $d = N_{\Delta t} - 1$, while the number of sample paths N determines the dimensionality of a single tuple, see Figure 10.6. Note that a single path can itself consist of many
stochastic processes. The main challenge in constructing low-discrepancy sequences in multiple dimensions is to avoid the multi-dimensional clustering caused by the correlations between
the dimensions. Low-discrepancy sequences should be independent for different points

---

Algorithm 8   The algorithm calculates a number of the van der Corput sequence in
basis b for input n. The filling of the gap at a maximum distance to neighboring points
is obvious.

Set basis b
$n_0 = n$
$c = 0$
$y = 1/b$
while $n_0 > 0$ **do**
> $n_1 = (\text{INT})(n_0/b)$
> $i = n_0 - n_1 * b$
> $c = c + y * i$
> $y = y/b$
> $n_0 = n_1$

end while
$x = c$

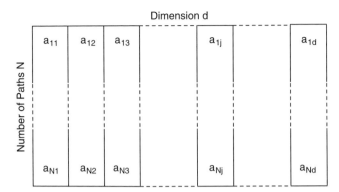

Figure 10.6   The figure explains the dimensionality of a QMC setup. The number of points used for the time discretization (number of columns) determines the dimensionality d, while the number of sample paths N (number of rows) determines the length of a single sequence. If we think of a Monte Carlo simulation of an option with maturity date in 1 year and a maximum time step length of 1 day $M = d$ would be 365. If we perform the simulation with $N = 1024$ sample paths each single sequence needs to be that long.

in time.[11] The major problem in using pure quasi-random sequences is their degradation – the breakdown of a uniform filling due to correlation – when the dimensionality becomes large (see Figure 10.8 as an example). The generation process of uniformly distributed points in $[0; 1[^d$ becomes increasingly hard – the space to fill becomes too large.

Halton Sequence

The Halton sequence uses van der Corput sequences with consecutive prime numbers as bases for consecutive dimensions. The first dimension is identical to the van der Corput sequence in base 2, for the second dimension, base 3 is used, for the third dimension base 5, and so on. A higher base results in a longer cycle and therefore in a higher computation time. Consequently, problems occur for high-dimensional problems: in dimension 50, for example, the Halton sequence uses base 229 (the 50th prime number), considerably increasing the cycle size. Figure 10.7 shows one thousand tuples of the Halton sequence in two dimensions. For the Halton sequence the high correlation of points in successive dimensions is shown in Figure 10.8. For comparison of the coverage of the unit square, a sample of one thousand 2-tuples of pseudo-random numbers generated with Mersenne Twister is shown in Figure 10.11.

Faure Sequence

The Faure sequence differs from the Halton sequence by using the same base for all dimensions and by permuting the vector elements for each dimension. It uses the smallest prime number larger than or equal to the number of dimensions in the problem, e.g., base 2 for a one-dimensional problem. For high-dimensional problems the Faure sequence thus works with van der Corput sequences of long cycle length, which increases the computational cost. However, the problem is not as severe as with Halton sequences – for a dimensionality of 50, the Faure

---

[11] Recalling the basic properties of a Wiener process, the increments of the Brownian motion (and also of other processes such as Poisson/jump processes) must be independently and identically distributed.

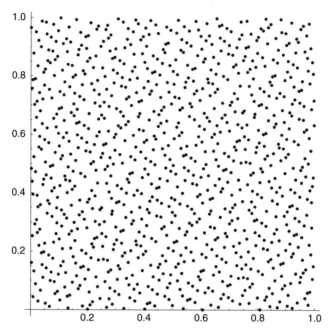

Figure 10.7   The figure shows the first one thousand 2-tuples of the Halton sequence, omitting n = 0.

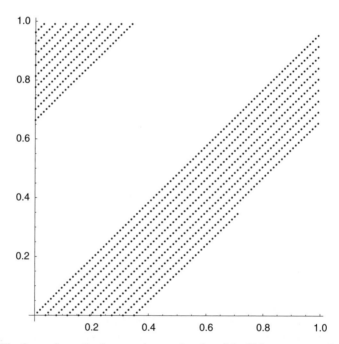

Figure 10.8   The figure shows the first one thousand tuples of the Halton sequence for dimensions 27 ($b = 103$) and 28 ($b = 107$). Points in successive dimensions are highly correlated. Furthermore, in high dimensions, the initial points are clustered close to zero. The second problem can be avoided by starting with $n_0 \neq 1$ (the sequence preserves its basic properties when starting from a different number), but the first problem can lead to poor estimates in the QMC simulation.

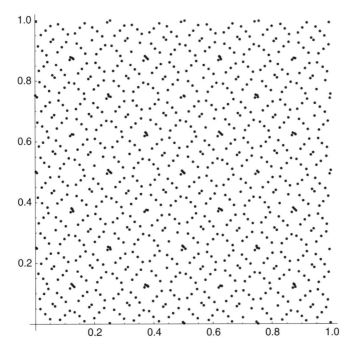

Figure 10.9   The figure shows the first one thousand 2-tuples of the Faure sequence, omitting n = 0.

sequence uses a base of 53, while the Halton sequence uses a base of 229. Several important issues are reported in connection with the Faure sequence. Galanti and Jung (1997), among others, point out that the Faure sequence suffers from the problem of start-up: in particular for high dimensionality and low values of n_0, the Faure numbers exhibit clustering around zero. In order to reduce this problem, Faure suggests to discard the first $n = (b^4 - 1)$ points, where b is the base. The start-up problem has also been reported for other sequences, and the same suggestion of discarding initial numbers holds there. In addition, the Faure sequence exhibits high-dimensional degradation at approximately the 25th dimension, and according to Galanti and Jung (1997), calculating the Faure sequence is significantly slower than generating Halton and Sobol sequences. Figure 10.9 shows one thousand tuples of the Faure sequence in two dimensions.

Sobol Sequence

Sobol sequences (Niederreiter, 1992) solve the problem of dependency in higher dimensions. Sobol sequences use only 2 as a base for construction. Just as in the Faure sequence, a reordering of the vector elements within each dimension is performed. The sequences are generated in such a way that the first 2^m terms for each dimension, for $m = 0, 1, 2, \ldots$, are permutations of the corresponding terms of the van der Corput sequence with base $b = 2$. If the permutation is chosen appropriately, the resulting S-dimensional sequence exhibits low discrepancy. High-dimensional clustering can be omitted by setting n_0 appropriately (Glasserman, 2003). Galanti and Jung (1997) showed that the problem of degradation is not as severe for Sobol sequences as it is for Halton sequences: Sobol sequences do not show degradation at all up to

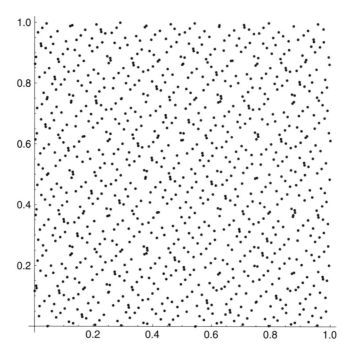

Figure 10.10   The figure shows the first one thousand 2-tuples of the Sobol sequence, omitting n = 0.

the dimension 260. Halton, Sobol and Faure sequences have been thoroughly tested, with the conclusion that for higher dimensionality Sobol sequences outperform the other two (Niederreiter, 1992). In general, Sobol sequences can be constructed significantly faster than other low discrepancy sequences, as a result of the short cycle length due to the overall use of $b = 2$. By virtue of their superior properties, Sobol sequences are widely used in quantitative finance. Figure 10.10 shows one thousand tuples of the gobol sequence in two dimensions.

10.2.2   Randomizing QMC

Randomizing QMC is considered to calculate statistical error measures, such as confidence intervals, while at the same time retaining much of the accuracy of standard QMC. There are even indications that in specific settings randomization improves the accuracy of the calculation (see Glasserman (2003) and the references therein). Different techniques for randomization exist – we start with a set of N d-dimensional points $X = \{X_1, \ldots, X_N\}$, where $X_i \in [0, 1[^d$. In the *random shift technique*, a random vector Y uniformly distributed over the unit hypercube is used to shift each point in X. The resulting point is taken modulo 1 coordinate-wise to assure that each coordinate is lying in $[0, 1[$. The *random permutation of digits technique* applies a random permutation of $0, 1, \ldots, b - 1$ to the coefficients of the base-b representation of the coordinates of each point. This technique is further improved in the *scrambled net* method, where a hierarchy of permutations is used. The permutation applied to the jth digit of a number in b-base representation depends on the first $j - 1$ digits.

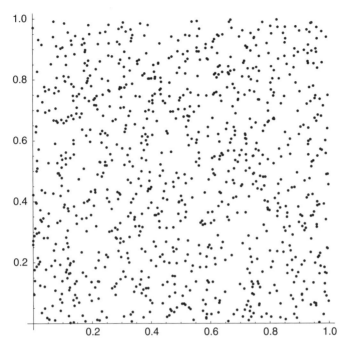

Figure 10.11   The figure shows one thousand 2-tuples of pseudo-random numbers generated with the Mersenne Twister.

10.3 BROWNIAN BRIDGE TECHNIQUE

The Brownian Bridge technique (Caflisch and Moskowitz, 1995) allows to improve Quasi Monte Carlo simulations by eliminating the dimensionality problem. A straightforward way to construct a sample path of a Brownian motion with M time steps t_m in the time interval $[0, T]$ is to start at $t_0 = 0$ and to add the increment $W_{t_{m+1}} - W_{t_m}$ to W_{t_m} in each time step,

$$W_{t_{m+1}} = W_{t_m} + \sqrt{t_{m+1} - t_m}\, z_{j+1}, \tag{10.28}$$

where $j = 0, \ldots, M - 1$ and $W_{t_0} = 0$.[12] This can be written in matrix notation,

$$\begin{pmatrix} W_{t_1} \\ W_{t_2} \\ \vdots \\ W_{t_M} \end{pmatrix} = \mathbf{A} \begin{pmatrix} z_1 \\ z_2 \\ \vdots \\ z_M \end{pmatrix}, \tag{10.29}$$

where $\mathbf{A}$ is the Cholesky factorization of the $M \times M$ matrix $\mathbf{C} = \mathbf{A}\mathbf{A}^T$ with

$$C_{i,j} = \min(t_i, t_j).$$

---

[12] For example for the valuation of an option with an expiry date $T = 1$ year $\Delta t = 1$ day resulting in $M = 365$ time steps.

For equidistant time discretization, $\Delta t = T/M$,

$$
\mathbf{A} = \sqrt{\Delta t}
\begin{pmatrix}
1 & & & \\
1 & 1 & & \\
\vdots & \vdots & \ddots & \\
1 & 1 & \cdots & 1
\end{pmatrix}.
\tag{10.30}
$$

For a path constructed this way, all dimensions are of equal importance, thus correcting the problem of low-discrepancy sequences, where low dimensions show more favorable distribution properties.

The Brownian bridge technique is an alternative way to generate a path of the Brownian motion by using the first elements of a sequence to construct the points with good distribution properties along the sample path. In the first step, W_T is generated, then using this value and $W_0 = 0$ we generate $W_{T/2}$. The construction proceeds by recursively filling in the mid points of each resulting subinterval, i.e., in the following step, $W_{T/4}$ is generated from W_0 and $W_{T/2}$, then $W_{3T/4}$ is generated from $W_{T/2}$ and W_T. In the end, the values of the sample path at $T, T/2, T/4, 3T/4, \ldots, (M-1)T/M$ are determined by

$$
W_T = \sqrt{T} z_1,
$$

$$
W_{T/2} = \frac{1}{2} W_T + \frac{\sqrt{T}}{2} z_2,
$$

$$
W_{T/4} = \frac{1}{2} W_{T/2} + \frac{\sqrt{2T}}{4} z_3,
$$

$$
W_{3T/4} = \frac{1}{2}(W_{T/2} + W_T) + \frac{\sqrt{2T}}{4} z_4,
\tag{10.31}
$$

$$
\vdots
$$

$$
W_{(M-1)T/M} = \frac{1}{2}(W_{(M-2)T/M} + W_T) + \frac{\sqrt{T}}{2M} z_M.
$$

This can again be written in matrix form, but obviously, the resulting matrix is different from the matrix $\mathbf{A}$ obtained by the Cholesky factorization above. The method can also be generalized to time intervals of unequal length: Again assuming $\Delta T = T/M$, $k > j$ and W_{t_k} are known, a future value can be calculated according to

$$
W_{t_k} = W_{t_j} + \sqrt{(k-j)\Delta t}\, z \quad z \sim N(0,1).
\tag{10.32}
$$

Furthermore, W_{t_i} can be calculated at any intermediate point in time $t_j < t_i < t_k$ (given W_{t_j} and W_{t_k}) using the Brownian bridge formula

$$
W_{t_i} = (1-\alpha) W_{t_j} + \alpha W_{t_k} + \sqrt{\alpha(1-\alpha)(k-j)\Delta t}\, z \quad z \sim N(0,1),
\tag{10.33}
$$

where $\alpha = (i - j)/(k - j)$. The Brownian bridge technique can be easily extended to D dimensions[13] by applying the one-dimensional random walk construction separately to each coordinate of the D-dimensional vector W, basically treating W as a matrix with D rows and M columns. To account for correlation, the vector z_i (vector of normally distributed random

---

[13] Be careful not to mix up d and D!

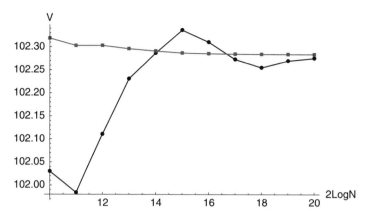

Figure 10.12 The figure shows the values of the Steepener instrument described in section 9.2.3 obtained under the Libor market model using Monte Carlo simulation (black circles) and Sobol sequences together with Brownian bridge technique for path construction (gray squares). N is the number of paths used for the simulation.

variables of dimension D – a slice in time) is multiplied with the matrix $\mathbf{A}$, the lower triangular matrix obtained from the Cholesky factorization of the $D \times D$ correlation matrix Σ,

$$X = \mathbf{A}Z. \tag{10.34}$$

An alternative to the Brownian bridge technique is to use principal component analysis for path construction (Ackworth, Broadie and Glasserman, 1998).

10.3.1 A Steepener under a Libor Market Model

We have valuated the Steepener instrument described in section 9.2.3 under a Libor Market model calibrated to the same market data as the two-factor Hull-White model in Chapter 9. The parameters of the calibrated volatility function (9.29) are $a = 2.72067$, $b = 0.871985$, $c = 1.21931$ and $d = 4.94402$, and the parameters of the correlation function (9.45) are $\beta_0 = 0.01$ and $\beta_1 = 0.01$ (note that $\rho_\infty = 0$). Figure 10.12 shows the Steepener values obtained under the the Libor Market Model using Monte Carlo simulation (black circles) and Quasi Monte Carlo simulation (Sobol sequence together with the Brownian bridge technique – gray squares). It is obvious that the estimator obtained with QMC is superior to the estimator obtained with plain Monte Carlo simulation especially for a small number of paths.

11

Valuation of Financial Instruments with Embedded American/Bermudan Options within Monte Carlo Frameworks

In contrast to European options, which can only be exercised at a fixed time, Bermudan options can be exercised at several points in time up to the maturity/expiry of the instrument. As explained before, we call an option which can be exercised at any time up to its expiration an American option. Consequently, finding the option value amounts to finding an optimal exercise rule, which is a matter of solving an optimal stopping problem and then computing the expected discounted payoff.

Pricing Bermudan and American derivatives with Monte Carlo methods is an area of both active academic research and great relevance in practice.[1] One technique is to use the least squares approach (Least Squares Monte Carlo (LSMC)), which has become popular through the seminal work of Longstaff and Schwartz (2001).[2] Several variations of the methodology have been proposed in the literature, see, for example, Rogers (2002), Glasserman and Yu (2004b), Cerrato (2008). In this chapter, we start by sketching the work of Longstaff and Schwartz (2001) and subsequently present a modification for Bermudan callable interest rate derivatives that improves the lower bound values.[3] This modification is an extension of the work presented in Piterbarg (2005) and Amin (2003); the basic idea is to use regressions for the holding and exercise values of the callable derivative.

11.1 PRICING AMERICAN OPTIONS USING THE LONGSTAFF AND SCHWARTZ ALGORITHM

The value of an American option is given by

$$V_0 = \sup_{\tau \in \mathcal{T}} \mathbb{E}\left[\frac{h_\tau}{D_\tau}|\mathcal{F}_0\right], \tag{11.1}$$

where $\mathcal{F}_0$ is an information process (filtration), h_τ is the payoff function and D_τ a bond process used for discounting. The calculation of V_0 boils down to finding the optimal stopping time $\tau^\star$ that achieves the supremum, which can be accomplished by a dynamic programming ansatz.

---

[1] See, for example, the SSRN website of Mark Joshi: http://papers.ssrn.com/sol3/cf_dev/AbsByAuth.cfm?per_id=550354, or current papers by Mark Broadie: http://www.columbia.edu/~mnb2/broadie/research_papers.html.

[2] The idea of using Monte Carlo simulations to price American options first published in Tilley (1993).

[3] Monte Carlo estimators typically will not find the strictly optimal exercise strategy and therefore underestimate the true option value.

Assume an option with M call/put dates has not previously been exercised: then, the value of interest $V_0(X_0)$ is determined by the recursion

$$V_M(x) = h_M(x), \tag{11.2}$$

$$V_{i-1}(x) = \max\left\{ h_{i-1}(x),\ \mathbb{E}\left[\frac{D_{i-1}}{D_i} V_i(X_i) \Big| X_{i-1} = x \right] \right\}, \tag{11.3}$$

for $i = 1, \ldots, M$, where X is the set of underlying stochastic processes.

The key challenge in valuing Bermudan derivatives with the Monte Carlo approach is the estimation of the continuation value

$$C_i(x) = \mathbb{E}\left[\frac{D_i}{D_{i+1}} V_{i+1}(X_{i+1}) \Big| X_i = x \right] \tag{11.4}$$

for $i = 0, \ldots, M - 1$. The key idea is to assume the continuation value to be a function of the current values of the state variables (Lamberton, Protter and Clement, 2002),

$$C_i(x) = \sum_{l=1}^{L} \beta_{i,l} \phi_l(x), \tag{11.5}$$

where $\beta_{i,l}$ are constants and ϕ_l is a set of basis functions, $\phi_l : \mathbb{R}^d \longrightarrow \mathbb{R}$. For each i, the set of $L + 1$ coefficients $\beta_i = \{\beta_{i,l=0,\ldots,L}\}$ can be estimated by a regression using all N Monte Carlo paths.

Step-by-step algorithm   (note that the superscript $\hat{}$ denotes the discounted value):

Step 1 Start by generating N independent sample paths $\{X_1, \ldots, X_N\}$. Each element in the set $\{X_1, \ldots, X_N\}$ is a matrix, where the number of rows is determined by the number of stochastic factors and the column index is determined by the underlying time discretization. That is, $X_{n,i}$ denotes the nth path (set of stochastic factors) at time step i. We do not distinguish individual stochastic factors by indices.

Step 2 For the final time step, assign each $\hat{V}_{n,M} = \hat{h}_M(X_{n,M})$, $n = 1, \ldots, N$.

Step 3 Apply the following backwards recursion for $i = M - 1, \ldots, 1$:
1. Calculate the set of regression coefficients β_i by least squares regression, using the estimated values $\hat{V}_{n,i+1}$,
2. Set

$$\hat{V}_{n,i} = \begin{cases} \hat{h}_i(X_{n,i}) & \hat{h}_i(X_{n,i}) \geq \hat{C}_i(X_{n,i}), \\ \hat{V}_{n,i+1} & \hat{h}_i(X_{n,i}) < \hat{C}_i(X_{n,i}), \end{cases} \tag{11.6}$$

with C_i defined as in (11.5).

Step 4 Finally, let $V_0 = (\hat{V}_{1,1} + \cdots + \hat{V}_{1,n})/N$.

To verify the least squares Monte Carlo algorithm proposed by Longstaff and Schwartz, we compare valuation results for an American put option with solutions of the corresponding Black-Scholes PDE in Figure 11.1.

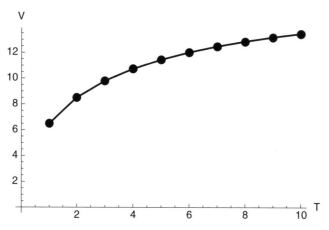

Figure 11.1   Comparison of valuation results for an American put option for different maturity dates using either a PDE (line) or least squares Monte Carlo (dots) in the Longstaff-Schwartz setup.

11.2   A MODIFIED LEAST SQUARES MONTE CARLO ALGORITHM FOR BERMUDAN CALLABLE INTEREST RATE INSTRUMENTS

In general, a swap is a contract between two parties to exchange periodic payments C^{PL} and C^{RL} (PL and RL denote the paid and received legs, respectively) that depend on a set of reference and exchange rates. In addition, we define a set of points in time $\tilde{T} = \{\tilde{T}_0, \tilde{T}_1, \ldots, \tilde{T}_{N_c+1}\}$, where $\tilde{T}_i$ (with i in 1 to $N_c + 1$) are coupon dates, $\tilde{T}_0$ is the valuation date, and $\tilde{T}_{N_c+1}$ is the maturity date, which is in most cases also a coupon date. The value of the swap at a coupon date $\tilde{T}_i$ can be calculated by

$$CV_i = \omega_i^{RL} C_i^{RL} - \omega_i^{PL} C_i^{PL}, \tag{11.7}$$

where ω_i^k ($k \in \{PL, RL\}$) denotes the respective set of coupon weights for coupon date T_i. Therefore, the value of the swap at date t is

$$SV_t = \sum_{i=\tilde{t}}^{N_c+1} \exp\left\{ -\int_t^{\tilde{T}_i} r_d(s)ds \right\} CV_i, \tag{11.8}$$

where $\tilde{t}$ denotes the index of the first coupon date after t and r_d denotes an interest rate process used for discounting.[4,5] The value at the valuation date is given by

$$SV_0 = \sum_{i=1}^{N_c+1} \exp\left\{ -\int_{\tilde{T}_0}^{\tilde{T}_i} r_d(s)ds \right\} CV_i. \tag{11.9}$$

---

[4] See Brigo and Mercurio (2006).
[5] Note that no expectation value is used in this place since r_d is not necessarily a stochastic process.

In a Monte Carlo simulation where underlying rates are modeled by stochastic variables, the value of the instrument at time $T_0 = \tilde{T}_0$ is approximated by taking the average of all instrument values realized in N different paths,

$$\mathbb{E}[SV_0] = \frac{1}{N} \sum_{n=1}^{N} SV_{n,0}. \qquad (11.10)$$

If the instrument is callable, one party has the additional opportunity to cancel the swap at specified dates (the call dates) for a specified amount of money (the call rates). The call dates $\mathcal{T} = \{T_1, \dots, T_M\}$ are typically a subset of the coupon dates; we will use this assumption in the following, although it is not a necessary requirement of the method. In order to simplify the notation and give a clear presentation of the algorithms, we omit practical financial industry settings such as business day conventions, rounding rules and day count conventions.

11.2.1 Algorithm: Extended LSMC Method for Bermudan Options

Step 1 Initialization during Monte Carlo simulation
- Call rate matrix C for every call date ($1 \times M$ matrix).
- Swap value matrix S ($N \times M$ matrix),

$$\begin{pmatrix} S_{1,1} & S_{1,2} & \cdots & S_{1,M} \\ \vdots & \vdots & \ddots & \vdots \\ S_{N,1} & S_{N,2} & \cdots & S_{N,M} \end{pmatrix}, \qquad (11.11)$$

where $S_{n,i}$ denotes the value of the swap at time T_i in the n-th path [compare (11.8) with t equal to the corresponding call date T_i]. During the algorithm the entries of this matrix will be replaced by the option values.
- Discount factor matrix D ($N \times M$ matrix), where

$$D_{n,i} = \exp \left\{ -\int_{T_0}^{T_i} r_d(s)ds \right\}$$

denotes the discount factor in the nth path from T_0 to T_i and r_d denotes the interest rate used for discounting. This integral is approximated numerically.
- Set of regressor matrices. For each stochastic factor j used for the regression analysis, $j = 1, \dots, J$, an $N \times M$ matrix is required.[6] We denote the set of these matrices with $R = \{R^1, \dots, R^J\}$ and the corresponding matrix entries with $R_{n,i}^j = X_{n,i,j}$.

Step 2 Start at the last call date T_M and perform the following steps:
   2.1 Compute the least squares regression of swap values as a function of the underlying variables,

$$\min_{\beta_M} \left\{ \sum_{n=1}^{N} \left(S_{n,M} - g\left(\beta_M, \{R_{\cdot,M}\} \right) \right)^2 \right\}, \qquad (11.12)$$

---

[6] Not all stochastic factors used for developing a single path need to be used as underlying variables for the regression analysis. This is especially important when multi-factor or market models are used for modeling rates. Thus, a subset of J stochastic variables is used here.

where $g(\beta_M, \{R_{.,M}\})$ is the regression function, β_M is the set of regression parameters to be determined and $\{R_{.,M}\}$ is the set of stochastic factors used for regression
at call date M. The "." indicates that all paths are taken into account.

2.2 Compute the current regression value $RV^g_{n,M}$ for each path using the optimal
parameter set $\beta^\star_M$ calculated in the previous step,

$$RV^g_{n,M} = g(\beta^\star_M, \{R_{n,M}\}). \tag{11.13}$$

2.3 Compare the regression value to the call rate for each path: If the latter is smaller
than $RV^g_{n,M}$, it is better to exercise the option and take the difference $SV_{n,M} - C_M$,
otherwise set $S_{n,M}$ to 0,

$$SV_{n,M} = \begin{cases} SV_{n,M} - C_M & \text{if } C_M < RV^g_{n,M} \\ 0 & \text{otherwise} \end{cases}.$$

At the end of these steps the swap value matrix typically look like

$$\begin{pmatrix} S_{1,1} & S_{1,2} & \cdots & S_{1,M-1} & S_{1,M} - C_M \\ S_{2,1} & S_{2,2} & \cdots & S_{2,M-1} & 0 \\ \vdots & \vdots & \ddots & \vdots & \vdots \\ S_{n-1,1} & S_{n-1,2} & \cdots & S_{n-1,M-1} & 0 \\ S_{n,1} & S_{n,2} & \cdots & S_{n,M-1} & S_{n,M} - C_M \\ S_{n+1,1} & S_{n+1,2} & \cdots & S_{n+1,M-1} & 0 \\ \vdots & \vdots & \ddots & \vdots & \vdots \\ S_{N,1} & S_{N,2} & \cdots & S_{N,M-1} & 0 \end{pmatrix}.$$

Step 3 Switch to the previous call date T_{M-1} and compute two least squares regressions; the
first is similar to the one above fitting current gains as a function of $\{R_{.,M-1}\}$,

$$\min_{\beta_{M-1}} \left\{ \sum_{n=1}^{N} \left(S_{n,M-1} - C_{M-1} - g(\beta_{M-1}, \{R_{.,M-1}\}) \right)^2 \right\}.$$

The second one regresses the sum of discounted future cashflows on a function
$f(\gamma_{M-1}, \{R_{.,M-1}\})$,

$$\min_{\gamma_{M-1}} \left\{ \sum_{n=1}^{N} \left(\left(S_{n,M} \frac{D_{n,M}}{D_{n,M-1}} \right) - f(\gamma_{M-1}, \{R_{.,M-1}\}) \right)^2 \right\},$$

where γ_{M-1} denotes the regression parameter set. Compute both regression values
using the optimal parameter sets $\beta^\star_{M-1}, \gamma^\star_{M-1}$ in each path

$$RV^g_{n,M-1} = g(\beta^\star_{M-1}, \{R_{.,M-1}\}),$$
$$RV^f_{n,M-1} = f(\gamma^\star_{M-1}, \{R_{.,M-1}\}),$$

and compare $RV^g_{n,M-1}$ to $RV^f_{n,M-1}$: If the first regression value is smaller than the second regression value, it is better to exercise the option and take the difference $SV_{n,M-1} - C_{M-1}$, otherwise set $S_{n,M-1}$ to $S_{n,M}\frac{D_{n,M}}{D_{n,M-1}}$:

$$
S_{n,M-1} = \begin{cases} S_{n,M-1} - C_{M-1} & \text{if } RV^g_{n,M-1} > RV^f_{n,M-1} \\ S_{n,M}\frac{D_{n,M}}{D_{n,M-1}} & \text{else} \end{cases}.
$$

Since all entries of S in column M are no longer needed, they are set to 0.[7] Now, the swap value matrix typically looks like

$$
\begin{pmatrix}
S_{1,1} & S_{1,2} & \cdots & (S_{1,M} - C_M)\frac{D_{n,M}}{D_{n,M-1}} & 0 \\
S_{2,1} & S_{2,2} & \cdots & S_{2,M-1} - C_{M-1} & 0 \\
\vdots & \vdots & \ddots & \vdots & \vdots \\
S_{n-1,1} & S_{n-1,2} & \cdots & S_{n-1,M-1} - C_{M-1} & 0 \\
S_{n,1} & S_{n,2} & \cdots & (S_{n,M} - C_M)\frac{D_{n,M}}{D_{n,M-1}} & 0 \\
S_{n+1,1} & S_{n+1,2} & \cdots & 0 & 0 \\
\vdots & \vdots & \ddots & \vdots & \vdots \\
S_{N,1} & S_{N,2} & \cdots & S_{N,M-1} - C_{M-1} & 0
\end{pmatrix}.
$$

Step 4 Repeat Step 3 for all remaining call dates T_i, $i = M - 2, \ldots, 1$ (replace $M - 1$ by i).
Step 5 After repeating Step 3 for all call dates our final swap value matrix typically looks like

$$
\begin{pmatrix}
(S_{1,M} - C_M)\frac{D_{1,M}}{D_{1,1}} & 0 & \cdots & 0 & 0 \\
(S_{2,M-1} - C_{M-1})\frac{D_{2,M-1}}{D_{2,1}} & 0 & \cdots & 0 & 0 \\
\vdots & \vdots & \ddots & \vdots & \vdots \\
S_{n-1,1} - C_1 & 0 & \cdots & 0 & 0 \\
(S_{n,2} - C_2)\frac{D_{n,2}}{D_{n,1}} & 0 & \cdots & 0 & 0 \\
0 & 0 & \cdots & 0 & 0 \\
\vdots & \vdots & \ddots & \vdots & \vdots \\
(S_{N,M-1} - C_{M-1})\frac{D_{N,M-1}}{D_{N,1}} & 0 & \cdots & 0 & 0
\end{pmatrix}.
$$

There is at most one entry per row in this matrix. Each of these values is discounted to the valuation date using the appropriate discount factors stored in D and the final value of the option is obtained by

$$
\mathbb{E}[CV] = \frac{1}{N}\sum_{n=1}^{N} D_{n,1} S_{n,i}. \tag{11.14}
$$

---

[7] This is not required for the implementation, but allows us to demonstrate the algorithm more clearly

11.2.2   Notes on Basis Functions and Regression

As pointed out in Piterbarg (2005), one should use very simple basis functions. Longstaff and Schwartz (2001) obtained virtually identical lower bound values for different kinds of parametric families. For valuating equities under a Black-Scholes model, Stentoft (2004) has found that the results are practically independent of the basis functions used. From a practical point of view, it is important to bear in mind the trade-off between accuracy and computational effort. For the examples in this book, we have used polynomial basis functions. Glasserman and Yu (2004a) advise choosing the number of basis functions – in our case, the degree of the polynomials – to be rather small. Our own numerical studies indicate that a degree of two or three is typically sufficient to obtain reasonable values for the lower bound. We have also found that the regressors used in the computation tend to have a much higher impact on the quality of the option value than the kind of basis functions. The optimal choice of regressor largely depends on the type of product. Typical regressors are forward or short rates, FX rates, inflation rates, but also coupon and swap rates.

Analysis of Regression for a Callable Snowball

To demonstrate the effect of choosing different variables as regressors, we examine the regression analysis involved in the valuation of a callable snowball instrument in more detail. In a snowball instrument, the value of a coupon does not only depend on a reference rate, but also on the value of the previous coupon. Figure 11.2 compares the option values obtained by one-dimensional regression for two different regressors (coupon rate and reference rate),

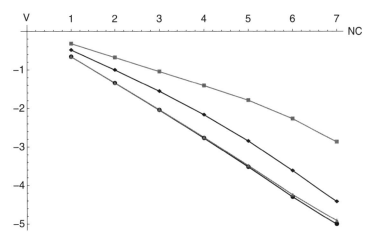

Figure 11.2   The figure shows the development of the option value of a callable snowball instrument as a function of the number of call dates for different underlyings chosen for the regression analysis. Gray squares indicate results obtained with a one-dimensional regression using polynomials of third order and the coupon rate of the snowball as a regressor. Black diamonds show the option values obtained with a one-dimensional regression with polynomials of third order where the reference rate is used as a regressor. Gray triangles indicate option values for a two-dimensional regression with both coupon and reference rates as regressors (two-dimensional polynomials of third order were used as regression functions). The results obtained by solving a two-dimensional PDE, shown as black circles, can be considered as practically exact. The two-dimensional regression evidently reproduces them very well.

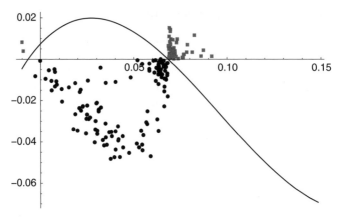

Figure 11.3 The figure shows all "wrong" points for the one-dimensional regression analysis for the callable snowball instrument with the reference rate used as regressor. The black line indicates the regression function. Gray squares and black dots indicate points on the "wrong" side of the regression – wrong sign compared to the regression function.

by two-dimensional regression, and by solving the corresponding PDE. As explained above, in the least squares Monte Carlo scheme the decision whether to exercise or not is taken with respect to the option value obtained from the regression function, but the value used for subsequent calculations is the actual value of the option in the path. This results in "wrong" points, see Figure 11.3. In this specific example, the total number of points was 1024. The number of "wrong" points was 376 for the one-dimensional regression with the coupon rate as a regressor, 174 for the one-dimensional regression with the reference rate as a regressor, and 104 for the two-dimensional regression. This explains the improvement of the option values seen in Figure 11.3.

11.3   EXAMPLES

In this section we focus on lower bounds computed by Monte Carlo least squares regressions. We valuate different instruments under different short rate models and compare these results to accurate solutions of the corresponding PDEs. Upper bound algorithms are closely related but not considered here. Instead, we refer the reader to Rogers (2002) and Haugh and Kogan (2008) (dual upper bounds), Andersen and Broadie (2004) (upper bounds from lower bounds with nested simulation) and Belomestny, Bender and Schoenmakers (2009) (upper bounds from lower bounds without nested simulations).

To show how the modified algorithm improves the results compared to the original Longstaff and Schwartz method, we have valuated a series of Bermudan reverse floaters with increasing maturities under a Vasicek model (Hull-White model with constant parameters). Coupons are paid quarter-annually (0.075-3M Euribor), and we have chosen an initial spot rate of 0.02, a drift of 0.0375, a speed of 1 and a volatility of 0.015. The results of this comparison are shown in Figure 11.4.

11.3.1   A Bermudan Callable Floater under Different Short-rate Models

As an example, we valuate a callable floater which starts on December 1, 2008 and matures after 10 years with a redemption rate of 100%. The bond pays quarterly coupons (C_{RL}) of the

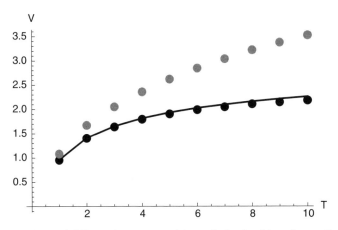

Figure 11.4   Comparison of different least squares Monte Carlo algorithms for ten Bermudan floaters with increasing maturities. The black line marks the PDE option value, the black dots indicate the modified Longstaff-Schwartz approach and the gray dots the original Longstaff-Schwartz method.

form $7.5\% - 1.5*(3M\ Libor)$; all coupons are set in advance. The first coupon rate is 5% and each coupon is floored by zero. Additionally, the payer of the receiving leg has the right to call the bond back on every December 1 for 100%.[8] We have valuated the floater under two models: First, a Hull-White model with the same parameters used in the comparison with the PDE. Second, a Black-Karasinski model where the short rate $r(0)$ is 3%, the drift θ is -0.10, the reversion speed α is 0.04 and the volatility of the process is 0.2. As basis functions, we choose cubic polynomials of the interest rate for both regression functions g and f,

$$g_i(r_i) = \beta_{i,0} + \beta_{i,1}r_i + \beta_{i,2}(r_i)^2 + \beta_{i,3}(r_i)^3,$$
$$f_i(r_i) = \gamma_{i,0} + \gamma_{i,1}r_i + \gamma_{i,2}(r_i)^2 + \gamma_{i,3}(r_i)^3,$$

where i denotes the ith call date. Indices identifying the path are omitted.

Table 11.1 shows the values of the bond and the Bermudan option under the Hull-White model; the results for the Black-Karasinski model are shown in Table 11.2. We have used up to 2^{19} paths in the Monte Carlo simulation. In order to verify the Monte Carlo results, we again compare them to the results obtained by solving the corresponding PDE using a finite difference algorithm:

Hull & White

PDE bond value : 103.1920
PDE option value : -1.4837

Black & Karasinski

PDE bond value : 100.0210
PDE option value : -3.8031

---

[8] The exact specifications of this instrument and of all others in the following examples can be obtained from the authors.

Table 11.1 Monte Carlo bond and option values for a callable floater under a Hull-White model. The symbol (s.e.) denotes the standard error for the callable bond. The last three columns show the differences to the results obtained by solving the corresponding PDE. The original least squares option values are computed with the algorithm published by Longstaff and Schwartz (2001).

Paths 2^x	Least squares bond	Least squares option	Original least squares	(s.e.)	Difference Bond	Difference Option	Callable bond
10	103.0476	−1.4495	−2.2124	(.2222)	−.1444	.0342	−.1102
11	103.1091	−1.4523	−2.1865	(.1552)	−.0829	.0314	−.0515
12	103.3264	−1.4994	−2.2148	(.1101)	.1343	−.0156	.1186
13	103.2745	−1.5066	−2.2202	(.0774)	.0824	−.0228	.0595
14	103.1916	−1.4584	−2.1827	(.0544)	−.0004	.0253	.0248
15	103.1668	−1.4536	−2.1868	(.0383)	−.0252	.0301	.0048
16	103.2098	−1.4694	−2.1911	(.0271)	.0177	.0143	.0320
17	103.1793	−1.4656	−2.1785	(.0192)	−.0127	.0181	.0053
18	103.1622	−1.4559	−2.1679	(.0136)	−.0298	.0278	−.0020
19	103.1678	−1.4621	−2.1694	(.0096)	−.0242	.0216	−.0026

The parameters of the PDE solution (365 time steps per year and a grid of 1000 points for the interest rate) have been chosen to achieve very accurate values.

11.3.2 A Bermudan Callable Steepener Swap under a Two Factor Hull-White Model

In this example, a callable Steepener swap which starts on January 1, 2008 and matures on January 1, 2018 is valuated. The instrument pays quarter-annual coupons (C_{PL}) of the form 0.5*(3M Libor)−0.5% set in advance and receives annual coupons (C_{RL}) of the form 10 ∗ (10YCMS−2YCMS) + 1%, set in advance too. All coupons are floored by zero. The first

Table 11.2 Monte Carlo bond and option values for a callable floater under a Black-Karasinski model. The symbol (s.e.) denotes the standard error of the callable bond. The last three columns show the difference to the results obtained by solving the corresponding PDE. The original least squares option values are computed with the algorithm published by Longstaff and Schwartz (2001).

Paths 2^x	Least squares bond	Least squares option	Original least squares	(s.e.)	Difference Bond	Difference Option	Callable bond
10	99.6719	−3.5569	−3.8928	(.4580)	−.3495	.2462	.1032
11	99.7827	−3.5543	−3.8947	(.3181)	−.2387	.2588	.0101
12	100.4040	−3.8305	−4.1052	(.2234)	.3828	−.0273	.3555
13	100.2300	−3.8027	−4.0723	(.1588)	.2083	.0004	.2088
14	100.0640	−3.7210	−4.0009	(.1127)	.0422	.0821	.1244
15	99.9717	−3.6831	−3.9582	(.0794)	−.0497	.1200	.0703
16	100.0850	−3.7393	−4.0156	(.0560)	.0631	.0638	.1270
17	99.9875	−3.7480	−4.0148	(.0399)	−.0339	.0551	.0021
18	99.9494	−3.7324	−3.9992	(.0282)	−.0720	.0707	.0012
19	99.9612	−3.7337	−4.0033	(.0199)	−.0602	.0694	.0092

Table 11.3 Monte Carlo swap and option values for a callable Steepener swap under a two factor Hull-White model. The symbol (s.e.) denotes the standard error of the callable swap. The last three columns contain the difference to the results obtained by solving the corresponding PDE. The original least squares option values are computed with the algorithm published by Longstaff and Schwartz (2001).

Paths 2^x	Least squares swap	Least squares option	Original least squares	(s.e.)	Difference Swap	Difference Option	Callable swap
10	−3.3334	−4.2784	−3.9019	(.2804)	.4464	.1686	−.2778
11	−3.5831	−4.1242	−3.7590	(.1993)	.1967	.0144	−.1823
12	−3.7474	−4.0524	−3.7129	(.1417)	.0324	−.0573	.0898
13	−3.9417	−4.0025	−3.6611	(.0993)	−.1618	−.1072	.0545
14	−3.7410	−4.0922	−3.7452	(.0702)	.0388	.0175	.0564
15	−3.7240	−4.0748	−3.7298	(.0497)	.0558	.0349	.0908
16	−3.7975	−4.0337	−3.6914	(.0350)	−.0176	.0760	.0584
17	−3.8185	−4.0149	−3.6824	(.0248)	−.0386	.0948	.0562
18	−3.7838	−4.0414	−3.7062	(.0175)	−.0039	.0683	−.0644
19	−3.8212	−4.0263	−3.6897	(.0124)	−.0413	.0834	−.0421

coupon rate is 3.5% for the paid leg and 5% for the received leg. Additionally, the payer of the receiving leg has the right to call the swap back on every January 1 for 0% starting on January 1, 2013. For valuation, we use a two factor Hull-White model where the short rate $r(0)$ is 5%, the drift is 6%, the reversion speed of r is 1, the reversion speed of u is 0.05, the volatility of r is 1%, the volatility of u is 1.5% and the correlation between the r and u process is 0.2. Again, we choose cubic polynomials of the interest rate as basis functions for both regression functions g and h. Table 11.3 shows the values of the bond and the Bermudan option. Again, we have used up to 2^{19} paths in the Monte Carlo simulation. For verification, we compare the Monte Carlo results to PDE solutions obtained with a streamline diffusion algorithm (Binder and Schatz, 2004):

$$\text{PDE swap value} : -3.7798$$
$$\text{PDE option value} : -4.1097$$

These values are again generated with 365 time steps per year and 1000 discretization points for the short rate and u processes.

11.3.3 A Bermudan Callable Steepener Cross Currency Swap in a 3D IR/FX Model Framework

In our final example we valuate an FX linked swap under a three-dimensional IR/FX model framework. The FX linked swap starts on January 1, 2009 and matures on January 1, 2014. The currency of the product is EUR, the currency of the paid leg is CHF and the currency of the received leg is EUR again. The swap pays annual coupons (C_{PL}) of the form 1.25 × (3M EURIBOR) set in arrears and receives annual coupons (C_{RL}) of the form (3M CHFLIBOR) + 0.02×FX, set in arrears too. All coupons are without floor. In addition, the payer of the receiving leg has the right to call the swap back on every January 1 for 0% starting on January 1, 2009.

The three-dimensional IR/FX model consists of two Hull-White models (the domestic and foreign interest rate processes) and one log-normal process for the exchange rate,

$$\text{EUR: } dr^1(t) = (0.0125 - 0.25\, r^1(t))dt + 0.01\, dW^1(t),$$
$$\text{CHF: } dr^2(t) = (0.00625 - 0.25\, r^2(t))dt + 0.015\, dW^2(t),$$
$$\text{CHF/EUR: } dfx(t) = (r^1(t) - r^2(t))fx(t)dt + 0.05\, fx(t)dW^3(t).$$

Here,

$$r^1(0) = 0.04, \; r^2(0) = 0.02, \; fx(0) = 0.62,$$

and the correlation matrix ρ is a matrix of constants,

$$\begin{pmatrix} \rho_{r1,r1} & \rho_{r1,r2} & \rho_{r1,fx} \\ \rho_{r2,r1} & \rho_{r2,r2} & \rho_{r2,fx} \\ \rho_{fx,r1} & \rho_{fx,r2} & \rho_{fx,fx} \end{pmatrix} = \begin{pmatrix} 1 & 0.8 & -0.2 \\ 0.8 & 1 & -0.15 \\ -0.2 & -0.15 & 1 \end{pmatrix}.$$

As basis functions for the function g we choose a constant, the first two powers of all underlyings (both interest rates and the exchange rate) and the mixed terms,

$$g\left(r_i^1, r_i^2, fx_i\right) = \beta_{i,0} + \beta_{i,1} r_i^1 + \beta_{i,2} \left(r_{k,.}^1\right)^2$$
$$+ \beta_{i,3} r_i^2 + \beta_{i,4}(r_i^2)^2$$
$$+ \beta_{i,5} fx_i + \beta_{i,6}(fx_i)^2$$
$$+ \beta_{i,7} r_i^1 r_i^2 + \beta_{i,8} r_i^1 fx_i + \beta_{i,9} r_i^2 fx_i.$$

For f, we choose a constant and the first two powers of the domestic interest rate (the rate which is used to discount the option values),

$$f\left(r_i^1\right) = \gamma_{i,0} + \gamma_{i,1} r_i^1 + \gamma_{i,2} \left(r_i^1\right)^2.$$

This choice of basis functions and the number of polynomials is heuristic and follows no strict rule. We have, however, performed extensive tests and in our experience simple power functions with an order of two or three work very well. In addition, our investigations indicate that g should only contain those underlyings that are necessary to determine the coupons, and that it is sufficient for f to contain only underlyings necessary for discounting the future option values. Table 11.4 shows the values of the bond and the Bermudan option. Up to 2^{19} paths are used in our Monte Carlo simulation.

Again, we have used a partial differential equation approach in order to verify the results. The PDE swap and option values are

$$\text{PDE swap value : } 8.9850$$
$$\text{PDE option value : } -7.1400.$$

For computational efficiency, we have restricted ourselves to the three-dimensional case in this example. With $\mathbf{x} = (fx, r_d, r_f)$, the corresponding initial value problem is (Reisinger (2004))

$$\frac{\partial u}{\partial t} - \frac{1}{2} \sum_{i,j=1}^{3} v_i v_j \rho_{ij} \frac{\partial^2 u}{\partial x_i \partial x_j} - \sum_{i=1}^{3} \mu_i \frac{\partial u}{\partial x_i} + \rho_{31} v_3 v_1 \frac{\partial u}{\partial x_3} + x_2 u = 0. \quad (11.15)$$

Table 11.4   Monte Carlo swap and option values for a callable FX linked swap under a multi-dimensional model. The symbol (s.e.) denotes the standard error for the callable swap. The last three columns contain the difference to the results obtained by solving the corresponding PDE. The original least squares option values are computed with the algorithm published by Longstaff and Schwartz (2001).

Paths 2^x	Least squares swap	Least squares option	Original least squares	(s.e.)	Difference Swap	Difference Option	Callable swap
10	9.0170	−7.1247	−6.7705	(.1429)	.0320	.0152	.0472
11	9.0608	−7.1815	−6.8324	(.1048)	.0758	−.0414	.0343
12	9.0454	−7.1661	−6.8225	(.0741)	.0604	−.0261	.0342
13	9.0183	−7.1523	−6.8259	(.0518)	.0333	−.0123	.0210
14	8.9658	−7.1072	−6.7939	(.0369)	−.0191	.0327	.0135
15	8.9887	−7.1324	−6.8229	(.0261)	.0037	.0075	.0113
16	8.9971	−7.1394	−6.8275	(.0183)	.0121	.0005	.0127
17	9.0165	−7.1592	−6.8460	(.0130)	.0315	−.0192	.0122
18	9.0288	−7.1687	−6.8537	(.0092)	.0438	−.0286	.0151
19	9.0188	−7.1595	−6.8532	(.0065)	.0338	−.0195	.0143

The parameters ρ_{ij} determine the correlations of the different Wiener processes, and μ_i, v_i are defined as

$$\mu_1(t) = 0.01250 - 0.25\, r^1(t), \quad v_1(t) = 0.01,$$

and

$$\mu_3(t) = (r^1(t) - r^2(t))f\,x(t), \quad v_3(t) = 0.1\,f\,x(t).$$

The initial value corresponds to the payoff structure at maturity T,

$$u(\mathbf{x}, 0) = SV(T), \tag{11.16}$$

and is propagated backwards in time. We have discretized equation (11.15) using finite differences for the derivatives and have included upwinding to avoid numerical instabilities. To maintain stability in the time domain, a fully implicit backward Euler scheme has been used. At each time step, the resulting system of linear equations has been solved using BICGSTAB (van der Vorst, 1992). We have used 365 time steps per year, 121 discretization points for the domestic rate, 101 points for the foreign rate and 251 points for the exchange rate.

12

Characteristic Function Methods

for Option Pricing

The conditional expectation of the value of a contract payoff function under the risk neutral measure can be linked to the solution of a partial (integro-) differential equation (PIDE) (Øksendal, 2007). This PIDE can then be solved using discretization schemes, such as Finite Differences (FD) and Finite Elements (FEM), or by Wavelet-based methods, together with appropriate boundary and terminal conditions. A direct discretization of the underlying stochastic differential equation, on the other hand, leads to (Quasi)Monte Carlo (QMC) methods. Both groups of numerical techniques – discretization of the P(I)DE as well as discretization of the SDE – are discussed elsewhere in the book. A third group of methods, which will be discussed in this chapter, directly applies numerical integration techniques to the risk neutral valuation formula for European options (Cox and Ross, 1976)

$$V(x, t_0) = e^{-r\Delta t}\mathbb{E}^Q[V(y, T)|x] = e^{-r\Delta t} \int_{\mathbb{R}} V(y, T) f(y \mid x) dy, \tag{12.1}$$

where V denotes the option value, Δt is the difference between the maturity T and the valuation date t_0, $f(y \mid x)$ is the probability density of $y = \ln(S_T/K)$ given $x = \ln(S_0/K)$, and r is the risk neutral interest rate. Direct integration techniques have often been limited to the valuation of vanilla options, but their efficiency makes them particularly suitable for calibration purposes. A large part of state of the art numerical integration techniques relies on a transformation to the Fourier domain (Carr and Madan, 1999). In Equation (12.1), the probability density function $f(y \mid x)$ appears in the integrand in the original pricing domain (for example the price or the log-price), but is not known analytically for many important pricing processes. The characteristic functions of these processes, on the other hand, can often be expressed analytically, where the characteristic function $\phi(\omega) = \mathbb{E}[e^{i\omega X}]$ of a real valued random variable X is the Fourier transform of its distribution. The probability density function and its corresponding characteristic function thus form a Fourier pair,

$$\phi(\omega) = \frac{1}{\sqrt{2\pi}} \int_{\mathbb{R}} e^{i x \omega} f(x) dx \qquad \text{and} \qquad f(x) = \frac{1}{\sqrt{2\pi}} \int_{\mathbb{R}} e^{-i x \omega} \phi(\omega) d\omega. \tag{12.2}$$

Many probabilistic properties of random variables correspond to analytical properties of their characteristic functions, making them a very useful concept for studying random variables. The characteristic function of a random variable completely characterizes its distribution law: two variables with the same characteristic function are identically distributed. Given the characteristic function of the stochastic process responsible for the propagation of the state variables, different techniques, such as Fourier inversion and series expansion methods, can be applied to obtain option prices of options written on these state variables. Before going deeper into this topic, we will present a number of advanced equity models.

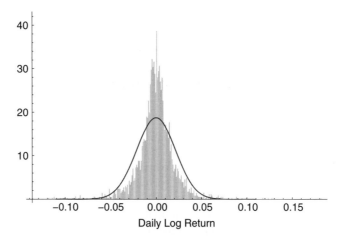

Figure 12.1 Histogram and fitted normal distribution of the daily log-returns of the General Electric stock between 2000-01-03 and 2012-12-07. The histogram and the overlaying normal distribution clearly show that the assumption of normally distributed daily log-returns does not properly describe the tail behavior of the empirical distribution.

12.1 EQUITY MODELS

The shortcomings of the Black-Scholes model are well known: First, the assumed normally distributed log-returns are not found in reality. Empirical studies show that returns of traded assets and indices are skewed[1] and fat tailed.[2] Figures 12.1 and 12.2 show these deviations from the normal distribution for the General Electric stock.[3] Second, the Black-Scholes model cannot reproduce the volatility smile as it has only one parameter, the volatility σ, to price a European option. All other parameters are either determined by the contract or by the imposed no-arbitrage conditions. Since there is a liquid market for such options, an implied volatility can be calculated from their prices,

$$S_t \Phi \left(d_+(\hat{\sigma}) \right) - e^{-r(T-t)} K \Phi \left(d_-(\hat{\sigma}) \right) = C^{\text{Market}}(S_t, K, t, T), \qquad (12.3)$$

where

$$d_{\pm}(\hat{\sigma}) = \frac{\log(S_t/K) + \left(r \pm \frac{1}{2}\hat{\sigma}^2 \right)(T-t)}{\hat{\sigma}\sqrt{T-t}}. \qquad (12.4)$$

Under the Black-Scholes model, all European options on the same underlying would have the same implied volatility $\hat{\sigma}$. In real markets, however, $\hat{\sigma}$ depends on the expiry of the instrument as well as on the strike price of the option, as shown in Figure 12.3 for options on the FTSE-100.

The Dupire local volatility model (see Chapter 15) has been introduced by Dupire, Derman and Kani in 1994 to represent the volatility smile in a more satisfying way. In contrast to the Black-Scholes model, where the volatility σ is kept constant over time, the basic idea is to

---

[1] Skewness is a measure of the asymmetry of the probability distribution of a real valued random variable. It is the third standardized moment of a random variable.
[2] The corresponding quantity to measure the "peakedness" and therefore the tail behavior of a probability distribution of a real valued random variable is the kurtosis. It is the fourth standardized moment of a random variable.
[3] Data (Provider: Yahoo Financial Data) for the General Electric stock between 2000-01-03 and 2012-12-07 is used.

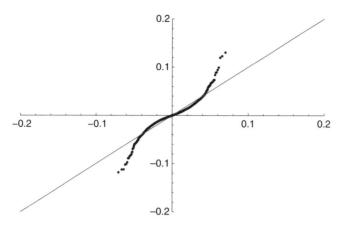

Figure 12.2 Quantile-Quantile plot of the daily log-returns of the General Electric stock between 2000-01-03 and 2012-12-07. For comparison, the fixed point line (quantile-quantile plot of the normal distribution) is plotted. Obviously, the normal distribution does not adequately describe the distribution of the daily log-returns. Especially the tail region (and therefore the occurrence of large up and down moves) is underestimated by the assumption of normally distributed log-returns.

regard the volatility as a function of the price of the underlying asset and the time, $\sigma = \sigma(S_t, t)$. Again, the underlying price process of the asset is modeled as an Ito process,

$$\frac{dS_t}{S_t} = \mu(S_t, t)dt + \sigma(S_t, t)dW_t.$$

Under the assumption that μ and σ are bounded and continuously differentiable, a solution for this stochastic differential equation is guaranteed to exist. The local volatility (Dupire) model allows to fit the observed volatility surface, but provides no more information into the

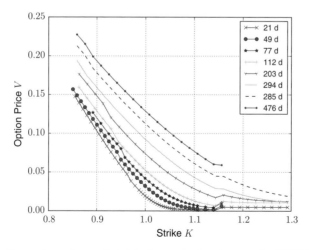

Figure 12.3 The figure shows the market data for a set of options on the FTSE-100 index for May 1st 2008. The forward rates (GBP) on that date ranged between 3.4% p.a. and 4.52% p.a. (continuous compounding). Each line corresponds to an expiry date for European call options.

underlying economic dynamics. A modification of the Black-Scholes model that allows for a better interpretation from an economical point of view is to use a second stochastic process for the volatility. As an example for this approach, we will discuss the Heston model below.

The models we discussed so far did not include the possibility of jumps, i.e., discontinuous asset price processes. In real markets, however, such jumps do occur. While small jumps can be satisfactorily explained by diffusion, this is no longer possible for the more pronounced breaks in market behavior that have happened several times in history (Black Monday, 9/11, Lehman Brothers, ...). There are two different categories of financial models with jumps: The first are so-called *jump diffusion models*, where a diffusion process responsible for the "normal" evolution of prices is augmented by additional jumps added at random intervals. In these models, jumps represent rare events, such as crashes and large drawdowns. This kind of evolution of the asset price can be represented by modeling the (log)-price as a Lévy process[4] (Cont and Tankov, 2003) with a non-zero Gaussian component and a jump part. The jump part is a compound Poisson process with finitely many jumps in every time interval. Depending on the distribution used for jump sizes, different jump diffusion models exist. The second category of jump models uses infinite activity Lévy processes for propagating the state variable. Examples for models in this category are the Variance Gamma (VG) model and the Normal Inverse Gaussian (NIG) model.

Although the class of Lévy processes is rich, it is insufficient for multi-period financial modeling due to the stationarity of increments (new market information cannot be taken into account in the return distribution) and due to the fact that moments and cumulants depend on time in a well-defined manner. This does not always coincide with the empirically observed time-dependence of these quantities (Bates, 1996). Bates added a jump term to the Heston model to introduce a diffusion model with stochastic volatility and a jump component.

12.1.1 Heston Model

The Heston stochastic volatility model (Heston, 1993) relaxes the constant volatility assumption in the classical Black-Scholes model by incorporating an instantaneous short-term variance process,

$$dS_t = (r(t) - q(t))S_t dt + \sqrt{v_t} S_t dW_t^1, \tag{12.5}$$

where r denotes the domestic yield curve, q the foreign yield or continuous dividend curve, v denotes the stock price variance and dW_t^1 is a standard Brownian motion. In the Heston model, the variance is stochastic and follows a classical Cox-Ingersoll-Ross (CIR) process,

$$dv_t = \kappa(\Theta - v_t)dt + \sigma\sqrt{v_t}dW_t^2, \qquad v_0 \geq 0. \tag{12.6}$$

The Heston model allows to reproduce a number of different smile and skew patterns of volatility surfaces with a comparatively small number of parameters:

- ρ, which is defined as $\rho dt = E[dW_t^1, dW_t^2]$ and can be interpreted as the correlation between the log-returns and the variance of the asset, affects the skewness of the distribution. Since the volatility tends to rise when asset prices are falling and tends to fall when asset prices are increasing (leverage effect), ρ is typically negative.

---

[4] A Lévy process is a stochastic process with independent, stationary increments.

- σ, the volatility of variance parameter, is responsible for the kurtosis (peak) of the distribution. With regard to the volatility surface, σ affects the intensity of the smile effect.
- κ, the mean reversion parameter, represents the degree of volatility clustering.
- Θ is the long-term level of the variance process and v_0 is the initial variance of the underlying.

The variance process is always positive if

$$2\kappa\Theta > \sigma^2 \tag{12.7}$$

(Feller condition) and mean reverting, i.e., the drift term $\kappa(\Theta - v_t)$ is positive if $v_t < \Theta$ and negative if $v_t > \Theta$. The process v_t will therefore, on average, tend to Θ (is fluctuating around the long-term mean Θ). The characteristic function of the Heston model (Albrecher, Mayer, Schoutens and Tistaert, 2007) is given by

$$\phi(\omega) = \exp\left(i\omega(\log S_0 + (r - q)t)\right)$$
$$\times \exp\left(\theta\kappa\sigma^{-2}\left((\kappa - \rho i\omega - d)t - 2\log\left(\frac{1 - ge^{-dt}}{1 - g}\right)\right)\right) \tag{12.8}$$
$$\times \exp\left(v_0\sigma^{-2}(\kappa - \rho\sigma i\omega - d)\left(\frac{1 - e^{-dt}}{1 - ge^{-dt}}\right)\right),$$

where

$$d = \sqrt{(\rho\sigma i\omega - \kappa)^2 + \sigma^2(i\omega + \omega^2)},$$
$$g = \frac{(\kappa - \rho\sigma i\omega - d)}{(\kappa - \rho\sigma i\omega + d)}.$$

Figure 12.4 shows the real part, the imaginary part and the absolute value of the characteristic function of the Heston model for a typical set of parameters.

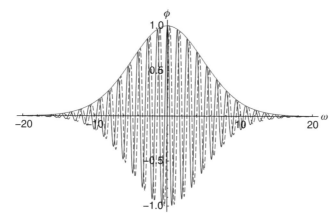

Figure 12.4 Real part (solid oscillating line), imaginary part (dashed oscillating line) and absolute value (solid envelope line) of the characteristic function of the Heston model for a typical set of parameters ($\theta = 0.05$, $\kappa = 1.5$, $\sigma = 0.1$, $\rho = -0.9$, $v_0 = 0.03$) and $t = 1$. Note the highly oscillatory behavior and the absolute value acting as an envelope function.

12.1.2 Jump Diffusion Models

Jump diffusion models add a jump process to the Brownian motion responsible for the "normal" propagation of the underlying. In such models, jumps represent rare events like crashes. The Black-Scholes model is extended through the addition of a compound Poisson jump process (Cont and Tankov, 2003) to capture the skewness and tail behavior observed in real world data. A compound Poisson process with intensity $\lambda > 0$ and a jump size distribution f is a stochastic process X_t,

$$X_t = \sum_{i=1}^{N_t} Y_i,$$

where N_t is a Poisson process with intensity λ independent from Y_i. The jump sizes Y_i are independent and identically distributed with distribution f. At a given time t the characteristic function of the compound Poisson process is given by

$$E\left[e^{i\omega X_t}\right] = \exp\left\{t\lambda \int_{\mathbb{R}} (e^{i\omega x} - 1) f(dx)\right\}. \tag{12.9}$$

Adding the drift and Brownian motion we end up with

$$X_t = \mu t + \sigma W_t + \sum_{i=1}^{N_t} Y_i, \tag{12.10}$$

where

$$S_t = S_0 \exp\{X_t\}. \tag{12.11}$$

The process in Equation (12.10) is again a Lévy process, since the Brownian motion part is independent of the jump part, and the characteristic function can thus be computed by multiplying the characteristic function of the Brownian motion with the characteristic function of the compound Poisson process,

$$E\left[e^{i\omega X_t}\right] = \exp\left\{t\left(i\omega\mu - \frac{\sigma^2\omega^2}{2} + \lambda \int_{\mathbb{R}} (e^{i\omega x} - 1) f(dx)\right)\right\}. \tag{12.12}$$

Merton Jump Diffusion Model

The Merton Jump Diffusion model (MJD) (Merton, 1976) uses a normal distribution for f, where $Y_i \sim \mu_j + Z\sigma_j$, with Z a standard normal random variable. This extension adds three additional parameters to the Black-Scholes model – the intensity of the compound Poisson process λ_j, the jump mean μ_j and the standard deviation of the jump size σ_j. In the risk neutral measure, μ in (12.10) becomes

$$\mu = r - \lambda\left(e^{\mu_j + \frac{\sigma_j^2}{2}} - 1\right). \tag{12.13}$$

The characteristic function of the MJD model (Cont and Tankov, 2003) is given by

$$\phi(\omega) = \exp\left\{i\omega\left(\mu - \frac{\sigma^2}{2}\right)t - \frac{\omega^2\sigma^2}{2}t + \lambda_j t\left(e^{i\omega\mu_j - \frac{\sigma_j^2\omega^2}{2}} - 1\right)\right\}. \tag{12.14}$$

Kou Model

Kou (2002) modeled the jump distribution f with an asymmetric double exponential distribution to distinguish between up and down moves. In the Kou model four additional parameters arise, namely the intensity of the compound Poisson process λ_j, the intensity of the exponential distribution for down jumps λ_-, the intensity of the exponential distribution for up jumps λ_+ and the probability for the up jump p. In the risk neutral measure μ in (12.10) becomes

$$\mu = r - \lambda\xi, \tag{12.15}$$

where

$$\xi = \frac{p\lambda_+}{\lambda_+ - 1} + \frac{(1-p)\lambda_-}{\lambda_- + 1} - 1. \tag{12.16}$$

The characteristic function of the Kou model (Cont and Tankov, 2003) is given by

$$\phi(\omega) = \exp\left\{ \iota\omega\left(\mu - \frac{\sigma^2}{2}\right)t - \frac{\omega^2\sigma^2}{2}t + \lambda t\left(\frac{p}{1 - \iota\omega\lambda_+} + \frac{1-p}{1 - \iota\omega\lambda_-} - 1\right)\right\}. \tag{12.17}$$

12.1.3 Infinite Activity Models

Infinite Activity Models are a category of jump models with an infinite number of jumps in every interval. The whole dynamics of the underlying is generated solely through jumps, there is thus no need for a separate diffusion process or a distribution of jump sizes. We will present two such models, the Variance Gamma (VG) model and the Normal Inverse Gaussian (NIG) model.

Variance Gamma Model

The Variance Gamma (VG) process (Geman, 2002) is a three-parameter generalization of the Brownian motion,

$$S(t) = S(0)\exp\left\{ \int_0^t r(s)ds + \kappa t + X(t, \eta, \Theta, \sigma)\right\}, \tag{12.18}$$

with

$$\kappa = \frac{1}{\eta}\log\left(1 - \Theta\eta - \frac{1}{2}\sigma^2\eta\right). \tag{12.19}$$

Here, the time t in the Brownian motion

$$B(t, \Theta, \sigma) = \Theta t + \sigma W(t), \tag{12.20}$$

where $W(t)$ is a Wiener process, has been replaced by a Gamma process γ with independent Gamma$(1, \eta)$-distributed time increments,

$$X(t, \eta, \Theta, \sigma) = B(\gamma(t, 1, \eta), \Theta, \sigma). \tag{12.21}$$

The process has infinitely many jumps in any time interval, but only finitely many of them are larger than any given positive size. The Brownian motion is determined by two parameters, the volatility σ and the drift Θ. As in the Black-Scholes model, σ can be interpreted as the volatility of the stock price process and Θ is responsible for the skewness. The parameter

η controls the Gamma-distributed time increments and is responsible for the kurtosis of the distribution. The characteristic function of the VG model (Cont and Tankov, 2003) is given by

$$\phi(\omega) = \left(\frac{1}{1 - \iota \Theta \eta \omega + \frac{\sigma^2}{2} \eta \omega^2} \right)^{\frac{t}{\eta}}. \tag{12.22}$$

Normal Inverse Gaussian Model

The Normal Inverse Gaussian (NIG) model (Rydberg, 1997) is also a generalization of the Brownian motion,

$$S(t) = S(0) \exp \left\{ \int_0^t r(s)ds + \kappa t + X(t, \eta, \Theta, \sigma) \right\}, \tag{12.23}$$

where

$$\kappa = \frac{1}{\eta} - \frac{1}{\eta} \sqrt{1 - \Theta \eta - \frac{1}{2} \sigma^2 \eta}. \tag{12.24}$$

In the NIG model, the time t in the Brownian motion is replaced by an inverse Gaussian process NIG with independent NIG$(t, \alpha, \beta, \delta, 0)$-distributed time increments,

$$X(t, \eta, \Theta, \sigma) = B(\text{NIG}(t, \alpha, \beta, \delta, 0), \Theta, \sigma), \tag{12.25}$$

with

$$\alpha = \sqrt{\frac{\eta^2}{\sigma^2} + \frac{\Theta^2}{\sigma^4}}, \quad \beta = \frac{\Theta}{\sigma^2}, \quad \delta = \sigma. \tag{12.26}$$

Again, the process has infinitely many jumps in any time interval, but only finitely many of them are larger than any given positive size. The parameter Θ is responsible for the skewness and the parameter η is responsible for the kurtosis of the distribution. The characteristic function of the NIG model (Cont and Tankov, 2003) is given by

$$\phi(\omega) = \exp \left\{ \delta \left(\sqrt{\alpha^2 - \beta^2} - \sqrt{\alpha^2 - (\beta + \iota \omega)^2} \right) \right\}. \tag{12.27}$$

12.1.4   Bates Model

The Bates model is an extension of the Heston model allowing for jumps in the stock price process. The jumps are modeled by a compound Poisson process N_t with intensity λ_j and jumps J, independent of the Brownian paths W_t^1 and W_t^2.

$$dS_t = (r_d(t) - r_f(t))S_t dt + \sqrt{v_t} S_t dW_t^1 + J_t dN_t, \tag{12.28}$$

$$dv_t = \kappa \left(\theta - v_t^2 \right) dt + \sigma \sqrt{v_t} dW_t^2, \quad v_0 \geq 0, \tag{12.29}$$

$$\text{Cov}\left(dW_t^1, dW_t^2 \right) = \rho dt. \tag{12.30}$$

J denotes the percentage jump size, which is lognormal and identically distributed,

$$\ln(1 + J) \sim N\left(\ln(1 + \mu_j) - \frac{1}{2}\sigma_j^2, \sigma_j^2\right). \tag{12.31}$$

The Bates model uses eight model parameters $(\kappa, \Theta, \sigma, \rho, v_0, \lambda_j, \mu_j, \sigma_j)$, where the first five parameters are identical to the corresponding parameters in the underlying Heston model, λ_j is the jump intensity, μ_j is the mean jump size and σ_j the mean jump volatility. The characteristic function of the Bates model (Cont and Tankov, 2003) is given by

$$\phi(\omega) = \exp\left(\iota\omega(\log S_0 + (r - q)t)\right)$$

$$\times \exp\left\{\frac{\Theta\kappa}{\sigma^2}((\kappa - \rho\sigma\omega\iota - d)t - 2\log\left(\frac{1 - ge^{-dt}}{1 - g}\right)\right.$$

$$+ \frac{v_0}{\sigma^2}(\kappa - \rho\sigma\omega\iota - d)\frac{1 - e^{-dt}}{1 - ge^{-dt}}$$

$$\left. - \lambda_j\mu_j\iota\omega T + \lambda_j T((1 + \mu_j)^{\iota\omega}\exp\left(\sigma_j^2\frac{\iota\omega}{2}(\iota\omega - 1)\right) - 1)\right\}, \tag{12.32}$$

with

$$d = ((\rho\sigma\omega\iota - \kappa)^2 - \sigma^2(-\iota\omega - \omega^2))^{\frac{1}{2}}, \tag{12.33}$$

$$g = \frac{\kappa - \rho\sigma\omega\iota - d}{\kappa - \rho\sigma\omega\iota + d}. \tag{12.34}$$

12.2 FOURIER TECHNIQUES

When their underlyings are driven by stochastic processes with known characteristic functions, options can be priced by applying Fourier inversion methods. Two main trends are found in the literature, applying Fourier inversion either to the cumulative distribution function, which leads to Black-Scholes-style formulae (Bakshi and Madan, 2000), or to the probability density function (Carr and Madan, 1999). Apart from using quadrature rules to directly evaluate the inversion of the Fourier integral, the integration can be performed by Fast Fourier Transform algorithms (Jackson, Jaimungal and Surkov, 2009) or series expansions (Fang and Oosterlee, 2008). Recently, characteristic function methods have been applied to options other than European vanilla options, see, for example, (Jackson, Jaimungal and Surkov, 2009; Fang and Oosterlee, 2009). Both methods discussed in this chapter offer good parallelizability (Surkov, 2010; Zhang, 2009) on CPUs as well as on graphics processing units.

12.2.1 Fast Fourier Transform Methods

To price an option with the Fast Fourier Transform technique (Jackson, Jaimungal and Surkov, 2009), we start by considering a truncated stock price domain $\Omega = [y_{min}, y_{max}]$, where $y = \log(S/K)$ (or, alternatively, $y = \log S/S_0$). This domain is partitioned into a finite mesh of points $y_0, \ldots, y_{N-1}$, where

$$y_n = y_{min} + n\Delta y, \qquad \Delta y = \frac{y_{max} - y_{min}}{N - 1}.$$

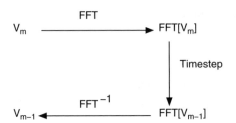

Figure 12.5 Schematic display of the Fourier time-stepping scheme for the propagation from t_m to t_{m-1}.

Furthermore, we consider a discretization of the time domain into $t_0, \ldots, t_M = T$ into M intervals. At maturity, we calculate the payoff of the option $V(y, t_M) = V(y, T)$. Then, at each time step, we repeat the following steps:

- for $m = M, \ldots 0$ do:
  - transform $V(y, t_m)$ to the Fourier domain using the FFT:

$$V(\omega, t_m) = \mathcal{F}[V(y, t_m)]. \tag{12.35}$$

  - multiply with the characteristic function $\phi(\omega)$ with $t = t_m - t_{m-1}$
  - apply the inverse Fourier transform back to the original pricing domain to calculate the set of prices at t_{m-1},

$$V(y, t_{m-1}) = \mathcal{F}^{-1}\left[\phi(\omega)V(\omega, t_m)\right]. \tag{12.36}$$

Figure 12.5 schematically shows the algorithm for propagating the prices from t_m to $t_m - 1$. The price at t_0 is obtained using interpolation on the grid. With the Fast Fourier Transformation, one transformation can be performed with a computational complexity of $O(N \log_2 N)$. A major drawback of the the FFT algorithm is the restriction to an equidistantly spaced grid in the price domain. In addition, the pricing of American/Bermudan and other exotic, in particular path-dependent, options can require long computation times.[5] Oosterlee and Fang overcame this drawback by using Fourier-Cosine expansions to replace the FFT (Fang and Oosterlee, 2008), a method we will discuss in the following section.

Pricing with the Fourier Transformation Method

To check the accuracy of the Fourier method, we calculate the price of a European call option with strike price $K = 100$ as a function of the number of discretization points N using the Black-Scholes model with $\sigma = 0.2$ (underlying: $S_0 = 100$, risk-free rate: $r = 0.02$). The results are shown in Figure 12.6. For comparison, the corresponding analytical value is also shown in the figure.

A key advantage of characteristic function methods is the ability to switch between different models by simply replacing the characteristic function in the algorithm. They are thus well suited to compare option prices between different models with a minimal method risk.

---

[5] For example when pricing a barrier or an American option at each time step the decision whether early exercise takes place or the barrier is hit can only be made in the original pricing domain. Therefore at each time step two extra Fourier transformations need to be applied significantly increasing the computation time.

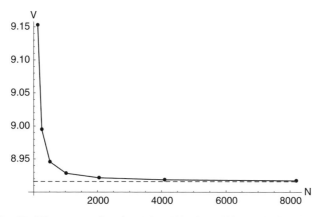

Figure 12.6 Price V of European call option ($K = 100$, $S_0 = 100$, $r = 0.02$) using the Black-Scholes model with $\sigma = 0.2$ as a function of the number of discretization points N (solid line). For comparison the corresponding analytical value is shown (dashed line).

Figure 12.7 shows the values for a European call option V as a function of the underlying S for the VG model (dashed line) and the Black-Scholes model (solid line) calculated with the Fourier transform algorithm.

12.2.2   Fourier-Cosine Expansion Methods

In a first step we present how to solve the inverse Fourier integral via cosine expansion (Fang and Oosterlee, 2008). For a function supported on $[a, b]$, the cosine expansion reads

$$f(x) = \frac{1}{2}A_0 + \sum_{k=1}^{\infty} A_k \cos\left(k\pi \frac{x - a}{b - a}\right),$$

(12.37)

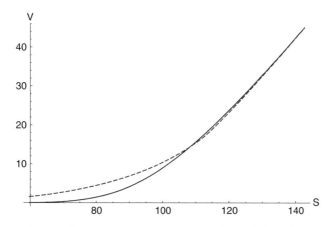

Figure 12.7 Price V of a European call option as a function of the price S of the underlying ($K = 100$, $S_0 = 100$, $r = 0.02$), calculated with the Fourier transform method using the Black-Scholes model with $\sigma = 0.2$ (continuous) and the VG model with $\Theta = 0.1$, $\eta = 2.0$, $\sigma = 0.2$ (dashed). The number of discretization points used for the calculation is $N = 8192$.

with expansion coefficients

$$A_k = \frac{2}{b-a} \int_a^b f(x) \cos\left(k\pi \frac{x-a}{b-a}\right) dx. \tag{12.38}$$

Due to the conditions for the existence of a Fourier transform, the integrands in (12.2) need to decay to zero at $\pm\infty$ and we can therefore truncate the infinite region to $[a, b]$, i.e., we choose $[a, b]$ in a such a way that

$$\int_a^b e^{\imath\omega x} f(x) dx \approx \int_{\mathbb{R}} e^{\imath\omega x} f(x) dx = \phi(\omega). \tag{12.39}$$

Comparing (12.38) with (12.39), we see that[6]

$$A_k = \frac{2}{b-a} \mathrm{Re}\left\{ \phi(\omega) \exp\left(-\imath \frac{k a \pi}{b-a}\right), \right\} \tag{12.40}$$

where $\mathrm{Re}\{\cdot\}$ denotes taking the real part of the argument. We now derive the Fourier-Cosine method by rewriting the risk neutral pricing formula (12.1), truncating the domain to the interval $[a, b]$,

$$V(x, t_0) = e^{-r\Delta t} \int_a^b V(y, T) f(y \mid x) dy. \tag{12.41}$$

Performing the Fourier-Cosine series expansion for the density $f(y \mid x)$ we obtain

$$f(y \mid x) = \sum_{k=0}^{\prime\infty} A_k(x) \cos\left(k\pi \frac{y-a}{b-a}\right), \tag{12.42}$$

where the prime in the sum indicates that the first element of the sum is weighted by $1/2$. The series' coefficients are defined by

$$A_k(x) = \frac{2}{b-a} \int_a^b f(y \mid x) \cos\left(k\pi \frac{y-a}{b-a}\right) dy. \tag{12.43}$$

Replacing $f(y \mid x)$ in (12.41) by (12.42) yields

$$V(x, t_0) = e^{-r\Delta t} \int_a^b V(y, T) \sum_{k=0}^{\prime\infty} A_k(x) \cos\left(k\pi \frac{y-a}{b-a}\right) dy. \tag{12.44}$$

Interchanging summation and integration and inserting the definition

$$V_k := \frac{2}{b-a} \int_a^b V(y, T) \cos\left(k\pi \frac{y-a}{b-a}\right), \tag{12.45}$$

we obtain

$$V(x, t_0) = \frac{1}{2}(b-a)e^{-r\Delta t} \sum_{k=0}^{\prime\infty} A_k(x) V_k. \tag{12.46}$$

The expression for V_k depends on the payoff of a European option at maturity T, where $y = \ln(S_T/K)$ with the strike price K and the stock price at maturity S_T. As shown in

---

[6] Basically this is an approximation due to the truncation. Nevertheless we use the equal sign at this point.

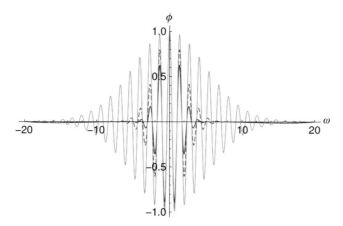

Figure 12.8 Characteristic function of the Heston model for a typical set of parameters ($\theta = 0.05$, $\kappa = 1.5$, $\sigma = 0.1$, $\rho = -0.9$, $v_0 = 0.03$) and $t = 10$ (continuous black), $t = 5$ (dashed) and $t = 1$ (continuous grey). Obviously, the rate of decay of the characteristic function depends on the time to maturity and the model parameters.

Figure 12.8, the decay[7] of the characteristic function allows us to truncate the summation from ∞ to N. Similar to the step leading to (12.40), we now use the characteristic function for the series coefficients. In the case of European options, one ends up with

$$L[v(x, t_0)] = e^{-r\Delta t} \sum_{k=0}^{N\prime} \mathrm{Re} \left\{ L\left[\phi\left(\frac{k\pi}{b-a}, x \right) \right] \exp\left(-i\frac{ka\pi}{b-a} \right) \right\} V_k, \qquad (12.47)$$

where the operator $L[\cdot]$ is the identity operator if the option value itself is to be calculated, or defined as $L = \frac{\partial}{\partial p_i}$ if the gradient of the option value with respect to the ith model parameter is to be calculated.[8] Note that for all processes considered in this chapter, we have

$$\phi\left(\frac{k\pi}{b-a} \right) = \phi\left(\frac{k\pi}{b-a}, x \right).$$

For European vanilla options, $V(y, T)$ in (12.45) is defined as

$$V(y, T) = [\alpha \cdot K(e^y - 1)]^+, \quad \text{with } \alpha = \begin{cases} 1 & \text{for a Call} \\ -1 & \text{for a Put} \end{cases}. \qquad (12.48)$$

Closed form solutions for the integral in (12.45) for different options can be found in (Fang and Oosterlee, 2008). Here, we provide the formulae for European call and put options,

$$V_k^{\mathrm{Call}} = \frac{2}{b-a} K \left(\chi_k(0, b) - \psi_k(0, b) \right), \qquad (12.49)$$

$$V_k^{\mathrm{Put}} = \frac{2}{b-a} K \left(-\chi_k(a, 0) + \psi_k(a, 0) \right). \qquad (12.50)$$

---

[7] Necessary for the existence of a Fourier transform.
[8] An analytic form of the derivative with respect to the model parameters is available and can be used in gradient-based optimization algorithms used for model calibration.

The expressions

$$\chi_k(c, d) = \int_c^d e^y \cos\left(k\pi \frac{y-a}{b-a}\right) dy \qquad (12.51)$$

and

$$\psi_k(c, d) = \int_c^d \cos\left(k\pi \frac{y-a}{b-a}\right) dy \qquad (12.52)$$

are known analytically,

$$\chi_k(c, d) = \frac{1}{1 + \left(\frac{k\pi}{b-a}\right)^2} \left[\cos\left(k\pi \frac{d-a}{b-a}e^d\right) - \cos\left(k\pi \frac{c-a}{b-a}e^c\right)\right.$$
$$\left. + \frac{k\pi}{b-a} \sin\left(k\pi \frac{d-a}{b-a}e^d\right) - \frac{k\pi}{b-a} \sin\left(k\pi \frac{c-a}{b-a}e^c\right)\right], \qquad (12.53)$$

$$\psi_k(c, d) = \begin{cases} \left[\sin\left(\pi \frac{d-a}{b-a}\right) - \sin\left(\pi \frac{c-a}{b-a}\right)\right] \frac{b-a}{k\pi} & k \neq 0 \\ (d-c) & k = 0 \end{cases}. \qquad (12.54)$$

From Equations (12.49) and (12.50) it follows that European call/put options can be computed simultaneously for many strike prices. Note that also the Greeks can be easily accessed using series expansion methods (Fang and Oosterlee, 2008).

Error Analysis and Stopping Criterion

Several approximations are used in the derivation of the cosine series expansion method for option pricing. First, the infinite integration domain in (12.1) is truncated to an interval $[a, b]$, which leads to an integration range truncation error. Second, the summation in the cosine expansion is truncated, motivated by the rapid decay of the coefficients as a result of the decay of the characteristic function. This leads to a series truncation error. A third source of error is the truncation of the integrals of the Fourier pair (12.2) to the interval $[a, b]$. The choice of the number of summands N considerably influences the computational demand. As shown in Figure 12.8, different maturities (and also different Heston parameters) strongly influence the form of the characteristic function. It turns out in practice that a good choice for the abortion of the summation in Equation (12.47) is to check whether the absolute of the characteristic function is smaller than a predefined value, $|\phi(\omega)| < \epsilon$.

Pricing a European Call Option Under the Heston Model

To show the influence of ϵ (and, in turn, the number of summands N) on the option price, we calculate the price of a European call option ($S_0 = 100$, $K = 100$, $r = 0.02$, $T = 365d$) under a Heston model with parameters $\theta = 0.05$, $\kappa = 1.5$, $\sigma = 0.1$, $\rho = -0.9$, $v_0 = 0.03$. For comparison, the analytical value of the call option, obtained with the pricing formula of the original paper (Heston, 1993), is $V = 8.84849$. The cosine series expansion method described in this section is highly parallelizable (see Chapter 18) and provides accurate results

Table 12.1   The table shows the number of summands N used in (12.47) for the abort criterion $|\phi(\omega)| < \epsilon$. The last column shows the corresponding option values. The analytical value of the call option is $V = 8.84849$.

ϵ	N	V
1e-2	108	7.67972
1e-3	139	8.85555
1e-4	170	8.86074
1e-5	200	8.8485
1e-6	231	8.84839
1e-7	262	8.8485

(see Table 12.1) for the calculation of Vanilla options. Furthermore, the method is flexible enough to incorporate time-dependent parameters (for example a yield curve instead of a flat risk free rate) and should thus be considered as the method of choice for the valuation of large sets of options, a task that is particularly relevant in the model calibration process (see Chapters 15 and 16).

Numerical Methods for the Solution
of PIDEs

Several models including jumps have been presented in Chapter 12. They provide extensions of flat volatility, local volatility and stochastic volatility models. In this chapter, we present an additional way for solving contingent claims under such jump models. Instead of using the characteristic function of the underlying probability density (mainly limited to the plain vanilla case) or the Monte Carlo method (see Chapter 9), the SDE can also be transformed into a partial integro-differential equation (PIDE). The discretization of such PIDEs requires special care: a naïve discretization of the integral term using finite differences or finite elements would lead to a dense coefficient matrix in the corresponding linear system of equations. We restrict the discussion to one-dimensional PIDEs; in our opinion, (Q)MC should be used for higher-dimensional problems.

Extensions to valuate American options and a survey of finite difference methods for option pricing under finite activity jump diffusion models are given in (Salmi and Toivanen, 2012). Recently, Kwon and Lee have presented a method based on finite differences with three time levels with a second-order convergence rate (Kwon and Lee, 2011). A finite element discretization of the PIDE resulting from a stochastic volatility jump diffusion model is discussed in (Zhang, Pang, Feng and Jin, 2012). Matache and Schwab used a wavelet Galerkin-based method for the pricing of American options on Lévy driven assets (Matache and Schwab, 2003). For a general overview of the topic and for an extension to infinite activity models we refer the reader to the monograph of Cont and Tankov (Cont and Tankov, 2003).

13.1 A PIDE FOR JUMP MODELS

For option pricing models where the risk neutral dynamics can be described by a diffusion process for the underlying – such as the Black-Scholes model – the value of a derivative (for example the value of a call option) $V(t, S_t)$ can be computed by solving a partial differential equation with appropriate boundary and terminal conditions. A similar result holds when the risk neutral dynamics is described by a jump model. The PIDE

$$\frac{\partial V}{\partial t}(t, S) + rS \frac{\partial V}{\partial S}(t, S) + \frac{\sigma^2 S^2}{2} \frac{\partial^2 V}{\partial S^2}(t, S) - rV(t, S)$$

$$+ \int v(dy) \left[V(t, Se^y) - V(t, S) - S(e^y - 1) \frac{\partial V}{\partial S}(t, S) \right] = 0,$$

(13.1)

defined on

$$[0, T) \times (0, \infty),$$ (13.2)

where $v(dy) = \lambda f(dx)$ is the Lévy density (f is the jump size distribution function and λ the intensity of the Poisson process; compare with section 12.1.2) describes the evolution of the price of a contingent claim under a jump diffusion model. Together with a terminal condition [for example $V(T, S) = \max(S - K, 0)$ for a European call option with strike price K] and boundary conditions, this PIDE determines the price of a contingent claim. Compared to the Black-Scholes equation, an additional integral term appears in the equation as a consequence of the presence of jumps. The integral term is nonlocal, i.e., it depends on the whole solution $V(S, t)$. A variable transformation of the form

$$\tau = T - t \quad x = \ln(S/S_0) \tag{13.3}$$

changes (13.1) to

$$
\frac{\partial u}{\partial \tau}(\tau, x) = \frac{\sigma^2}{2} \frac{\partial^2 u}{\partial x^2}(\tau, x) + \left(r - \frac{\sigma^2}{2} - \lambda \xi \right) \frac{\partial u}{\partial x}(\tau, x)
$$

$$
- (r + \lambda) u(\tau, x) + \lambda \int u(\tau, z) f(z - x) dz, \tag{13.4}
$$

with

$$u(\tau, x) = V(T - \tau, S_0 e^x) \tag{13.5}$$

and

$$\xi = \int (e^x - 1) f(x) dx. \tag{13.6}$$

The domain of the transformed PIDE is now

$$(0, T] \times (-\infty, \infty), \tag{13.7}$$

and the terminal condition becomes an initial condition (for instance $u(0, x) = \max(S_0 e^x - K)$ in the case of a European call option).

13.2   NUMERICAL SOLUTION OF THE PIDE

To solve a PIDE under given terminal and boundary conditions, the following preparation steps need to be performed:

1. Truncation of large jumps: the integration boundaries in Equation (13.4) are actually $-\infty$ and ∞. In order to apply numerical schemes, a truncation to a finite interval $]B_l; B_u]$ is necessary. As long as the tails of the corresponding density v decrease exponentially – that is, the probability of large jumps is very small – this truncation will not significantly alter the results.

2. Introduction of artificial boundaries in the spatial domain $[-A; A]$: to obtain a bounded computational domain in case the problem is initially given on an unbounded domain. The procedures involved here are discussed in Chapter 6. For many options, there is a natural choice for this localization procedure. For a double barrier option, for instance, the value of the option at the barriers is the rebate (or 0 if no rebate exists), imposing Dirichlet boundary conditions. Both steps (1) and (2) induce an approximation error that is usually called "localization error". When the Lévy density decays exponentially, both errors, the error induced by the truncation of the domain and the error induced due to the truncation of large jumps, are exponentially small in the truncation parameters.

3. Discretization: operators in (13.4) are replaced by their corresponding finite difference or finite element representation. The spatial domain is replaced by a discrete grid and the differential operators are discretized using appropriate finite difference schemes (see Chapter 3). The integral operator can be approximated using a quadrature rule.

13.2.1 Discretization of the Spatial Domain

We discretize the spatial domain $[-A, A]$ using $N + 1$ grid points with indices $j \in \{0, 1, \ldots, N\}$ and an equidistant grid spacing

$$h = \frac{2A}{N}.$$ (13.8)

The coordinate of a point with index i is thus given by

$$x_i = -A + ih.$$ (13.9)

For discretizing the differential operators in (13.4), we use finite difference operators (see Chapter 3) and the upwinding techniques discussed in Chapter 5. We choose the following finite difference formulae for the spatial derivatives[1]

$$\left(\frac{\partial^2 u}{\partial x^2}\right)_i = \frac{u_{i+1} - 2u_i + u_{i-1}}{h^2},$$

$$\left(\frac{\partial u}{\partial x}\right)_i = \begin{cases} \dfrac{u_{i+1} - u_i}{h}, & \text{if } \quad r - \sigma^2/2 - \lambda\xi < 0 \\ \dfrac{u_i - u_{i-1}}{h}, & \text{if } \quad r - \sigma^2/2 - \lambda\xi \geq 0 \end{cases}.$$ (13.10)

To approximate the integral term of (13.4) on the grid, the trapezoidal rule is used (see Appendix 13.3),

$$\int u(\tau, z) f(z - x_i) dz = \frac{h}{2} \left(u_0 f_{i,0} + 2 \sum_{j=1}^{N-1} u_j f_{i,j} + u_N f_{i,N} \right),$$ (13.11)

where $f_{i,j} = f(x_i - x_j)$.

13.2.2 Discretization of the Time Domain

The time domain $[0, T]$ is discretized using $M + 1$ grid points with indices $j \in \{0, 1, \ldots, M\}$ and an equidistant grid spacing

$$\Delta t = \frac{T}{M}.$$ (13.12)

The discrete time points are thus given by

$$T_j = j\Delta t.$$ (13.13)

---

[1] Note that we are omitting the error terms but nevertheless use the equals sign. Furthermore, we omit the index for the time discretization.

We use the forward difference quotient for the time derivative operator at spatial point x_i (note that again we use the equals sign although we omit the error term),

$$\frac{\partial u}{\partial \tau} = \frac{u_i^{j+1} - u_i^j}{\Delta \tau}. \tag{13.14}$$

We further denote the discretized differential operators of the right hand side of (13.4) by the matrix $\mathbf{D}$, and the discretized integral part by the matrix $\mathbf{J}$. Different time-stepping schemes can be constructed; in Chapter 3 we have shown that a fully explicit scheme imposes stringent conditions on the size of the time step Δt, considerably increasing the computation time. A fully implicit time-stepping scheme is given by

$$\frac{\mathbf{u}^{j+1} - \mathbf{u}^j}{\Delta \tau} = \mathbf{D}\mathbf{u}^{j+1} + \mathbf{J}\mathbf{u}^{j+1}. \tag{13.15}$$

At each time step, a system of linear equations must be solved[2]

$$(\mathbf{I} - \Delta t(\mathbf{D} + \mathbf{J}))\mathbf{u}^{j+1} = \mathbf{u}^j \tag{13.16}$$

in order to obtain $\mathbf{u}^{j+1}$. While $\mathbf{D}$ is a banded matrix, $\mathbf{J}$ is dense, and the linear system of equations is thus expensive to solve. Also mixing schemes of the form

$$\frac{\mathbf{u}^{j+1} - \mathbf{u}^j}{\Delta \tau} = \Theta(\mathbf{D}\mathbf{u}^j + \mathbf{J}\mathbf{u}^j) + (1 - \Theta)(\mathbf{D}\mathbf{u}^{j+1} + \mathbf{J}\mathbf{u}^{j+1}) \tag{13.17}$$

suffer from this drawback. Operator splitting (Cont and Tankov, 2003) can be used to obtain a banded structure of the coefficient matrix of the resulting system of linear equations.[3] The integral operator is computed using the solution $\mathbf{u}^j$, whereas the differential term is treated implicitly. This explicit-implicit time-stepping scheme is given by

$$\frac{\mathbf{u}^{j+1} - \mathbf{u}^j}{\Delta \tau} = \mathbf{D}\mathbf{u}^{j+1} + \mathbf{J}\mathbf{u}^j. \tag{13.18}$$

where

$$(\mathbf{I} - \Delta t\mathbf{D})\mathbf{u}^{j+1} = (\mathbf{I} + \Delta t\mathbf{J})\mathbf{u}^j \tag{13.19}$$

needs to be solved for $\mathbf{u}^{j+1}$.

13.2.3 A European Option under the Kou Jump Diffusion Model

We calculate the value of a European call option (strike price $K = 100$, maturity $T = 0.25$, value of underlying $S_0 = 100$, risk free rate $r = 0.05$) under the Kou model (see section 12.1.2) with parameters[4]

$$\sigma = 0.15,$$
$$\lambda_+ = 3.0465,$$
$$\lambda_- = 3.0775, \tag{13.20}$$
$$p = 0.3445,$$
$$\lambda = 0.1.$$

---

[2] We do not discuss the incorporation of boundary conditions here, and instead refer the reader to Chapters 3 to 6.
[3] Basically, the structure of $\mathbf{D}$ is retained.
[4] We have chosen the same parameters as Kwon and Lee (2011).

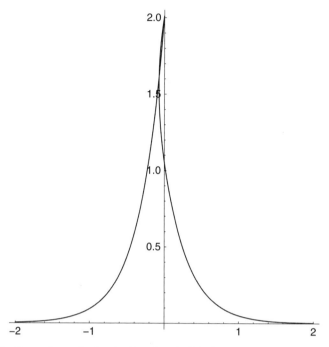

Figure 13.1   The figure shows the density function f of the Kou model for the parameter set (13.20).

Table 13.1   The table shows the option values for combinations of N (spatial discretization points) and M (time discretization points) without splitting the integral. The computational domain is given by the interval $[-5, 5]$.

N	M	V
1000	20	3.92617
1000	100	3.9429
1000	200	3.945
2000	200	3.959

The density f of the jump model is shown in Figure 13.1. The prices of the option for different combinations of N and M are reported in Tables 13.1 and 13.2. For all calculations, homogenous Neumann boundary conditions have been used. The reference value is 3.97348 (Kwon and Lee, 2011). If the spatial domain is localized to the interval $[-4, 4]$ we obtain the values given in Table 13.1. The efficiency of the method can be dramatically increased by improving the localization by splitting[5] the integral term into

$$\int_{\mathbb{R}} u(\tau, z) f(z - x_i) dz = \int_{-A}^{A} u(\tau, z) f(z - x_i) dz + \int_{\mathbb{R} \setminus [-A, A]} u(\tau, z) f(z - x_i) dz. \quad (13.21)$$

---

[5] The option price asymptotically behaves like the payoff function for large $|x|$. Therefore we set $u(\tau, x) = h(x)$, where $h(x)$ is the payoff function.

Table 13.2 The table shows the option values for combinations of N (spatial discretization points) and M (time discretization points) with a splitting of the integral. The computational domain is given by the interval $[-1.5, 1.5]$.

N	M	V
400	50	3.96095
400	100	3.96514
600	100	3.97445
600	200	3.97654

For the Kou model, the residual integral is given by

$$\int_{\mathbb{R}\setminus[-A,A]} u(\tau, z) f(z - x_i) dz = S_0 \frac{p\lambda_+}{\lambda_+ - 1} e^{\lambda_+ x - (\lambda_+ - 1)A} - Kp e^{-r\tau - \lambda_-(A-x)}. \quad (13.22)$$

We restrict the computational domain to the interval $[-1.5, 1.5]$ and obtain the values displayed in Table 13.2.

13.3 APPENDIX: NUMERICAL INTEGRATION VIA NEWTON-COTES FORMULAE

The Riemann definition of the definite integral is

$$\int_a^b f(x) dx = \lim_{h \to 0} \left[h \sum_{i=1}^{(b-a)/h} f(x_i) \right], \quad (13.23)$$

where the interval $[a, b]$ is split into N segments of equal length h,

$$h = \frac{b - a}{N}, \qquad x_i = a + ih, \quad i \in \{0, \dots, N\}. \quad (13.24)$$

An obvious numerical approximation for the definite integral is thus

$$\int_a^b f(x) dx \approx \sum_{i=0}^{N-1} f(x_i) \omega_i. \quad (13.25)$$

Integration formulae of the form (13.25) can be obtained (Abramowitz and Stegun, 1972) using interpolation polynomials of different orders between the node points x_i. The weights ω_i and the order of the leading error term depend on the order of the interpolation polynomials:

- The 0th-order approximation results in the rectangle rule (also called mid-point rule). In this case, the weights ω_i are equal to h and the approximation of the definite integral is thus given by

$$\int_a^b f(x) dx \approx f_0 h \quad (13.26)$$

for $N = 1$. The error term is

$$E = \frac{(b-a)^3}{24} f^{(2)}(\xi),$$ (13.27)

where ξ is an arbitrary (but unknown) point in the interval $[a, b]$. For $N \geq 1$, the different rectangles are summed up, resulting in

$$\int_a^b f(x)dx \approx h \sum_{i=0}^{N-1} f_i$$ (13.28)

as an approximation of the integral.
- As the 1st order approximation, the trapezoidal rule (compare Figure 13.2) is obtained,

$$\int_a^b f(x)dx \approx \frac{h}{2}(f_0 + f_1),$$ (13.29)

with a leading error term of

$$E = -\frac{(b-a)^3}{12} f^{(2)}(\xi)$$ (13.30)

for a single segment ($N = 1$). For $N \geq 1$, the approximation of the integral is given by

$$\int_a^b f(x)dx \approx \frac{h}{2}f_0 + h \sum_{i=1}^{N-1} f_i + \frac{h}{2}f_N.$$ (13.31)

- The 2nd order approximation leads to the Simpson rule,

$$\int_a^b f(x)dx \approx \frac{h}{3}(f_0 + 4f_1 + f_2),$$ (13.32)

with a leading error term

$$E = -\frac{(b-a)^5}{2880} f^{(4)}(\xi)$$ (13.33)

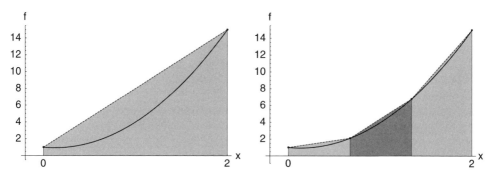

Figure 13.2   The figure shows the application of the trapezoidal rule for the approximation of the integral of a quadratic function f. The left picture shows the approximation for $N = 1$ and the right picture the approximation for $N = 3$.

for a single segment ($N = 1$). For $N \geq$ the Simpson formula is

$$\int_a^b f(x)dx \approx \frac{h}{3}f_0 + \frac{4h}{3}f_1 + \frac{2h}{3}f_2 + \ldots + \frac{2h}{3}f_{N-2} + \frac{4h}{3}f_{N-1} + \frac{h}{3}f_N. \quad (13.34)$$

Such Newton-Cotes formulae can be constructed for any degree p of the interpolating function. For large p, however, Newton-Cotes rules can become unstable. For further reading and a comprehensive collection of Newton-Cotes formulae we refer the reader to (Abramowitz and Stegun, 1972).

14

Copulas and the Pitfalls of Correlation

The problem of finding and quantifying dependencies between time series of observables frequently occurs in quantitative finance and econometrics.[1] Here, by "dependence" we refer to any situation in which random variables are not probabilistically independent. Even though the term "correlation" is often used in the same sense, we use it in a technically more strict sense in this work to refer to particular types of dependencies, as detailed below. In addition to the correlation between two or more variables, a signal can also show cross-correlation with itself. This so-called autocorrelation describes, loosely speaking, the similarity between observations as a function of the time Δt separating them. Autocorrelation is also linked to the mean reversion property many of the models discussed in this book display, for example, the Hull-White models and the Black-Karasinski model.

Many financial models for dependent risk are based on the assumption of normally distributed factors (multivariate normality), and linear correlation is usually employed as a measure for dependence. However, as pointed out in Chapter 12, financial data are rarely normally distributed, but tend to follow distributions with heavier tails. Furthermore, synchronized extreme downturns, which are observed in reality, cannot be modeled using multivariate normal distributions. To correctly reproduce these properties, other elliptical distributions[2] are used. Estimators for linear correlation are still used as a natural measure for dependence of elliptical distributions.[3] In addition to Pearson's ρ, we will also introduce Spearman's ρ and Kandall's τ as measures of correlation. In contrast to Pearson's ρ, which can be calculated directly from the two data series, the latter require the rank or position of the variables in each series.[4]

During recent years, the use of copulas in different fields of quantitative finance has grown steadily. A copula is a distribution function that describes the dependence between two or more random variables. But more than for any other mathematical concept used in quantitative finance, the model and method risk induced by the use of copulas is said to have led to financial turmoil and market deteriorations. In our view, problems of this kind should not lead to abandoning sophisticated quantitative methods in analyzing the complexity of financial markets; on the contrary, the applied models should be even more rigorously analyzed and thoroughly tested under extreme scenarios, in order to use them in a sensible and meaningful way.[5]

---

[1] A time series is a sequence of data points with a natural temporal order. This allows us to distinguish time series analysis from the analysis of observations without natural ordering (for instance, explaining the life income of people in reference to their education level) or from spatial data analysis (observations relate to geographical locations).

[2] The reason why elliptical distributions are used is their support for standard methods of risk management (Value at Risk, see Chapter 17) and portfolio construction (see Chapter 16).

[3] Note, though, that the widely used Pearson product-moment correlation estimator exhibits bad performance for heavier-tailed data. Also for contaminated data – data including measurement errors and other errors leading to outliers – it turns out that using the Pearson ρ leads to poor estimates of dependence.

[4] As a consequence, the value of the Pearson ρ will change when the value of a single observation in one of the time series is changed, while the rank correlation coefficient will remain unchanged as long as the position of the observation in the data series is not changed.

[5] Although it is well known that Gaussian distributions and copulas underestimate the tail behavior of many observables, they are used because of their analytic tractability.

14.1 CORRELATION

Financial correlations[6] measure the degree of co-movement of two or more financial observables in time – a well-known example is the negative correlation between stocks and bonds. Correlations are a critical ingredient of risk measurement and management (see Chapter 17); the lower the correlation between assets in a portfolio, the lower the risk expressed in terms of Value at Risk (VaR) or Expected Shortfall (ES). Note that all correlation coefficients introduced in this chapter are in the range between -1 and 1.

14.1.1 Pearson's ρ

Pearson's ρ, also known as the linear correlation coefficient, is a nonparametric measure of statistical dependence. It is given by

$$\rho_{x,y} = \frac{\text{cov}(x, y)}{\sigma_x \sigma_y},$$ (14.1)

where $\text{cov}(x, y)$ is the population covariance and σ_x and σ_y are the standard deviations of the population. The covariance $\text{cov}(x, y)$ is calculated as

$$\text{cov}(x, y) = \frac{1}{N} \sum_{i=1}^{N} (x_i - \mu_x)(y_i - \mu_y),$$ (14.2)

where μ_x and μ_x are the population means. For a sample with sample size N, the correlation coefficient can be calculated using

$$\rho_P = \frac{\sum_{i=1}^{N} (x_i - \bar{x})(y_i - \bar{y})}{\sqrt{\sum_{i=1}^{N} (x_i - \bar{x})^2} \sqrt{\sum_{i=1}^{N} (y_i - \bar{y})^2}},$$ (14.3)

where $\bar{x}$ and $\bar{y}$ are the sample means. Pearson's ρ is only a valid measure of correlation if the marginal distributions are jointly elliptical, i.e., they are related to the multivariate normal distribution.

14.1.2 Spearman's ρ

Spearman's rank correlation coefficient (also Spearman's ρ or ρ_S) is a nonparametric measure of statistical dependence. It assesses how well the dependence of two variables is described by a monotonic, but not necessarily linear, function (in fact, $\rho_S = 1$ if the variables x and y are strictly monotonically related). To calculate Spearman's ρ for a sample of size N, Equation (14.3) is also used, but with the row outcomes x_i and y_i replaced by the corresponding ranks r_{x_i} and r_{y_i},

$$\rho_S = \frac{\sum_{i=1}^{N} (r_{x_i} - \bar{r}_x)(r_{y_i} - \bar{r}_y)}{\sqrt{\sum_{i=1}^{N} (r_{x_i} - \bar{r}_x)^2} \sqrt{\sum_{i=1}^{N} (r_{y_i} - \bar{r}_y)^2}}.$$ (14.4)

---

[6] Nowadays, correlations play an important role in finance. For example, the capital asset pricing model (CAPM) states that an increase in diversification (inverse correlation) increases the return/risk ratio.

Table 14.1   The table displays a sample of two observables x and y, the corresponding ranks r_{x_i} and r_{y_i} and d_i. Note that in the case of equal observations the rank is calculated using the arithmetic mean. For the values in the sample $\rho_S = -0.975$.

i	x_i	y_i	r_{x_i}	r_{y_i}	d_i
1	1.2	0.97	1	5	−4
2	1.1	0.98	3	3.5	−0.5
3	1.18	0.98	2	3.5	−1.5
4	0.98	1.01	5	1	4
5	0.99	0.99	4	2	2

Here, the rank r_i is the position of i-th element in the ordered sample of observations. Alternatively, ρ_S can be calculated using

$$\rho_S = \frac{6 \sum_{i=1}^{N} d_i^2}{n(n^2 - 1)}, \tag{14.5}$$

where $d_i = r_{x_i} - r_{y_i}$. A short example of how to determine the ranks for the calculation of Spearman's ρ is given in Table 14.1. In contrast to Pearson's ρ, Spearman's ρ is independent of the statistical distribution of the underlying data, but depends only on the order of the observations. ρ_S is positive for an increasing monotonic trend between x and y and is negative for a decreasing monotonic trend, as shown in Figure 14.1. Compared to Pearson's ρ, Spearman's ρ is less sensitive to outliers in the tails, as shown in Figure 14.2.

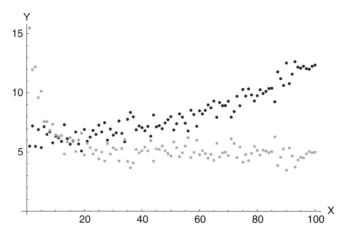

Figure 14.1   The figure shows two sets of dependent variables: The round point set displays an increasing monotonic trend with $\rho_S = 0.928$, the square point set displays a decreasing monotonic trend with $\rho_S = -0.392$.

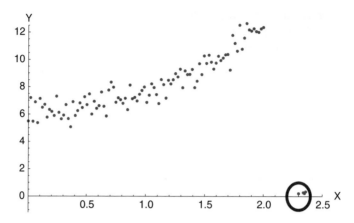

Figure 14.2   The figure shows a set of dependent variables x and y with outliers (points in the circle). For the point set excluding the outliers, the Pearson and the Spearman correlation coefficients are given by $\rho_P = 0.93$ and $\rho_S = 0.938$. If the outliers are included, the Pearson correlation is affected much more compared to the Spearman rank correlation, $\rho_P = 0.386267$ and $\rho_S = 0.722864$.

14.1.3   Kendall's τ

Kendall's τ (or τ_K) is also a rank correlation coefficient, and is calculated by comparing pairs of data points. For two variables x and y, we refer to the combination (x_i, y_i) as an "observation". Two observations (x_1, y_1) and (x_2, y_2) are said to be concordant if $x_2 - x_1$ and $y_2 - y_1$ have the same sign, and are said to be discordant for different signs, see Figure 14.3. For a set of N observations, Kendall's τ is given by

$$\tau_k = \frac{2(N_c - N_d)}{N(N-1)}, \tag{14.6}$$

where N_c is the number of concordant pairs and N_d is the number of discordant pairs, respectively.

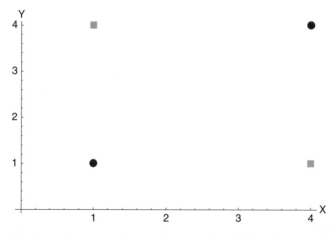

Figure 14.3   The figure shows a set of concordant (round) and discordant (square) observations.

14.1.4   Other Measures

The information delivered by a correlation coefficient (or a correlation matrix) often fails to sufficiently describe the dependency structure between two or more random variables.[7] Pearson's ρ can be zero even for dependent random variables; to overcome this drawback, distance correlation (also Brownian covariance or Brownian distance) (Szekely and Rizzo, 2009) has been introduced, where zero distance correlation guarantees independence of the random variables. A number of additional dependence measures has been introduced in the literature: The correlation ratio, for instance, is able to detect almost all functional dependencies. Multi-moment correlation measures such as entropy-based mutual information, total correlation or dual total correlation are capable of detecting even more general dependencies. We will not address these measures here, but will use copulas to obtain a more complete view of the dependency structure of two or more variables.

14.2   COPULAS

Copulas allow to model the nature of dependencies and to consider the dependencies of extreme events, and therefore overcome some of the shortcomings of the linear correlation concept:

- In particular in times of financial turmoil, applying linear correlation to calculate the dependence structure among different assets can be problematic as the variance of returns of these assets tends to be infinite.[8]
- Obviously, linear correlation does not take into account nonlinear effects.
- The linear correlation is not invariant under nonlinear strictly increasing transformations. As a consequence, for a given sample the prices may be correlated while the returns are uncorrelated.
- Linear Correlation does not provide insight into the structure of the dependence.[9]

During the financial crisis of 2007–2008, a number of articles blamed the copula approach for the financial turmoil (Salmon, 2009). We believe the reasons of the financial crisis are rather rooted in inadequate or missing risk management, and the failure of financial models was rather caused by calibrating them with overly benign input data (garbage in – garbage out). Yet, a number of critical remarks on the use of copulas are in order at this point:

- Due to its simplicity and analytical tractability, the Gaussian copula is the most widely used type. It has relatively low tail dependence and is therefore not suited to describe systematic risk.
- The basic approach to model dependencies with copulas is static (i.e., time-independent) and therefore allows only limited risk management (Donnelly and Embrechts, 2010). Several attempts with time-dependent copula variables have been made (Hull, Predescu and White, 2010) but have not been able to create a fully dynamic stochastic process including drift

---

[7] A complete description of the dependence structure between two variables with a correlation coefficient (or a correlation matrix) is only possible in very specific cases, for example when the distribution is a multivariate normal distribution.

[8] The linear correlation between assets is undefined if frequent observation of extreme events takes place.

[9] During the financial crisis, for example, markets crashed in different countries during the same time period, although the correlation between the markets had been quite low before. The structure of dependence also effects the benefits obtained by diversification based on linear correlation.

and noise, as required for flexible hedging and risk management. Albanese overcame this drawback by introducing the concept of dynamic copulas (Albanese and Vidler, 2008).

14.2.1 Basic Concepts

The joint cumulative distribution function $F(x_1, \ldots, x_d)$ for d Variables X_1 to X_d is defined as

$$F(x_1, \ldots, x_d) = P(X_1 \leq x_1, | \ldots |, X_d \leq x_d). \tag{14.7}$$

A copula $C : [0, 1]^d \rightarrow [0, 1]$ for modelling the dependence of two or more variables is a joint cumulative distribution function with marginal cumulative distribution functions $F_i(x_i) = u_i$ as inputs,

$$F(x_1, \ldots, x_d) = C(F_1(x_1), F_2(x_2), \ldots, F_{d-1}(x_{d-1}), F_d(x_d)). \tag{14.8}$$

The copula C is required to have the following three properties:

- A copula must be an increasing function of its marginal distributions: if $F(x_i^*) > F(x_i)$ then

$$C(F_1(x_1), F_2(x_2), \ldots, F_i(x_i^*), \ldots F_{d-1}(x_{d-1}), F_d(x_d)) >$$
$$C(F_2(x_1), F_2(x_2), \ldots, F_i(x_i), \ldots F_{d-1}(x_{d-1}), F_d(x_d)).$$

- If all but one of the marginal distribution functions are 1, then the value of the copula must be equal to the value of the remaining marginal distribution,

$$C(1, 1, \ldots, 1, F_i(x_i), 1, \ldots, 1, 1) = F_i(x_i).$$

- A copula always needs to return a non-negative probability.

Sklar's theorem (Sklar, 1959) states that not only a multivariate cumulative distribution function with marginals can be written in the form of (14.8), but that also the converse is true: Given a copula $C : [0, 1]^d \rightarrow [0, 1]$ and d marginal cumulative distribution functions $F_i(x_i)$, then $C(F_1(x_1), \ldots, F_d(x_d))$ defines a d-dimensional cumulative distribution function. As the probability density function is the gradient of the cumulative distribution function, a copula density function gives the rate of change of the copula distribution function. Restricting ourselves to continuous distribution functions, the copula density function $c(F_1(x_1), \ldots, F_d(x_d))$ is given by

$$c(F_1(x_1), \ldots, F_d(x_d)) = \frac{f(x_1, \ldots, x_d)}{f_1(x_1)f_2(x_2) \ldots f_d(x_d)}, \tag{14.9}$$

where $f(x_1, \ldots, x_d)$ is the joint density function of the joint cumulative distribution function $F(x_1, \ldots, x_d)$, and $f_i(x_i)$ are the marginal density functions of the marginal cumulative distribution functions $F_i(x_i)$.

14.2.2 Important Copula Functions

Copulas can be classified into three families: elliptical copulas, Archimedean copulas and extreme value copulas.

Elliptical Copulas

Elliptical copulas can be derived from elliptical multivariate distribution functions. The most important copulas in this family are the Gauss copula and the t-copula (derived from the multivariate normal and the multivariate t-distribution, respectively). A Gauss copula for d marginal cumulative distribution functions is given by

$$C(F(x_1), \ldots, F(x_d)) = \Phi_\rho \left(\Phi(x_1), \ldots \Phi(x_d) \right), \tag{14.10}$$

and therefore

$$C(u_1, \ldots, u_d) = \Phi_\rho \left(\Phi^{-1}(u_1), \ldots \Phi^{-1}(u_d) \right), \tag{14.11}$$

where Φ_ρ is the multivariate cumulative normal distribution function with correlation matrix (or correlation coefficient if $N = 2$) ρ and Φ^{-1} is the inverse of the univariate normal distribution. In the bivariate case, the Gauss copula is given by

$$C(u_1, u_2) = \int_{-\infty}^{\Phi^{-1}(u_1)} \int_{-\infty}^{\Phi^{-1}(u_2)} \frac{1}{2\pi\sqrt{1-\rho^2}} \exp\left\{ -\frac{s^2 - 2\rho st + t^2}{2(1-\rho^2)} \right\} ds\, dt. \tag{14.12}$$

Typical realizations of bivariate Gauss copulas for different ρ are shown in Figure 14.4. The t-copula can be defined analogously to the Gauss copula,

$$C(F(x_1), \ldots, F(x_d)) = t_{\rho,v} \left(t_v(x_1), \ldots t_v(x_d) \right), \tag{14.13}$$

and therefore

$$C(u_1, \ldots, u_d) = t_{\rho,v} \left(t_v^{-1}(u_1), \ldots t_v^{-1}(u_d) \right), \tag{14.14}$$

where $t_{\rho,v}$ is the multivariate cumulative t-distribution function with correlation matrix (or correlation coefficient if $N = 2$) ρ, v is the number of degrees of freedom and t_v^{-1} is the inverse of the univariate t-distribution. In the bivariate case the t-copula is given by

$$C(u_1, u_2) = \int_{-\infty}^{t_v^{-1}(u_1)} \int_{-\infty}^{t_v^{-1}(u_2)} \frac{1}{2\pi\sqrt{1-\rho^2}} \left(1 + \frac{s^2 - 2\rho st + t^2}{2v(1-\rho^2)} \right)^{-\frac{v+2}{2}} ds\, dt. \tag{14.15}$$

Typical realizations of bivariate t-copulas with $v = 1$ and $v = 10$ for different ρ are shown in Figure 14.5. As shown in Figure 14.6, the t-copula exhibits stronger tail dependence than the Gaussian copula, where tail dependence expresses the probability of having a high (low) extreme value for x_2 given that a high (low) extreme value for x_1 has occurred. Tail dependence is increasing with the correlation ρ and decreasing with the degrees of freedom v of the copula. Figure 14.6 compares the tail dependence of a bivariate Gaussian and a bivarate t-copula for $x_1, x_2 \sim U[-1, 1]$.

Archimedean Copulas

Archimedean copulas are derived from a generator function γ with the following properties:

- $\gamma : [0, 1] \longrightarrow [0, \infty)$,
- $\gamma(1) = 0$,
- γ is continuous, convex and strictly monotonically decreasing.

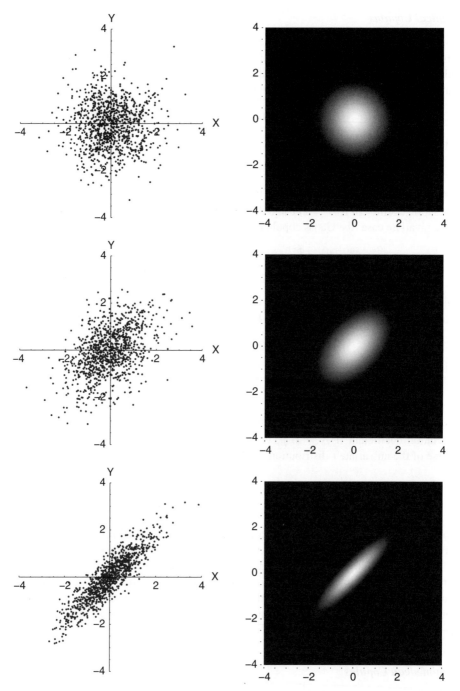

Figure 14.4 The figure shows scatter and density plots of Gauss copulas for $\rho = 0.0$, $\rho = 0.5$ and $\rho = 0.9$.

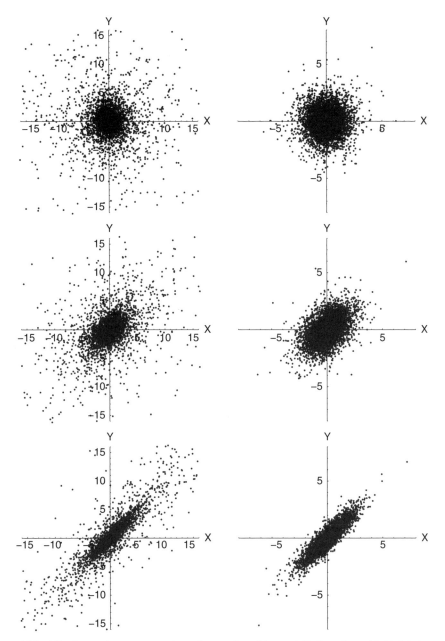

Figure 14.5   The figure shows scatter plots of *t*-copulas with $v = 1$ (left) and $v = 10$ (right) degrees of freedom for $\rho = 0.0$, $\rho = 0.5$ and $\rho = 0.9$ (from top to bottom). Note the different length scales, as all the marginal distributions have fatter tails compared to the Gaussian distributions. For increasing v, the marginal *t*-distributions approach the Gaussian distribution. In addition, the *t*-copula exhibits stronger tail dependence than the Gaussian copula (compare Figure 14.6).

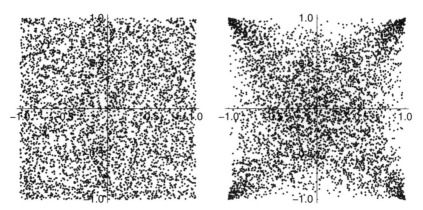

Figure 14.6   The figure compares the tail dependence of the bivariate Gaussian (left) and the bivariate
t-copula (right) for $\rho = 0$ and x_1, $x_2 \sim U[-1, 1]$.

A d-dimensional Archimedean copula can be written as

$$C(U_1, U_2, \dots, u_d) = \gamma \left(\gamma^{-1}(u_1) + \cdots + \gamma^{-1}(u_d) \right). \qquad (14.16)$$

The most important Archimedean copulas are the Gumbel copula (see Figure 14.7), the Frank
copula (see Figure 14.9) and the Clayton copula (Figure 14.8). Their generator functions,
the corresponding inverses, the range for the parameter λ and the relationship with Kendall's
τ are shown in Table 14.2. Different copulas exhibit different symmetries and dependence
behaviors: The Gumbel copula (also Gumbel-Hougard copula) is asymmetric and shows
greater dependence in the positive tail than in the negative, as can be seen in Figure 14.7. The
Clayton copula is asymmetric, too, but shows greater dependence in the negative tail than in
the positive, see Figure 14.8. Finally, the Frank copula is symmetric, compare Figure 14.9.
   In the bivariate case, the Gumbel copula is given by

$$C(u_1, u_2) = \exp \left\{ -\left((-\ln u_1)^\lambda + (-\ln u_2)^\lambda \right)^{\frac{1}{\lambda}} \right\}, \qquad (14.17)$$

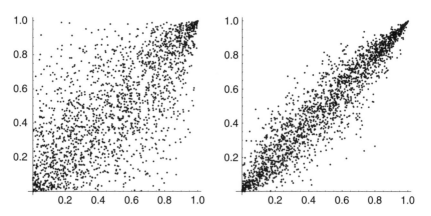

Figure 14.7   The figure shows Gumbel copulas with parameter $\lambda = 2$ ($\tau = 0.5$) on the left hand side
and $\lambda = 5$ ($\tau = 0.8$) on the right hand side.

Table 14.2 The table shows the generator functions and their inverse, the range of the parameter λ and the relationship between λ and Kendall's τ for the Gumbel, the Clayton and the Frank copulas. Note that the relationship between Kendall's τ and the copula parameter λ only holds in the bivariate case and does not extend to multivariate cases, where multiple values of τ exist. A workaround is to average the values for τ.

Copula	γ	γ^{-1}	λ-range	Relationship with Kendall's τ
Gumbel	$\gamma(x) = (-\ln(x))^{\lambda}$	$\gamma^{-1}(x) = \exp\left\{-x^{\frac{1}{\lambda}}\right\}$	$\lambda \in [1, \infty)$	$\lambda = \dfrac{1}{1 - \tau}$
Clayton	$\gamma(x) = \frac{1}{\lambda}\left(x^{-\lambda} - 1\right)$	$\gamma^{-1}(x) = (\lambda x + 1)^{-\frac{1}{\lambda}}$	$\lambda \in [-1, \infty)\backslash\{0\}$	$\lambda = \dfrac{2\tau}{1 - \tau}$
Frank	$\gamma(x) = -\ln\left(\dfrac{\exp\{-\lambda x\} - 1}{\exp\{-\lambda\} - 1}\right)$	$\gamma^{-1}(x) = -\frac{1}{\lambda}\ln\left(1 + \exp\{-x\}(\exp\{-\lambda\} - 1)\right)$	$\lambda \in (-\infty, \infty)\backslash\{0\}$	$\dfrac{1 - \tau}{4} = \dfrac{\frac{1}{\lambda}\left(\int_0^{\lambda} \frac{t}{e^t - 1} dt\right) - 1}{\lambda}$

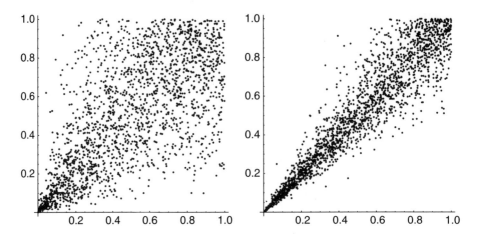

Figure 14.8   The figure shows Clayton copulas with parameter parameter $\lambda = 2$ ($\tau = 0.5$) on the left hand side and $\lambda = 8$ ($\tau = 0.8$) on the right hand side.

the Clayton copula by

$$C(u_1, u_2) = \max\left((u_1^{-\lambda} + u_2^{-\lambda} - 1)^{-\frac{1}{\lambda}}, 0\right), \qquad (14.18)$$

and the Frank copula by

$$C(u_1, u_2) = -\frac{1}{\lambda} \ln\left(1 + \frac{\left(\exp\{-\lambda u_1\} - 1\right)\left(\exp\{-\lambda u_2\} - 1\right)}{\exp\{-\lambda\} - 1}\right). \qquad (14.19)$$

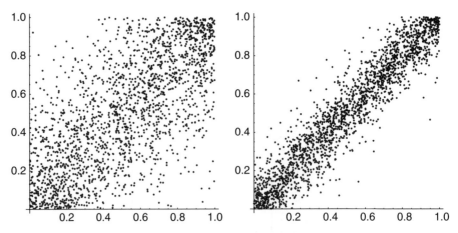

Figure 14.9   The figure shows Frank copulas with parameter $\lambda = 5.735$ ($\tau = 0.5$) on the left hand side and $\lambda = 3.2$ ($\tau = 0.8$) on the right hand side.

Other Copula Functions

Extreme-value copulas are derived from multivariate extreme value distributions,[10] and are appropriate models for the structure of the dependence between rare events. In addition, they can be used to model data with positive dependence. The Gumbel copula is the only copula that is Archimedean and an extreme-value copula at the same time. For multivariate data with unknown marginal distribution functions, empirical copulas can be used. Suppose we have N observations in d dimensions,

$$X_{ij} \text{ with } i \in 1, \ldots, N, \quad j \in 1, \ldots, d. \tag{14.20}$$

Then, one can construct pseudo-copula observations by using the empirical marginal distribution functions

$$F_{Nj}(x_1, x_2, \ldots, x_d) = \frac{1}{N} \sum_{i=1}^{N} 1 \left(X_{ij} \leq x_j \right), \tag{14.21}$$

where 1 is the counting operator. The corresponding empirical copula is then given by

$$C^N(u_1, \ldots, u_d) = \frac{1}{N} \sum_{i=1}^{N} 1 \left(F_{N1}(X_{i1}) \leq u_1, F_{N2}(X_{i2}) \leq u_2, \ldots, F_{Nd}(X_{id}) \leq u_d \right), \tag{14.22}$$

where

$$F_{Nj}(x_j) = \frac{1}{N} \sum_{i=1}^{N} 1 \left(X_{ij} \leq x_j \right) \tag{14.23}$$

is the estimator of the empirical marginal distribution.

14.2.3 Parameter Estimation and Sampling

Before a copula can be used to generate samples of random variates, the parameters of the copula function need to be estimated.

Estimation of Copula Parameters to Historical Data

In general, three different methods exist to estimate a copula from a given set of data:

- parameter-free estimation,
- semi-parametrical estimation,
- parametrical estimation.

The parameter-free estimation of the copula corresponds to the empirical copula described in section 14.2.2. We illustrate this estimation for a small data set with $N = 4$ and $d = 2$,

$$\mathbf{X} = \{(5, 8), (1, 5), (4, 7), (2, 9)\}.$$

---

[10] Extreme-value distributions are distributions of the maximum values of continuous random variables for a large number of observations, similar to the central limit theorem.

Table 14.3   The table shows the ranks of the observations X_1 and X_2.

X_1	5	1	4	2
X_2	8	5	7	9
R_1	4	1	3	2
R_2	3	1	2	4

We assign probabilities for all possible values $u_1 = i_1/N$ and $u_2 = i_2/N$ with $i_1 \in \{1, \ldots, N\}$ and $i_2 \in \{1, \ldots N\}$. For example, for $u_1 = 1/4$ and $u_2 = 1/4$, the value of the empirical copula is

$$C\left(\frac{1}{4}, \frac{1}{4}\right) = \frac{1}{4}.$$

This value is obtained by inserting u_1 and u_2 into the estimators of the marginal distributions (14.23),

$$F_{41}(x_1) = \frac{1}{4}, \quad F_{42}(x_2) = \frac{1}{4},$$

and finding the observations occurring in both counting processes. A second possibility is to use the ranks R_i of the observations shown in Table 14.3: For $i_1 = 1 = R_1$ and $i_2 = 1 = R_2$ we find the observation $(1, 5)$ in Table 14.3 (that is, $x_1 = 1$ and $x_2 = 5$, taking into account the estimators of the marginal distributions). Therefore, the assigned probability is $1/4$. The total empirical copula is then given by

$$C\left(\frac{i_1}{4}, \frac{i_2}{4}\right) = \begin{cases} 0 & i_1 = 0, i_2 = 0 \\ \frac{1}{4} & i_1 = 1, i_2 = 1 \\ \frac{1}{4} & i_1 = 1, i_2 = 2 \\ \frac{1}{4} & i_1 = 1, i_2 = 3 \\ \frac{1}{4} & i_1 = 1, i_2 = 4 \\ \frac{1}{4} & i_1 = 2, i_2 = 1 \\ \frac{1}{4} & i_1 = 2, i_2 = 2 \\ \frac{1}{4} & i_1 = 2, i_2 = 3 \\ \frac{1}{2} & i_1 = 2, i_2 = 4 \;. \\ \frac{1}{4} & i_1 = 3, i_2 = 1 \\ \frac{1}{2} & i_1 = 3, i_2 = 2 \\ \frac{1}{2} & i_1 = 3, i_2 = 3 \\ \frac{3}{4} & i_1 = 3, i_2 = 4 \\ \frac{1}{4} & i_1 = 4, i_2 = 1 \\ \frac{1}{2} & i_1 = 4, i_2 = 2 \\ \frac{3}{4} & i_1 = 4, i_2 = 3 \\ 1 & i_1 = 4, i_2 = 4 \end{cases}$$

To obtain values for the empirical copula between the discrete points, multilinear interpolation can be used.

In the semi-parametric estimation method, only the copula parameters are estimated, without any assumptions on the marginal distributions. We have discussed different dependence measures in the first part of this chapter. These measures are used as input parameters; for example, the correlation matrix is used as an input to the Gaussian and t-copulas, or Kendall's τ can be used to estimate the parameter of the Archimedean copulas as shown in Table 14.2. In the multivariate case, using a Pseudo-Maximum-Likelihood method is an alternative to averaging Kendall's τ over the data (Genest, Ghoudi and Rivest, 1995).

For the parametric estimation method, the copula parameters and the parameters for the marginal distributions are estimated. The most common method here is to maximize the Log-Likelihood function (Kim, Silvapulle and Silvapulle, 2007). The likelihood function is a function of the parameters of a statistical model defined as

$$L(\alpha|x) = P_\alpha(X = x) \tag{14.24}$$

in the discrete case and as

$$L(\alpha|x) = f_\alpha(x) \tag{14.25}$$

in the continuous case, where f_α is a density function depending on parameter α. This means that the likelihood of a set of parameter values given the observed outcomes is equal to the probability of the observed outcomes given the parameter values. The value of a likelihood function bears no meaning on its own, its use lies solely in comparing one value to another. Given the outcome of the sample, one value of the parameter may be more likely than another. Suppose a d-dimensional data sample with N observations is given, then the multivariate distribution function is (Sklar's theorem)

$$F(x_1, \ldots, x_d, \alpha_1, \ldots, \alpha_d; \lambda) = $$
$$C(F_1(x_1, \alpha_1), F_2(x_2, \alpha_2), \ldots, F_{d-1}(x_{d-1}, \alpha_{d-1}), F_d(x_d, \alpha_d); \lambda), \tag{14.26}$$

where the α_i are parameters (or sets of parameters) for the marginal distributions and λ is the copula parameter. The Log-Likelihood function for the joint distribution is

$$L(\alpha_1, \ldots, \alpha_d; \lambda) = \sum_{i=1}^{N} \sum_{i=1}^{N} \log(f(x_1(i), \ldots, x_d(i), \alpha_1, \ldots, \alpha_d; \lambda))$$

$$= \sum_{i=1}^{N} \log(c(F_1(x_1(i); \alpha_1), \ldots, F_d(x_d(i); \alpha_d); \lambda)) \tag{14.27}$$

$$+ \sum_{j=1}^{d} \sum_{i=1}^{N} \log(f_j(x_j(i); \alpha_j)),$$

where $f(\cdot)$ denotes the multivariate density function, $f_j(\cdot)$ denotes the univariate density function and $c(\cdot)$ the density function of the copula. Searching for a global maximum of (14.27) has two drawbacks. First, it can be computationally very demanding to find a global maximum, if one is found at all. Second, if the number of observations for the different marginal distributions is different, one needs to reduce the affected data sets in order to get an equal number of observations. This can lead to substantial data loss. Both drawbacks can be circumvented by applying a multistep optimization procedure: In a first step, the parameters of the marginal distributions are maximized using their respective Log-Likelihood functions,

$$L(\alpha_j) = \sum_{i=1}^{N} \log(f_j(x_j(i); \alpha_j)), \tag{14.28}$$

taking into account the whole amount of data for each optimization. In a second step, (14.27) is maximized using the already optimized parameters α_i for the marginal distributions.

Sampling

The simplest method for generating a sample of dependent random variates of dimension d under a copula C is the Monte Carlo inversion method:

1. generate d independent uniformly distributed random variates $v_1, v_2, \ldots, v_d$
2. use the copula C to transform the $v_1, v_2, \ldots, v_d$ into a set of dependent uniformly distributed random variates $u_1, u_2, \ldots, u_d$
3. to calculate the dependent realizations $x_1, x_2, \ldots, x_d$, use the inverse of the marginal cumulative distribution function $x_i = F_i^{-1}(u_i)$, where $i \in \{1, \ldots, d\}$

We will now explain step 2 from above in more detail for the bivariate Gaussian copula. First, the independent uniformly distributed random variates v_1 and v_2 are transformed into standard normal distributed random variates z_1 and z_2,

$$z_i = \Phi^{-1}(v_i), \quad i \in \{1, 2\}. \tag{14.29}$$

To obtain two correlated standard normally distributed random variates we multiply with the Choleksy decomposition of the correlation matrix,

$$\begin{pmatrix} y_1 \\ y_2 \end{pmatrix} = \begin{pmatrix} 1 & 0 \\ \rho & \sqrt{1 - \rho^2} \end{pmatrix} \begin{pmatrix} z_1 \\ z_2 \end{pmatrix}. \tag{14.30}$$

The vector of the dependent random variates (u_1, u_2) is then obtained by applying the cumulative distribution function of the standard normal distribution,

$$u_i = \Phi(y_i), \quad i \in \{1, 2\}. \tag{14.31}$$

A very similar algorithm can be applied to obtain a sample of the t-copula for v degrees of freedom. After performing the steps described in (14.29) and (14.30), we obtain a sample of a bivariate t-distributed random variable with v degrees of freedom through the transformation

$$\begin{pmatrix} w_1 \\ w_2 \end{pmatrix} = \sqrt{\frac{v}{s}} \begin{pmatrix} y_1 \\ y_2 \end{pmatrix}, \tag{14.32}$$

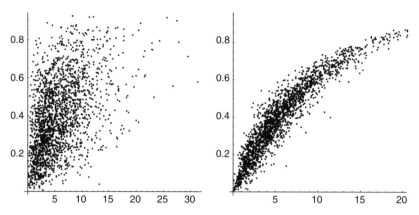

Figure 14.10   The figure shows a bivariate Gaussian copula with $\rho = 0.5$ (left) and a Gumbel copula with $\lambda = 0.5$ (right). In these cases, the marginal distributions are a gamma Ga(2, 3) distribution and a beta $\beta(2, 3)$ distribution.

where $s \sim \chi_\nu^2$ independent of z_i.[11] The vector of the dependent random variates u_1, u_2 is obtained by applying the cumulative distribution function of the t-distribution with ν degrees of freedom,

$$u_i = t_\nu(w_i), \quad i \in \{1, 2\}. \tag{14.33}$$

The generalization of this procedure to d dimensions is straightforward for both copulas.

For the Archimedean Gumbel, Clayton and Frank copulas presented above, the inverse of the generator, γ^{-1}, has an analytically tractable representation, namely the Laplace transformation[12] of a cumulative distribution function F (see Table 14.2). Therefore, a possible sampling algorithm for a d-dimensional random variate is to generate a random variable s with cumulative distribution function F, and d uniformly distributed random variables $v_1, v_2, \ldots, v_d$. Then, the vector with the components

$$u_i = \gamma^{-1}\left(-\frac{\ln v_i}{s}\right), \quad i \in 1, \ldots, d \tag{14.34}$$

is a vector with the desired Archimedean copula dependence structure with generator γ (McNeil, Frey and Embrechts, 2005). For the Gumbel copula, s is stable St$(1/\lambda, 1, \alpha, 0)$-distributed, where $\alpha = (\cos(\pi/2/\lambda))^\lambda$. For the Clayton copula, s is gamma Ga$(1/\lambda, 1)$-distributed, and for a Frank copula s is discrete with $P(s = k) = (1 - e^{-\lambda})^k/(k\lambda)$ for $k = 1, 2, \ldots$. In (McNeil, Frey and Embrechts, 2005) algorithms to simulate gamma, stable or discrete distributions are presented in detail.

For all copulas, realizations x_i of any marginal distribution can be calculated by simply applying the inverse cumulative distribution functions, see, for example, Figure 14.10.

---

[11] A simple algorithm for producing a random variate s from a χ_ν^2 distribution is given by

$$s = \sum_{i=1}^{\nu} y_i^2,$$

where y_i are independent standard normally distributed random variates.

[12] The Laplace transform is an integral transformation with a variety of applications in physics and engineering. The Laplace transform resolves a function into its moments (Davies, 2002).

Table 14.4 Comparison of joint default probabilities for Gauss copula and t-copulas for different degrees of freedom v for $\rho_{ij} = 0$. The number of draws in the simulation is $N = 10\,000$. The joint default probabilities have been calculated for 5 underlyings for 5 years. A constant hazard rate $h_i(t) = 0.05$ is assumed.

Gaussian	0	1	2	3	4	5
1Y	0.7776	0.2002	0.0215	0.0007	0.	0.
2Y	0.6067	0.3176	0.0692	0.0061	0.0004	0.
3Y	0.4747	0.3802	0.1271	0.0163	0.0017	0.
4Y	0.3718	0.4018	0.1861	0.0364	0.0036	0.0003
5Y	0.2891	0.4027	0.2341	0.065	0.0085	0.0006
Student $v = 1$						
1Y	0.8596	0.0733	0.0428	0.017	0.0059	0.0014
2Y	0.7229	0.147	0.082	0.0359	0.0098	0.0024
3Y	0.5956	0.2086	0.1199	0.0574	0.0156	0.0029
4Y	0.4868	0.2544	0.1573	0.0759	0.0222	0.0034
5Y	0.3893	0.2837	0.1969	0.0971	0.0286	0.0044
Student $v = 5$						
1Y	0.8003	0.1622	0.0308	0.0056	0.0011	0.
2Y	0.6385	0.2688	0.0744	0.0148	0.0035	0.
3Y	0.5041	0.3383	0.1206	0.0313	0.0056	0.0001
4Y	0.3927	0.3765	0.1679	0.0543	0.0081	0.0005
5Y	0.3064	0.3852	0.2206	0.0722	0.0146	0.001
Student $v = 10$						
1Y	0.7931	0.1728	0.0309	0.0031	0.0001	0.
2Y	0.6267	0.285	0.0735	0.0136	0.0011	0.0001
3Y	0.4948	0.3498	0.1227	0.0287	0.0038	0.0002
4Y	0.3917	0.3767	0.1762	0.0482	0.0066	0.0006
5Y	0.3091	0.385	0.2203	0.0726	0.0122	0.0008
Student $v = 20$						
1Y	0.7781	0.1955	0.0247	0.0015	0.0002	0.
2Y	0.605	0.3128	0.0721	0.0097	0.0004	0.
3Y	0.4762	0.3688	0.129	0.0237	0.0022	0.0001
4Y	0.3661	0.4008	0.1832	0.0441	0.0055	0.0003
5Y	0.2853	0.4041	0.2293	0.0692	0.0114	0.0007
Student $v = 30$						
1Y	0.7901	0.1847	0.0236	0.0015	0.0001	0.
2Y	0.6207	0.3002	0.0705	0.0082	0.0004	0.
3Y	0.4855	0.3673	0.1238	0.022	0.0014	0.
4Y	0.3773	0.3987	0.1786	0.0411	0.0042	0.0001
5Y	0.2923	0.4043	0.2264	0.0669	0.0092	0.0009

14.2.4 Default Probabilities for Credit Derivatives

The price of multi-name credit derivatives such as collateralized debt obligations (CDOs)[13] or n-th to default baskets[14] depends on the joint default probabilities and therefore on the choice

---

[13] A CDO is a type of a structured asset-backed security with tranches, where each tranche offers a different degree of risk (and therefore return) to the investors.

[14] Basket default swaps are derivative securities tied to an underlying portfolio (or "basket") of corporate bonds or other assets subject to credit risk. A basket default swap provides one party in the swap (the protection buyer) with a type of insurance against the possibility of default in exchange for regular payments made to the other party (the protection seller). Insuring a basket of

Table 14.5 Comparison of joint default probabilities for Gauss copula and t-copulas for different degrees of freedom v for $\rho_{ij} = 0.25$. The number of draws in the simulation is $N = 10\,000$. The joint default probabilities have been calculated for 5 underlyings for 5 years. A constant hazard rate $h_i(t) = 0.05$ is assumed.

Gaussian	0	1	2	3	4	5
1Y	0.8082	0.1486	0.0351	0.0073	0.0007	0.0001
2Y	0.6637	0.2325	0.0739	0.0251	0.0045	0.0003
3Y	0.5513	0.2771	0.1109	0.0464	0.0119	0.0024
4Y	0.4597	0.2972	0.1462	0.0694	0.0234	0.0041
5Y	0.3829	0.3103	0.1763	0.0865	0.0364	0.0076
Student $v = 1$						
1Y	0.8743	0.059	0.0319	0.0202	0.0107	0.0039
2Y	0.7576	0.1137	0.0607	0.0394	0.0206	0.008
3Y	0.6488	0.1604	0.0924	0.0578	0.0276	0.013
4Y	0.5497	0.2009	0.1188	0.0764	0.0378	0.0164
5Y	0.4665	0.2243	0.1479	0.093	0.0484	0.0199
Student $v = 5$						
1Y	0.8276	0.1206	0.0379	0.0098	0.0033	0.0008
2Y	0.6861	0.202	0.0722	0.0291	0.008	0.0026
3Y	0.573	0.2511	0.1086	0.0477	0.0144	0.0052
4Y	0.4729	0.2823	0.146	0.0667	0.0241	0.008
5Y	0.3985	0.29	0.1772	0.0852	0.0383	0.0108
Student $v = 10$						
1Y	0.8177	0.1388	0.03	0.0106	0.0024	0.0005
2Y	0.6753	0.2209	0.0703	0.0251	0.0077	0.0007
3Y	0.5619	0.2682	0.1106	0.0411	0.0158	0.0024
4Y	0.4697	0.2907	0.1478	0.0645	0.0223	0.005
5Y	0.3906	0.2997	0.1809	0.0859	0.0363	0.0066

of a dependence structure between default times of the underlying bonds or loans. The default time τ_i for each of the N_u underlyings is assumed to be a random variable and is defined as the first time the default countdown process,

$$\lambda_i(t) = \exp\left\{ -\int_0^t h_i(s)ds \right\}, \tag{14.35}$$

reaches the level of the trigger variable U_i

$$\tau_i = \inf\left\{ \tau \geq 0 : \lambda_i(t) \leq U_i \right\}. \tag{14.36}$$

Here, $h_i(t)$ is the hazard rate which can either be a deterministic or a stochastic process itself (Schönbucher, 2005). In both cases, credit default swaps are used to obtain either the deterministic hazard rate or the parameters of the stochastic models. In Tables 14.4–14.7, the default probabilities for Gauss copulas and t-copulas for different degrees of freedom v and

---

assets is typically less expensive than insuring each asset separately. For example, in a first-to-default swap, the protection buyer is compensated if one asset in the basket defaults but receives no compensation for any subsequent defaults. This is less expensive than buying insurance against all possible defaults and may provide adequate protection if multiple defaults are very unlikely.

Table 14.6 Comparison of joint default probabilities for Gauss copula and t-copulas for different degrees of freedom v for $\rho_{ij} = 0.5$. The number of draws in the simulation is $N = 10\,000$. The joint default probabilities have been calculated for 5 underlyings for 5 years. A constant hazard rate $h_i(t) = 0.05$ is assumed.

Gaussian	0	1	2	3	4	5
1Y	0.8489	0.1009	0.0318	0.0142	0.0034	0.0008
2Y	0.7329	0.1556	0.066	0.0276	0.0135	0.0044
3Y	0.6381	0.1891	0.0916	0.0454	0.0259	0.0099
4Y	0.557	0.2089	0.1142	0.0654	0.0373	0.0172
5Y	0.4926	0.2158	0.1313	0.0837	0.0497	0.0269
Student $v = 1$						
1Y	0.8899	0.0433	0.0273	0.0188	0.0121	0.0086
2Y	0.7886	0.083	0.0498	0.0376	0.0244	0.0166
3Y	0.6941	0.118	0.0726	0.0533	0.0361	0.0259
4Y	0.606	0.1477	0.0944	0.0701	0.0487	0.0331
5Y	0.5297	0.1685	0.1138	0.0836	0.0614	0.043
Student $v = 5$						
1Y	0.8573	0.0885	0.029	0.0138	0.0076	0.0038
2Y	0.7404	0.1439	0.0609	0.0292	0.0174	0.0082
3Y	0.6439	0.1778	0.0878	0.0481	0.027	0.0154
4Y	0.5621	0.1985	0.1081	0.0675	0.0411	0.0227
5Y	0.4907	0.2106	0.1281	0.0852	0.0519	0.0335
Student $v = 10$						
1Y	0.8405	0.0983	0.0362	0.0159	0.007	0.0021
2Y	0.7259	0.1499	0.0638	0.0342	0.0188	0.0074
3Y	0.6355	0.181	0.0887	0.0495	0.0303	0.015
4Y	0.5541	0.2004	0.11	0.0679	0.0442	0.0234
5Y	0.4853	0.2136	0.1259	0.0848	0.0569	0.0335

Table 14.7 Comparison of joint default probabilities for Gauss copula and t-copulas for different degrees of freedom v for $\rho_{ij} = 0.75$. The number of draws in the simulation is $N = 10\,000$. The joint default probabilities have been calculated for 5 underlyings for 5 years. A constant hazard rate $h_i(t) = 0.05$ is assumed.

Gaussian	0	1	2	3	4	5
1Y	0.8809	0.0602	0.0278	0.0163	0.0085	0.0063
2Y	0.7907	0.0907	0.0457	0.0326	0.0223	0.018
3Y	0.7111	0.1145	0.061	0.0455	0.0355	0.0324
4Y	0.6448	0.1251	0.0764	0.0542	0.0468	0.0527
5Y	0.5871	0.1343	0.0857	0.0649	0.0555	0.0725
Student $v = 1$						
1Y	0.9062	0.0278	0.0183	0.0124	0.0144	0.0209
2Y	0.8247	0.0515	0.0324	0.027	0.0234	0.041
3Y	0.75	0.0736	0.0468	0.035	0.0363	0.0583
4Y	0.6766	0.0938	0.0603	0.0472	0.0484	0.0737
5Y	0.6121	0.11	0.068	0.0599	0.0595	0.0905
Student $v = 5$						
1Y	0.8882	0.0509	0.0242	0.0135	0.0116	0.0116
2Y	0.7995	0.0836	0.0411	0.0292	0.0216	0.025
3Y	0.7199	0.1079	0.0582	0.0389	0.0337	0.0414
4Y	0.6499	0.1252	0.0679	0.0521	0.047	0.0579
5Y	0.5895	0.1336	0.0803	0.0613	0.059	0.0763
Student $v = 10$						
1Y	0.8788	0.0602	0.0251	0.0161	0.011	0.0088
2Y	0.7867	0.0904	0.0439	0.033	0.0235	0.0225
3Y	0.7119	0.112	0.0552	0.0459	0.0362	0.0388
4Y	0.646	0.1221	0.0758	0.0519	0.0473	0.0569
5Y	0.5881	0.1297	0.0852	0.0625	0.0609	0.0736

different ρ are shown. The number of underlyings is fixed at 5 and the hazard rate $h_i(t) = 0.05$ for each underlying. In this example, all ρ_{ij} are assumed to be equal for $i \neq j$. Due to the higher tail dependence of the t-copula, the probability of default for an increasing number of defaulting underlyings is higher than for the Gauss copula, in particlular for small degrees of freedom v. As expected, for increasing v the probabilities of default predicted by the t-copula approach the values obtained using the Gauss copula.

15

Parameter Calibration and Inverse Problems

Up to this point, we have considered various models for the movement of the underlying(s), and have assumed their parameters to be provided by an unspecified external source. The typical workflow in practical quantitative finance simulations is as follows:

1. Choose an appropriate model for the movement of the underlying.
2. Determine the parameters of this model such that model prices fit given market data, or, alternatively, manually choose the parameters.
3. Use one of the numerical methods described in the previous chapters to calculate a fair value or a Greek of a derivative or structured financial instrument.
4. (optional) Modify the market data to run scenario analyses or stress tests for risk management purposes.

In the present chapter, we will focus on step 2 above. Note that there is a huge difference between applications based on, say, thermodynamics and quantitative finance problems: The heat conductivity of a specific material at room temperature is, within measurement errors, the same when measured by different engineers at different times. In finance, on the other hand, the market prices of bonds are possibly made by the same market participants who want to determine model parameters. As a result, self-fulfilling prophecies or overreaction of markets may occur. Here, we do not take into account such important behavioral aspects of price formation, but accept the market prices of the instruments used for calibration at face value.

15.1 IMPLIED BLACK-SCHOLES VOLATILITIES

The simplest example of a calibration problem is the determination of a constant Black-Scholes volatility σ from the price $V_{market}(K, T)$ of an option with given strike K and expiry T (let us assume a call option for simplicity). When the spot price of the underlying, S_0, and the interest rate r between times 0 and T are known, this amounts to solving the equation

$$F(\sigma) = BSC(\sigma; S_0, K, r, T) - V_{market}(K, T) = 0 \qquad (15.1)$$

for the unknown volatility σ. By analyzing formula (2.13) for the Black-Scholes call value BSC, it can be shown in a fairly straightforward manner that the Black-Scholes Vega introduced in (3.24) is strictly positive for all positive S_0, K, T, σ, and that

$$\lim_{K \to 0} \text{Vega} = \lim_{K \to \infty} \text{Vega} = 0 \qquad (15.2)$$

for all positive S_0, T, σ. This implies that a solution σ of (15.1), if it exists, is necessarily unique. Given σ, one can thus calculate the fair Black-Scholes value, and, the other way round, from the Black-Scholes price the uniquely determined so-called *implied volatility* can be calculated.

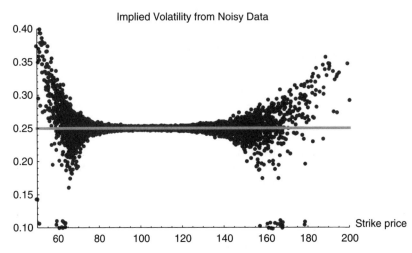

Figure 15.1   Implied flat volatility from noisy option prices. $S_0 = 100, T = 1/2$ year, $r = 2\%$ (continuous compounding). The call option values for $\sigma = 0.25$ are perturbed by a normally distributed noise with mean 0 and standard deviation of (absolute) 0.03. The quality of the implied volatility is, as expected, good at the money (Vega is high), and poor if Vega is small.

Applying Newton's method for solving the (one-dimensional) equation $F(\sigma) = 0$, using σ_1 as a starting point, yields

$$\sigma_{n+1} = \sigma_n - F(\sigma_n)/F'(\sigma_n), \qquad n = 1, 2, \ldots, \tag{15.3}$$

which can be iterated until satisfied with the convergence of the result. Note that this scheme may not converge at all, for instance when the call price is not admissible, i.e., outside the interval $(S_0 - Ke^{-rt}, S_0)$.

A more challenging difficulty arises when the option contract used for determining the implied volatility either lies deep in the money (exercise at expiry is very likely) or deep out of the money (exercise is very unlikely). In these cases, the option Vega ($F'(\sigma)$) is close to zero, and a wide range of volatilities lead to almost the same option values. Prices of options (or of warrants[1]) are quoted within a bid-ask-spread range, and therefore are not known exactly. When the market values are noisy, this noise is amplified by ($1/F'(\sigma)$) due to the glancing intersection, and may lead to unreliable results. Figure 15.1 shows scattered implied volatilities when (synthetic) market values of 6 month call options for a 25% volatility carry a normally distributed error with mean 0 and standard deviation 0.03 (for comparison: The at-the-money call value for $K = S_0 = 100$ is 7.516).

15.2 CALIBRATION PROBLEMS FOR YIELD CURVES

As an introduction to model calibration in the fixed income world, we start with the following model problem: Assume that at time 0, we can, for all T, obtain quotes for the fair values $Z(0, T)$ of the risk-free zero coupon bonds maturing at maturities T. We would like to derive

---

[1] Options are exchange traded, whereas warrants are issued (typically by investment banks) and therefore carry the risk of a credit event of the issuer.

the fair (continuously compounded) forward short rates $r(t)$ for all $t \in (0, T)$. The bond values fulfill

$$Z(0, T) = e^{-\int_0^T r(t) \, dt}, \tag{15.4}$$

and therefore, with the notation $y(T) = -\ln Z(0, T)$, we obtain

$$r(t) = \frac{d}{dt} y(t). \tag{15.5}$$

Now assume that the zero coupon bond prices and, in turn, the data $y_\delta(t)$ are noisy and can be obtained only within a spread level δ. Can we derive an error estimate for the short rate? With the following ansatz for the noise,

$$y_\delta^{(n)}(t) = y(t) + \delta \cdot \sin(nt/\delta), \tag{15.6}$$

we obviously have $\max |y_\delta^{(n)}(t) - y(t)| \leq \delta$, but the corresponding forward short rates r and $r_\delta^{(n)}$ differ by n. Arbitrarily small errors in the data may thus lead to arbitrarily large errors in the results. The reason for this behavior lies in the differentiation: when oscillations with small amplitude (δ) but high frequency (n/δ) are contained in the data, then the derivative of this noise becomes unbounded. The above example is of only limited relevance to practice: typically, one is not interested in forward short rates, but in forward rates of a finite tenor, say, 3, 6, or 12 months. Nevertheless, if one wants to calculate the 12 month forward rate between 20 and 21 years, and if the 20 year rate is assumed to be fairly accurate, then an error of one basis point in the annualized 21 year rate is amplified by a factor of 21.

A more realistic example pertains to the (one factor) Hull–White model presented in section 4.4. Assume that the reversion speed b and the volatility σ in the Hull–White model are both constant and known. Then the drift term $a(t)$ can be utilized to fit market data of yield rates. Using (4.22) and the subsequent equations, with $y(T) = -\ln B(0, T)$, we obtain

$$y(T) = -r(0)C(0, T) - A(0, T), \tag{15.7}$$

where the unknown function $a(.)$ appears in the integrand of $A(0, T)$. Equation (15.7) is thus a linear integral equation (to be more specific, a Volterra integral equation) of the first kind.[2] The Volterra property means that the fair present value of a bond maturing at time T is influenced only by parameter values $a(t)$ for $t \in (0, T)$. If we assume $a(.)$ to be piecewise constant with values a_i in $((i-1) \cdot h, i \cdot h)$, we could determine a_i iteratively from the yield values $y(i \cdot h)$. In this context, it is guaranteed that the system of linear equations for the vector (a_i) is a triangular system with non-zero diagonal elements, and therefore possesses a unique solution.

For the following example, we assume $b = 0.08$, $\sigma = 0.7\%$ and the drift function $a(.)$ to be a constant with value 0.0048, thus reverting the short rate to an equilibrium rate of 6%. The initial short rate r_0 is assumed to be 3%. Neglecting day-count conventions, we obtain the yield curve (with continuous compounding) shown in Figure 15.2. To demonstrate the calibration of the drift rate $a(.)$, we perturb this yield curve in Figure 15.2 by a relative error of up to 0.01%, such that an accurate yield rate of 5% would be quoted between 4.9995 and 5.0005%. A typical result of solving the triangular system for given monthly rates is shown in Figure 15.3.

---

[2] The term "integral equation of the first kind" denotes an equation where the unknown function appears in the integrand only, but not outside the integral. For a detailed analysis of integral equations of the first kind and their proper treatment, see (Engl, Hanke and Neubauer, 1996) or (in German) (Engl, 1997).

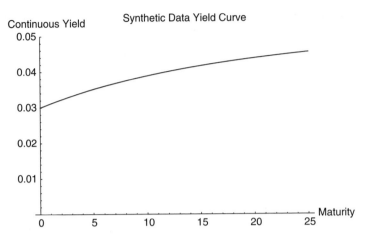

Figure 15.2 Synthetic Hull-White yield curve for $r_0 = 3\%$, $b = 0.08$, $\sigma = 0.7\%$, $a(t) = 0.0048$. Maturity ranges up to 25 years.

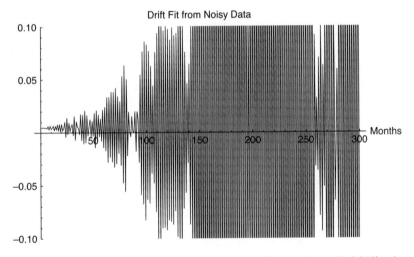

Figure 15.3 Drift rate $a(.)$ obtained from monthly yield curve data with 0.01% noise.

What is the reason for these heavy oscillations? In the finite dimensional setting of discrete yield curve data, the reason lies in the high condition number of the system matrix.[3] In the example shown here, the condition number grows cubically with the number of discretization points as indicated in Table 15.1. For monthly data ($N = 300$), the condition number is 1.8E+07: a relative error of 0.01%, that is, a noise-to-signal ratio of 0.0001 in the data thus typically leads to a noise-to-signal ratio of 1800 (!) in the result, rendering it practically useless.

---

[3] The condition number of a real matrix A is the quotient of the largest singular value over the smallest one. This condition number measures how much relative errors in the right hand side b may be amplified in the solution x, when $AX = b$ is solved. See, e.g., Stoer and Bulirsch (2002).

Table 15.1   Condition number of discretized Hull-White curve fitting.

Number of time intervals used	Condition number
1	1.00E+00
5	8.89E+01
25	1.06E+04
50	8.43E+04
100	6.72E+05
150	2.26E+06
300	1.81E+07

Well-posed and Ill-posed Problems

The term "well-posed problem" was introduced by Jacques Hadamard in 1923. A mathematical problem is called well-posed if the following conditions hold:

1. A solution exists for any (reasonable) data.
2. The solution is unique.
3. The solution depends continuously on the data, in some reasonable topology.

Hadamard believed that "correct modeling of a physically relevant problem leads to a well-posed problem." It has turned out that many inverse problems, in finance as well as in technical applications, are not well-posed in the above sense when treated in an infinite-dimensional setting. The finite-dimensional discretizations of such ill-posed problems are then typically ill-conditioned.

For the following treatment, we formally write the integral equation as

$$Kx = y. \tag{15.8}$$

When the kernel of an integral equation of the first kind on finite intervals is not degenerate (Engl, Hanke and Neubauer, 1996; Engl, 1997) and is square integrable, then the operator K is compact (see, e.g., Dunford and Schwartz (2009)), which is an abstract way of saying that it is smoothing, its singular values converge to zero, and the range of the operator is infinite-dimensional and not closed. The inversion of K is then ill-posed and unbounded in the topology of square-integrable functions. This implies that finite dimensional approximations of the inversion are ill-conditioned, and their instability increases with dimension.

Regularization of Ill-posed Problems

One way to stabilize the problem (15.8) is to solve (Tikhonov regularization)

$$x_\alpha^\delta = \arg\min(\|Kx - y^\delta\|^2 + \alpha\|x\|^2) \tag{15.9}$$

instead of $Kx = y^\delta$, with α chosen depending on the noise level $\delta = \|y^\delta - y\|$. For a linear equation, this is equivalent to solving

$$(K^*K + \alpha I)x_\alpha^\delta = K^*y^\delta, \tag{15.10}$$

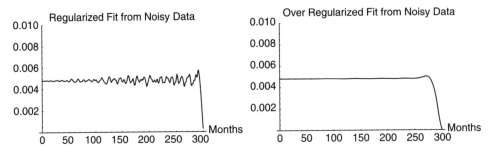

Figure 15.4 Drift rate $a(.)$ obtained from monthly yield curve data with 0.01% noise. Left pane: regularization parameter $\alpha = 0.001$. Right pane: regularization parameter $\alpha = 0.1$.

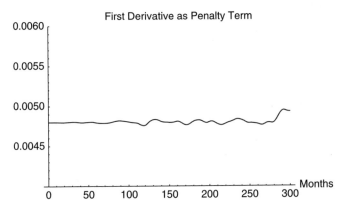

Figure 15.5 Drift rate $a(.)$ obtained from monthly yield curve data with 0.01% noise. Regularization parameter $\alpha = 0.5$ in the penalty term $\alpha \| \frac{dx}{dt} \|^2$. Note that the regularization parameters for different penalty terms are not comparable.

with K^* being the adjoint operator of K.[4] Linear ill-posed problems are well-analyzed, and optimal a priori and a posteriori strategies for choosing the regularization parameter α (Engl, Kunisch and Neubauer, 1989) are known. Figure 15.4 shows the curve fit results obtained with the regularization parameters $\alpha = 0.001$ and $\alpha = 0.1$ for the same noisy data used for 15.3.

It turns out that regularization by applying the penalty term $\alpha \|x\|^2$ in (15.9) tends to pull the regularized solution closer to zero than the true solution. One way to avoid this phenomenon (if desired) is to use $\alpha \| \frac{dx}{dt} \|^2$ (or other penalty functions containing derivatives) instead. Figure 15.5 shows the result.

An appropriate choice of the regularization parameter for a linear problem such as the Hull-White curve fit can be obtained by analyzing the spectrum (i.e., the eigenvalues) of the normal equation $K^*Kx = K^*y$. The operator K^*K is positive semidefinite; by adding αI, the spectrum is shifted away from zero. An easy and robust strategy is to choose α in such a way that the condition number of $K^*K + \alpha I$ is, say, less then 1E+06. Of course, this threshold should depend on the noise level. If derivatives are used in the penalty term, a modified regularization matrix has to be used instead of the identity matrix.

---

[4] In the finite-dimensional linear setting, the adjoint operator is just the matrix transpose.

Yield Curve Fitting for the Two Factor Hull-White Model

If the reversion speeds, the volatilities and the correlation in the two factor Hull-White model (see (7.86)) are assumed to be known, the determination of the drift parameter $\theta(.)$ again leads to a linear integral equation of the first kind, which should be treated by the same techniques used for the one factor case.

15.3 REVERSION SPEED AND VOLATILITY

In the previous section, we have seen how a given yield curve can be fit by solving the integral equation for the drift term $a(t)$ using appropriate regularization techniques. To calibrate the reversion speed – which is, in general, time-dependent – and the volatility function, additional information on fixed-income options is needed. Typically, cap data (for various strikes and various maturities) and swaption data (for different combinations of expiries of the swap option and of the underlying swap rate), either at the money or also in/out of the money, can be obtained for liquid currencies. These data are usually quoted by their Black76 volatilities (see Chapter 4).

Assume that only at-the-money cap data is given and the reversion speed is known. Then, for each additional caplet in the future, a unique Hull-White volatility (piecewise constant on the respective time intervals) can be determined as described in section 4.4. The higher the reversion speed, the higher the corresponding Hull-White volatility has to be to attain given Black76 volatilities. In order to also obtain reversion speeds, additional information must be drawn from swaption data.

15.4 LOCAL VOLATILITY

The Black-Scholes model for equities assumes that the volatility of the underlying is constant, which allows the derivation of closed form solutions for call, put and single barrier options (in this case only if the barrier and the interest rate are constant). However, market reality quotes different volatilities for different strikes and different expiries of options. One way to obtain a more realistic volatility surface is, as pointed out in Chapter 12, to introduce jump processes or a stochastic volatility like the Heston model does. An alternative approach is to use a *local volatility* function $\sigma(S, t)$, such that the random walk for the underlying is given by

$$dS_t = S_t(\mu(S_t, t)\,dt + \sigma(S_t, t)\,dW_t). \tag{15.11}$$

Under reasonable assumptions on μ and σ,[5] Itô's lemma can be applied, and with the same arguments as in the Black-Scholes case, we obtain for the fair value of a call option:

$$\frac{\partial C}{\partial t} + \frac{\sigma^2(S, t)S^2}{2}\frac{\partial^2 C}{\partial S^2} + rS\frac{\partial C}{\partial S} - rC = 0. \tag{15.12}$$

Again, r is the risk-free interest rate, which may depend on time. The only difference to the Black-Scholes PDE is the dependence of σ on S and t. If σ actually depends on S, there is no closed-form solution available, and the forward valuation of derivatives must be carried out by numerical techniques as presented in previous chapters (finite elements or Monte Carlo).

---

[5] If μ and σ are bounded and continuously differentiable, these assumptions are satisfied. For weaker conditions, see, e.g., (Øksendal, 2007).

15.4.1 Dupire's Inversion Formula

Bruno Dupire (1994) showed in (1994) that the call value $C(S, K, t, T)$, with the strike price K, does not only satisfy (15.12) interpreted as a partial differential equation in (S, t), but also the *dual equation*

$$-\frac{\partial C}{\partial T} + \frac{\sigma^2(K, T)K^2}{2}\frac{\partial^2 C}{\partial K^2} - rK\frac{\partial C}{\partial K} = 0, \tag{15.13}$$

with the initial condition $C(K, 0) = (S_0 - K)^+$. This dual equation is a PDE forward in expiry time T and must be solved for $C(S_0, K, 0, T)$.[6]

To obtain $\sigma(K, T)$, one could formally manipulate (15.13) to obtain

$$\sigma(K, T) = \sqrt{\frac{\frac{\partial C}{\partial T} + rK\frac{\partial C}{\partial K}}{\frac{K^2}{2}\frac{\partial^2 C}{\partial K^2}}}. \tag{15.14}$$

If the option values $C(K, T)$ were known in functional form for all relevant (K, T), one could use Dupire's formula (15.14) to obtain the local volatility function. However, the following important points must be considered regarding this procedure:

1. Accurate call values and, even more relevant, accurate derivatives of the call values with respect to T (first order) and to K (first and second order) are required.
2. For K far away from S_0 (deep in the money or deep out of the money), the second derivative $\frac{\partial^2 K}{\partial K^2}$ tends to zero, which amplifies errors in the denominator. Thus, a method for stabilizing this calculation is required, even more so as the market data far away from the money are typically less liquid.

15.4.2 Identifying Local Volatility

Due to the above concerns, determining the local volatility by directly applying Dupire's formula is not recommended. A stable algorithm, presented by Egger and Engl (2005), consists of the following steps:

1. Translate implied volatilities (for different strikes and different expiries) as quoted by market data providers into market prices of call options.
2. Choose a finite dimensional ansatz for the local volatility to be identified, e.g., piecewise constant or piecewise linear, and choose an initial guess $\sigma^0(S, t)$ for the local volatility. Set an iteration counter $k = 0$.
3. For the current k, use $\sigma^k(S, t)$ to calculate the option values. Note that the PDE needs to be solved only once in each iteration step, but for a vector of options with different strikes and expiries. Calculate the residual (market prices minus model prices) and calculate a penalty term for penalizing oscillations in σ^k. Combine them to a Tikhonov functional.
4. If the result is satisfactory, or if the iteration counter has exceeded its maximal value, then stop. Otherwise go to 5.
5. Calculate an updated volatility $\sigma^{k+1}(S, t)$ by using an optimization step as presented in Chapter 16. Go to 3.

---

[6] The derivation of the dual equation is not trivial and requires the Fokker-Planck equation for the probability density. For a step-by-step manipulation that is more readable than Dupire (1994), see, e.g. Rouah (1997).

The calculation of the increment in 5 typically requires the gradient or the Hessian of the Tikhonov functional with respect to the coefficients of the local volatility ansatz function. A naïve numerical differentiation approach could need hundreds of function evaluations per iteration step, each one requiring the numerical solution of a PDE. By utilizing techniques from adjoint functionals, the calculation of the gradient can be reduced to the same complexity as the function evaluation itself. For details, see Egger and Engl (2005).

15.4.3   Results

In order to quantify the calibration error obtained by the two methods presented in sections 15.4.1 and 15.4.2, we set up the following experiment: A flat volatility of 30% should be identified, but the data are perturbed randomly so that the implied Black volatilities lie between 29 and 31%. These volatility data are given for expiries $T = 35, 70, 105, \ldots, 3500$ days and strike prices $K = 50, 52, \ldots, 150$ (with the spot price $S = 100$). The annualized interest rate is assumed to be 2% (continuous compounding). The surface of the perturbed call prices is shown in Figure 15.6.

Figure 15.7 compares the local volatilities obtained by Dupire's inversion formula and by the algorithm described in section 15.4.2 for a noise level of (absolute) 1% in the implied volatility. The diffentiation in (15.14) was carried out by finite differences using the neighbouring points. Even for a noise level of (absolute) 0.01%, Dupire's inversion formula does not deliver reasonable results, see Figure 15.8. The reason lies in the fine grid of strike prices; a pre-smoothing of data would improve the results.

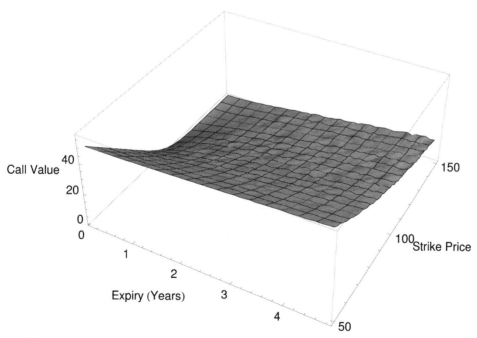

Figure 15.6   Realization of call price data for implied volatility in the interval $(0.29, 0.31)$.

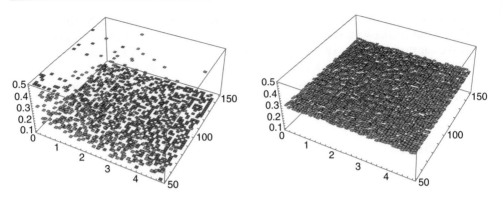

Figure 15.7   Local volatility identified by the Dupire inversion formula (left) and by Egger-Engl (right) from the data of Figure 15.6.

15.5   IDENTIFYING PARAMETERS IN VOLATILITY MODELS

In Chapter 12, a number of equity models that improve upon the Black-Scholes model were presented. The Heston model (cf. subsection 12.1.1), for instance, reads

$$dS_t = (r(t) - q(t))S_t dt + \sqrt{v_t}S_t dW_t^1,$$

$$dv_t = \kappa\left(\Theta - v_t^2\right)dt + \lambda\sqrt{v_t}dW_t^2 \qquad v_0 \geq 0.$$

In addition to the parameter functions $r(.)$ (interest rate) and $q(.)$ (dividend yield), which are assumed to be known, it requires five additional parameters that need to be determined:

- the inital variance v_0,
- the long-term variance level Θ,
- the reversion speed κ of the (Cox-Ingersoll-Ross) variance process,
- the volatility σ of the variance process,
- and the correlation ρ of the two Wiener processes.

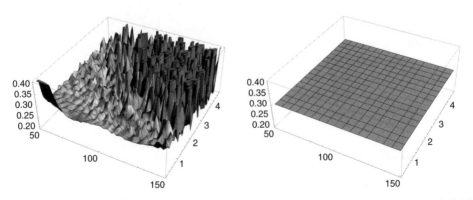

Figure 15.8   Local volatility identified by the Dupire inversion formula (left) and by Egger-Engl (right). Absolute error level in volatility data was 0.01%.

Typically, the Feller condition $2\kappa\Theta > \sigma^2$ is required in order to guarantee the positiveness of the variance. Again, the Heston parameters need to be identified from market prices for call or put options, similar to the local volatility in the previous section. In this case, the number of options quoted in the market is usually much higher than the number of free parameters (five), and therefore one can only expect to find a least squares solution. The non-linearity – or, to be more specific, the non-convexity – of the mapping of the Heston parameters to the option prices, however, makes the problem more intricate than one would normally expect from a five-dimensional identification problem.[7]

For calibration, the differences between the model prices and the market prices of the quoted options are expressed by a suitable error functional that should be minimized; typically, a weighted sum of squares of residuals is used. In Chapter 16, we present a more detailed description of various optimization techniques that are either based solely on function evaluations, or also on additional gradient information. When several (or many) local minima are expected, time consuming global optimization techniques may be required. In both cases, the calibration of a Heston model can require the calculation of millions of vanilla option prices; it is therefore essential that such options can be valuated efficiently. Here, characteristic function methods are certainly the method of choice.

15.5.1 Model Calibration for the FTSE-100

The FTSE-100 is a share index of the 100 companies with the highest market capitalization listed at the London Stock Exchange. Obviously, it is one of the most liquid equity indices, and therefore many options on the FTSE-100 with different strike prices and different expiries are traded. In the following example, we try to calibrate

- the parameters of the Heston model,
- the parameters of a Variance Gamma model,
- and the parameters of a normal inverse Gaussian model,

all from the same market data for 304 options, which were traded in May/June 2008 on 25 consecutive business days. Their implied volatilities are shown in Figure 15.9.

By applying the hybrid method discussed in Chapter 16, Fürst (2013) obtained the time series of Heston model parameters for the 25 trading days shown in Figure 16.6. As can be seen, these parameters are quite robust over the time interval under consideration. For the variance gamma model and the normal inverse Gaussian model, similar time stability results of the model parameters were obtained. With these parameter sets, the market prices of vanilla call options can be reproduced with very good quality, cf. Figure 15.10. Note that there are artefacts in the market prices that cannot be reproduced, and even, in the specific case, would allow arbitrage. Again, the good fit quality for vanilla options is not only achieved for the Heston model, but also for the variance gamma and normal inverse Gaussian models.

Model Uncertainty

What happens if we use the parameters obtained for the models in the calibration above to valuate an exotic option, say, an up-and-out barrier option? The results of such a valuation

---

[7] Binder et al showed in (Binder, Engl, Groetsch et al, 1994) that already for a one-parameter example, minimizing sequences need not converge.

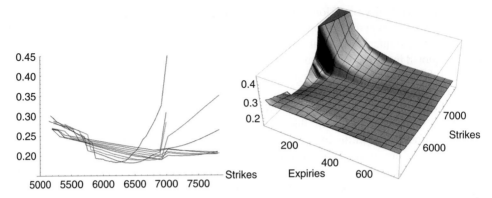

Figure 15.9 Left: Implied volatility for the FTSE-100 in May 2008. Each curve represents one expiry date. Right: Same data shown in a 3D plot.

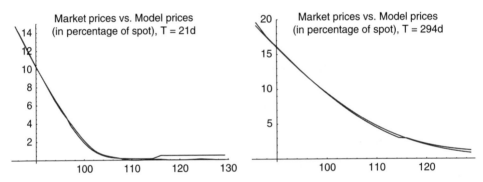

Figure 15.10 Heston model prices vs. market prices for different strikes. Left: Expiry 21d. Right: Expiry 294d. With the exception of the hump artefacts, the fit quality is excellent.

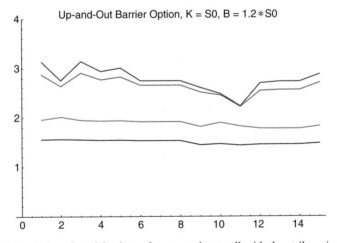

Figure 15.11 Time series of model prices of an up-and-out call with the strike price being the spot price and a continuously observed barrier at 120% of spot. From the top: Variance Gamma, Normal Inverse Gaussian, Heston, Black-Scholes with constant volatility.

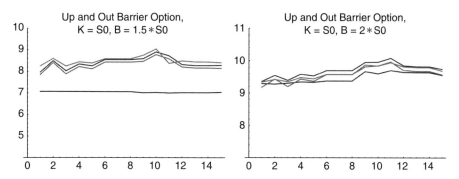

Figure 15.12 If the barrier levels are increased (left: 150% of spot, right: 200% of spot), then the options become more vanilla-like and their model prices get closer.

are shown in Figures 15.11 and 15.12. The time series of model prices is again stable, but the prices predicted by different models significantly differ. When only prices of vanilla options are available, then it cannot be argued which of the advanced volatility models should be the model of choice. By valuating an exotic option under more than one model for the equity movement, model uncertainty can be discovered. Of course, it is up to the market participant if she is prepared to bear this type of model risk.

Optimization Techniques

Efficient numerical optimization techniques play a key role in many of the calculation tasks in modern financial mathematics. Optimization problems occur for example in asset allocation, risk management and model calibration problems.

From a more theoretical point of view, the problem of finding an $\mathbf{x}^* \in \mathbb{R}^n$ that solves

$$\min_{\mathbf{x}} f(\mathbf{x}) \quad \text{subject to} \, \mathbf{x} \in S \tag{16.1}$$

is called an optimization problem for a given function $f(\mathbf{x}) : \mathbb{R}^n \to \mathbb{R}$. The function f is called the objective function and S is the feasible region. When S is empty, the problem is called infeasible. If it is possible to find a sequence $\mathbf{x}^0 \in S, \mathbf{x}^1 \in S, \ldots$ such that $f(\mathbf{x}^k) \to -\infty$ for $k \to \infty$, then the problem is called unbounded. For problems that are neither infeasible nor unbounded it may be possible to find a solution $\mathbf{x}^*$ satisfying

$$f(\mathbf{x}^*) \leq f(\mathbf{x}), \forall \mathbf{x} \in S. \tag{16.2}$$

Such an $\mathbf{x}^*$ is called a global minimizer of the optimization problem (16.1) (see Figure 16.1).[1]

On some occasions, one may only find an $\mathbf{x}^*$ satisfying

$$f(\mathbf{x}^*) \leq f(\mathbf{x}), \forall \mathbf{x} \in S \cap D(\mathbf{x}^*, \epsilon), \tag{16.3}$$

where $D(\mathbf{x}^*, \epsilon)$ is an open sphere with radius ϵ and midpoint $\mathbf{x}^*$. In this case, $\mathbf{x}^*$ is called a local minimizer of the optimization problem (see Figure 16.2). Typically, the feasible region S is described by equalities and inequalities, leading to the following form of the optimization problem:

$$\min_{\mathbf{x}} f(\mathbf{x})$$
$$g_i(\mathbf{x}) = 0, \quad i \in U, \tag{16.4}$$
$$h_i(\mathbf{x}) \geq 0, \quad i \in V.$$

Here, U denotes the index set for equality constraints and V denotes the index set for inequality constraints.

The type of optimization problem is determined by the properties of the functions f, g_i and h_i. Here, we list a number of problem types common in computational finance:

- Linear Programming (LP): A linear programming problem is the problem of optimizing a linear objective function f subject to linear equality and inequality constraints g_i,

$$\min_{\mathbf{x}} \mathbf{c}^T \mathbf{x}$$
$$A\mathbf{x} \leq \mathbf{b} \tag{16.5}$$
$$\mathbf{x} \geq \mathbf{0},$$

---

[1] A sufficient condition for the existence of a global minimizer is that S is compact and f is continuous.

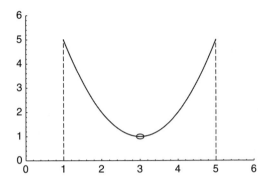

Figure 16.1 The global minimum of a one-dimensional function f is marked by a circle. The dashed lines indicate the boundaries of the assumed feasible interval.

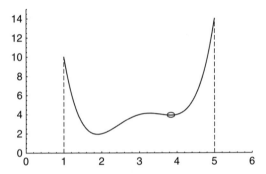

Figure 16.2 A local minimum of the function f is marked by a circle. The dashed lines indicate a possible feasible and bounded region.

where $\mathbf{c} \in \mathbb{R}^n$, $\mathbf{b} \in \mathbb{R}^m$ and $\mathbf{A} \in \mathbb{R}^{m+n}$ are given and $\mathbf{x} \in \mathbb{R}^n$ is the vector of unknowns. Note that in (16.5) the inequalities are to be understood component-wise. Possible algorithms for the solution of linear programming problems are the simplex algorithm and the interior point method.

- Quadratic Programming (QP): In a quadratic programming problem, the objective function is quadratic in the unknown variables,

$$\min_{\mathbf{x}} \frac{1}{2}\mathbf{x}^T \mathbf{Q}\mathbf{x} + \mathbf{c}^T\mathbf{x}$$
$$\mathbf{A}\mathbf{x} \leq \mathbf{b} \qquad (16.6)$$
$$\mathbf{x} \geq 0,$$

where $\mathbf{c} \in \mathbb{R}^n$, $\mathbf{b} \in \mathbb{R}^m$, $\mathbf{A} \in \mathbb{R}^{m\times n}$ and $\mathbf{Q} \in \mathbb{R}^{n\times n}$ are given and $\mathbf{x} \in \mathbb{R}^n$ is the vector of unknowns.[2] If $\mathbf{Q}$ is a positive semidefinite matrix the objective function f is convex.

---

[2] Note that due to

$$\frac{1}{2}\mathbf{x}^T(\mathbf{Q} + \mathbf{Q}^T)\mathbf{x} = \mathbf{x}^T(\mathbf{Q})\mathbf{x}$$

$\mathbf{Q}$ can be assumed to be symmetric.

A convex optimization problem can be solved in polynomial time[3] using interior point methods.

- Integer Programming: In integer programming problems, the variables are required to take integer values,

$$\mathbf{x} \in \mathbb{Z}^n. \tag{16.7}$$

If this is required only for a subset of variables,

$$x_j \in \mathbb{N} \quad \text{for } j = 1, \dots, p, \quad p < n, \tag{16.8}$$

the problem is called mixed integer programming. If the variables x_j represent binary decision variables, i.e., $x_j \in \{0, 1\}$, the optimization problem is called a $0 - 1$ linear program.

- Nonlinear Programming (NLP): In nonlinear programming problems, the objective function f and/or the equality and inequality constraints g_i and h_i are nonlinear functions mapping from $\mathbb{R}^n \to \mathbb{R}$. In contrast to, for example, the simplex method for an LP problem, there is no single preferred algorithm for solving general nonlinear problems. We will discuss gradient-based algorithms and heuristically inspired methods for the solution of such problems in the next section.

The type of optimization problem, the dimension n and the number of equality and inequality constraints m are good indicators for the difficulty of the optimization problem.

16.1 MODEL CALIBRATION AND OPTIMIZATION

Before complex instruments can be priced, the model parameters x_i ($\mathbf{x} = (x_i)_i$) must be calibrated to the market prices of liquid instruments (for details see Chapter 15), e.g., by minimizing the least squares error of model prices compared to market prices (objective function),

$$\sum_j ||V_j^{Mod}(\mathbf{x}) - V_j^{Mar}||^2 \to \min. \tag{16.9}$$

Here, the V_j are single calibration instruments, e.g., European call/put options with different strike prices and different expiries. The corresponding optimization problem, formulated as a minimization problem of a least squares functional, is not necessarily convex as a function of the model parameters and is therefore hard to solve. Several, or even a large number of local minima may exist. In addition, even if there is only one unique minimum, the objective function can exhibit extremely "flat" behavior such that a parameter set far away from the true optimum may be still accepted as optimal.

Two groups of algorithms can be applied to solve such optimization problems. Both have in common that the optimization starts from an arbitrary initial state $\mathbf{s} = \mathbf{x}_0$ (point in the parameter space) or a set of such arbitrary initial states and tries to propagate this state/these states through the search space in search for the minimum of the objective function. During the propagation procedure neighbors are created; new states that are produced by altering a given state in a particular, algorithm dependent way,

$$\mathbf{s} \to \mathbf{s}' \to \mathbf{s}'' \to \cdots \to \mathbf{s}^{opt}. \tag{16.10}$$

---

[3] Polynomial time algorithms always find an optimal solution in an amount of time that is at most a polynomial function of the input size.

The iterations are stopped after a suitably defined stopping criterion is reached, and the final state $\mathbf{s}^{opt}$ is taken as an approximation for the solution, $\mathbf{x}^* = \mathbf{s}^{opt}$. The first group are locally convergent algorithms (e.g., Levenberg-Marquardt), which are guaranteed to find a (numerical) minimum, albeit not necessarily the global one. The second group are based on meta-heuristic methods and are considered to be acceptably good solvers for the problem of finding the global minimum (Osman and Kelly, 1996) (simulated annealing, particle swarm methods, evolutionary algorithms, ...). The disadvantage of the latter group is the enormous amount of computation time required to obtain a result in comparison to the algorithms of the first group. Hybrid methods combine meta-heuristic methods with local search methods. The goal is to design algorithms with improved convergence properties compared to pure heuristic methods that are still not as easily trapped in local minima as pure local search methods. Several realizations of such hybrid algorithms exist – see, for example, (Hedar and Fukushima, 2002) and the references therein.

16.1.1 Gradient-Based Algorithms for Nonlinear Least Squares Problems

The most intuitive and simplest technique to find the minimum of a function is probably the steepest descent method. The update step from $\mathbf{x}^k$ to $\mathbf{x}^{k+1}$ consists of adding a negative multiple of the gradient,

$$\mathbf{x}^{k+1} = \mathbf{x}^k - \lambda \nabla f. \tag{16.11}$$

Simple gradient descent may exhibit bad convergence and zigzagging of the minimization path due to the curvature of the error surface (consider, for instance, flat valleys with steep walls).

In contrast to a steepest descent method, which uses only information about the first order derivatives, Newton's method also incorporates information about the curvature, i.e., the function's second order derivatives. Let us consider an objective function $f(\mathbf{x})$. In order to find the minimum, a system of equations

$$\nabla f(\mathbf{x}) = \mathbf{F}(\mathbf{x}) = \mathbf{0} \tag{16.12}$$

needs to be solved, where

$$F_i = \frac{\partial f}{\partial x_i}(\mathbf{x}). \tag{16.13}$$

Introducing an iteration index k, the first order Taylor expansion of $\mathbf{F}$ around $\mathbf{x}^k$ is

$$\mathbf{F}(\mathbf{x}^k + \delta) \approx \mathbf{F}(\mathbf{x}^k) + \nabla \mathbf{F}(\mathbf{x}^k)\delta. \tag{16.14}$$

With the Hessian matrix $\mathbf{H}(\mathbf{x}^k)$ of the function $f(\mathbf{x}^k)$,[4]

$$\mathbf{H}(\mathbf{x}) = \nabla \mathbf{F}(\mathbf{x}) = \begin{pmatrix} \frac{\partial^2 f}{\partial x_1 \partial x_1} & \cdots & \frac{\partial^2 f}{\partial x_1 \partial x_n} \\ \vdots & \ddots & \vdots \\ \frac{\partial^2 f}{\partial x_n \partial x_1} & \cdots & \frac{\partial^2 f}{\partial x_n \partial x_n} \end{pmatrix}, \tag{16.15}$$

we can rewrite (16.14),

$$\mathbf{F}(\mathbf{x}^k + \delta) \approx \mathbf{F}(\mathbf{x}^k) + \mathbf{H}(\mathbf{x}^k)\delta. \tag{16.16}$$

---

[4] Note that we omit the index k in the next formula for reasons of simplicity.

To find a solution for (16.12), we need to set the left hand side of (16.16) equal to **0** and solve for δ,

$$\mathbf{0} = \mathbf{F}(\mathbf{x}^k) + \mathbf{H}(\mathbf{x}^k)\delta, \tag{16.17}$$

$$\delta = \mathbf{H}(\mathbf{x}^k)^{-1}\mathbf{F}(\mathbf{x}^k) = \mathbf{H}(\mathbf{x}^k)^{-1}\nabla f(\mathbf{x}^k). \tag{16.18}$$

This is the (n-dimensional) Newton's method for solving (16.12), and the Newton update formula becomes

$$\mathbf{x}^{k+1} = \mathbf{x}^k + \delta, \tag{16.19}$$

with δ taken from (16.18). Close to the optimum, the Newton method converges quadratically (under smoothness assumptions on f). However, it also has a number of drawbacks: First, Newton's method is sensitive to the starting point and may not converge if the starting point is not chosen appropriately. Second, it is expensive to compute the Hessian matrix in each iteration, in particular for large scale optimization problems. Approximations are therefore used instead of the Hessian to make the solution of the linear system in (16.18) computationally cheaper. Such approaches are known as Quasi-Newton methods (Bonnans, 2009).

Sequential Quadratic Programming

Sophisticated methods are available for solving quadratic programs. The Sequential Quadratic Programming (SQP) method tries to use them to solve general nonlinear programs. At the current feasible point $\mathbf{x}^k$, where k is the iteration number, the NLP is approximated by a quadratic program:

- a quadratic approximation of the objective function is computed.
- linear approximations of the equality constraints and of the active inequality constraints are computed.

This approximation results in the problem

$$\min_{\mathbf{x}} \mathbf{r}^k(\mathbf{x} - \mathbf{x}^k) + \frac{1}{2}(\mathbf{x} - \mathbf{x}^k)^T \mathbf{B}^k (\mathbf{x} - \mathbf{x}^k),$$
$$\nabla g_i(\mathbf{x}^k)^T(\mathbf{x} - \mathbf{x}^k) + g_i(\mathbf{x}^k) = 0, \qquad i \in U, \tag{16.20}$$
$$\nabla h_j(\mathbf{x}^k)^T(\mathbf{x} - \mathbf{x}^k) + h_j(\mathbf{x}^k) \leq 0, \qquad \text{for all active } j.$$

The key ingredients in the approximation of the NLP by a quadratic program are the choices of the vector $\mathbf{r}^k$, which should approximate $\nabla f(\mathbf{x}^k)$, and the matrix $\mathbf{B}^k$, which should approximate the Hessian $\mathbf{H}$ of $f(\mathbf{x}^k)$ in (16.20). For $\mathbf{B}^k = \mathbf{1}$, one obtains a steepest-descent-like method, if $\mathbf{B}^k$ is the Hessian of f, one obtains a Newton-like method (Bonnans, 2009).

Levenberg-Marquardt Algorithm

The Levenberg-Marquardt algorithm (LMA) is an iterative technique for finding the minimum of a sum of squares of nonlinear functions, i.e., for an objective function of the form

$$f(\mathbf{x}) = \frac{1}{2}\sum_{i}^{N} r_i^2(\mathbf{x}) = \frac{1}{2}||\mathbf{r}(\mathbf{x})||^2, \tag{16.21}$$

where N is the number of data points. It has become a standard technique for nonlinear least squares problems and can be thought of as an interpolation between a steepest descent and a

Gauss-Newton method (Nocedal and Wright, 2000).[5] The gradient of the objective function in (16.21) is

$$\nabla f(\mathbf{x}) = \sum_i^N r_i(\mathbf{x}) \nabla r_i(\mathbf{x}) = \mathbf{J}^T(\mathbf{x}) \mathbf{r}(\mathbf{x}). \tag{16.22}$$

If the residuals are small or the second derivatives of the residuals with respect to the parameters vanish, the Hessian can be calculated from the Jacobians by

$$\mathbf{H}(\mathbf{x}) = \mathbf{J}^T(\mathbf{x}) \mathbf{J}(\mathbf{x}). \tag{16.23}$$

The update step in each iteration of the LMA is

$$\mathbf{x}^{k+1} = \mathbf{x}^k - (\mathbf{H}(\mathbf{x}) + \lambda \mathbf{I})^{-1} \nabla f(\mathbf{x}^k), \tag{16.24}$$

where $\lambda \geq 0$ is a scaling parameter that is adjusted according to the evolution of the error during the iterations. It has been a common way to determine λ via a line search in the negative gradient direction. When the error is large, λ is increased and the algorithm behaves like a steepest descent method (see (16.11)): slow, but guaranteed to converge. When the current guess approaches the correct solution, λ is decreased and the algorithm becomes a Gauss-Newton method (see (16.19)). The LMA is thus more robust than a pure Gauss-Newton algorithm, in the sense that it finds a minimum even if it is started far from the solution. The update step can be further improved by scaling each component of the gradient according to the curvature, resulting in a bigger movement along the directions where the gradient is small, in order to circumvent the valley problem (see steepest descent method),

$$\mathbf{x}^{k+1} = \mathbf{x}^k - (\mathbf{H}(\mathbf{x}) + \text{diag}[\mathbf{H}])^{-1} \nabla f(\mathbf{x}^k). \tag{16.25}$$

In modern implementations, the scaling parameter is not determined via line search, but a trust region approach is used. A trust region refers to the subset of the region of the objective function that is well approximated by a model function (often quadratic). The trust region is expanded if an adequate model of the objective function is found, otherwise, if the approximation is poor, the region is contracted. Different techniques exist to incorporate box constraints (Kanzow, Yamashita and Fukushima, 2004) or linear constraints (Nocedal and Wright, 2000).

16.2 HEURISTICALLY INSPIRED ALGORITHMS

Meta-heuristic methods are robust and applicable to a wide range of problem areas, but suffer, in particular when they are applied to complex problems, from slow convergence and high computational cost. The better part of these methods creates random movements to explore the global parameter space without using local information to determine the most promising search direction. While this strategy avoids getting trapped in local minima, it also results in relatively slow convergence.

---

[5] Note that Gauss-Newton methods (and therefore also the LM algorithm) are special forms of Quasi-Newton methods only usable for nonlinear least squares problems, whereas a general Quasi-Newton method can be applied to minimize general real-valued functions.

16.2.1   Simulated Annealing

Simulated Annealing (SA) is a meta-heuristic method rooted in annealing in metallurgy, a technique that uses heating and controlled cooling for crystal growth in a material. From a more general, but still physically motivated point of view, SA can be seen as a method to minimize the internal energy $E(s)$ of a physical system, where s describes the state of the system.[6] When applying SA algorithms to the optimization problem (16.1), we associate the point s of the search space with the state of the physical system, and the value of the objective function at this point with the energy $E(s)$. During the evolution process, the state s^k can be updated to s^{k+1} even if the value of the energy function E increases. This avoids becoming stuck in a local minimum. The probability accepting a new state s^{k+1} if $E^{k+1} > E^k$ depends on the energy difference $\Delta E = E^{k+1} - E^k$ and a parameter T that describes the optimization strategy,[7]

$$P(\Delta E) \sim \exp\left(-\frac{\Delta E}{T}\right).\qquad(16.26)$$

A candidate for the updated state s^{k+1} can be calculated from s^k for example by adding a random shift. The acceptance of s^{k+1} as the new state is then calculated using the Metropolis algorithm (Metropolis, Rosenbluth, Rosenbluth et al., 1953). Given s^k, the guess s^{k+1}, the corresponding values of the objective function E^k and E^{k+1} and the acceptance probability $p = P(\Delta E)$ from (16.26), s^{k+1} is accepted if either

$$E^{k+1} \leq E^k,\qquad(16.27)$$

or if $E^{k+1} > E^k$ and the following relation holds:

$$p \geq p_a \quad \text{where } p_a \sim U[0, 1](\text{uniform distribution}).\qquad(16.28)$$

The acceptance rate r_a, i.e., the fraction of accepted moves, is an important quantity to monitor during the iteration process. The effectivity of SA algorithms strongly depends on the optimization strategy $T = T(k)$, the starting temperature $T(0)$ and the algorithm used to calculate s^{k+1}.[8] The acceptance rate r_a can be used to formulate a stopping criterion (other than simply stopping after a predefined maximum number of iterations): stop if $r_a < x$, where x depends on the problem type. Due to its simplicity, SA can be easily combined with direct search methods (Hedar and Fukushima, 2002). We have applied SA and a version of such a hybrid algorithm, the Direct Search Simulated Annealing algorithm (DSSA) (Hedar and Fukushima, 2002), to the calibration of the Heston model in section 16.3 of this chapter. The typical evolution of the residual as a function of the iteration number k is displayed in Figure 16.3.

---

[6] Consider a simple diatomic molecule where the distance between the two atoms is used to describe the state of the system. The energy as a function of the state will be minimized at the bond length. SA tries to bring the system from an arbitrary initial state to this state with the minimum possible energy.

[7] In the physical analogy, T is the temperature (or kinetic energy) of the particle ensemble, and the optimization strategy corresponds to a cooling scheme.

[8] The starting temperature $T(0)$ is usually adjusted in a way to have an acceptance rate r_a between 40% and 60%. Many techniques exist to calculate a guess for s^{k+1}: random shift, permutations, combine gradient-based information with the previous two, . . .

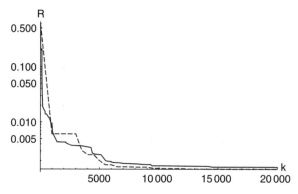

Figure 16.3 The figure shows the evolution of the residual for the calibration of the Heston model to a data set of 286 Vanilla options on the DAX from 2009-03-02 for the SA (solid line) and the DE (dashed line) algorithm.

16.2.2 Differential Evolution

Differential Evolution (DE) belongs to a family of biologically inspired algorithms that draw from an evolutionary metaphor. For the wide field of biologically inspired algorithms and their application to financial problems, we refer the reader to the book of Brabazon and O'Neill (2006) and the references therein.[9] From a biological point of view, evolution is the process of positive or negative selection of species, depending on their relative success to survive and reproduce in their environment. Concepts of mutation, recombination and fitness-based selection are used to manipulate a population of solution encodings in order to find a good solution.

Several variants of DE algorithms exist. They are usually described using the shorthand notation DE/x/y/z, where x specifies how the base vector of real values is chosen, y is the number of difference vectors used and z denotes the crossover scheme. For example, DE/rand/1/bin means the base vector is chosen randomly, the number of chosen difference vectors is 1 and bin indicates that the crossover is based on independent binomial experiments. A DE algorithm consists of the following steps:

1. Create a population of N vectors of dimension n,

$$\{\mathbf{x}_1, \dots, \mathbf{x}_N\} \quad \text{where } \mathbf{x}_i \in \mathbb{R}^n, \tag{16.29}$$

where each vector encodes a possible solution (a point in the region S). The vector is (quasi-)randomly initialized and evaluated using a "fitness function", the objective function f.

2. For each $\mathbf{x}_i$:

    2a. Create a variant vector $\mathbf{v}_i$ using randomly selected members of the population (mutation step). Ensure that the variant vector encodes a valid solution candidate, i.e., that the vector is in S.

    2b. Create a trial vector $\mathbf{t}_i$ by combining the variant vector with vector $\mathbf{x}_i$ (crossover step)

    2c. Perform a selection process to determine whether the trial vector replaces the vector $\mathbf{x}_i$ of the population

---

[9] Popular members of the family of evolutionary algorithms are Genetic Algorithms (GA), Differential Evolution (DE) and Genetic Programming (GP).

3. Repeat steps 2a to 2c until the stopping criterion is fulfilled or the maximum number of iterations is reached.

The variant vectors $\mathbf{v}_i$ are calculated by randomly selecting indices $k, l, m \in \{1, \ldots, N\}$, where i, k, l, m are mutually distinct:

$$\mathbf{v}_i = \mathbf{x}_m + \lambda(\mathbf{x}_k - \mathbf{x}_l). \qquad (16.30)$$

Here, the vector $\mathbf{x}_k - \mathbf{x}_l$ is called the difference vector, and λ is a scaling parameter responsible for amplification or damping of the difference vector, which is necessary to avoid stagnation of the search process.[10] A different possibility to calculate $\mathbf{v}_i$ is to use the highest-fitness member (the vector leading to the lowest value for the objective function) of the current population $\mathbf{x}_b$ instead of $\mathbf{x}_m$ in (16.30), leading to a DE/best/y/z algorithm.

The trial vector $\mathbf{t}_i$ is obtained by

$$\mathbf{t}_i = \begin{cases} v_{ij} & \text{if } u_j \le c \text{ or } j = p, \\ x_{ij} & \text{else,} \end{cases} \qquad (16.31)$$

where $j = 1, \ldots, n$, $u_j \sim U(0, 1)$, $c \in (0, 1)$ is a user defined crossover constant and $p \sim \{1, \ldots, n\}$. The random index p ensures that the trial vector $\mathbf{t}_i$ differs in at least one component from $\mathbf{x}_i$. The resulting trial vector $\mathbf{t}_i$ replaces $\mathbf{x}_i$ in the population if it has higher fitness, i.e., if the objective function $f(\mathbf{t}_i) < f(\mathbf{x}_i)$. The key parameters of a DE algorithm are the population size N (typically five to ten times the number of dimensions of a solution vector), the crossover rate c (typically around 0.5) and the scaling factor λ (typically between 0.4 and 0.9). These parameters need to be adapted for a given problem to ensure high efficiency. The typical evolution of the residual as a function of the iteration number k is displayed in Figure 16.3.

16.3 A HYBRID ALGORITHM FOR HESTON MODEL CALIBRATION

In this section, we discuss how to find the optimal parameters for a Heston model for reproducing given market data. We use a hybrid algorithm that propagates walkers through the parameter space using the Levenberg-Marquardt algorithm: N_I starting points are chosen from quasi-random low discrepancy sequences to achieve good coverage of the parameter space. We evaluate the objective function for each of these parameter sets in parallel (see also Chapter 18). Increasing N_I allows us to improve the best residual. Assume two sets of starting points S_{I_1} and S_{I_2}, then using quasi-random low discrepancy sequences (here Sobol points) ensures that $S_{I_1} \subset S_{I_2}$, if $|S_{I_2}| > |S_{I_1}|$. Then the N_B points with the lowest residuals are used as starting points and propagated through the parameter space using the Levenberg-Marquardt algorithm. Unfortunately, for the Heston model the optimal parameter set may violate the Feller condition (12.7), as shown in Figure 16.4. We overcome this drawback by introducing a second optimization performed on the 4d region determined by the boundary of the Feller condition. We use the best point in the parameter space obtained from this optimization, and compare it to the points obtained by the full 5d optimization – a huge gain in speed (see Table 16.3) results from the fact that it is no longer necessary to use projections but that one can

---

[10] Also algorithms utilizing more than one difference vector exist. For example, a DE/x/2/z algorithm uses two difference vectors that are created using five indices mutually distinct from each other and mutually distinct to i.

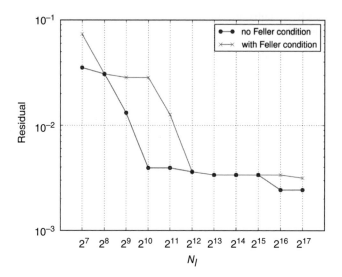

Figure 16.4 This figure shows the residual as a function of N_I Sobol points. If the minima coincide for a certain N_I, the optimal parameter set does not violate the Feller condition (Fürst, Aichinger, Binder and Kletzmayr, 2012).

Table 16.1 This table shows the residual for different combinations of initial points N_I and Levenberg-Marquardt starting points N_B.

N_I	1	2	4	8	16	32	64	128
2^7	0.00441	0.00383	0.00359	0.00353	0.00316	0.00297	0.00293	0.00285
2^8	0.01350	0.01350	0.00343	0.00306	0.00300	0.00287	0.00287	0.00287
2^9	0.01350	0.01202	0.00364	0.00306	0.00297	0.00290	0.00288	0.00288
2^{10}	0.00394	0.00325	0.00311	0.00311	0.00311	0.00293	0.00288	0.00285
2^{11}	0.00328	0.00328	0.00313	0.00303	0.00308	0.00279	0.00279	0.00279
2^{12}	0.00311	0.00311	0.00311	0.00299	0.00290	0.00286	0.00275	0.00275
2^{13}	0.00286	0.00286	0.00286	0.00286	0.00279	0.00279	0.00279	0.00279
2^{14}	0.00286	0.00286	0.00286	0.00286	0.00285	0.00285	0.00283	0.00282
2^{15}	0.00286	0.00286	0.00286	0.00286	0.00286	0.00286	0.00284	0.00284
2^{16}	0.00286	0.00286	0.00286	0.00286	0.00286	0.00283	0.00283	0.00283
2^{17}	0.00279	0.00279	0.00279	0.00279	0.00279	0.00279	0.00274	0.00274

simply destroy the walker.[11] Table 16.1 shows the dependence of the residual and the optimal parameters on the number of starting points N_I and the number of points N_B chosen after sorting to start the gradient-based algorithm from.

We now focus on the gradient part of the calibration algorithm and explore whether using analytical derivatives is superior to using numerical derivatives calculated via finite differences (see Chapter 3) by comparing the optimization results. Analytical derivatives of the objective function with respect to the model parameters can be calculated using 12.47. We have

---

[11] When the Feller condition is violated, the parameter set needs to be projected to the admissible domain, which considerably slows down the performance of the whole algorithm.

Table 16.2   This table shows the residual and the corresponding calibrated parameter set using the Levenberg Marquardt algorithm starting from $(2.5, 0.5, 0.5, 0.5, -0.5)$ and fixing the number of iterations at 50. The different lines correspond to the different methods used for calculating the derivatives with respect to the Heston parameters: analytic refers to calculation using (12.47), bd refers to using a simple backward difference quotient (first order), fd to a forward difference quotient (first order), cd to central difference quotient (second order) and cd2 to a higher order central difference quotient (fourth order).

Method	Residual	κ	θ	σ	ρ	v_0
analytic	0.00181063	0.092252	0.486551	0.695210	−0.384361	0.048140
fd	0.00181035	0.090878	0.493407	0.694971	−0.384394	0.048132
bd	0.00181089	0.093595	0.480052	0.695447	−0.384329	0.048147
cd	0.00181063	0.092256	0.486530	0.695211	−0.384361	0.048140
cd2	0.00181063	0.092249	0.486566	0.695210	−0.384361	0.048137

started from a point in the five-dimensional parameter space, $(\kappa = 2.5, \theta = 0.5, \sigma = 0.5, \rho = -0.5, v_0 = 2.5)$, and performed 50 iterations of the Levenberg-Marquardt algorithm. Results are reported in Table 16.2. The evolution of the residuum (16.9) during the iterative process is shown in Figure 16.5. It turns out that using analytical derivatives does not improve the calibration results.

Validation of Results

To compare different algorithms and to check the validity of the results of our hybrid method (HM), we have used a simulated annealing (SA) algorithm, a direct search simulated annealing (DSSA) algorithm and a differential evolution (DE) algorithm (Brabazon and O'Neill, 2006; Hedar and Fukushima, 2002) to calibrate a Heston model. Table 16.3 shows the results of these optimizations: All algorithms arrive at comparable results for the value of the objective function (16.9), but the found parameter sets are slightly different. Note the enormous speed advantage of the hybrid method.

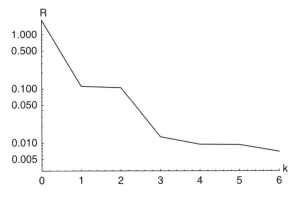

Figure 16.5   The figure shows the evolution of the residuum during the iterative process. As a starting point we have chosen $(4.375, 0.125, 0.625, -0.875, 0.625)$.

Table 16.3   This table shows results obtained with SA, DSSA, DE and our hybrid method (HM) for the Heston model. For the results obtained with the hybrid method we have used $N_I = 16384$, $N_B = 8$ and report the parameters of the best three points. Note that the calibration time with reflecting boundaries instead of the $4d/5d$ optimization is around 10 minutes.

Method	Time	κ	θ	σ	ρ	v_0	Residuals
SA	$> 1h$	1.37489	0.0659624	0.42583	−0.521524	0.0442002	0.0026999
DSSA	$> 1h$	3.326651	0.056260	0.609410	−0.528481	0.045514	0.002731
DE	$> 1h$	2.19221	0.0606641	0.515656	−0.52504	0.0442017	0.002674
HM	$20s$	2.110270	0.060529	0.503548	−0.532090	0.045330	0.002684
HM	$20s$	2.851548	0.057947	0.574742	−0.512623	0.045789	0.002700
HM	$20s$	4.487206	0.054525	0.699049	−0.509853	0.045819	0.002808

Robustness of Parameters

A key point in the validation of a calibration algorithm is the robustness of parameters as a function of time, i.e., whether small (random) perturbations of market data also lead to small changes in the parameter sets. To demonstrate the robustness of the hybrid method, we compare time series of Heston model parameters calibrated by the global differential evolution algorithm and the hybrid method in Figure 16.6.

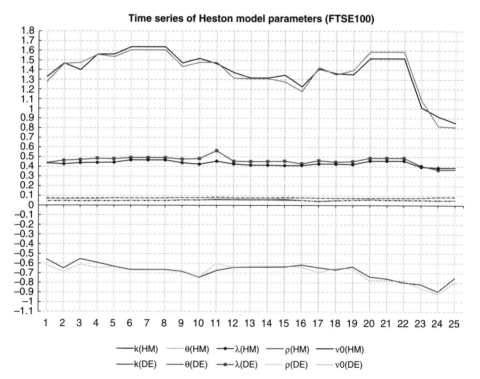

Figure 16.6   This figure shows time series of calibrated parameters for the Heston model obtained with differential evolution (DE) and our hybrid method (HM).

16.4 PORTFOLIO OPTIMIZATION

The theory of optimal portfolio selection was developed in the 1950s by Harry Markowitz (1952). Suppose one wants to invest a given amount of money in a number N of different securities (e.g., stocks) with returns μ_i and variance σ_i^2 with $i \in \{1, \dots, N\}$. The correlation between two securities i and j is given by ρ_{ij}.[12] The vector $\mathbf{x}$ is the weight vector describing the fraction of the total funds invested, i.e., x_i is the fraction invested in security i. The expected return of the portfolio is then given by

$$E[\mathbf{x}] = x_1 \mu_1 + \cdots + x_n \mu_n = \mu^T \mathbf{x}. \tag{16.32}$$

The variance of the portfolio is

$$\mathrm{Var}[\mathbf{x}] = \sum_{ij} \rho_{ij} \sigma_i \sigma_j x_i x_j = \mathbf{x}^T \mathbf{Q} \mathbf{x}, \tag{16.33}$$

where $Q_{ij} = \rho_{ij} \sigma_i \sigma_j$. In addition to the constraint

$$\sum_i x_i = 1, \tag{16.34}$$

additional equality and inequality constraints may be present. If no short sales are permitted, for instance, $x_i \geq 0$ for $i \in \{1, \dots, N\}$.

To determine the vector $\mathbf{x}$ minimizing the risk for a given return R, one needs to solve a QP program (16.6) of the form

$$\begin{aligned} \min_{\mathbf{x}} \ & \frac{1}{2} \mathbf{x}^T \mathbf{Q} \mathbf{x} \\ & \mu^T \mathbf{x} = R \\ & \mathbf{A} \mathbf{x} = \mathbf{b} \\ & \mathbf{C} \mathbf{x} \geq \mathbf{d}, \end{aligned} \tag{16.35}$$

where $\mathbf{A}$ is an $m_A \times n$ matrix describing the m_A equality constraints, and $\mathbf{C}$ is an $m_C \times n$ matrix describing the m_C inequality constraints. The right hand side vectors $\mathbf{b}$ and $\mathbf{d}$ are of length m_A and m_C. This problem can be efficiently solved with the interior point method. Interior point techniques for constrained convex minimization rely on approximating the constrained problem (16.6) by the smooth unconstrained problem

$$\min_{\mathbf{x}} \ \mu \frac{1}{2} \mathbf{x}^T \mathbf{Q} \mathbf{x} + a(\mathbf{x}), \tag{16.36}$$

where $a(\mathbf{x})$ is a barrier for the feasible region S of the original problem. That means $a(\mathbf{x})$ is a convex function with the property that $a(\mathbf{x}) \to \infty$ when $\mathbf{x}$ approaches the boundary of S from its interior. A commonly used barrier function is

$$a(\mathbf{x}) = \frac{1}{2} \mathbf{x}^T \mathbf{Q} \mathbf{x} - \mu \sum_{i=1}^{m} \log(-g_i(\mathbf{x})), \tag{16.37}$$

where m is the number of constraints $g_i(\mathbf{x})$ and $\mu > 0$ is a small parameter. Interior point algorithms solve a sequence of unconstrained problems with decreasing values of μ. For a detailed description of the method, we refer the reader to Nocedal and Wright (2000) and the references therein.

---

[12] Note that μ_i, σ_i^2 and ρ_{ij} can be estimated using the time series of the stock data.

The matrix $\mathbf{Q}$ is, as a variance-covariance matrix, theoretically guaranteed to be positive semidefinite. If that is not the case numerically, one can apply an eigenvalue decomposition of $\mathbf{Q}$. Since $\mathbf{Q}$ is real and symmetric this decomposition is

$$\mathbf{Q} = \mathbf{V}\mathbf{\Lambda}\mathbf{V}^T, \tag{16.38}$$

where $\mathbf{V}$ is an $N \times N$ matrix whose i^{th} column is the ith eigenvector of $\mathbf{Q}$. The matrix $\mathbf{\Lambda}$ is a diagonal matrix whose diagonal entries are the corresponding eigenvalues λ_i. To ensure the positive definiteness of $\mathbf{Q}$, we lift all non-positive eigenvalues $\lambda_i \leq 0$ to ϵ where $\epsilon > 0$ and small and calculate $\mathbf{Q}$ according to (16.38). For real and symmetric matrices, the Householder algorithm can be used to reduce the matrix to tridiagonal form. For this tridiagonal matrix, the eigenvalues and eigenvectors can easily be determined using the QL algorithm. Both algorithms are described in detail (including code listings) in (Press, Teukolsky, Vetterling and Flannery, 2007).

An Example for $N = 9$ Assets

Let the following returns, volatilities and covariances be given:

- Returns $\mu = \{0.017, 0.017, 0.018, 0.019, 0.028, 0.018, 0.019, 0.028, 0.06\}$.
- Volatilities: $\sigma = \{0.076; 0.077; 0.073; 0.117; 0.015; 0.073; 0.117; 0.015; 0.187\}$.
- The covariance matrix is given in (16.41) at the end of the chapter.

The following equality and inequality constraints are present for the weights x_i:

$$\begin{aligned}
0.02 &\leq x_i \leq 0.2 \quad \text{for } i \in \{1, \dots, 9\}, \\
x_1 + x_2 + x_3 &\leq 0.4, \\
x_7 + x_8 &\leq 0.3, \\
2x_7 - x_8 - x_9 &= 0.
\end{aligned} \tag{16.39}$$

An additional constraint is imposed on the problem by defining a target return

$$\mu^T \mathbf{x} = R_j, \tag{16.40}$$

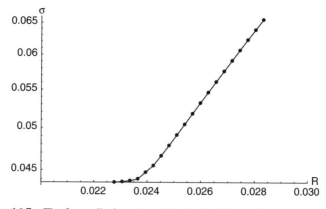

Figure 16.7   The figure displays the minimal volatilities σ_j for target returns R_j.

Table 16.4 The covariance matrix for the example with N = 9 assets.

$$\text{Cov} = \begin{pmatrix}
0.005776 & 0.00585011 & 0.00540333 & 0.00275795 & 0.000156552 & 0.00540333 & 0.00275795 & 0.000156552 & 0.00233333 \\
0.00585011 & 0.005929 & 0.00547007 & 0.00282608 & 0.000158676 & 0.00547007 & 0.00282608 & 0.000158676 & 0.00238746 \\
0.00540333 & 0.00547007 & 0.005929 & 0.00547007 & 0.00282608 & 0.000158676 & 0.00547007 & 0.00282608 & 0.000158676 \\
0.00275795 & 0.00282608 & 0.00547007 & 0.005929 & 0.00547007 & 0.00282608 & 0.000158676 & 0.00547007 & 0.00282608 \\
0.000156552 & 0.000158676 & 0.00282608 & 0.00547007 & 0.005929 & 0.00547007 & 0.00282608 & 0.000158676 & 0.00547007 \\
0.00540333 & 0.00547007 & 0.000158676 & 0.00282608 & 0.00547007 & 0.005929 & 0.00547007 & 0.00282608 & 0.000158676 \\
0.00275795 & 0.00282608 & 0.00547007 & 0.000158676 & 0.00282608 & 0.00547007 & 0.005929 & 0.00547007 & 0.00282608 \\
0.000156552 & 0.000158676 & 0.00282608 & 0.00547007 & 0.000158676 & 0.00282608 & 0.00547007 & 0.005929 & 0.00547007 \\
0.00233333 & 0.00238746 & 0.000158676 & 0.00282608 & 0.00547007 & 0.000158676 & 0.00282608 & 0.00547007 & 0.005929
\end{pmatrix}$$

(16.41)

where the portfolio return R_j is set between R_{min} and R_{max}. R_{min} can be calculated applying the interior point method to the problem without the last constraint in (16.40). R_{max} can be obtained by maximizing $\mu^T x$ under the constraints given in (16.39); obviously, the constraint (16.40) is not included. The resulting problem is LP but can nevertheless be solved using the interior point method. The resulting pairs of returns R_j and the corresponding minimal portfolio volatilities (risk) σ_j are displayed in Figure 16.7. As an example we report the portfolio weights x for $R = 0.0254$ with an optimized $\sigma = 0.0504$:

$$x = \{0.1799999999478, 0.0200000000657, 0.1999999999867,$$
$$0.0200000000004, 0.1607259524278, 0.0200000000003,$$
$$0.1330913491904, 0.1669086508109, 0.0992740475700\}$$

The method used in this example has successfully been applied to portfolio optimization problems with several hundred assets.

17

Risk Management

In order to manage risk, it is important to be aware of the different kinds of risks an institution may face. The list of particular risks will evolve over time as the institution's environment and internal processes change. In this chapter, we focus solely on the market risk and how it can be measured. For an introduction to financial enterprise risk management, we refer the reader to Sweeting (2011). Market risk is present for all institutions that have an exposure to or interact with capital markets. Underlying risk factors such as interest rates, foreign exchange rates, credit spread and credit score have direct influence on both the asset (bonds, equities, . . .) and the liability side. Interest rate risk arises when unanticipated developments shift the yield curve or change its shape. Foreign exchange risk arises when cashflows of a financial institution are in different currencies. Credit spread risk arises due to changes in the credit spread, affecting the value of assets. The term credit risk itself often refers to default risk. For credit institutes with a large number of loans to individuals and small businesses, the credit risk is often the largest risk. Counter-party risk is also a form of credit risk, and refers to the fact that the counterparty of a financial transaction may not be able to deliver the payment. With the appearance of credit linked derivatives such as CDOs, n^{th} to default bonds and swaps, credit risk and its accurate modeling became even more important.

17.1 VALUE AT RISK AND EXPECTED SHORTFALL

Different measures of risk, from deterministic to probabilistic, are used. A typical example for a deterministic risk measure is the scenario sensitivity. It combines the stresses to single risk factors into a scenario; the portfolio[1] is then valuated under this scenario. For example, such a scenario could be a $50bp$ decrease in the interest rate and a 20% increase of the volatility of equity markets.

The industry standard measure for assessing risk is the Value at Risk (VaR). It is defined as the maximum amount of loss over a given holding period for a given level of confidence. A 95% one week VaR of −100, for instance, means that the maximum loss for a week is +100 with a 95% level of confidence. Unfortunately, different terminology is used for reporting the VaR, thus the same situation could be expressed as a 5% one week VaR of +100. To be specific, it is neither standardized whether $\alpha\%$ or $(100 - \alpha)\%$ is used to indicate the level of confidence, nor is it standardized whether the maximum loss is expressed as a positive or negative number. In this book, will use $\alpha\%$ for the level of confidence and report the VaR as a typically negative number.

Three approaches exist to calculate the VaR:

- parametric approach
- historical approach
- Monte Carlo approach

---

[1] We use the term portfolio here to refer to a group of instruments as well as a single instrument.

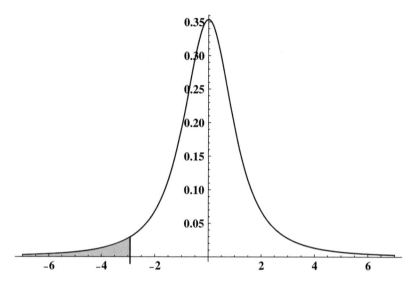

Figure 17.1 The figure shows a profit and loss distribution with the 95% VaR indicated by the black line. The ES is the expected value of the tail beyond the VaR indicated by the shaded area. ES would be the integral over the shadowed region.

The time horizon is an important part of the VaR calculation. For all methods presented in the next three sections, quantities like indices and loop limits are set up for the calculation of a d-day VaR. If, for example, the time series data for the risk factors for $N + d$ days are given, we can generate N historical scenarios. An additional measure for risk closely related to VaR is the Expected Shortfall (ES), also called conditional Value at Risk (CVaR). The ES is the expected value of the tail below the VaR as shown in the profit and loss distribution displayed in Figure 17.1. It describes the expected loss in the case where the value falls below the VaR. Expected shortfall can be calculated as the expected value of all possible losses exceeding the VaR. For an introduction to the broad topic of VaR, ES and other risk measures we refer the reader to the book of Jorion (2006).

17.1.1 Parametric VaR

Parametric VaR, also known as linear VaR or variance-covariance VaR, is a parametric approach to VaR calculation where a probability distribution is assumed for the risk factors (calculation of variance and covariance using historical data). It is a linear approach, as it is assumed that instrument prices change linearly with respect to changes in the risk factors. It is therefore not capable of capturing nonlinear effects, such as nonlinear payoffs or calls. The computation of the parametric VaR is fast (simple matrix algebra) and can capture events not present in historical data.

Workflow

1. Define a set of risk factors $\beta = \{\beta_1, \ldots, \beta_{N_\beta}\}$
2. For all N_P instruments in the portfolio, calculate the derivatives with respect to each risk factor

$$d_{l,i} = \partial V_l / \partial \beta_i. \tag{17.1}$$

A $1 \times N_\beta$ matrix $\mathbf{D}_l$ can be generated for each of the N_P instruments,

$$\mathbf{D}_l = [d_{l,1}, d_{l,2}, \ldots, d_{l,N_\beta}]. \tag{17.2}$$

The matrix for the overall portfolio is then

$$\mathbf{D}_P = \sum_{l=1}^{N_P} \mathbf{D}_l \omega_l, \tag{17.3}$$

where ω_l is the weight of instrument l in the portfolio.

3. Calculate the N changes (for $N + d$ historical data points) $\Delta\beta_{i,k}$ for each risk factor, where k is the time index. The change $\Delta\beta_{i,k}$ depends on the risk factor and may either be of the form

$$\Delta\beta_{i,k} = \beta_{i,n+d} - \beta_{i,n}, \tag{17.4}$$

or of the form

$$\Delta\beta_{i,k} = \frac{\beta_{i,n+d}}{\beta_{i,n}}, \tag{17.5}$$

where k ranges from 1 to N and the index n is given by $n = k - 1$. Next, calculate the standard deviation and the correlations between the changes,

$$\sigma_{\beta_i}^2 = \frac{1}{N-1} \sum_{k=1}^{N} (\Delta\beta_{i,k})^2, \tag{17.6}$$

$$\rho_{\beta_i \beta_j} = \frac{1}{N-1} \left(\frac{\sum_{k=1}^{N} \Delta\beta_{i,k} \Delta\beta_{j,k}}{\sigma_{\beta_i} \sigma_{\beta_j}} \right). \tag{17.7}$$

4. Build up the variance-covariance matrix

$$\mathbf{C} = \begin{pmatrix} \sigma_{\beta_1}^2 & \rho_{\beta_1\beta_2}\sigma_{\beta_1}\sigma_{\beta_2} & \cdots & \rho_{\beta_1\beta_{N_\beta}}\sigma_{\beta_1}\sigma_{\beta_{N_\beta}} \\ \rho_{\beta_1\beta_2}\sigma_{\beta_1}\sigma_{\beta_2} & \sigma_{\beta_2}^2 & \cdots & \rho_{\beta_2\beta_{N_\beta}}\sigma_{\beta_2}\sigma_{\beta_{N_\beta}} \\ \vdots & \vdots & \cdots & \vdots \\ \rho_{\beta_1\beta_{N_\beta}}\sigma_{\beta_1}\sigma_{\beta_{N_\beta}} & \rho_{\beta_2\beta_{N_\beta}}\sigma_{\beta_2}\sigma_{\beta_{N_\beta}} & \cdots & \sigma_{\beta_{N_\beta}}^2 \end{pmatrix}. \tag{17.8}$$

5. Calculate the VaR using

$$\text{VaR} = \alpha_z \sqrt{\mathbf{D}_P \mathbf{C} \mathbf{D}_P^T}, \tag{17.9}$$

where α_z is calculated using the desired percentile (for example, for a 99%-VaR, $\alpha_z \approx 2.33$ assuming a standard normal distribution)

For scalar risk factors (equity prices, fx rates, inflation indices, equity volatilities, fx volatilities, interest rate/interest rate correlation, interest rate/fx rate correlation), the calculation of standard deviations and correlations is straightforward. For non-scalar risk factors (yield curves, credit curves, equity yield curves and inflation swap curves), principal component analysis (PCA) can be used, see section 17.2.

17.1.2 Historical VaR

Time series of the risk factors β are used to calculate the historical VaR by creating "real" market data scenarios that have occurred in the past. Using the time series of the given risk factors, their historical changes are calculated. Historical scenarios are then generated by applying them to today's risk factors. We now consider a single risk factor β omitting the index for the different risk factors. A scenario s_i for this risk factor can be created by

$$s_i = \bar{\beta} + \beta_{l+d} - \beta_l \qquad (17.10)$$

or by

$$s_i = \bar{\beta}\frac{\beta_{l+d}}{\beta_l}, \qquad (17.11)$$

where $\bar{\beta}$ is today's value of the risk factor. Examples of a risk factor where scenarios are generated using (17.10) are the projections μ of the PCA, whereas examples of risk factors where scenarios are generated using (17.11) are equity prices, fx rates or inflation indices.[2] The index $i \in \{1, \ldots, N_S\}$ is called the scenario index,[3] the index l is given by $l = i - 1$. Each individual instrument of the portfolio is then valuated under every historical scenario; the differences between these scenario values and today's value are the scenario delta values ΔV_i,

$$\Delta V_i = V(s_i) - V(\bar{\beta}). \qquad (17.12)$$

The $x\%$ historical VaR is then given as the $(100 - x)\%$ quantile of the sorted scenario deltas ΔV_i. Expected shortfall can easily be calculated by averaging over the values below the VaR quantile. The portfolio scenario deltas and the portfolio VaR are calculated by aggregation. Figure 17.2 shows the scenario delta values ΔV_i of a historical VaR simulation for $N_S = 700$. The VaR can be obtained by applying the quantile function as shown in Figure 17.3. For the given data, the one day 95% VaR is -52182.0 and the ES is -70698.6. The valuation of the instruments under each generated scenario can be performed using either a full valuation or principal component analysis. A full valuation yields the exact values of the instrument under each scenario (we refer to this value as the scenario value) but is computationally demanding.[4] Principal component analysis (PCA) (see section 17.2) can be used to obtain a fast approximation of the scenario values by the use of Taylor series expansions for certain types of instruments.[5] PCA is a local approximation, i.e., the smaller the historical changes, the better the approximation is. We draw our motivation to use the PCA from the well-known fact that time-dependent changes in risk factors, for example in the yield curve, can be described by few factors (Binder, 2007).

---

[2] Note that for some risk factors additional constraints need to be applied. If, for example, a correlation is used as a risk factor it needs to be ensured that for the whole scenario the correlation is in $[-1, 1]$.

[3] To create N_S scenarios, we take into account N_S historical time intervals and therefore we need $N_S + d$ points in time. Time points start with index 0 indicating today's date and increase backwards in time, i.e. $\mathbf{x}_1$ is the change of the risk factor between yesterday and today in the case of one day VaR calculation.

[4] Assume a portfolio of 1000 instruments under 1000 different scenarios. Then the number of single instrument valuations is 10^6.

[5] The PCA is most effective for instruments with a small number of risk factors (or only one). For more than one risk factor, one needs to take care of correlations between the risk factors and thus needs to use higher order mixed differentiation.

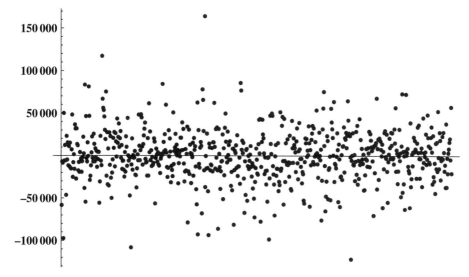

Figure 17.2 The figure shows the scenario delta values ΔV_i of a historical VaR simulation.

17.1.3 Monte Carlo VaR

To calculate the Monte Carlo VaR, the time series of the changes $\Delta\beta$ for each risk factor β, as defined in (17.4) and (17.5), is used to fit N_β marginal distributions F, where N_β is the number of risk factors. The correlation between the risk factors is then calculated using (17.7). The matrix of correlations between the risk factors and the marginal distributions are

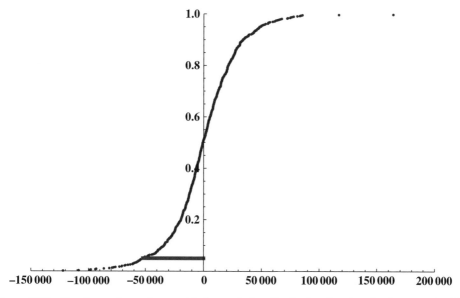

Figure 17.3 The figure shows the empirical cumulative distribution function for the scenario delta values ΔV_i shown in Figure 17.2. The horizontal line indicates the quantile function.

used to create a multivariate distribution function, i.e., a copula.[6] A typical setup would be to assume Gaussian distributions for the marginal distributions and to use a Gaussian copula. For scalar risk factors the fitting procedure is straightforward; for non-scalar risk factors PCA (see section 17.2) can be used. By drawing N_S random variates $\mathbf{p}$, where each variate is of dimension N_β, from the copula, one can generate N_S scenarios. A scenario $\mathbf{s}$ is a vector of size N_β, where each component of the vector is a risk factor[7] and is calculated by

$$\mathbf{s} = f(\mathbf{s}_0, \mathbf{p}), \tag{17.13}$$

where $\mathbf{s}_0$ is today's market scenario. Note that f is a function that acts differently in each component of the vector, and depends on the type of risk factor (adding or multiplying). As soon as the scenarios are available, the Monte Carlo VaR is calculated in the same way as the historical VaR, including the valuation utilizing the PCA (see section 17.2).[8]

17.1.4   Individual and Contribution VaR

To assess and manage the risk of a portfolio, it is important to know how the single instruments and the different risk factors contribute to the VaR. Suppose we created a list of scenario delta values for each instrument in a portfolio using either Monte Carlo VaR or the historical VaR. Then the $x\%$ portfolio VaR is the $(100 - x)\%$ quantile of the list of portfolio scenario delta values, where the portfolio scenario delta values are calculated by summing up the weighted single instrument scenario deltas. The weights are determined by the position, and if portfolio currency and single instrument currency do not coincide, the corresponding fx rate VaR scenario.[9] The $x\%$ individual VaR is the $(100 - x)\%$ quantile of the list of single instrument scenario deltas of a single instrument. These are calculated by taking into account all risk factors assigned to the instrument.[10] The contribution VaR is defined as the delta scenario value of the underlying instrument which is used in the calculation of the portfolio VaR.

Example

Assume a portfolio (P) comprised of a fixed rate bond (FRB, Coupon: 5%, $T \approx 10y$) and a callable reverse floater (F, $T \approx 5y$) with weights $\omega_1 = 1$ and $\omega_2 = 1$ (both are interest rate instruments of the same currency). We calculate the scenario deltas for a one-day time horizon for the following three situations:

1. We use two risk factors (β_1: interest rate curves and β_2: credit spreads) that lead to overall (all risk factor) deltas.[11]
2. We only take into account β_1 (interest rate curve deltas)
3. We only take into account β_2 (credit spread deltas)

---

[6] Note that the correlation matrix is a valid description of the dependence structure between the risk factors only for the Gaussian and the t-copula. To obtain input parameters for other copulas see Chapter 14.

[7] Non-scalar risk factors such as yield curves are reduced to scalar risk factors, i.e., the projections μ.

[8] As in the Monte Carlo VaR the projections μ are risk factors drawn from the joint distribution, the fast evaluation (given the sensitivities δ) is reduced to the summation in (17.18).

[9] If portfolio currency and single instrument currency do not coincide, the single instrument scenario delta must be multiplied with the fx rate that transforms one unit of the currency of the instrument to the currency of the portfolio.

[10] Not every risk factor affecting the portfolio needs to affect each single instrument of the portfolio.

[11] To simplify the notation, we assume a single risk factor for the interest rate curve and a single risk factor for the credit spread here.

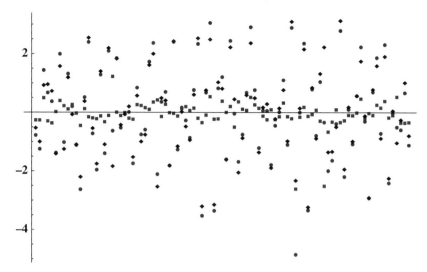

Figure 17.4   The figure shows the scenario delta values ΔV_i for the all risk factor scenarios (circle), the interest rate scenarios (square) and the credit spread scenarios (diamond) for the fixed rate bond.

The resulting scenarios are shown in Figure 17.4 for the fixe rate bond and in Figure 17.5 for the floater. The single risk factor scenario delta values do not add up to the all risk factor scenario delta values due to the correlations between the risk factors, but the single instrument scenario delta values add up to the portfolio scenario delta values when taking into account the portfolio weights. From these generated scenarios one can calculate the following numbers

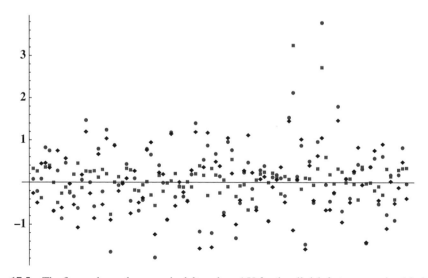

Figure 17.5   The figure shows the scenario delta values ΔV_i for the all risk factor scenarios (circle), the interest rate scenarios (square) and the credit spread scenarios (diamond) for the floater.

for a 95% level of confidence, where we use $\beta = \{\beta_1, \beta_2\}$ to indicate an all risk factor scenario and β_k, $k \in \{1, 2\}$ for the single risk factors:

- Individual VaRs of all underlying instruments taking into account all risk factors β or single risk factors β_k:

Instrument	β	β_1	β_2
FRB	−2.9341	−0.4625	−2.5227
F	−0.9001	−0.4203	−1.5732

- Portfolio VaRs taking into account all risk factors β or single risk factors β_k:

Instrument	β	β_1	β_2
P	−3.915	−0.1525	−3.7505

Note that the all/single risk factor individual VaRs do not sum up to the portfolio VaRs (different scenarios are responsible for the VaR values).

- Contribution VaR of all underlying instruments taking into account all risk factors β or single risk factors β_k:

Instrument	β	β_1	β_2
FRB	−2.12457	0.4101	−2.5227
F	−1.79042	−0.5626	−1.2278

Note that the contribution VaRs sum up to the portfolio VaRs (same scenarios are responsible for the VaR values).

17.2 PRINCIPAL COMPONENT ANALYSIS

The principal component analysis (PCA) is a technique for the reduction of multidimensional data through the calculation of an eigensystem $\{v_i, \lambda_i\}$, with eigenvectors v_i and eigenvalues λ_i. From a mathematical point of view, the principal component analysis is an orthogonal transformation into a new coordinate system such that the variance of the projected data is sorted from highest (first coordinate axes direction) to lowest.

17.2.1 Principal Component Analysis for Non-scalar Risk Factors

For a non-scalar risk factor w the PCA is therefore the optimal transformation in the least squares sense. Let us start with a matrix X whose entries x_{ij} are calculated from the changes in market data. The change in market data x_i is given by $x_i = w_{l+d} - w_l$ with the index l given by $l = i - 1$. The index j ranges from 1 to M, where M is the dimension of the vector (M is, for example, the number of bucket points of a yield curve). The principal components are then calculated by

$$\{\mathbf{v}_m, \lambda_m\} = \text{Eigensystem}\{\mathbf{X}^T\mathbf{X}\}. \tag{17.14}$$

Note that $\mathbf{X}^T\mathbf{X}$ is a quadratic $M \times M$ matrix and the index m ranges from 1 to m and enumerates the eigenvectors/eigenvalues.[12] The eigenvectors $\mathbf{v}_m$ (column vectors) can then be used to calculate the projection μ_m of the change of the market data in the direction of the mth principal component (we omit the scenario index i and set $\mathbf{x} = \mathbf{x}_i$),

$$\mu_m = \mathbf{x}\mathbf{v}_m. \tag{17.15}$$

For N_S scenarios, a number of N_{PCA} vectors of projections can be calculated,

$$\boldsymbol{\mu}_m = \{\mu_{m1}, \dots, \mu_{mN_S}\}, \quad m \in \{1, \dots, N_{\text{PCA}}\}. \tag{17.16}$$

Each projection μ_m is used as a risk factor in all parametric and Monte Carlo VaR calculations. For the parametric VaR, the time series of μ_m (the vector $\boldsymbol{\mu}$) is required to calculate standard deviation and covariance. For the Monte Carlo VaR calculation, a distribution function is fitted to the values $\{\mu_{m1}, \dots, \mu_{mN_S}\}$. The eigenvalues λ_m calculated in (17.14) are sorted from largest (high 'explanatory value' for changes in market data) to lowest (low 'explanatory value' for the changes in market data).[13] A number N_{PCA} of most influential risk factors from the PCA is then taken into account in further calculations.

17.2.2   Principal Components for Fast Valuation

To apply Taylor series expansion for the valuation of a product under a scenario, we need to calculate the sensitivities δ_m of the value V with respect to the eigenvectors $\mathbf{v}_m$ calculated via PCA in (17.14)

$$\delta_m = \frac{\partial V(\mathbf{w})}{\partial \mathbf{v}_m} \approx \frac{V(\mathbf{w} + \epsilon\mathbf{v}_m) - V(\mathbf{w} - \epsilon\mathbf{v}_m)}{2\epsilon}. \tag{17.17}$$

With the sensitivities δ_m and the projections μ_m at hand, the valuation under a scenario using a first order Taylor expansion is given by

$$V(\mathbf{w} + \mathbf{x}) = \sum_{r=1}^{N_{\text{PCA}}} \delta_r \mu_r, \tag{17.18}$$

where N_{PCA} is the number of principal components used. This kind of valuation is extremely fast as it only requires simple vector and matrix manipulations. For each of the N_{PCA} calculations of the sensitivities δ with respect to the eigenvectors $\mathbf{v}$ in (17.17), two full valuations are necessary, i.e., one for a shift up in the direction of the eigenvector and one for a shift down in the direction of the eigenvector. For example, for a single instrument with $N_{\text{PCA}} = 5$, only $10 + 1$ (the $+1$ stems from the valuation with today's market data) full valuations are required, independent of N_S.

---

[12] Be careful not to mix up j, the index of the components of a vector of dimension M, with the eigenvalue index m.

[13] For example, Binder (2007) reported that in his analysis of weekly yield curve changes the first three unit vectors exhibit the "shift, twist, butterfly" behavior. Unit vector 1 explains 77% of interest rate changes, 1 and 2 explain 92%, and $1, 2,$ *and* 3 explain 96.88% of the weekly interest rate changes.

17.3 EXTREME VALUE THEORY

In the historical and Monte Carlo VaR approaches, the VaR is calculated by applying the quantile function to the calculated scenario delta values (see 17.12). In risk management, however, the extreme scenarios are often of particular interest. These extreme scenarios are rare (they are in the tails of the distribution) or not present at all (if such scenarios did not occur in the time series used to calculate the historical VaR). Under a standard normal distribution, the probability of an event $\Phi(X \leq -4) = 0.0000316712$ is considered to be small. It is impossible to calculate the huge numbers of scenarios required to obtain reliable results for the tails of the distribution. Here, extreme value theory allows us to gain deeper insight into the tail behavior of the distribution of scenario delta values ΔV_i. Two broad approaches for modeling such extreme events exist: the generalized extreme value distribution and the generalized Pareto distribution (de Haan and Ferreira, 2006). We will focus on the generalized Pareto distribution in this section. For historical reasons, the threshold value is positive and the analysis is made for the right tail. As we are only interested in the tails of the distribution, we only use the absolute value of data points indicating a loss (negative scenario delta value), reducing the size of the dataset to N_n entries. We define the random variable X to be the absolute value of the loss above the threshold u. N_u is the number of data points exceeding the threshold. Then,

$$F_u(x) = P(X - u \leq x | X > u) = \frac{F(x+u) - F(u)}{1 - F(u)} \tag{17.19}$$

describes the conditional distribution for X given that the threshold u is exceeded no more than x. The Gnedenko-Pickands-Balkema-deHaan (GPBdH) theorem (de Haan and Ferreira, 2006) states that as u increases in size, the distribution $F_u(x)$ converges to a generalized Pareto distribution (GPD) $G_{\xi,\beta}(x)$ such that:

$$G_{\xi,\beta}(x) = \begin{cases} 1 - \left(1 + \frac{\xi x}{\beta}\right)^{-\frac{1}{\xi}} & \text{if} \quad \xi \neq 0, \\ 1 - \exp\left(\frac{-x}{\beta}\right) & \text{if} \quad \xi = 0. \end{cases} \tag{17.20}$$

Here, β is called the scale parameter and ξ is the shape parameter. The probability density function is given by

$$g_{\xi,\beta}(x) = \frac{1}{\beta}\left(1 + \frac{\xi x}{\beta}\right)^{-\frac{1}{\xi}-1}. \tag{17.21}$$

Figures 17.6 and 17.7 show the cumulative distribution function (17.21) and the probability density function (17.20) of the GPD. The parameters β and ξ can be estimated using a maximum likelihood method (see Chapter 14) or with the method of probability weighted moments,[14] where

$$\xi = 2 - \frac{w_0}{w_0 - 2w_1} \tag{17.22}$$

and

$$\beta = \frac{2w_0 w_1}{w_0 - 2w_1}. \tag{17.23}$$

---

[14] A detailed discussion of the maximum likelihood method, the method of probability weighted moments and other methods for estimating the parameters β and ξ can be found in de Haan and Ferreira (2006) and the references therein.

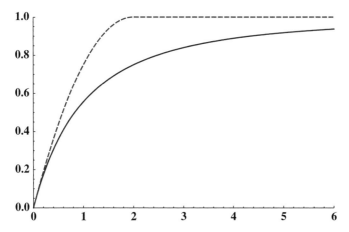

Figure 17.6   The figure shows the cumulative distribution function of the GPD (17.21) for $\beta = 1$ and $\xi = 1/2$ (continuous) and $\xi = -1/2$ (dashed).

Suppose we are given a vector containing the absolute values of the losses. We exclude all points smaller than the threshold u and sort the remaining N_u data points from large to small, i.e., the greatest loss is in the first position of this list L. Then, w_0 is given by

$$w_0 = \frac{1}{N_u} \sum_{i=1}^{N_u} L_i,\tag{17.24}$$

and w_1 is given by

$$w_1 = \frac{1}{N_u} \sum_{i=1}^{N_u} \left(1 - \frac{N_u + 1 - i}{N_u}\right) L_i.\tag{17.25}$$

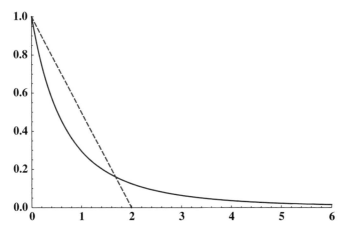

Figure 17.7   The figure shows the probability density function of the GPD (17.20) for $\beta = 1$ and $\xi = 1/2$ (continuous) and $\xi = -1/2$ (dashed).

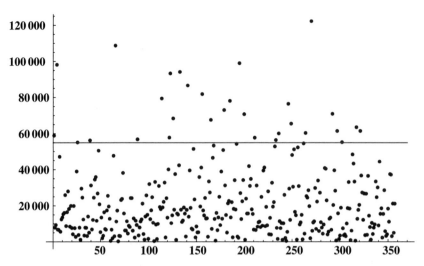

Figure 17.8 The figure shows the absolute of the scenario delta values that result in a loss. The line indicates the threshold u. All data points exceeding the threshold are used for the estimation of parameters β and ξ.

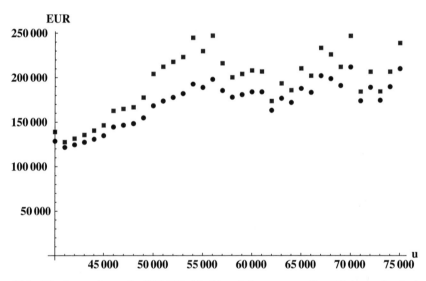

Figure 17.9 The figure shows the 95% VaR (circle) and the corresponding ES (square) calculated for different thresholds u. Note the stable region between $u \approx 55\,000$ and $u \approx 65\,000$. On the left hand side of this region points which are not in the tails of the distribution are included (see Figure 17.10 and Figure 17.11), causing the trend in the values of VaR and ES. On the right hand side of $u \approx 65\,000$ the number of available points N_u used to fit is too small (see Table 17.1) to obtain reliable results for the parameters β and ξ.

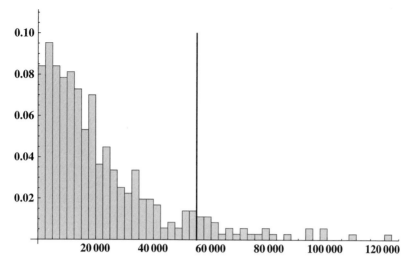

Figure 17.10   The figure shows a histogram estimating the probability distribution function. The black line indicates the assumed beginning of the tail region.

With these estimated parameters, the VaR and the ES can be calculated,

$$\text{VaR} = u + \frac{\beta}{\xi}\left(\left(\frac{N_n}{N_u}(1-p)\right)^{-\xi} - 1\right),$$ (17.26)

$$\text{ES} = \frac{\text{VaR}}{1-\xi} + \frac{\beta - \xi u}{1-\xi}.$$ (17.27)

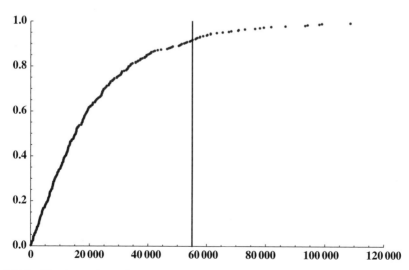

Figure 17.11   The figure shows the empirical cumulative distribution function for the loss distribution. The black line indicates the assumed beginning of the tail region.

Table 17.1   The table shows the number of points N_u for different threshold values u used for fitting the parameters β and ξ.

u	N_u
40000	52
41000	48
42000	47
43000	46
44000	45
45000	44
46000	44
47000	42
48000	40
49000	39
50000	39
51000	37
52000	35
53000	33
54000	32
55000	29
56000	28
57000	25
58000	23
59000	22
60000	21
61000	20
62000	18
63000	18
64000	17
65000	17
66000	16
67000	16
68000	15
69000	14
70000	14
71000	12
72000	12
73000	11
74000	11
75000	11

All distributions of excess losses converge to the GPD, therefore it seems to be the natural model for excess losses. The selection of the threshold u determines the number of observations N_u in excess of the threshold value. Choosing the threshold involves a trade-off: on the one hand, it needs to be high enough such that GPBdH theory can be applied, but on the other hand it must be sufficiently low, so that there will be enough observations to apply estimation techniques to the parameters. One approach for choosing the threshold u is to consider the mean excess function,

$$e(u) = E[X - u | X > u], \quad u \geq 0. \tag{17.28}$$

The empirical mean excess function is given by

$$e(u) = \frac{1}{\#\{i\ :\ X_i > u, i = 1, \ldots N_n\}} \sum_{i=1}^{N_n} \max(X_i - u, 0). \qquad (17.29)$$

For distributions with short tails $e(u)$ decreases to zero for increasing u. Distributions with fat tails show a mean excess $e(u)$ that increases for increasing u (a linear increase is observed for the Pareto distribution). A reasonable threshold u can be chosen such that the value where $e(u)$ starts increasing linearly is taken. In practice a number of different thresholds is often chosen, as the identification of a unique threshold u may not be possible. We refer the reader to the book of de Haan and Ferreira (2006) for a discussion of methods to estimate reasonable values for u.

Example

For the scenario delta values ΔV_i shown in Figure 17.2, the number of data points is $N_{tot} = 700$ and the number of scenarios values indicating a loss is $N_n = 357$. Figure 17.8 shows a typical setup for the calculation of VaR and ES where the N_u points that exceed the threshold u are used to fit the parameters β and ξ. Figure 17.9 shows values for the VaR and the ES for different thresholds u calculated using (17.26) and (17.27).

18

Quantitative Finance on Parallel Architectures

For many years, parallel computing has been restricted to expensive supercomputers only available to a relatively small high-performance computing community. This situation has drastically changed in recent years: physical and technological limits to serial processing speed have initiated a paradigm shift towards parallel computing, also in inexpensive commodity hardware. Today, multicore CPUs and programmable GPUs are common even in desktop computers and notebooks. In this chapter, we want to give a rough overview of parallel programming models and their application in quantitative finance. We cannot go into programming details, but instead refer the reader to the broad range of available online tutorials; see, e.g., Barney.

18.1 A SHORT INTRODUCTION TO PARALLEL COMPUTING

For the greater part of computer history, software has been written with a serial von Neumann computer architecture in mind, where a computer program – in whatever programming language it is written – is ultimately translated into a stream of instructions that is executed sequentially. Writing parallel programs is fundamentally different: The software developer is responsible for identifying parts of an algorithm that can be run concurrently, or for transforming a given serial algorithm into an algorithm suitable for concurrent execution.

A wide range of parallel computing hardware with very different characteristics is available today. One important criterion of distinction is their method of memory access. In shared memory architectures, all processors have access to the whole available memory as a global address space, albeit access speeds to different parts of the memory may not be uniform on some architectures. In distributed memory architectures, each processor has its own local memory, and communicates with others by sending messages via a communication network. Distributed memory systems are often comprised of smaller shared memory systems connected by a fast network. Another way of classifying parallel architectures is by their execution model. Flynn's taxonomy (Barney) distinguishes between four classes – the two most relevant for present hardware are MIMD (multiple instruction, multiple data) and SIMD (single instruction, multiple data). In MIMD systems, the processing units are capable of executing different instruction streams on different data independently, as schematically shown in Figure 18.1. Multicore CPUs, for instance, fall into this class. In SIMD architectures, on the other hand, all processing units execute the same instruction at any given time, but each processing unit can operate on different data. This way, certain problems can be parallelized very efficiently, as shown in Figure 18.2. Streaming multiprocessors contained in modern GPUs are of this type.

As a consequence of the variety in hardware, different high-level programming frameworks and APIs (application programming interfaces) have evolved. Here, we only discuss a number of widely used ones, and again refer the reader to Barney for a more exhaustive list. In the Message Passing Interface (MPI) programming model, for instance, each process only has

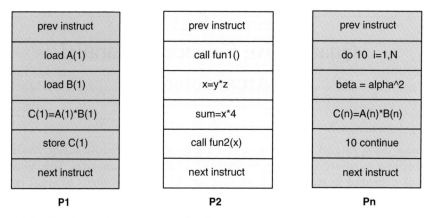

Figure 18.1 The figure shows the principle of MIMD processors, where every processor may be executing a different instruction stream. Currently, computers built on the MIMD architecture are the most common type of parallel computers. Note that many MIMD architectures nowadays also include SIMD execution sub-components.

access to its own local memory; multiple processes can be executed either on the same physical machine and/or on an arbitrary number of machines connected via a network. Processes can communicate and exchange data by sending and receiving messages. This is a cooperative operation, i.e., data is sent by one process and explicitly received by another; any change in the receiving process's memory is thus made with its explicit participation. MPI has originated from distributed memory architectures, but can also be used on shared memory systems. An excellent tutorial for MPI can be found in Barney. The OpenMP framework is designed for shared memory MIMD systems and accomplishes parallelism by using threads, where a thread is the smallest unit of processing that can be scheduled by the operating system. It uses the fork-join model of parallel execution: A master thread creates a team of parallel threads (fork). The directives of the program enclosed in the parallel region (for example in a loop) are then executed in parallel. All threads have unrestricted access to the same shared memory,

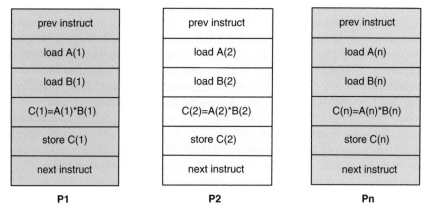

Figure 18.2 The figure shows the working principle of SIMD processors for the example of an element-wise multiplication of two arrays A and B. Note how a single instruction stream is executed on multiple data. Modern GPUs are often wide SIMD implementations which are capable of branches, loads, and stores on 128 or 256 bits at a time.

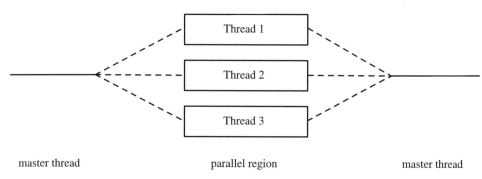

master thread   parallel region   master thread

Figure 18.3   The figure shows the fork-join model schematically. A master thread starts a team of parallel threads which execute the statements of the parallel region. After finishing they synchronize and terminate, leaving only the master thread.

which is also used for communication between the threads. When the team's threads complete the execution of the parallel region they synchronize and terminate, leaving only the master thread (join). The fork-join model is schematically displayed in Figure 18.3. The OpenCL and CUDA frameworks have been designed to program streaming multiprocessors in GPU cards, see section 18.3. OpenCL can also be used on shared memory MIMD architectures in a way similar to OpenMP.

For a given serial algorithm, the maximum theoretical speed-up s that can be achieved through parallelization on N cores depends on the fraction p of parallelizable code,

$$s = \frac{1}{(1 - p) + \frac{p}{N}}. \tag{18.1}$$

This relation is known as Amdahl's law. If, for example, 90% of a code can be parallelized, $p = 0.9$, the asymptotical theoretical speed-up is $s = 10$ for $N \to \infty$ as shown in Figure 18.4. Since parallelization of an algorithm requires human work – and thus a considerable amount

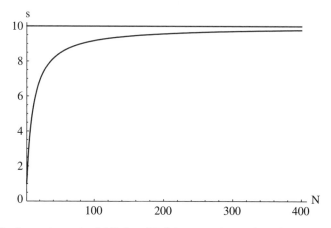

Figure 18.4   The figure shows Amdahl's law (18.1) between the number of cores N and the speed-up s for an amount of parallellizable code of $p = 0.9$. The straight line shows the asymptotical speed-up ($s = 10$) for $N \to \infty$.

Valuation pool   **Compute nodes**

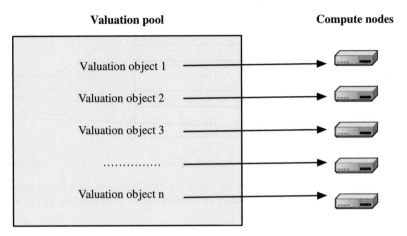

Figure 18.5 The figure shows a valuation pool which collects valuation objects. These valuation objects are distributed to compute nodes. At these nodes fine grain parallelization can be used to further speed up the calculations.

of time and money – it is advisable to first estimate p in order to decide whether the potential speed-up is worth the effort.

18.2 DIFFERENT LEVELS OF PARALLELIZATION

A variety of applications in quantitative finance are computationally extremely demanding. For VaR or CVA calculations, for instance, hundreds of millions of single instrument valuations may need to be performed. From our experience, one can meet these computational demands by following a two-level strategy of coarse- and fine-grained parallelization.

At the coarse parallelization level, each valuation is represented by a valuation object that holds all necessary information for the calculation task. These objects are collected in a "valuation pool" that is responsible for distributing the valuations throughout the parallel hardware environment as displayed in Figure 18.5. Little communication between different instrument valuations is required; the coarse parallelization level is thus well suited for the MPI programming model and distributed memory architectures.

The fine-grained parallelization level aims at the efficient valuation of single instruments on multi-core CPUs (using OpenMP or OpenCL) and GPU cards (using CUDA or OpenCL). An analysis of the fine-grained parallelization of the Quasi Monte Carlo method for valuating financial instruments is presented in section 18.4.

18.3 GPU PROGRAMMING

In contrast to multi-core CPUs, which are of the MIMD type, GPUs are throughput-oriented SIMD processors. If an algorithm is interpreted as a prescription to transform one piece of input data into a corresponding piece of output data, CPUs try to perform the instructions of this algorithm as quickly as possible for one piece of data. GPUs take a more holistic approach: They focus on transforming a whole parallel stream of input data into the corresponding stream of output data with as much total data throughput as possible.

Due to the fundamentally different nature of their execution models, there is no straight-forward way to efficiently use existing CPU algorithms on GPUs. Moreover, not all algorithms are suitable for the type of parallelization required by the SIMD model. Algorithms that involve a lot of branching, for instance, are ill-suited: on GPUs, threads are organized in groups, so-called "warps", and for optimal performance threads in each warp should execute identical code. If control instructions, such as if-statements, force the threads in a warp to execute different code, so-called "control divergence" occurs: in this case, all threads in the warp execute all branches of the if-statement one after another, in a serial way. Control divergence thus seriously impairs performance. GPUs provide a hierarchy of different memory types with very different speed/size trade-offs. Efficiently using these different memories in the design of an algorithm is key to utilizing the performance of GPUs, see section 18.3.2. For many developers starting to write code for GPUs, the first question is which programming framework to use. Currently, two main frameworks are available: CUDA and OpenCL.

18.3.1   CUDA and OpenCL

CUDA is a proprietary parallel programming model developed by NVIDIA.[1] The CUDA software API gives developers access to the virtual instruction set and memory of the parallel computational elements on CUDA GPUs. CUDA provides both a low-level and a higher-level API. OpenCL (Open Computing Language) is an open framework for developing programs that execute on heterogeneous platforms consisting of CPUs, GPUs or other processors and is not tied to a specific hardware vendor. OpenCL is maintained by a technology consortium called the Khronos group.[2] While performance may significantly change from one hardware or software generation to the next, at the time of writing this book, OpenCL and CUDA offered similar performance on systems where an optimized OpenCL implementation is available (Fang, Varbanescu and Henk, 2011).

18.3.2   Memory

Different types of memory with different trade-offs between memory size on the one hand and latency and memory bandwith on the other hand are available on a GPU:

- **host memory** refers to the memory of the GPU card's host computer. This memory is controlled by the CPU and cannot be accessed by the GPU.
- **global memory** is the largest memory located on the graphics card.[3] It can be accessed by all threads, but has relatively high latency and modest bandwidth. Access to the global memory can be coalesced: If a certain memory location is accessed, a whole chunk of contiguous memory can be transferred at little or no additional cost. One of the most important points in code design is to ensure that access to global memory is coalesced.

---

[1] http://www.nvidia.com.
[2] http://www.khronos.org/opencl.
[3] At the time of writing the book, high-end cards with several GB of memory are available.

- **constant memory** is a small area of cached memory with fast read-only access for the GPU, and write access for the CPU. It is well suited for storing look-up tables that can be set up on the CPU and then copied to the device.
- **shared memory** is a small[4] area of very fast (low latency and high throughput) memory with shared access to all threads in a thread block.[5] Each thread block has its own shared memory, but threads in one block can not access shared memory of a different block.

In order to approach a GPU's high theoretical peak performance in practice, algorithms must be designed to exploit these different memory types in order to hide the low bandwidth and high latency of the large global memory. Data transfer between host and device should be avoided whenever possible, as it represents, in most cases, the tightest bottleneck.

18.4   PARALLELIZATION OF SINGLE INSTRUMENT VALUATIONS USING (Q)MC

In Chapter 10, we discussed the (Quasi)Monte Carlo (QMC) method and its application to the valuation of financial instruments. We briefly recap the main steps required to perform such simulations, using the valuation of an exotic option under a Black-Scholes or a Heston model as an example:

1. generate Sobol numbers (QMC) or uniformly distributed random variates (MC);
2. convert to normally distributed random variates;
3. convert the normals using the Brownian bridge technique (see section 10.3);
4. generate the paths for the underlying;
5. compute the discounted pay-off of the exotic option in each path;
6. calculate the QMC estimator by averaging across all the paths.

In a CPU program, one would typically carry out all of these steps for one path after the other (except for the last step, where one would update a running sum instead). In the GPU implementation, on the other hand, we perform each of the above steps for all paths at once.

As an example, we will now discuss the valuation of the following Barrier option under a Heston model in detail:

- Maturity: 1 Year
- Strike: 6000
- Call/Put: Call
- Barrier Type: Up&Out
- Barrier Up: 6400
- Rebate Type: Maturity
- Rebate: 14
- Observation Period: Day

The parameters of the Heston model are $\kappa = 1.329959$, $\Theta = 0.0672071$, $\lambda = 0.43525$, $\rho = -0.55819$ and $v_0 = 0.044053$. The reference value of the option (calcuated using MC) is $V = 13.18$. We have ported all steps of the above valuation algorithm to the GPU and have

---

[4] At the time of writing, 16 kB is a typical size.

[5] Threads on a GPU are organized in thread blocks. The maximum number of thread blocks and the maximum number of threads per block are hardware-dependent.

Table 18.1 Time in milliseconds. Each time value is the average of 100 evaluations. CPU: Double precision, GPU: Single precision.

1×CPU Thread Part	Mersenne Twister		Sobol	
	Time (ms)	%	Time (ms)	%
Pre-Processing	0.20	0.0%	0.21	0.0%
Memory Allocation	0.14	0.0%	0.12	0.0%
Random Numbers Generation Uniform to Gaussian	5,784.02	86.4%	6,855.58	88.3%
Option Valuation	839.59	12.5%	837.00	10.8%
Memory Deallocation	66.82	1.0%	67.12	0.9%
Post-Processing	0.13	0.0%	0.12	0.0%
Σ	6690.89	100%	7760.14	100%

1×CPU Thread Part	Mersenne Twister		Sobol	
	Time (ms)	%	Time (ms)	%
Pre-Processing	1.44	1.8%	0.99	1.0%
Memory Allocation	0.39	0.5%	0.39	0.4%
Random Numbers Generation	28.17	34.7%	9.75	9.8%
Uniform to Gaussian	28.33	34.9%	65.15	65.7%
Option Valuation	12.11	14.9%	12.10	12.2%
Memory Deallocation	10.69	13.2%	10.68	10.8%
Post-Processing	0.11	0.1%	0.11	0.1%
Σ	81.24	100%	99.16	100%

measured the time spent in each step for both the GPU and CPU version of the code. Note that in practice, one would of course first analyze the CPU version and only port those steps to the GPU that pose a significant computational demand. The recorded times are shown in Table 18.1 and Figure 18.6; the different strategies (all tasks for one path after another versus a single task for all paths) imposed by hardware restrictions (processor type, memory layout) result in considerable time differences.

The valuation results for the option, elapsed time, difference of the calculated option value to the reference value and the speed-up for MC and QMC settings are shown in Table 18.2 for the CPU algorithm and in Table 18.3 for the GPU.

18.5 PARALLELIZATION OF HYBRID CALIBRATION ALGORITHMS

We have implemented the hybrid calibration routine presented in Chapter 16 on two parallel hardware platforms: First, an SGI Altix 4700 CPU server with 256 cores in clusters of four with one terabyte memory. Second, a GPU server with two C1060 (240 streaming processor cores) and one GTX 260 (192 CUDA cores) graphic cards from Nvidia, and two Intel E5520 CPUs and 24 gigabyte memory. For parallelization, OpenMP has been used on the SGI machine and a combination of Open-MP and the Nvidia CUDA framework on the GPU server. All GPU

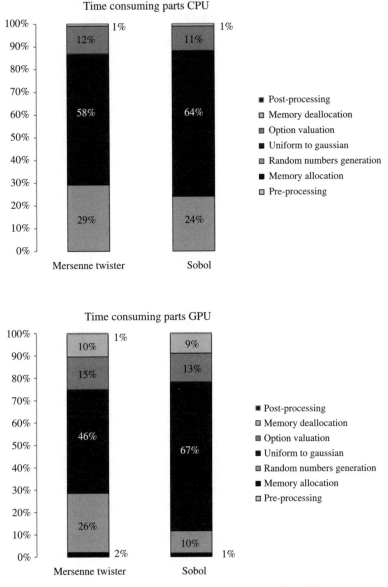

Figure 18.6   The figure shows the analysis of the time consumption of the different tasks necessary for the valuation of the Barrier option.

computations have been performed in double precision to ensure the accuracy necessary for calibration purposes.

18.5.1   Implementation Details

On both platforms, the function evaluations for the N_I starting points are distributed to the processing units (GPUs or cores). Parallelization is straight-forward in the CPU case; details

Table 18.2 Time in milliseconds. Each time value is the average of 100 valuations. Speed-up compared to 1 CPU thread. CPU: double precision.

Reference Value	13.18							
1×CPU	Mersenne Twister				Sobol			
Paths	Value	Time (ms)	Speed-up	Diff	Value	Time (ms)	Speed-up	Diff
2^8	12.09	7.53	1.00	1.10	13.16	9.45	1.00	0.02
2^9	12.26	13.36	1.00	0.92	13.18	17.29	1.00	0.00
2^{10}	12.52	27.61	1.00	0.66	13.45	33.86	1.00	−0.27
2^{11}	12.84	55.37	1.00	0.34	13.84	63.13	1.00	−0.65
2^{12}	13.05	106.61	1.00	0.14	13.74	124.37	1.00	−0.55
2^{13}	13.10	212.74	1.00	0.09	13.37	247.22	1.00	−0.18
2^{14}	13.03	417.93	1.00	0.16	13.25	488.76	1.00	−0.07
2^{15}	13.24	835.94	1.00	−0.05	13.24	978.56	1.00	−0.06
2^{16}	13.16	1,672.92	1.00	0.02	13.18	1,956.32	1.00	0.01
2^{17}	13.24	3,341.51	1.00	−0.06	13.15	3,897.40	1.00	0.04
2^{18}	13.22	6,678.95	1.00	−0.03	13.18	7,787.68	1.00	0.00
2^{19}	13.20	13,353.06	1.00	−0.02	13.18	15,562.84	1.00	0.01
2^{20}	13.24	26,721.99	1.00	−0.06	13.18	31,142.07	1.00	0.01
2^{21}	13.24	53,509.50	1.00	−0.06	13.18	62,246.17	1.00	0.00

of the implementation on the GPU can be found in Figure 18.7. The residuals (16.9) are sorted on the CPU, and Levenberg-Marquardt algorithms are started from the N_B points with the lowest residuals. On the CPU machine, each core is used to perform a Levenberg-Marquardt optimization, and the residual and derivatives are computed sequentially. On the GPU server, each GPU card concurrently performs an optimization, and the streaming processor cores on each GPU are used to parallelize the summation in (12.47). The main difference between

Table 18.3 Time in milliseconds. Each time value is the average of 100 valuations. Speed-up against 1 CPU thread. GPU: single precision.

Reference Value	13.18							
1×GPU	Mersenne Twister				Sobol			
Paths	Value	Time (ms)	Speed-up	Diff	Value	Time	Speed-up	Diff
2^8	14.13	4.83	1.56	−0.95	13.62	5.32	1.78	−0.44
2^9	14.52	4.63	2.88	−1.33	13.76	5.35	3.23	−0.57
2^{10}	13.76	4.71	5.86	−0.58	13.65	5.41	6.26	−0.46
2^{11}	12.86	4.87	11.37	0.32	13.42	5.64	11.20	−0.23
2^{12}	13.35	5.23	20.40	−0.16	13.42	5.99	20.75	−0.24
2^{13}	13.09	6.36	33.44	0.10	13.36	6.88	35.92	−0.18
2^{14}	13.17	8.36	49.99	0.02	13.24	11.15	43.82	−0.06
2^{15}	13.48	13.39	62.43	−0.29	13.17	16.62	58.88	0.02
2^{16}	13.22	23.50	71.20	−0.03	13.18	28.26	69.23	0.00
2^{17}	13.18	42.55	78.53	0.00	13.22	53.01	73.53	−0.04
2^{18}	13.23	80.73	82.73	−0.04	13.18	98.60	78.98	0.00

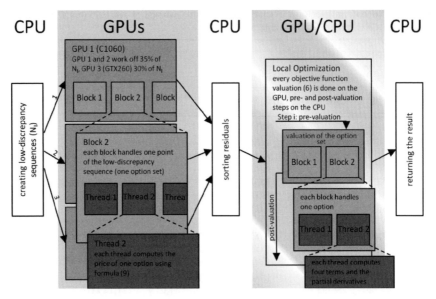

Figure 18.7   Implementation details of the calibration algorithm: a combination of quasi-random low-discrepancy sequences and a gradient-based Levenberg-Marquardt algorithm.

the GPU and CPU implementations is the number of summands used in (12.47). For optimal performance on the GPU, all threads should be equally busy; it is therefore advantageous to keep the number of summands N fixed. On a CPU system, on the other hand, a processing unit can start with the next parameter set after finishing a valuation task; it is therefore advantageous to have a stopping criterion. We use the absolute value of the characteristic function, i.e., the envelope function, as stopping criterion and abort the summation if $|\phi(u)| < \epsilon$.

Table 18.4   This table shows the average computation time (in milliseconds) for one option set (256 options) on the GPU (C1060), on a single core of the GPU server, on three GPUs (2×C1060+ 1GTX260) and for 8 and 32 cores on the Altix for a fixed number of summands denoted by $N = 512$ as well as for an abort criterion denoted by $\epsilon = 10^{-8}$.

N_I	CPU N	GPU N	CPU ϵ	8-CPU N	32-CPU N	8-CPU ϵ	32-CPU ϵ	3-GPU N
2^7	217.24	4.05	15.59	9.46	3.52	1.40	1.42	4.19
2^8	217.02	3.29	16.29	9.55	2.75	1.41	0.68	2.34
2^9	217.07	3.00	17.22	9.30	2.43	1.19	0.58	1.56
2^{10}	216.97	2.85	16.92	9.26	2.39	1.14	0.50	1.30
2^{11}	216.92	2.75	17.28	9.22	2.42	1.08	0.68	1.13
2^{12}	217.03	2.71	17.10	9.27	2.38	1.05	0.47	1.02
2^{13}	217.00	2.69	17.10	9.19	2.36	0.99	0.49	0.99
2^{14}	217.00	2.68	16.96	9.20	2.34	1.03	0.47	0.97
2^{15}	216.98	2.67	16.92	9.17	2.33	0.97	0.48	0.95
2^{16}	216.96	2.67	16.94	9.23	2.33	0.93	0.45	0.95

Table 18.5 Time required for the overall calibration algorithm in seconds for the dataset DS. The speed-up compared to 1 CPU thread is reported for different hardware configurations. All calculations have been performed in double precision.

	1 CPU Thread Time (Speed-up)	2 CPU Threads Time (Speed-up)	4 CPU Threads Time (Speed-up)	8 CPU Threads Time (Speed-up)
DS	780.9 (1.00)	440.5 (1.77)	275.8 (2.83)	204.0 (3.83)

	16 CPU Threads Time (Speed-up)	1×C2050 Time (Speed-up)	option valuations	function valuations
DS	139.9 (5.58)	8.5 (**92.23**)	1140608	3752

18.5.2 Results

All results presented in this section are calculated for a set of options (DS) on the FTSE-100 index for May 1, 2008 (see Figure 12.3). We report the performance of the first part of our hybrid algorithm – the evaluation of the residual for a large number of points in the five-dimensional parameter space – for different hardware platforms in Table 18.4. Table 18.5 shows the time required for the overall calibration on different hardware configurations and the speed-up compared to a single CPU.

19

Building Large Software Systems for the Financial Industry

The bigger part of this book has focused on numerical methods for either the valuation of financial instruments (trees, finite differences, finite elements, Monte Carlo, and Fourier techniques) or for the calibration of financial models (inverse problems and regularization, optimization). Building a large software system for the financial industry requires, from the authors' point of view, combining these methods with data management techniques in order to obtain a robust system able to run continuously for years. The design and development of the UnRisk FACTORY, in which the authors have been involved, was driven by commercial users from the finance industry interested in a more server-oriented and persistent solution than the valuation and calibration library mentioned above. On the following pages, we will highlight key aspects of such a solution.

Database

The financial database comprises the central hub of the application. Foremost, it needs to store the mathematical transcriptions of the termsheets of all instruments that are valuated on a regular basis. This may be necessary for either risk management and control, or because legislation forces the institution to carry out such a regular valuation; typically, both reasons are relevant. For a bond paying fixed rate coupons, this transcription will contain the currency, maturity date, coupon rate and coupon frequency, day count conventions and, for credit or limit considerations, the issuer. More complex instruments require additional information. A callable FX-linked note, e.g., will add at least a second currency and rules for the callability – on which dates may the issuer early-redeem the instrument? For what price? Is there a call notice period of several business days before a call may be exercised?

For primary (and liquidly traded) instruments, such as equities and foreign currencies, the valuation amounts to a straightforward application of the market price. Instruments that are structured, less liquidly traded or not traded at all (over-the-counter instruments like swaps), on the other hand, require rules on which valuation procedure is to be applied. Consequently, at least one model for the underlying must be specified; the parameters of this model typically need to be calibrated from market data of liquid instruments by a suitable procedure (such as those described in Chapter 15). It is desirable that a software system allows us to valuate financial instruments under different models. This way, model uncertainty in the valuation of complex instruments can be revealed. There is also a more pragmatic argument for this multi-model feature: when interest rates are low (as was the case in the year 2012), certain forward rates are negative. In this case, the valuation of a simple cap under a Black76 model breaks down, but its valuation under a Hull-White model is still possible.

Market Data

Market data are offered by different providers; the license fees for such a service are usually quite high. When different employees of one firm request the same market data (with the same time stamp), it is thus advantageous to obtain the data from the market data provider only once, and to subsequently store it in an in-house market database (provided the licensee is allowed to do so). Let us, for example, assume the requested market data is the interest rate data of one currency, i.e., money market and swap rates, cap volatilities and swaption volatilities for different combinations of strikes, expiries and underlying swap rates. Then, a bootstrapping process for the zero rate curves and the parameter calibration for different models can be performed immediately after obtaining these data. If the calibrated model parameters are stored as well, the calibration process, which may be time-consuming, only needs to be performed once per model for each set of market data fetched.

If the firm under consideration is, say, a capital management company performing low-frequency trading only, a daily update of market data may be sufficient. For risk management and risk reporting purposes, this market data import can be run fully automatized in overnight batch jobs. Here, rules on how to handle errors in the import of market data have to be defined: How will the system react if no market data can be obtained at all (e.g., due to a downtime of the internet connection, or due to a bank holiday that had not been considered before)? What if only an incomplete set of market data could be obtained (e.g., not all strike rates may be quoted for certain expiries of caps)?

Roles and User Administration

The question of user administration goes hand in hand with the definition of the users' roles and their corresponding role-related rights. In the authors' opinion, the prototypical financial software system is a client-server architecture accessible from the intranet of a firm, where a user must log on in order to gain access. Different user roles – such as trading, risk management, accounting, auditing, administrators – typically have different associated rights. Questions that should be answered in this context are, for example:

- Who is allowed to add/remove user roles and specific users? (Likely answer: User administrator)
- Who is allowed to add/remove/change market data sources?
- Who is allowed to manually import market data?
- Who is allowed to set up automated market data imports?
- Who is allowed to input financial instruments for testing purposes (to analyze whether a possible trade makes sense)?
- Who is allowed to change a possible trade into an actual trade?
- How can limits be observed?
- Who is allowed to set up scenario analyses or stress tests?
- Who is allowed to set up Value at Risk calculations?
- Who creates risk reports? Who is allowed to view these?
- Is there an audit trail to log changes of instrument data?
- Can parts of the application be accessed by the firm's customers via the internet? Is it guaranteed that a customer cannot see the positions of a different customer?

Load Balancing and Computing Scalability

The previous paragraphs considered the import of instrument and market data into the system and security aspects of the user administration. The main purpose of a risk management system

UnRisk FACTORY Architecture Overview

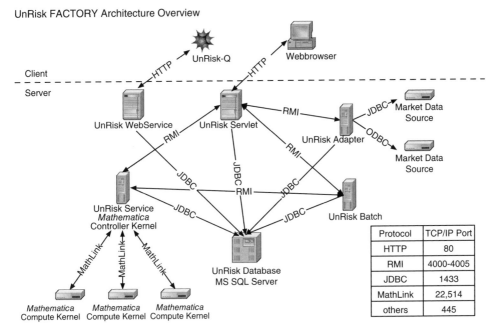

Figure 19.1 UnRisk FACTORY architecture: The UnRisk FACTORY can (on the client side) be accessed either via (web)Mathematica or via web browsers and dynamically generated forms. On the server side, it requires an UnRisk database server, the UnRisk adapter to fetch market data, the UnRisk service for controlling the workflow (manual calculations or batch jobs) and for balancing the load on the compute kernels. The application is scaleable through the number of compute kernels.

is, however, to analyze the value of a portfolio of financial instruments under different scenarios and/or stress tests and to calculate key risk numbers, such as Value at Risk or expected shortfall, for specific risk factors or combinations of risk factors. For the full valuation of a historical VaR with a time series of two years (500 business days), each instrument in the portfolio needs to be valuated 500 times, night by night by night. A capital management firm of moderate size (say, 10 billion USD under management) may have several thousand instruments among their assets; consequently, several million valuations must be carried out every night. For calculating a Monte Carlo VaR, the number of valuations is even higher.

The possibility of coarse grain parallelization is a key factor for obtaining high throughput: The valuation of an instrument and of its VaR deltas does not require additional information from the other instruments of the portfolio, and can thus be performed independently of the valuations of other instruments, with no or only very little communication. This is an ideal case for parallelization, with a speed-up scaling almost linearly with the number of CPUs added.

Open Architecture and Multi-library Approach

The modular approach outlined in the previous paragraphs has the big advantage that subtasks can be replaced fairly easily: If a market data provider is replaced by a different one for certain markets, only the import interface to the market database needs to be changed. If, for some reason, a certain instrument cannot be valuated reasonably by one valuation library (or by one interest rate model implementation), its valuation call is replaced by a different library call or by importing the external valuation result as a sort of a market data import. This is of particular relevance if alternative instruments with unknown composition (think of hedge funds) are part of the portfolio.

All of these principles have been observed in the design of the UnRisk FACTORY.[1] Figure 19.1 gives an overview of the FACTORY's software architecture.

[1] http://www.unrisk.com/index.php/products/unrisk-factory.

Bibliography

Abramowitz, M. and Stegun, I.A. (1972) *Handbook of Mathematical Functions with Formulae, Graphs, and Mathematical Tables*, Dover Publications.

Acklam, P.J. (n.d.) An algorithm for computing the inverse normal cumulative distribution function, http://home.online.no/~pjacklam/notes/invnorm/.

Ackworth, P., Broadie, M. and Glasserman, P. (1998) *A Comparison of some Monte Carlo and Quasi Monte Carlo Techniques for Option Pricing*, Springer-Verlag, New York.

Ahrens, J.H., Dieter, U. and Greenberg, H. (1982) Generating gamma variates by a modified rejection technique, *Communications of the ACM*, 25(1), 47–54.

Albanese, C. and Vidler, A. (2008) Dynamic conditioning and credit correlation baskets, MPRA Paper 8368, University Library of Munich, Germany, January.

Albrecher, H., Mayer, P., Schoutens, W. and Tistaert, J. (2007) The Little Heston Trap, *Wilmott Magazine*, January, 83–92.

Amin, A. (2003) Multi-Factor Cross Currency Libor Market Models: Implementation, Calibration and Examples. Social Science Research Network Working Paper Series, available at SSRN: http://ssrn.com/abstract=1214042.

Andersen, L. and Broadie, M. (2004) A Primal-Dual Simulation Algorithm for Pricing Multi-Dimensional American Options, *Management Science*, 50(9), 1222–1234.

Anderson, D.A., Tannehill, J.C. and Pletchter, R.H. (1997) *Computational Fluid Mechanics and Heat Transfer*, 2nd edn, Taylor & Francis, Washington, DC.

Bakshi, G. and Madan, D. (2000) Spanning and derivative-security valuation, *Journal of Financial Economics*, 55, 205–238.

Barney, B. (n.d.) Introduction to parallel computing. https://computing.llnl.gov/tutorials/parallel_comp/.

Barney, B. (n.d.) Message passing interface (mpi). https://computing.llnl.gov/tutorials/mpi/.

Bates, D.S. (1996) Testing Option Pricing Models, in Maddala, G.S. and Rao, C.R. (eds) *Handbook of Statistics*, vol 14, Elsevier, Singapore.

Beasley, J.D. and Springer, S.G. (1977) Algorithm AS 111: The Percentage Points of the Normal Distribution, *Applied Statistics*, 26(1), 118–121.

Bell, J. (1968) Algorithm 334: Normal random deviates, *Communications of the ACM*, 11(7), 498.

Belomestny, D., Bender, C. and Schoenmakers, J.G.M. (2009) True upper bounds for Bermudan products via non-nested Monte Carlo, *Mathematical Finance*, 19(1), 53–71.

Best, D.J. (1983) A note on gamma variate generators with shape parameter less than unity, *Computing* 30(2), 185–188.

Binder, A. (2007) A clever handful is enough, *Wilmott Magazine*, January, 10–14.

Binder, A. (2013) Boundary layers in mean reverting interest rate models, in preparation.

Binder, A. and Schatz, A. (2004) Finite Elements and Streamline Diffusion for the Pricing of Structured Financial Instruments, *Wilmott Magazine*, November, 97–103.

Binder, A. and Schatz, A. (2006) Finite elements and streamline diffusion for the pricing of structured financial instruments, in Wilmott, P. (ed.) *The Best of Wilmott 2*, John Wiley & Sons, Chichester, 351–363.

Binder, A., Engl, H.W., Groetsch, C.W., Neubauer, A. and Scherzer, O. (1994) Weakly closed nonlinear operators and parameter identification in parabolic equations by Tikhonov regularization, *Appl. Anal.*, 55(3-4), 215–234.

Bonnans, J.-F. (2009) *Numerical Optimization*, Springer.

Boyle, P., Broadie, M. and Glasserman, P. (1997) Monte Carlo methods for security pricing, *Journal of Economic Dynamics and Control*, 21, 1267–1321.

Brabazon, A. and O'Neill, M. (2006) *Biologically Inspired Algorithms for Financial Modelling*, Springer.

Brigo, D. and Mercurio, F. (2006) *Interest Rate Models – Theory and Practice: With Smile, Inflation and Credit*, Springer.

Caflisch, R.E. and Moskowitz, B. (1995) *Modified Monte Carlo Methods Using Quasi-Random Sequences*, Springer-Verlag, New York.

Carr, P. and Madan, D. (1999) Option valuation using the Fast Fourier Transform, *Journal of Computational Finance*, 2(4), 61–73.

Cerrato, M. (2008) Valuing American Style Derivatives by Least Squares Methods, Glasgow University, Department of Economics, Discussion Paper Series in Economics.

Cont, R. and Tankov, P. (2003) *Financial Modelling with Jump Processes*, Chapman and Hall, Boca Raton, CA.

Cox, J.C. and Ross, S.A. (1976) The valuation of options for alternative stochastic processes, *Journal of Financial Economics*, 3(1–2), 145–166.

Davies, B. (2002) *Integral Transforms and their Applications*, Springer-Verlag, New York.

Delbaen, F. and Schachermayer, W. (2006) *The Mathematics of Arbitrage*, Springer-Verlag, Berlin.

Devroye, L. (1986) *Non-Uniform Random Variate Generation*, Springer, New York.

DiDonato, A.R. and Alfred Jr, M.H. (1986) Computation of the incomplete gamma function ratios and their inverse, *ACM Transactions on Mathematical Software*, 12(4 December), 377–393.

Donnelly, C. and Embrechts, P. (2010) The devil is in the tails: Actuarial mathematics and the subprime mortgage crisis, *ASTIN Bulletin*, 40(1), 1–33.

Doust, P. (2007) Modelling discrete probabilities, Technical report, Quantitative Analysis Group, RBS.

Duffy, D.J. (2006) *Finite Difference Methods in Financial Engineering: A partial differential equation approach*, John Wiley & Sons, Chichester.

Dunford, N. and Schwartz, J.T. (2009) *Linear Operators Set*, John Wiley & Sons, New York.

Dupire, B. (1994) Pricing with a smile, *RISK*, 7, 18–20.

Egger, H. and Engl, H.W. (2005) Tikhonov regularization applied to the inverse problem of option pricing: Convergence analysis and rates, *Inverse Problems*, 21(3), 1027–1045.

Elshegmani, Z.A., Ahman, R.R., Jaaman, S.H. and Zakaria, R.H. (2011) Transforming Arithmetic Asian Option PDE to the Parabolic Equation with Constant Coefficients, *International Journal of Mathematics and Mathematical Sciences*.

Engl, H., Hanke, M. and Neubauer, A. (1996) *Regularization of Inverse Problems*, 2nd edn, Kluwer, Dordrecht.

Engl, H.W. (1997) *Integralgleichungen*, Springer Verlag.

Engl, H.W., Kunisch, K. and Neubauer, A. (1989) Convergence rates for Tikhonov regularization of nonlinear ill-posed problems, *Inverse Problems*, 5(4), 523–540.

Fang, F. and Oosterlee, C.W. (2008) A novel pricing method for European options based on Fourier-Cosine series expansions, *SIAM J. Sci. Comput.*, 31(2 November), 826–848.

Fang, F. and Oosterlee, C.W. (2009) Pricing early-exercise and discrete barrier options by Fourier-Cosine series expansions, *Numerische Mathematik*, 114(1), 27–62.

Fang, J., Varbanescu, A.L. and Henk, J. (2011) Comprehensive performance comparison of CUDA and OpenCL, *International Conference on Parallel Processing*, 216–225.

Fürst, J. (2013) *An Empircial Investigation on Fast and Stable Methods for the Calibration of Financial Models*, PhD thesis, JKU.

Fürst, J., Aichinger, M., Binder, A. and Kletzmayr, C. (2012) A fast and stable Heston model calibration on the GPU, *Lecture Notes in Computer Science, Euro-Par 2010 Parallel Processing Workshops*, 431-438.

Fusai, G. and Meucci, A. (2008) Pricing discretely monitored Asian options under Lévy processes, *J. Bank. Finan.*, 32(10), 2076–2088.

Galanti, S. and Jung, A. (1997) Low-discrepancy sequences: Monte Carlo simulation of option prices, *Journal of Derivatives*, 5(1), 63–83.

Geman, H. (2002) Pure jump Lévy processes for asset price modelling, *Journal of Banking and Finance*, 26(7), 1297–1316.

Genest, C., Ghoudi, K. and Rivest, L.P. (1995) A semiparametric estimation procedure for dependence parameters in multivariate families of distributions, *Biometrika*, 82(3), 543–552.

Gentle, J.E. (2003) *Random Number Generation and Monte Carlo Methods*, Springer.

Giles, M. (2010) Approximating the erfinv function, *GPU Computing Gems*, 2.

Glasserman, P. (2003) *Monte Carlo Methods in Financial Engineering*, Springer.

Glasserman, P. and Yu, B. (2004a) Number of paths versus number of basis functions in American option pricing, *Annals of Applied Probability*, 14(4), 2090–2119.

Glasserman, P. and Yu, B. (2004b) Simulation for American Options: Regression Now or Regression Later? in Niederreiter, H. (ed.) *Monte Carlo and Quasi Monte Carlo Methods 2002*, Springer Verlag, 213–226.

Gould, N., Hu, Y. and Scott, J. (2005) A numerical evaluation of sparse direct solvers for the solution of large sparse, symmetric linear systems of equations, Technical report, Computational Science and Engineering Department, Rutherford Appleton Laboratory.

de Haan, L. and Ferreira, A. (2006) *Extreme Value Theory: An Introduction*, Springer.

Hackbusch, W. (2003) *Multi-Grid Methods and Applications*, Springer.

Harten, A. (1983) High resolution schemes for hyperbolic conservation laws, *Journal of Computational Physics*, 49(3), 357–393.

Haug, E.G. (1998) *The Complete Guide to Option Pricing Formulas*, McGraw-Hill.

Haugh, M.B. and Kogan, L. (2008) Pricing American Options: A Duality Approach, *Operations Research* 52(2), 258–270.

Hedar, A.-R. and Fukushima, M. (2002) Hybrid simulated annealing and direct search method for nonlinear unconstrained global optimization annealing and direct search method for nonlinear unconstrained global optimization, *Optimization Methods and Software*, 17(5), 891–912.

Heston, S. (1993) A closed-form solution for options with stochastic volatility with applications to bond and currency options, *Review of Financial Studies*, 6(2), 327–343.

Hull, J. (2002) *Options, Futures and Other Derivatives*, 5th edn, Prentice Hall, London.

Hull, J., Predescu, M. and White, A. (2010) The valuation of correlation-dependent credit derivatives using a structural model, *The Journal of Credit Risk*, 6(3), 99–132.

Jackson, K.R., Jaimungal, S. and Surkov, V. (2009) Fourier space time-stepping for option pricing with Lévy models, *The Journal of Computational Finance*, 12(2), 1–28.

Jacobson, M.Z. (1999) *Fundamentals of Atmospheric Modeling*, Cambridge University Press.

Jäckel, P. (2002) *Monte Carlo Methods in Finance*, John Wiley & Sons, Chichester.

Jöhnk, M.D. (1964) Erzeugung von betaverteilten und gammaverteilten zufallszahlen, *Metrika*, 8(1), 5–15.

Jorion, P. (2006) *Value At Risk: The New Benchmark for Managing Financial Risk*, McGraw-Hill Professional.

Kabanov, Y. and Safarian, M. (2010) *Markets with Transaction Costs*, Springer.

Kallenberg, O. (2006) *Foundations of Modern Probability*, Springer.

Kanzow, C., Yamashita, N. and Fukushima, M. (2004) Levenberg-Marquardt methods for constrained nonlinear equations with strong local convergence properties, *Journal of Computational and Applied Mathematics*, 172(2), 375–397.

Kemna, A.G.Z. and Vorst, A.C.F. (1990) A pricing method for options based on average asset values, *Journal of Banking and Finance*, 14(1), 113–129.

Kim, G., Silvapulle, M.J. and Silvapulle, P. (2007) Comparison of semiparametric and parametric methods of estimating copulas, *Computational Statistics & Data Analysis*, 51(6), 2836–2850.

Knopp, R. (1969) Remark on algorithm 334, *Communications of the ACM*.

Knuth, D.E. (1998) *The Art of Computer Programming Volume II, Seminumerical Algorithms*, Addison Wesley Longman.

Korn, R. and Muller, S. (2010) Binomial trees in option pricing – history, practical applications and recent developments, in Devroye, L., Karasozen, B., Kohler, M. and Korn, R. (eds) *Recent Developments in Applied Probability and Statistics*, Springer, Heidelberg, 119–138.

Kou, S.G. (2002) A jump-diffusion model for option pricing, *Management Science*, 48(8), 1086–1101.

Kundu, D. and Gupta, R.D. (2007) A convenient way of generating gamma random variables using generalized exponential distribution, *Computational Statistics and Data Analysis*, 51(6), 2796–2802.

Kwon, Y.H. and Lee, Y. (2011) A second-order finite difference method for option pricing under jump-diffusion models a second-order finite difference method for option pricing under jump-diffusion models, *SIAM J. Numer. Anal.*, 49(6), 2598–2617.

Lamberton, D., Protter, P. and Clement, E. (2002) An analysis of a least square regression method for American option pricing, *Finance and Stochastics*, 6(4), 449–471.

Landau, R., Paez, M.J. and Bordeianu, C. (2011) *A Survey of Computational Physics: Python Multimodal eBook*, Princeton University Press.

L'Ecuyer, P. and Simard, R. (2007) TestU01: A C library for empirical testing of random number generators, *ACM Transactions on Mathematical Software*, 33(4).

Lehmer, D.H. (1951) Mathematical methods in large-scale computing units, Proceedings of the Second Symposium on Large Scale Digital Computing Machinery.

LeVeque, R.J. (1992) *Numerical Methods for Conservation Laws*, Lectures in Mathematics. ETH Zürich, Birkhäuser.

Lewis, R.W., Nethariasu, P. and Seetharamu, K. (2004) *Fundamentals of the Finite Element Modeling for Heat and Fluid Flow*, John Wiley & Sons, Chichester.

Longstaff, F. and Schwartz, E. (2001) Valuing American options by simulation: a simple least-squares approach, *Review of Financial Studies*, 14(1), 113–147.

Markowitz, H. (1952) Portfolio selection, *Journal of Finance*, 7(1), 77–91.

Marsaglia, G. (1968) Random numbers fall mainly in the planes, *Proceedings of the National Academy of Sciences*, 61(1), 25–28.

Marsaglia, G. (1972) The structure of linear congruental generators, in Zaremba, Z.K. (ed.) *Applications of Number Theory to Numerical Analysis*, Academic Press, New York, 249–285.

Marsaglia, G. (2003) Random number generators, *Journal of Modern Applied Statistical Methods*, 2(1), 2–13.

Marsaglia, G. and Bray, T.A. (1964) A convenient way of generating gamma random variables using generalized exponential distribution, *SIAM*, 6, 260–264.

Marsaglia, G. and Tsang, W.W. (2000) A simple method for generating gamma variables, *ACM Transactions on Mathematical Software*, 26(3), 363–372.

Matache, A.M. and Schwab, C. (2003) Wavelet Galerkin pricing of American options on Lévy driven assets, *Quant. Finance*, 5(4), 403–424.

Matsumoto, T. and Nishimura, M. (1998) Mersenne Twister: A 623-dimensionally equidistributed uniform pseudo-random number generator, *ACM Transactions on Modeling and Computer Simulation*, 8(1), 3–30.

McNeil, A., Frey, R. and Embrechts, P. (2005) *Quantitative Risk Management: Concepts, Techniques and Tools*, Princeton University Press.

Merton, R.C. (1976) Option pricing when underlying stock returns are discontinuous, *Journal of Financial Economics*, 3(1–2), 125–144.

Metropolis, N., Rosenbluth, A.W., Rosenbluth, M.N., Teller, A.H. and Teller, E. (1953) Equation of state calculations by fast computing machines, *Journal of Chemical Physics*, 21(6), 1087–1092.

Moro, B. (1995) The full monte, *RISK*, 8(2), 57–58.

Niederreiter, H. (1992) *Random Number Generation and Quasi-Monte Carlo Methods*, Society for Industrial and Applied Mathematics (SIAM), Philadelphia, PA.

Nocedal, J. and Wright, S.J. (2000) *Numerical Optimization*, Springer.

Øksendal, B. (2007) *Stochastic Differential Equations: An Introduction with Applications*, Springer, Berlin.

Osman, I.H. and Kelly, J.P. (1996) *Meta-Heuristics: Theory and Applications*, Kluwer Academic Publishers.

Paskov, S. and Traub, F. (1995) Faster valuation of financial derivatives, *Journal of Portfolio Management*, 22(1), 113–123.

Piterbarg, V. (2005) Pricing and Hedging Callable Libor Exotics in Forward Libor Models, *Journal of Computational Finance*, 8(2), 65–119.

Press, W.H., Teukolsky, S.A., Vetterling, W.T. and Flannery, B.P. (2007) *Numerical Recipes*, Cambridge University Press.

Protter, M.H. and Weinberger, H.F. (1967) *Maximum principles in differential equations*, Prentice-Hall.

Protter, P.E. (2004) *Stochastic Integration and Differential Equations*, Springer.

Quarteroni, A., Sacco, R. and Saleri, F. (2002) *Numerische Mathematik 2*, Springer.

Rebonato, R. (2004) *Volatilty and Correlation: The Perfect Hedger and the Fox*, John Wiley & Sons, Chichester.

Rebonato, R. (2009) *The SABR Libor Market Model*, John Wiley & Sons, Chichester.

Reisinger, C. (2004) *Numerical Techniques for High Dimensional Parabolic Equations with Applications in Option Pricing*, PhD thesis, Ruprecht-Karls-University Heidelberg, http://www.ub.uni-heidelberg.de/archiv/4954.

Roe, P.L. (1986) Characteristic-based schemes for the Euler equations, *Ann. Rev. Fluid Mech*, 18, 337–365.

Rogers, L.C.G. (2002) Monte Carlo Valuation of American Options, *Mathematical Finance*, 12(3), 271–286.

Ross, S.M. (2006) *Simulation*, Elsevier, Singapore.

Rouah, F.D. (1997) Derivation of local volatility, Lecture notes, unpublished.

Rukhin, A., Soto, J., Nechvatal, J., Barker, E., Leigh, S., Levenson, M., Banks, D., Heckert, A., Dray, J., Vo, S., Smid, M., Vangel, M., Bassham III, L.E. (2001) A statistical test suite for random and pseudo-random number generators for cryptographic applications, *NIST special publication*.

Rydberg, T.H. (1997) The normal inverse Gaussian Lévy process: Simulation and approximation, *Comm. Stat.: Stoch. Models*, 13(4), 887–910.

Saad, Y. (2003) *Iterative Methods for Sparse Linear Systems*, 2nd edn, SIAM.

Salmi, S. and Toivanen, J. (2012) Comparison and survey of finite difference methods for pricing American options under finite activity jump-diffusion models, *International Journal of Computer Mathematics*, 89(9), 1112–1134.

Salmon, F. (2009) Recipe for disaster: The formula that killed Wall Street, *Wired Magazine*.

Schoenmakers, J.G.M. and Coffey, B. (2000) Stable implied calibration of a multi factor Libor model via a semi-parametric correlations structure, *Weierstrass Institut Working Paper*, 611.

Schönbucher, P.J. (2005) *Credit derivatives pricing models: Models, Pricing and Implementation*, John Wiley & Sons, Chichester.

Segerlind, L.J. (1984) *Applied Finite Element Analysis*. John Wiley & Sons, Hoboken.

Shaw, W.T., Luu, T. and Brickman, N. (2011) Quantile mechanics II: Changes of variables in Monte Carlo methods and GPU-optimized normal quantiles, arxiv.org, http://arxiv.org/pdf/0901.0638.pdf.

Shreve, S.E. (1997) Stochastic calculus and finance, lecture notes, unpublished.

Shreve, S.E. (2008) *Stochastic Calculus for Finance II: Continuous Time Models*. 2nd printing, Springer, Berlin.

Sklar, A. (1959) Fonctions de répartition á n dimensions et leurs marges, 8 *Publ. Inst. Statist. Univ. Paris*, 229–231.

Steinbrecher, G. and Shaw, W.T. (2007) Differential equations for quantile functions, http://www.mth.kcl.ac.uk/~shaww/web_page/papers/QuantileODE.pdf.

Stentoft, L. (2004) Convergence of the least squares Monte Carlo approach to American option valuation, *Management Science*, 50(9), 1193–1203.

Stoer, J. and Bulirsch, R. (2002) *Introduction to numerical analysis*, Springer.

Surkov, V. (2010) Parallel option pricing with Fourier space time-stepping method on graphics processing units, *Parallel Computing*, 36(7), 372–380.

Sweeting, P. (2011) *Financial Enterprise Risk Management*, Cambridge University Press.

Szekely, G. and Rizzo, M.L. (2009) Brownian distance covariance, *The Annals of Applied Statistics*, 3(4), 1236–1265.

Thomas, J.W. (1995) *Numerical Partial Differential Equations: Finite Difference Methods*, Springer.

Tilley, J.A. (1993) Valuing American options in a path simulation model, *Transaction of the Society of Actuaries*, 45, 83–104.

van der Vorst, H.A. (1992) Bi-CGSTAB: A Fast and Smoothly Converging Variant of Bi-CG for the Solution of Nonsymmetric Systems, *SIAM Journal on Scientific and Statistical Computing*, 13(2), 631–644.

Veiga, C. and Wystup, U. (2009) Closed formula for options with discrete dividends and its derivatives, *Applied Mathematical Finance*, 16(6), 517–531.

Wichura, M.J. (1988) Algorithm as 241: The percentage points of the normal distribution, *Applied Statistics*, 37, 477–484.

Wilmott, P. (1998) *Derivatives*, John Wiley & Sons, Chichester.

Zhang, B. (2009) Option pricing with COS method on graphics processing units, *Parallel & Distributed Processing, 2009, IPDPS 2009*, IEEE.

Zhang, Y.Y., Pang, H.K., Feng, L.M. and Jin, X.Q. (2012) Quadratic finite element and preconditioning for options pricing in the SVCJ model, *Journal of Computational Finance*, in preparation.

Zienkiewicz, O.C. and Taylor, R.L. (2000a) *The Finite Element Method: The Basis*, Butterworth Heinemann.

Zienkiewicz, O.C. and Taylor, R.L. (2000b) *The Finite Element Method: Fluid Dynamics*, Butterworth Heinemann.

Index

Index compiled by Terry Halliday